Make It Italian

NEW YORK · ALFRED A. KNOPF · 2002

Make It Italian

THE TASTE AND TECHNIQUE
OF ITALIAN HOME COOKING

NANCY VERDE BARR

This Is a Borzoi Book
Published by Alfred A. Knopf, Inc.

Copyright © 2002 by Nancy Verde Barr
All rights reserved under International and Pan-American Copyright
Conventions. Published in the United States by Alfred A. Knopf,
a division of Random House, Inc., New York, and simultaneously
in Canada by Random House of Canada Limited, Toronto.
Distributed by Random House, Inc., New York.

www.aaknopf.com

Knopf, Borzoi Books, and the colophon are registered trademarks
of Random House, Inc.

Library of Congress Cataloging-in-Publication Data

Barr, Nancy Verde.
Make it Italian : The taste and technique of Italian home cooking /
by Nancy Verde Barr.—1st ed.
p. cm.
Includes index.
ISBN 0-375-40226-8
1. Cookery, Italian.   I. Title.

TX723 .B258 2002
641.5945—dc21   2001054519

Manufactured in Singapore
First Edition

For Brad and Andrew—"the song is you"

CONTENTS

ACKNOWLEDGMENTS

I am first and foremost grateful to the cooks who worked with me. Virginia Koster and Karl Schoonover were as excited about this book as I was, and each brought a great sense of taste, tireless energy, and an understanding of and a passion for Italian food. Jehanne Burch, McCartney Kay, Nancy Carr Starziano, and Lydia Bailey chopped, mixed, measured, weighed, tested, and made it fun. Ken Schneider, Knopf editorial assistant, tried some of the recipes at home, made very helpful observations, and always answered my calls as though he were truly happy to hear from me—again! Thank you all.

A cook needs inspiration and, in my case, Italian inspiration. I didn't expect to find it when I moved from Rhode Island to the island of Nantucket three years ago. But then Italian-trained chefs —Italian-Americans—Ron Suhanosky and his wife, Colleen Marnell-Suhanosky, opened their trattoria, Sfoglia. Oh happy day! It has been a challenge for my inspiration to keep up with their enthusiasm.

I am grateful to the designer, Johanna Roebas, whose artful eye graphically captured the concept of the book, and especially to the very talented photographer Christopher Hirsheimer, who not only gave visual life to my ideas, but also, with her husband Jim, warmed my being by sharing their home and hearth.

I will forever be indebted to Alexandra Nickerson, not only for providing me with a clear, attentive index but also for agreeing to do so on such short notice, and for caring about what I wanted it to be.

I don't think there can be any better gift to a writer than an editor who is able to draw out what the writer was trying to say and make her say it better. Judith Jones is that kind of editor. And she was mine. How lucky can a girl get!

And speaking of luck, it arrived with my fiancé, Roy. He loves food. Loves to cook. Loves me. He never minded all those people in the kitchen. He schlepped to the market again and again. He ate the same dish over and over until we got it right. Just a few of the reasons I love having him in my life.

As ever, I am deeply grateful to Julia Child, "Without whom . . ."

INTRODUCTION

I am never surprised when I read the numerous culinary surveys that proclaim Italian food as the favorite ethnic cuisine of Americans. I knew that! What does surprise me is how many people think they have to wait for a restaurant meal to enjoy it. With a basic understanding of the tastes and techniques of Italian food, you can make it Italian every day right in your own kitchen.

Taste and technique. They are the basic elements of good Italian cooking, indeed of all good cooking. It's the way all the cooks in my family prepared meals. There were no bookshelves crammed with cookbooks, no food-smeared recipe cards or ragged pages torn from culinary magazines. Equipped with an inherited awareness of Italian taste and technique, we simply cooked.

If you have grown up in an Italian home, or have cooked your way through Marcella Hazan, Giuliano Bugialli, and Lorenza de' Medici, or eaten your way through Italy, you most likely recognize what tastes Italian. Perhaps you discovered it in an Italian-American grocery store—a *salumeria*—where salted anchovies, plump capers, aged provolone, and cured salami awakened your senses. Or maybe an Italian-American restaurant with aromas of sizzling sausages, roasting peppers, and tomatoes simmering with basil was your introduction to the Italian home kitchen. If, on the other hand, you have never experienced good Italian cooking, I hope this book will begin your love affair with the enticing sensations of this timeless cuisine.

Italian technique—that is, the knowledge of how to work with ingredients—is a birthright passed down through generations of Italian homemakers. My grandmother Nonna learned by watching her mother, her grandmother, and her mother-in-law, and I learned by watching her. When I was not much more than table height, she showed me how to pound scaloppine, trim peppers, salt eggplant, make ravioli. Like most Italian grandmothers, Nonna never verbalized why she was doing what she was doing. She would only say, "Like this," and "That's enough," and "Cook it until it does this." My Italian heritage taught me the "how"; culinary training taught me the "why." I have since studied cooking in many parts of the United States, Italy, and France. I had the great advantage of working for many years with Julia Child, who always knew or found out exactly why any culinary step was necessary. Whether you are making a simple hamburger or an elaborate pasta timbale, the success of the dish depends on both how and why.

Make It Italian is my way of blending the magic of Nonna's kitchen with the schooled techniques of accomplished teachers, cooks, and chefs. This is not an exhaustive compilation of all the regional and classic recipes of Italy. It is intended to be a primer of techniques and taste that, once internalized, will become *your* Nonna in the kitchen. Absorbing this book and thinking of recipes in terms of technique will enable you to prepare many dishes spontaneously, and to improve on recipes that you do follow.

About This Book

I had one hesitancy in writing this book. Italian cooking is musical, diverse, impassioned—more like playing a symphony than practicing scales. I did not want to seem to be reducing it to a formula. But, in reality, most everything in cooking comes down to the principle of theme and variation. The Primary Recipes are the themes—the basic techniques; the additions and changes, whether they are classic Italian or your own innovations, are merely variations. Knowing what techniques connect one recipe to another will free you from rigid adherence to ingredients lists and step-by-step instructions. Recipes will become inspirations, not inflexible instructions.

Throughout, I give you numerous suggestions for substitutions and variations. Many Italian cookbooks are quite rigid about what is genuinely Italian and rely only on classic dishes. These traditional dishes should indeed be preserved, but there is room for more. Where would music and art be if we enjoyed only the classics? This book is not intended to be about classic Italian cooking. It is about good cooking with an Italian taste and Italian techniques. Our Italian ancestors, who brought their regional cuisine to this country, had to learn to improvise and substitute, so kitchen flexibility was one of my early lessons. It came in mighty handy when I had to squeeze marketing and dinner preparations into my sons' schedules of sports practice, music lessons, and homework. Such a challenge not only makes cooking practical—it makes it fun.

The recipes in this book are simple and uncomplicated. Some are personal favorites from my childhood; some are garnered from the boundless reserve of classic Italian food; others I have simply invented. The dishes represent home cooking—daily fare, not restaurant food. As you cook your way through them, I hope you will absorb the rhythm of Italian taste and technique so that you think no longer in terms of recipes but in terms of cooking.

About the Italian Meal

Italians divide the nucleus or entrée of their meal into two courses—*primo piatto* and *secondo piatto* (first and second plates). With spaghetti and meatballs, for example, the spaghetti is served first, followed by a separate plate of meatballs accompanied by a vegetable. The common American family practice is to have one main dish, and I have taken the liberty of accommodating Italian food to American meal formats. The recipes are portioned with this in mind. Whereas pasta and soup are primarily first courses in Italy and consequently small servings, they are often the whole meal for Americans. So I have developed them to be served as such.

If, on the other hand, you wish to serve your meal in the Italian fashion, recipes in this book for four people will serve six. One mistake many people make in serving a traditional Italian meal is to serve too much. The first and second courses added together should be equal in amount to one American course.

> The trouble with eating Italian food is that five or six days later you're hungry again.
> —GEORGE MILLER

Typical Italian Meal Format

The following outline lists the "soup to nuts" of a rather elaborate Italian dinner. A typical everyday family meal includes a *primo piatto,* a *secondo piatto,* and perhaps a salad. Dessert, if it were served at all, would be a lush, ripe piece of fruit. Antipasti and a sweet dessert were reserved for holiday or restaurant meals or when company was present.

All Italian families in Nonna's day seemed large enough to populate small villages on their own, and there was nothing more joyous than the times when mine gathered around the Verde family table for a festive meal. The celebration was opulent, but the food was simple and just kept coming. If you want a joyful, memorable evening, invite a large group and serve all nine courses—with bread and wine, of course.

1. APERITIVI (APERITIFS)

Drinks to stimulate the appetite served before guests sit at the table. Typical Italian choices are vermouth, Campari, white wine, or, for the more adventuresome, such cocktails as a Negroni or an Americano. Hors d'oeuvres, *stuzzichini* in Italian, are always light, such as a bowl of olives or salted almonds or simple *crostini.*

2. ANTIPASTI (APPETIZERS—LITERALLY, "BEFORE THE MEAL")

Served at the table, *antipasti* can be hot or cold dishes. Marinated fish or vegetables, prosciutto draped over fruit, *mozzarella in carrozza* (breaded and fried mozzarella cheese), *supplì al telefono* (deep-fried balls of rice with a runny cheese filling), or the common Italian-American plate of assorted cold cuts, sharp cheese, olives, celery, and anchovies are all possibilities.

3. PRIMO PIATTO (FIRST PLATE)

Choose from the gloriously large selection of Italian pasta, risotto, polenta, gnocchi, or soup dishes.

4. PIATTO DI MEZZO (HALF-PLATE)

This "in-between" course is served at very special celebratory meals. It is most often an elaborate treatment of vegetables, such as *sformato* (molded vegetables), *budino* (vegetable pudding), or stuffed vegetables—artichokes and zucchini are common.

5. SECONDO PIATTO (SECOND PLATE)

Serve either meat, fish, or poultry with a vegetable side dish, *contorno*. Sometimes the vegetable is a simple salad, if one is not served as a separate course.

6. INSALATA (SALAD)

Nonna always insisted that we follow the second plate with a salad. She called it the stomach's toothbrush and said it would make us feel less full—a necessity after a large meal. The salad can be as minimal as mixed greens or can be a combination of lettuces with tomatoes, onions, carrots, raw fennel, and peppers. The dressing is always good olive oil and vinegar poured on separately.

7. FRUIT, NUTS, AND/OR CHEESE

Bowls of fruit and nuts in their shells with appropriate nutcrackers are a lovely way to linger over dinner. A plate of cheese adds to the pleasure of nibbling. If I have made a very simple salad of mixed greens, I often add the cheese to that plate.

8. DOLCE (DESSERT)

If your guests have lingered long enough, they will be happy to indulge in a few biscotti, a slice of cake, a scoop of gelato, or a piece of poached fruit drizzled with *crema*.

9. ESPRESSO

Small cups of strong Italian coffee are usually served away from the table with an offering of liqueurs for *caffè corretto* (corrected espresso). The stalwart may take grappa.

Using This Book

When I was part of the culinary team working with Julia Child, preparing back-to-back two-minute cooking spots for *Good Morning America,* we suffered the occasional kitchen calamity. We'd all look at each other and chorus, "When all else fails, read the recipe!" My suggestion to you is that you begin there. Read Chapter 1 in its entirety. It will introduce you to terms and ingredients. If you have a good memory, it will save you from having to cross-reference later in the book. When you are ready to cook, prepare or at least read attentively the Primary Recipe in each section. That will provide you with the techniques you need to execute all the recipes in that part of the chapter. Next, try the variations. Finally, put the book aside and work out your own recipes. When you are trying Italian recipes from other cookbooks or from magazines, remember what you learned here. If an otherwise delicious-sounding recipe omits an important step that you learned here, or adds a flavor that is not Italian, you'll know better.

Above All

I do hope this book will enable you to prepare Italian meals with ease. I have tried to impart a sense of the Italian kitchen through the tastes and techniques that are most common to it. Yet there is an essential dimension to Italian food that only you can give. Food means more than eating to Italians. It means love, friendship, sharing, family, and tradition. It is a regular gathering around the table to compliment, celebrate, criticize, and remember. Italians say, *"La cucina piccola fa la casa grande"*—a little kitchen makes a large home. That is what makes food truly Italian.

Make It Italian

CHAPTER 1

Flavors That Say "Italian"

Years ago, I read a recipe for "Italian Spaghetti Sauce" that used canned tomato soup as the base. Like many American children, I had eaten my share of that reconstituted staple, so I could imagine the look and taste of the finished sauce. It would be sort of pinky red and oddly "tomatoey," but its flavor would not remotely resemble Italian tomato sauce.

Whether dishes are classic Italian, or Italian-American, or even Italian-inspired innovations, they share some unmistakable characteristics that make them Italian. No matter how widely the foods of the twenty regions of Italy may vary—not only from each other, but from Italian-American food—they share certain characteristics that just say "Italian."

For a finished dish to taste Italian, it must have Italian beginnings. If you stock your kitchen with some basic ingredients, you will not only produce Italian food, you'll do it quickly.

Keep in mind the Italian expression "What you put in there you will find" (*Quello che si mette, si trova*), meaning that the ingredients you add to a dish will be tasted, so they must be good. In this case, they should taste Italian.

Stocking an Italian Pantry

When I think back on it, my grandmother's pantry wasn't a single room. It rambled throughout the house. A large alcove, just off the kitchen, held colorful cans, jars, and bottles of foods she had preserved or purchased. Hanging strings of sausages and netted cheeses swung from basement beams above bottles of my grandfather's homemade wine. On Sundays, Nonna's bed might be covered with a clean sheet dotted with homemade ravioli. Tucked into bedroom and hall closets were baskets and sewing boxes filled with sweet biscotti and *wandi*. With a few purchases from the pushcart outside her door, the makings of a meal were always close at hand.

Such pantries are not merely romantic memories of bygone days. My own kitchen holds most of the same staples that Nonna had on hand and I have spent many a happy hour exploring the larders of contemporary Italian friends. Ceramic jars of green and black olives, tins of salted anchovies, tiny tomatoes strung up to dry, and salamis left to cure—their food storerooms are marvels of texture, color, and taste.

Following are some of the items that I think you should have on hand—though not necessarily all over the house—and suggestions for choosing and using them.

> *Il cuoco non muour di fame.*
> A three-year drought will not starve a cook.
> —ITALIAN PROVERB

Cooking Fats
GRASSO

Cooking fat not only coats the pan but serves as a flavor carrier, so the fat you choose will influence the flavor of the entire dish. Typical Italian choices, alone or in combination, are olive oil, seed oil, butter, and pork. In most cases you can substitute one for the other and create remarkably different dishes with otherwise identical ingredients.

OLIVE OIL
OLIO D'OLIVA

When I use olive oil, I want to taste olive, so I use only extra-virgin olive oil. Many affordable, very fine-tasting brands are available in American markets or specialty stores, and through the Internet. Depending on where and how it was produced, the oil may be fruity, peppery, full-bodied, or mild. Which one you choose should depend on your taste, but I suggest you avoid any that taste overly unctuous. I think such oils make a dish heavy and unappealing.

All regions of Italy except for Piedmont produce some olive oil. My preferences are for those from Apulia, Tuscany, and Umbria. Italian olive oils are graded according to the amount of oleic acid they contain and whether or not heat or solvents were used in the processing.

Storage: Store the oil away from the heat and the light. If you have a large can, transfer some of it to a smaller oil decanter or a clean, dark wine bottle for easier handling. You can buy cork-bottomed stoppers with pouring spouts at kitchen-supply stores or even liquor stores, which are helpful in controlling the flow. Olive oil will keep for at least a year if stored properly.

EXTRA-VIRGINE: "EXTRA-VIRGIN," OR, AS LISTED ON TRENDY RESTAURANT MENUS, EVO

These oils are the result of the first cold pressing of the olives; no heat or chemicals are involved in the process. Hence, they have the richest olive flavor. They can be filtered or unfiltered, so don't be dismayed by a cloudy appearance. By Italian law, the acid can be no more than 1 percent.

Occasionally you may buy or receive as a gift a truly extraordinary and costly bottle of extra-virgin olive oil. Don't use it for cooking. The flavor will break down and be lost. Just use a splash on top of the finished dish. I know many Italians, Tuscans especially, who have large ready supplies of best-quality olive oils and use them for everything—even deep-frying. I have never felt that extravagant.

VIRGINE: "VIRGIN" OR *SOPRAFFINO* (FINE)

Like extra-virgin olive oils, virgin olive oils are processed without heat or chemicals. The difference is that their acidity can range from 1½ to 4 percent.

OLIO DI OLIVE: PURE OLIVE OIL

Pure olive oils are made from the second or third pressing of olives and are usually treated with heat, to encourage flow, and with chemicals, to reduce acidity. Sometimes a bit of extra-virgin oil is added to the beleaguered lot to improve its flavor.

PIQUANT OIL
OLIO AL PEPERONCINO

Hot-pepper oil is olive oil that has been steeped with hot peppers. The Italians from Apulia call it "holy oil" (*olio santo*), because in ancient times this red-tinged oil was used to anoint those who deserved such accolades. It is used primarily to finish dishes, added at the last minute to a hot plate of pasta or bowl of soup or drizzled on pizza. Many Italian-American restaurants put a shaker bottle of red-pepper flakes on the table for the same purpose, but I think the oil is better, because its flavor is more evenly dispersed. It is available in Italian markets and specialty-food stores, but you can make your own. A week before you plan on using it, steep ½ to 1 teaspoon hot red-pepper flakes in 2 cups of extra-virgin olive oil. As the Apulians say, it will add "a tear or two" to your dish.

Storage: Store as for other oils.

SEED OIL
OLIO DI SEMI

When you do not want the flavor of olive oil in the dish, use a neutral vegetable oil such as sunflower, canola, or corn. Some Italian chefs working in America mix two parts corn oil with one part sunflower oil to approximate the taste of Italian seed oil.

Storage: Store the oil away from heat and light. As with any oil, smell it before using. You never know how long it may have sat in a delivery truck or on a market shelf, and oils will go rancid after a while. The rancidity is obvious to the nose.

BUTTER
BURRO

All my recipes that call for butter mean unsalted butter, which is all I use for cooking. If butter is used to cook foods over a high heat such as in frying and sautéing, it should be mixed with a small amount of olive or vegetable oil to prevent it from burning.

Storage: If you do not use unsalted butter often, keep it in the freezer, since the absence of salt shortens its shelf life.

PORK
MAIALE

Italians often use pork, both cured and fresh, for cooking fat. There are a number of choices.

PANCETTA

Pancetta is cured pork belly. Since this is the same cut of meat as bacon, many cookbooks translate pancetta to mean "Italian bacon," an unfortunate reference, since bacon is smoked and pancetta is dry-cured. Their flavors are decidedly different. If you can't find pancetta, an acceptable substitute is fatty prosciutto or prosciutto ends.

Some Italian recipes do call for smoked pork belly, *pancetta affumicata,* which is similar to our bacon but does not contain the sweeteners used in the American product. If you are substituting bacon for smoked pancetta, try to find one that is not sweetened, or tame the sweetness by blanching it for about 1 minute in boiling water before frying it.

If you live in an area with a large Italian population, you may find pancetta in two forms—rolled and flat; the two are interchangeable.

Storage: Pancetta will keep 3 weeks in the refrigerator wrapped well in plastic, and at least 3 months in the freezer. I chop pancetta into small pieces before freezing, so I can remove small amounts if that is all I need.

PROSCIUTTO

Prosciutto is Italian ham, the cured leg of the pig. Usually prosciutto is sliced to order at meat or deli counters, and there will be a meaty bone or end pieces left. If you are in an Italian market, these pieces may well be on the counter for the taking; if not, ask if they have any you can buy. Remove the meat from the bone and chop it up, with the fat, into ¼-inch pieces.

If you cannot find end pieces, buy slices, but not the most expensive brands, such as *prosciutto di Parma* and San Danielle. They are sublime for eating but too costly for cooking. There are good domestic brands, but beware of something called *prosciutini,* which is overly seasoned and far from the real thing.

Storage: Refrigerate for 4 or 5 days, or freeze for up to 3 months.

SAUSAGE

Sausage (*salsiccia*) is the most convenient way to use fresh pork as a flavoring for other dishes. Good Italian sausage is made from ground or chopped pork butt and has no filler mixed in. The best Italian sausage is said to be made *al punto del coltello*—i.e., with the point of a knife. In other words, it should not be homogeneous but have a coarse texture, as though it had been hand-chopped, which we all used to do long ago around Nonna's table. Italian sausage is usually flavored with fennel seed and may be made either "sweet" or "hot." "Hot" sausage has bits of red-pepper flakes; sweet does not. I buy only "sweet" sausage, and add hot pepper to the recipe if I want it.

"Crumble" seems to be the standard recipe term for handling sausage when the cook is supposed to break it up. But, unlike the cookie, which will indeed crumble, sausage crushed in one's hands just becomes mashed sausage. The goal is to break it into pieces of whatever size you choose. First slit the casing down the side, slip it off, and discard it. Then, even in a hot pan, if you work very fast, you can actually put the entire skinned sausage in the pan and quickly break it up with the tip of a wooden spoon or the back of a fork. I usually break it into large pieces as I drop it into the pan and then continue to poke it with my spoon until I like the size. The trick is to get the meat broken into the size you want before it browns, at which point it is difficult to split any further, so start it in a pan over medium to medium-low heat.

Storage: Fresh sausage will keep in the refrigerator for 3 days, and in the freezer for about 3 months. I wrap two pieces per package for freezing.

LARD

Olive oil and/or pancetta have largely replaced lard, *strutto,* which was once a mainstay of southern-Italian cooking. *Strutto* is refined, pure pork fat. *Lardo* is lean, streaky pork fat much like our salt pork, which, if you use it as a substitute, should be blanched briefly (that is, immersed in boiling water for 2 minutes or so) to remove the excess salt. Lard is quite flavorful, so you may choose to substitute it in recipes that call for pancetta or prosciutto. You will need less of it, and may have to drain excess fat from the pan before proceeding with the recipe.

Storage: Unless you use it daily, cut lard into small pieces and freeze. Frozen, it will keep for 3 or 4 months.

Aromatics
SOSTANZE AROMATICHE

A great majority of recipes start by cooking aromatic vegetables such as onions, garlic, carrots, shallots, celery, hot pepper, and herbs in the chosen fat. The combinations can be simple or close to opulent. The cooking of southern Italy, for example, is sometimes referred to as "*aglio, olio, prezzemolo*" (garlic, oil, and parsley), because every dish seems to begin with the cooking of this threesome. In other regions, many dishes begin with a generous assortment of aromatic vegetables sautéed in butter. Both preparations are unmistakably Italian.

The Start

SOFFRITTO

Your choices of cooking fat and aromatics form the flavor base of your recipe. The success of your finished dish depends on how you handle these primary ingredients. Throughout this book, I refer to this step as "The Start." The Italian word is *soffritto* (underfried), indicating that the ingredients are to be cooked at a lower temperature and to a lesser degree than frying requires. (Those of you with a southern-Italian heritage, especially from the areas around Naples, may be confused, since you will remember *soffritto* as a dense, rich stew of animal innards. This is different.)

The first step in preparing the *soffritto* is the actual chopping of the ingredients, and my recipes indicate whether the aromatics should be coarsely chopped, meaning somewhat irregular pieces ½ to ¾ inch; or diced into even ¼-inch pieces; or finely minced, as small as you can manage without turning them into mush. Remember, the smaller the chop, the more pronounced its flavor would be.

Battuto is the Italian term used to indicate that the aromatic beginnings are all very finely chopped—that is, minced. The word means "beaten," to indicate that the items are so small they seem to have been pummeled. Italians usually accomplish this with the aid of a *mezzaluna,* a two-handled moon-shaped knife. It is the perfect tool for the task. To use it, first coarsely cut all the vegetables, herbs, pancetta, etc., that are called for, then pile them all together and begin the rhythmic, rocking motion of the *mezzaluna,* which will mince them together. A large chef's knife will also do the trick, but use a food processor with caution, since it can turn the ingredients to paste.

With the ingredients chopped, you are ready to prepare a proper *soffritto.* Put the vegetables in the pan when the oil is still warming. Warm, rather than hot, is crucial for certain aromatics such as onions and garlic whose natural, residual sugars can caramelize and burn very quickly in a pan that is too hot. Once they have burned, the bitterness will permeate the entire dish, so you might just as well discard everything and start again—slowly. Season the aromatics with a pinch of salt—especially helpful when onions are present, since salt draws out their juices and further discourages scorching. Cook the aromatics slowly, over the lowest heat that will allow the pan's contents to just barely flutter, and pay attention to them with an occasional stir. Be patient. It may be 15 or 20 minutes before the vegetables are tender and translucent. Don't be tempted to rush this initial step. The aromatics should be carefully and attentively cooked so that they gradually, meltingly soften and release their flavors without browning.

GARLIC
AGLIO

I've always loved garlic, but now I am so happy to know that it is also good for us. Garlic pills. Imagine! How much better just to cook with it.

Choose either pink or white heads that are very firm and meaty. Old garlic will feel lightweight and crushable and perhaps have some green shoots poking out the tops of the cloves.

Some people say they object to garlic's strong flavor, but the strength of its taste depends on how you use it. Left in its skin and slowly cooked, garlic is actually sweet. The classic

French dish of chicken with forty cloves of garlic, and the current popularity of a whole roasted head served to a single diner, are proof. Peeled garlic that is left whole and sautéed in oil until lightly browned and then discarded will leave only a delicate hint of its presence. Minced garlic cooked only until golden but left in the dish will leave a more pronounced flavor. Remember as you cook that it is not so much how many cloves you use, but whether you slice, chop, mince, or leave them whole.

How to Prepare Garlic

I have watched too many students struggling with peeling and mashing garlic not to include here my method of handling it. To peel garlic, lightly smash it with the side of a chef's knife. The clove will split and the skin will break open, making it easy to lift off. Remove the root end. Many chefs insist on removing the green shoot in the middle if it is present. I don't worry about it if the garlic is going to be cooked; if the garlic is going raw into a dish, I do pick it out with the tip of a knife, since it may be slightly bitter when uncooked.

Sometimes you will want the garlic to be pureed, and I suggest you avoid a garlic press, which spits out the juices but leaves a great deal of pulp behind. Instead, chop the cloves until they are fine, and then sprinkle them with a little salt. Rub and firmly press the side of the blade of a heavy chef's knife back and forth over the garlic until it has turned into a puree.

Storage: Although I have read recommendations to the contrary, I always store garlic, uncovered, in the vegetable crisper of the refrigerator.

ONIONS

Red and yellow onions are the most common varieties called for in Italian cooking. Scallions (green onions) and leeks are less usual. Red onions are reserved mostly for salads, because of their sweetness. As sweet as they are, I always peel them, chop or slice them, and soak them in three changes of very cold water for 45 minutes, then drain and dry them, before I use them raw. The soaking removes their sharpness. You can substitute red onions in recipes that call for yellow ones, but their sweetness will change the flavor of the finished dish.

Recipes usually specify onions by size—small, medium, or large. A little more or less will not make a difference. Use the following merely as a guide.

Small onion—about 6 ounces = about 1 cup chopped
Medium onion—about 7 ounces = about 1¼ cups chopped
Large onion—about 9 ounces = about 1½ cups chopped

Storage: Store onions uncovered in the vegetable crisper of the refrigerator. A cold onion will be less apt to draw tears when you peel and chop it.

PARSLEY
PREZZEMOLO

I always, always have a large bunch of parsley on hand. How can one cook without it, even if it is not part of the recipe? Flat-leaf parsley, also called "Italian parsley," is the best one to use for Italian cooking. It is more aromatic, and its flavor is less startling than that of curly parsley. Because the leaves are more tender than those of the curly variety, they can be tossed whole into a dish. If you cannot find it in your area or grow your own, then substitute curly parsley. To use either kind of parsley, rinse it well in cold water, spin or pat it dry, and remove the large stems. The smaller stems, at the leaf end of flat-leaf parsley, are tender enough to be chopped and used in the dish.

Storage: Store parsley in a glass of water, like cut flowers, in or out of the refrigerator. It will keep at least a week, especially if you give the stems an occasional trimming.

Dried, Preserved, and Packaged Flavors
L'ERBE

I use fresh herbs whenever possible, growing my own sage, basil, oregano, marjoram, rosemary, and parsley when the season is right. I wish I had the green thumb that others seem to have, enabling them to keep pots of herbs alive on windowsills all winter. As the frost steals my crop's greenery, I pore over what the market has to offer at reasonable prices. When the pickings are slim, I rely on certain dried herbs—my own or store-bought—that maintain some flavor in a jar. I find dried oregano (the Greek variety is particularly good), thyme, marjoram, and rosemary acceptable. Dried basil and dried parsley are little more than musty, green sawdust. When substituting dried herbs for fresh, use a third of the amount—1 teaspoon dried equals 3 teaspoons (1 tablespoon) fresh. Crush dried herbs between your palms to release their flavor, or put them in a small strainer and pour a small amount of boiling water over them.

Storage: To dry herbs for storage, lay them out on paper towels until they are completely dry. Then, remove their stems and put the leaves in tightly closed jars. Store dried herbs away from heat and light. When the color has faded from bright green to a dull olive green, it is time to discard them.

SALT AND PEPPER
SEL E PEPE

I keep three types of salt on hand—iodized table salt; coarse, kosher salt; and sea salt—but I am not fanatical about having to use one or the other. I do like the bit of texture that coarse salt gives to fried foods. If you substitute coarse salt for fine salt, you will need slightly more. I am more compulsive about peppercorns. I buy black Tellicherry peppercorns and grind them myself. As for other spices, I regularly stock fennel seed, fennel powder, and sweet paprika.

Storage: Keep seasonings away from the heat, and check them regularly for both flavor and infestation. They keep about a year away from the heat and light.

HOT PEPPER
PEPERONCINO

Italian food is seldom so hot and spicy as to draw a sweat, but a bit of hot pepper is used a lot, especially to punch up flavor and add another dimension. I always keep a jar of red-pepper flakes in the cupboard, and bottles of large pickled red peppers and of small, pickled green peppers (*peperoncini*) in the refrigerator. I slice and use the pickled peppers when I want acid as well as heat in a recipe.

Today, most supermarkets carry at least a small selection of fresh hot peppers, and though they are not quite the same as those grown in Italy, they are an acceptable substitute. Choose firm, unblemished, and unwrinkled peppers. To use them, remove the stems, cut them in half, and scoop out the seeds with a small spoon. Be careful in handling them, since the hot oil can remain on your hands and will burn your eyes if you touch them.

Storage: Store fresh hot peppers, uncovered, in the vegetable crisper of the refrigerator. Store pepper flakes away from the heat and light. Discard any jars of flakes that have lost their vibrant color.

Vinegars
ACETI

Italians use only unpasteurized wine vinegars, both red and white. The quality of vinegars can vary greatly, since they are a wine product, and the better the wine the better the vinegar. Look for white wine vinegar that is transparent with a pale-golden color. Depending on the grapes, red-wine vinegar, which should also be unclouded, may be pale red or deep garnet in color. I have been happiest with the red vinegars from anywhere in Tuscany. Balsamic vinegar, *aceto balsamico,* is a special, highly aromatic vinegar made from cooked, concentrated, and aged juices of Trebbiano grapes. There are many grades of balsamic vinegar, and I keep less costly ones on hand for cooking, and savor a few drops of the more expensive ones on bowls of ripe strawberries, or as the last anointment of a special dish.

Storage: Vinegars will keep, unopened, a very long time. Once they are opened, they will begin to pale and lose flavor after about 6 months.

Olives, Anchovies, Capers
OLIVE, ACCIUGHE, CAPPERI

I can't imagine my kitchen without all three of these staples on hand. I may nibble on them for snacks or use them to garnish sandwiches or add them to a *soffritto*. I'm just happy they are there.

Olives are only edible after they are cured; right off the tree, they are bitter beyond belief. The two primary curing techniques are brining and dry-curing. Good Italian brine-cured olives are soaked in water, not lye, and then fermented in brine. Lye, used in most canned olives, leaches the flavor from the fruit. Dry-cured olives are packed in salt to leach the bitterness and then soaked in olive oil. Dry-cured olives have a stronger flavor than brine-cured, but I use them interchangeably. I keep both green and black olives on hand.

Ethnic markets are your best source, but I have been pleasantly surprised by the selections many supermarkets offer. Large brownish-green Sicilian olives and the small black Gaeta olives are the most common ones you will find, but look also for the large, sweet, green Bella di Cerignola.

Store olives in their brine or covered with olive oil in the refrigerator. To pit olives, position the flat side of a heavy chef's knife on top of one, and firmly press down or gently pound with your fist. The olive will immediately split open, and you can squeeze out the pit. You may be able to smash two or three at a time, but doing any more is inviting olive missiles to shower your kitchen.

A number of Italian recipes call for anchovies, either as a subtle flavor or as a dominant ingredient. In either case, the best anchovies to use are those from Italy preserved in salt. Many specialty-food stores and some sophisticated markets carry them loose and sell them by the pound. They are also available in cans, which are themselves works of art. You can order them through the Internet; see pages 27–29. Don't worry about buying too many, because they will last under salt in the refrigerator for a very, very long time. To use them, peel off the number of anchovies you need, rinse the salt away under running water, and gently separate the fish into two fillets. Pull out and discard the long bone that is clinging to one fillet. Any tiny little bones left behind will disintegrate during cooking—or chewing. If you are planning to eat rather than cook them, clean them as above and lay them out on a shallow dish. Cover them completely with olive oil.

If you cannot find salted anchovies, substitute the same quantity of anchovies packed in oil. Look for anchovies from Italy that are packed in olive oil, and drain the oil away before using the fish. Oil-packed anchovies will keep refrigerated for a long time as long as the fish are submerged.

Capers are the flower buds of bushes that are abundant all over the Mediterranean. Like anchovies, the best capers for Italian cooking are the large, salted ones from Italy. To use, measure the amount of capers you need into a strainer and run cold water over them until all the salt is washed away. Pat the capers dry, and leave whole or chop according to the recipe. If you can only find small capers packed in brine (nonpareils), you can successfully substitute them, but rinse them instead in warm water to remove any excess acid.

Dried Mushrooms
FUNGHI SECCHI

It used to be that when I traveled to Italy I reserved a bit of return-suitcase space for a supply of dried porcini mushrooms. They just were not to be had anyplace I shopped at home. Today, you can often find them—and numerous other varieties—at the local grocery store. Unfortunately, as with all items that become "trendy," the quality has suffered. Look for Italian-grown porcini that have been dried and packaged with care. The pieces should be relatively large and still have a good deal of white surface. Small brown pieces will taste old and musty. Store the mushrooms, airtight, in the refrigerator, and use them within 9 months to a year. They will darken as they get older. Page 58 describes how to soak and use them.

Breadcrumbs
MOLLICA

A frugal Italian cook sees a leftover loaf of bread as a valuable ingredient for another meal. It may be sliced and toasted and find its way into bread pudding or a bowl of *zuppa*. Perhaps the not-yet-hard center will be crumbled, softened with milk, and used as a binder for meatballs or stuffed peppers. A thoroughly dried loaf will be run over a box grater to make *pangrattato* (dried breadcrumbs) to be used as a binder, to coat fried food, or as a substitute for grated cheese. Bread is never wasted.

To make fresh breadcrumbs, pull out the white center of day-old but still-malleable Italian or other firm coarse-textured bread. Pulse the pieces in the food processor until you have an even crumb.

For dried breadcrumbs, grate totally dry and hard Italian bread on the small holes of a box grater or by pulsing it in a blender or food processor. Unless you need perfectly white crumbs, grate the crust as well. If the recipe calls for "fine dried breadcrumbs"—the best for breading food to be fried—pour the grated crumbs through a sieve and use the fine pieces that fall through. Many Italian bakeries sell breadcrumbs made from their own dry bread. They are usually very good, but be sure they have not been sitting on the shelf for weeks. Commercially packaged ones can do in a pinch, as long as they are unflavored and you have checked the expiration date—and the smell—to be sure the taste has not gone off.

To make dried breadcrumbs from bread that is not completely dry, pulse it in a food processor with a steel blade until the pieces are tiny. Scatter them on a cookie sheet and bake them in a 325° F oven for about 15 minutes, until they are dry and lightly colored.

Italian pasta recipes sometimes call for a sprinkling of toasted breadcrumbs in place of grated cheese. For each pound of pasta, sauté about 1 cup of fresh or dried breadcrumbs in 2 tablespoons of olive oil or butter until they are lightly browned.

Storage: Keep breadcrumbs refrigerated in an airtight container. They will keep for 2 to 3 months. They can also be frozen, well wrapped, for 4 months.

Pasta, Rice, and Grains

My pantry is never without a selection of dried pasta. I keep several assorted boxes and bags of short macaroni, long noodles, and sheets of lasagne. Pages 93–94 in the pasta chapter detail my preferences. Arborio rice is always present, and less crucial but nice to have are bags or boxes of Vialone Nano and Carnaroli rices for soups and risotto. My shelves hold a few boxes of quick-cooking yellow cornmeal (polenta) and bags of the longer-cooking variety from the Italian grocer. I keep couscous, semolina, and farro on hand. With all of these grains and pasta, monitor the date of purchase vigilantly, because old products are the breeding ground for annoying moths that will take up residence in your cupboard.

Tomatoes

Although tomatoes are not as omnipresent in Italian cooking as most people believe, they are an important staple. When a recipe calls for tomatoes, I usually give the option of fresh or canned. I expect you to choose the best that is available at that particular time of year in your location. If tomatoes are not in season locally, I always use canned.

READING TOMATO DIRECTIONS

- "Tomatoes, chopped" means cut up with their skins, juices, and seeds.
- "Tomatoes, peeled and chopped" means the skins are removed and the juices and seeds remain.
- "Tomatoes, peeled and seeded" means that the skins and seeds are removed but the juices are reserved.
- "Tomatoes, peeled, seeded, and juiced" means all is discarded but the pulp.

MEASURING TOMATOES

The following equivalents will help you determine how many tomatoes or cans you need. Use the weight or can size for buying, and the cup measure for cooking. Until recently, I always lived within spitting distance of the Italian section of Providence. I could buy cans, jars, and boxes of Italian tomatoes in all sizes. I know that in many areas of the country this is not the case. If a recipe calls for 3¼ cups of tomatoes—a 28-ounce can—and all you can find are 35-ounce cans that hold 4 cups, you have options. For sauces, increase the amount of all the ingredients slightly; freeze whatever sauce you don't need, even small amounts, since they are always good to add to soups, braises, or other sauces. Or use 3¼ cups from the 35-ounce can and freeze the rest. If you keep adding to them, you will soon have another 3¼ cups.

- 1 pound tomatoes = 8 to 10 fresh plum or 2 large or 3 medium round salad tomatoes
- 1 pound fresh plum tomatoes, with their skins and juices = about 2 cups chopped
- 1 pound fresh tomatoes, peeled, seeded, but with juices = about 1½ cups chopped

- 1 pound fresh tomatoes, peeled, seeded, and juiced = about 1 cup chopped
- 28-ounce can tomatoes, undrained = about 3¼ cups chopped
- 28-ounce can tomatoes, drained = about 1⅓ cups chopped
- 35-ounce can tomatoes, undrained = about 4 cups chopped
- 35-ounce can tomatoes, drained = about 1⅔ cups chopped

Golden Apples

The Italian word for "tomato," *pomodoro,* translates to "golden apple." When the first tomatoes were brought to Italy from the New World, in the mid–sixteenth century, they were yellow and the size of cherries. The name was appropriate. It took about two centuries before a brave Neapolitan dared to eat one, since the world believed them to be poisonous. Once their safety was assured, the Italians brought the lowly yellow fruit to extraordinary heights by cultivating numerous varieties.

FRESH TOMATOES
POMODORI FRESCHI

The best fresh tomato is one that is in season. No matter how red and lush those February tomatoes look on the outside, they will be pale and tasteless within. Whenever possible, especially for tomato sauce, choose either the pear-shaped Italian plum tomatoes or the slightly larger, similarly shaped Roma tomatoes. These meaty tomatoes have a larger proportion of pulp to juice than do other varieties. Consequently, a tomato sauce made with plum or Roma tomatoes will have good body. I have also made very tasty tomato dishes from round salad tomatoes when they are at their seasonal best. Because round tomatoes have a higher ratio of juice to flesh than do plum tomatoes, you may need more of them to yield the required amount of pulp when the recipe calls for them to be peeled, seeded, and juiced.

Storing Fresh Tomatoes

Never refrigerate fresh tomatoes or buy any that have been refrigerated. Temperatures below 50° F forever halt the ripening process, so all hope of good taste and juicy texture are lost. Keep tomatoes on the counter in a sunny spot. If any have ripened completely and you are not ready to use them, they can be refrigerated, but, truthfully, I am always suspicious of a cold tomato. It's better to make a sauce and refrigerate or freeze that.

If you have a particularly large crop of ripe plum tomatoes—and only when they are ripe—which you can't consume before they go bad, freeze them. Rinse them off and store them in plastic freezer bags. Thaw them, out of the bag, in warm water, and pull the skin away as they soften. Thawed whole tomatoes are suitable only for cooking.

PEELING AND SEEDING FRESH TOMATOES

In most cases, peeling the tomatoes is optional. I peel them when I want a more refined dish. To peel tomatoes, first be sure they are ripe; they should be fragrant and yield slightly to the gentle pressure of your thumb. Next, rinse them off and lower one or two into boiling water. Once the water begins to bubble again, count 15 seconds, then remove them from the hot water with a slotted spoon and plunge them into a bowl of ice water. Cut out the core, and pull the skin away with your fingers or the cutting edge of a paring knife held at an angle. It should release easily. If it does not, put the tomatoes back into the boiling water for another 10 seconds and test again. When you have determined the approximate amount of boiling time needed to shed the peel, you can work with a larger number of tomatoes, but do not put so many into the water that it does not immediately return to the boil, or the pulp will begin to cook.

Unless they are needed for the liquid part of a recipe, the juices should be removed. Seeds should be removed when recipes call for long cooking, since they can become bitter—or if their presence simply bothers you. To remove the juice and the seeds from peeled or unpeeled tomatoes, cut them in half through the round middle, not the stem, and squeeze them well, so the juice and seeds are forced out. You may have to flick a few stubborn seeds away with your finger. If you wish to remove the seeds but save the juice, squeeze the tomatoes over a sieve set atop a bowl, which will collect the juices. Then chop the tomatoes as called for and reunite them with their juices.

CANNED TOMATOES
POMODORI PELATI

When it is not tomato season, preserved whole Italian plum tomatoes, in cans or glass jars, are the best choices. If they are imported from Italy, look for the words "Genuine San Marzano" on the label. This area of Italy just happens to produce one of the world's sweetest plum tomatoes. Taste one next to another canned tomato and you will easily detect the flavor that makes them so prized. "San Marzano *Style*" on the can means exactly that—the same style as those of San Marzano, but not the real McCoy. It doesn't mean that they are not perfectly good, but you will have to determine that by your own sampling.

There are excellent domestic brands of plum tomatoes on the market. New Jersey tomatoes—fresh or preserved—are particularly flavorful. To judge the quality of a canned or jarred tomato, look at the label; it should state that the tomatoes are whole and packed in their own juice, without any fillers such as tomato puree or paste. The opened can should reveal whole, plump tomatoes with a slightly firm as opposed to mushy texture. Sometimes there is that insipid-looking basil leaf in the can; toss it out.

SEEDING AND CHOPPING CANNED TOMATOES
Canned tomatoes are already peeled but not seeded. This is not a problem for recipes that call for cooking the tomatoes 25 minutes or less. If, however, the

tomatoes will undergo longer cooking, the seeds can become bitter, so they should be removed. Squeeze the tomatoes over a sieve atop a bowl, just as with fresh tomatoes; chop the pulp, and add it to the juice in the bowl. If a recipe calls for canned tomatoes with their juices to be seeded and very finely chopped, you can run them through a food mill or push them through a coarse sieve. The seeds will remain behind, while the juices and tiny pieces of tomato pulp will flow through.

If I want to chop the tomatoes with their juices and don't care about the seeds, I empty the entire contents into a bowl and break them up with my hands. You can also use a food processor and pulse them until they are chopped. Some canned tomatoes are labeled "Kitchen Ready" and are already chopped. Since they are usually packed in heavy puree, I always shun them. Not long ago, my fiancé, Roy, unaware of my long-held prejudice, brought a can home. They were not horrific, and the resulting sauce had a familiar and typical Italian-American flavor unlike the light, sweet flavor produced by tomatoes packed in their own juices. Since these cans of chopped tomatoes still have seeds that need to be removed for long cooking, I'm not sure how much time they save—chopping or simply crushing with your hands is quite easy.

TOMATO PASTE

It is quite common for Italian recipes to call for tomato paste, especially recipes from southern Italy and Sicily in particular. My grandmother never used it, and I suspect it was because the American brands, which are tomatoes boiled down to a paste, taste nothing like the Italian brands, made from tomatoes that are dried in the sun. She had no access to the Italian variety, and the sun was neither strong enough nor around long enough in Rhode Island for her to make her own. I tasted my first real tomato paste in Sicily at Anna Tasca Lanza's lovely wine estate, Regaleali. She and her staff make their own, and it is not only delicious but also a delight to see made. If you have seen the movie *Cucina Paradiso,* you may recall the scene in the Italian piazza in which Sicilian women appear to be painting door-size boards red. They're actually spreading the pulp and juices from chopped tomatoes onto the boards to dry in the hot sun. A *donna* with an average-size southern-Italian crop of tomatoes begins with about twelve boards. Each day she scrapes the drying tomatoes down and spreads them out again, and since some of the juices will have evaporated, she will need fewer boards. When the process is finished, she is usually left with one board and a pure and luscious tomato paste. Anna gave me some to take home, and it lasted a long time in the refrigerator even though I dipped into it often to perk up tomato sauces, stews, and soups.

I have never found anything close to that tomato paste, but those from Italy, packed in tubes and with no additives other than maybe salt, are very good.

Cheese
FORMAGGIO

This is by no means an exhaustive list of Italian cheeses. Each region of Italy produces its own special cheeses, many of which are never exported to the United States. For a more complete compilation and excellent description, look to Steven Jenkins's book, *Cheese Primer*. The cheeses listed below are those that I use for

cooking and that are readily available in American markets. I have divided them into categories according to their characteristics, to help you when you want or need to make substitutions in recipes. As well as a cooking ingredient, cheese is a delicious, simple ending to a meal. Some of my favorite cheese and fruit combinations are listed on pages 448–49 in the dessert chapter.

HARD GRATING CHEESE
GRANA

Used primarily for stirring into sauces, sprinkling on top of finished dishes, and mixing into stuffings, grated hard cheeses melt into the dish, adding their own distinctive flavors.

Good Italian markets will cut grating cheeses to order from large prime-condition wheels. Supermarkets usually sell precut pieces that are wrapped in plastic. Look the pieces over carefully and reject any that have dry, white spots. Neither the flavor nor the meltability will be the same. Do not buy pregrated cheeses. They are little more than sawdust.

Grate only as much cheese as is called for in the recipe, and then pass a piece with a hand grater at the table. Four ounces of hard cheese will yield approximately 1 cup of grated cheese, depending on how finely you grate it and how tightly you pack the cup. A favorite new addition to my kitchen batterie is the microplane, a handheld flat, stainless-steel rasp with rows of ultra-sharp tiny holes. It quickly and effortlessly turns a wedge of cheese into a mound of snowy flakes.

I keep wedges of grating cheeses in small, tightly zipped plastic bags in the vegetable bin of the refrigerator.

- Parmigiano Reggiano—cow's milk. Considered the king of grating cheeses, the real McCoy will always have "Parmigiano Reggiano" stamped clearly on the rind. A good piece will be golden-colored and slightly moist.
- Grana Padano—cow's milk. Aged a shorter time than Parmesan and consequently more delicately flavored and less expensive, grana padano is an excellent cheese, and the one that sustained Italian-Americans long before Parmigiano Reggiano was so readily available. The name is stamped on the rind.
- Pecorino—sheep's milk. Pecorino Romano is the most commonly found in American markets, but there are other hard pecorino cheeses available that can be substituted. Sharper and tangier than Parmesan, pecorino is a good choice for piquant recipes. Locatelli is an excellent and readily available brand.
- Asiago—made from partly skimmed cow's milk. Italian Asiago that is aged for about 9 months (*Asiago vecchio*) is a good grating cheese with a slightly sharp flavor. Well-made American Asiago is considerably sharper than the Italian variety, somewhat like provolone.
- Montasio—cow's milk. Italian Montasio has a very mild flavor.

STRETCHED OR KNEADED CHEESE
PASTA FILATA

These cheeses are stretched or kneaded and then molded. They are the ones commonly used in baked dishes, such as lasagna, because of their ability to melt and yet retain some texture.

- Mozzarella—Italian mozzarella may be made from buffalo's milk, *mozzarella di bufala,* or from cow's milk, *il fiore di latte.* Freshly made American mozzarella is cow's milk. Avoid hard supermarket varieties. Freshly made mozzarella has a shelf life of about 1 week. I prolong its shelf life by replacing the whey in which it is sold with salted water.
- Scamorza—cow's-milk cheese that is molded into forms the size and shape of fresh pears. It is made exactly like mozzarella but is then cured in brine, which intensifies its flavor, renders it slightly salty and a bit chewy, and prolongs its shelf life. There is a smoked variety that bears a brown rind and can be used in the same way.
- Caciocavallo—brine-cured cow's-milk cheese that is formed into large pear-shaped cheeses usually displayed in red string bags tied two by two. This venerable cheese of southern Italy dates back to at least the fourteenth century. Young caciocavallo has a mild and tangy flavor that becomes sharper with age. It has a long shelf life, and aged caciocavallo can be grated and used as the *grana* above.
- *Manteca burrata* and *burrino*—cow's-milk kneaded cheese with a small nugget of butter and/or salami inside.
- Provolone—cow's-milk cheese formed into sausage shapes that range from a few feet to a few yards. This is the cheese most often seen hanging from the ceilings of Italian markets. Depending on its source and age, its flavor will be mild or pungent, so ask to taste it before you buy. Some are smoked and these may be used in the same way.
- Provola—cow's-milk cheese similar to mozzarella but ripened longer, so the texture is firmer and flavor fuller. It is sometimes smoked.

Soft fresh cheeses add creaminess to a dish. They can be added to baked dishes or stirred into stovetop creations. These cheeses will keep only a week or so in the refrigerator.

- Mascarpone—cow's milk. This very rich, buttery, double-cream Italian cheese is most commonly sold in plastic tubs. It is soft in texture and pale ivory in color. One is tempted just to stand back and enjoy its velvety beauty. The flavor resembles a thick, sweet cream; hence it is often used in desserts as well as savory dishes. Good American-made mascarpone is also available in some areas. Regular American cream cheese is not the same and will neither behave nor taste like the real thing.

- Ricotta—cow's milk and, in some lucky parts of the country, sheep's milk. Italian markets usually sell freshly made ricotta. The supermarket variety does not have the same flavor but is perfectly acceptable. Ricotta is actually a cheese by-product, since it is made from the whey that is left after another cheese is made. The whey is recooked, or, in Italian, *ri-cotta*—hence the name.

SPECIALTY CHEESES

- Gorgonzola—cow's-milk Italian blue cheese that can be *dolce* (sweet) or mountain. The sweet variety has excellent melting qualities and becomes quite creamy when stirred into pasta or soup. The mountain is sharper and more robust.

- Fontina—this cow's-milk cheese with its earthy flavor is one of Italy's most elegant and distinctive cheeses. Authentic Italian Fontina has a brown-gold rind and purple trademark stamped on it. Avoid the imitations in red plastic wrappers. Fontina melts beautifully, and I often mix it with mozzarella to use in baked pasta dishes.

- Ricotta Salata—sheep's-milk ricotta, which is salted and briefly cured, so that it is slightly firm. Its mild, nutty flavor makes it a good accompaniment to olives for a simple antipasto dish. Most often it is grated into pasta dishes, although it will not melt into a dish the way true *grana* cheeses do.

Shopping Online

I realize that you may live in an area of the country where quality Italian products are not easy to come by, but the advent of the amazing Internet makes it possible to create an impressive Italian pantry without ever leaving home. These are just some of the Web addresses I have used for products. Since the Internet is growing, changing, appearing, and disappearing on a regular basis, I apologize in advance for changes or omissions.

TODARO BROTHERS. 555 2nd Avenue, New York, New York 10016; local phone, 212-679-7766. Toll free, 877-472-2767. http://www.todarobros.com

This venerable New York *salumeria* has long been a reliable source of Italian products to those fortunate enough to live nearby. Now their extensive line of reasonably priced merchandise is a mere dotcom from your doorstep.

ITALIAN FOOD EXPERIENCE. Esperya USA, 1715 West Farms Road, Bronx, New York 10460; local phone, 718-860-2949; fax, 718-860-4311. Toll free, 877-907-2525. http://www.esperya.com

A super shopping guide for a wide range of products imported from many regions of Italy but shipped from New York, so delivery time is usually 24 hours. They offer a wide and excellent selection of foods, including my favorite brands of dried pasta—Latini, Rustichella d'Abruzzo, and Martelli.

URBANI TRUFFLES AND CAVIAR ONLINE. 800-281-2330. http://www.urbani.com

Think of Urbani's as the Tiffany's of food. Nothing comes cheap here, and nothing cheap comes from here. For years they have been the primary source of Italian black and white truffles, but they also offer a fabulous selection of dried mushrooms and other hard-to-find Italian items. Some items can be purchased only in bulk, so if you want prosciutto you must buy the entire leg. It's not a bad idea if you can entice a number of friends to share it with you.

MOZZARELLA COMPANY. 2944 Elm Street, Dallas, Texas 75226; 800-798-2954. http://www.mozzco.com

When Dallas native Paula Lambert returned to Texas from a long stay in Italy and could not find the mozzarella cheese with which she had fallen in love, she returned to the Italian source and learned to make her own. She was quickly supplying a long list of in-the-know restaurants with her constantly evolving selections. Her fresh mozzarella has won more awards than I can count, but also try her caciotta, scamorza, and—well, get the sample package.

IDEAL CHEESE SHOP, LTD. 942 1st Avenue (at 52nd Street), New York, New York 10022; 800-382-0109. http://www.idealcheese.com

One of the finest sites for quality Italian cheeses. Products come well wrapped, and usually contain instructions for storing and suggestions for using.

FORTUNA'S SAUSAGE CO. 975 Greenville Avenue, Greenville, Rhode Island 02828; 800-427-6879. http://www.soupy.com

This homespun site is produced by a Rhode Island–based family company, Fortuna's. "Soupy" is the pet Italian name for soppressata, a dry-cured, dense, and flavorful sausage popular for centuries with Italians. In addition to their family's own soupy, Fortuna's sells other family-made dry-cured sausages and salamis, as well as olives and Italian cheeses.

JAMISON FARM. 171 Jamison Lane, Latrobe, Pennsylvania 15650; 800-237-5262. http://www.jamisonfarm.com

Lamb has always been a favorite with Italians, especially for spring celebrations. We have an excellent source in the persons of John and Sukey Jamison. They have been raising animals on natural feed (bluegrass and white clover in the hills of Appalachia) for the past 25 years.

NIMAN RANCH. East 12th Street, Oakland, California 94696; 510-808-0340. http://www.nimanranch.com

Niman's oversees a network of sustainable family farms that raise animals naturally and humanely. This 20-year-old California provider of quality meats to fine restaurants and markets is now directly accessible to home cooks through this easy-to-navigate Web site. A wide selection of lamb, pork, and beef products, including the sometimes hard to find caul fat, are efficiently packaged and shipped.

SALUMERIA ITALIANA. 151 Richmond Street, Boston, Massachusetts 02109; 800-400-5916. http://salumeriaItaliana.com

The Salumeria Italiana in Boston's old North End has long been a Mecca for shoppers in search of the best and most authentic Italian products. I know people who make regular long-distance trips to stock up on prosciutto, pancetta, polenta, risotto, San Marzano tomatoes, imported pasta, vinegars, oils, and so much more from many regions of Italy. And now it's all available to you wherever you are.

CONSTANTINO'S VENDA RAVIOLI. 265 Atwells Avenue, Providence, Rhode Island 02903; 401-421-9105, or contact them at *venda265@aol.com.*

Why am I giving you this when I have no online address? As this book goes to press, they are working on a Web site, and I would hate for you to miss it. Venda is my hands-down favorite Italian *salumeria*. The atmosphere, the products, the staff—many who have been there as long as I can remember—will instantly show you what Italian food, family, and tradition are all about; at the most reasonable prices I've found anywhere. Venda's motto—"Every day is Sunday"—will strike a chord with Italians who remember that Sundays meant homemade pasta, family, and more Italian food than could be consumed in the allotted four-hour meal. If the site is not ready at this time, make a trip to Providence. It's worth it—and tell Betty hello.

GASBARRO'S. 361 Atwells Avenue, Providence, Rhode Island 02903; 401-421-4170, or fax, 401-274-WINE (9463). Web site in progress.

Another of my favorite Providence haunts, Gasbarro's, has the largest selection of Italian wines and spirits in this country. So don't worry if I call for something that sounds difficult to find, such as Malvasia di Lipari, Alchermes, and Maraschino. It is sure to be right there on his shelves. Until the site is up and running, telephone or fax my friend Lombard Gasbarro and, if your state allows, he will ship the bottle to you. As a matter of fact, if you are a true Italian food–aphile, call him anyway. Lombard is in Italy as much as he is here, and he is always ready to tell you what he ate where and which of Italy's latest wine treasures he drank with it.

Cooked Ingredients to Have on Hand

In addition to the raw staples listed at the beginning of the chapter, a well-stocked Italian larder contains such prepared foods as tomato and white sauces, boiled beans, and a selection of broths. Having such items on hand will allow you to prepare dishes quickly. The flavor of these cooked staples is as important as the quality of all the raw ingredients that you've taken such care to purchase. Although many of them are available in cans or jars in the market, your own homemade will be infinitely better. When you have the time, turn on a Verdi opera and prepare your own market of Italian products.

Making Ahead

To save you the frustration of beginning to prepare a recipe only to find that it requires an ingredient that needs to be cooked ahead, I have listed such ingredients first in each recipe, under the heading "Making Ahead." Of course, if you have stocked your freezer with the suggested cooked items, you'll be ready in the bleep of a microwave.

The Two Basic Tomato Sauces

In Italian cooking, tomato sauce is not only something served over pasta, but also an integral part of other recipes—one of the ingredients.

Italian cuisine has a great variety of tomato-based sauces, most of which are variations of two main types: *marinara,* a quick, meatless sauce, and *ragù,* a long-cooking sauce with meat. What is important to note is the difference in flavor and uses between a sauce made with meat and one without. *Marinara* is light and toma-toey; *ragù* is rich and meaty.

Marinara Sauce

MAKES ABOUT 9 CUPS

I grew up calling a meatless tomato sauce *marinara* because that was the name my grandparents used. They grew up in Ischia, off the coast of Naples, and their food and dialect was basically Neapolitan. *Marinara* is Italian for "seaside" or "mariner," but this classic Neapolitan sauce does not have seafood in it. Some say it was named for Neapolitan fishermen who often came in hungry from a day at sea. They would gather on the beach and quickly throw tomatoes and herbs into a skillet over an open fire. Others claim that it was named for the fishermen's wives; having spotted her husband's fishing boat approaching shore, a wife would start this sauce and have his dinner on the table by the time he reached her door. Still others credit the name to the fact that this sauce is the base in which Neapolitans poached seafood. Whatever the lore, this style of quick tomato sauce is always credited to Naples and is to me the one that best retains the character of the tomato. It is, however, only one style of Italian meatless tomato sauce. Others may contain carrots and celery; some call for pureeing or straining the cooked tomatoes. They may be called *pommarola* (or *pummarola*) or *sugo di pomodoro*.

Canned Italian tomatoes are fine, but keep your eye out for local tomatoes in season. Buy the ripest you can find and make large quantities of sauce. Use what you need and then store the remainder in the refrigerator for up to four days, or freeze in 1-to-4-cup portions for up to four months. If you develop a passion for cooking Italian, you will need that sauce. You will use it in place of canned tomatoes in soups for a deeper, richer flavor, or poach fish in it, or use it to braise meats, chicken, and vegetables. You can use it to build other, more complex tomato sauces. And, of course, you'll want it for pasta.

When I make *marinara* in large quantities, I use a minimum of olive oil to begin the recipe—just enough to coat the pan. Then, when I am ready to use the sauce, I reheat it with a little fresh oil or butter, deciding then which flavor will best complement the dish. I also add more fresh basil to a thawed sauce.

About 3 tablespoons extra-virgin olive
  oil
5 large garlic cloves, thinly sliced, or
  1 large onion, finely chopped
¼ to ½ teaspoon hot red-pepper flakes
  or paprika

About 10 cups peeled, seeded, and
  chopped fresh or canned tomatoes,
  with their juices (pages 21–22)
About 1 tablespoon salt
¾ cup basil leaves, torn into small pieces
Small pinch sugar, if necessary

Coat the bottom of a deep saucepan with the oil and set it on medium-low heat. Add the garlic or onion and cook, stirring often, until it is golden in color and softened; do not allow it to brown, or it will become bitter. Add the pepper flakes or paprika, and stir for 15 seconds, then pour in the tomatoes with their juice and bring to a boil. Reduce the heat to low, season with salt and basil, and simmer 20 to 25 minutes. The sauce will have thickened and you may notice small pools of orange where the oil has separated from the tomatoes. Stir in the basil, taste carefully, and adjust the seasoning if necessary. Whether or not you need the pinch of sugar will depend on your tomatoes. If the sauce lacks the natural sweetness of perfectly ripe, fresh tomatoes, then add the sugar.

Bottled Sauces

Nothing could be simpler to make than *marinara*, and yet the proliferation of bottled sauces on the market tells me that many cooks don't want to bother or don't know how easy it is. I find most bottled sauces are too often overcooked, taste unpleasantly pasty, and have a disturbing number of dried herbs fighting one another. Many Italian markets and specialty-food stores sell freshly made tomato sauces that I wouldn't hesitate to use as part of other recipes. Alone on pasta, I use only my own freshly made sauce.

Long-Simmering Meat Sauce

Ragù

MAKES ABOUT 7 CUPS

Neapolitan *ragù,* or "gravy," as some Italian-Americans translated it, is an abundant sauce flavored with fist-size pieces of beef and pork, long links of sausages, at least a dozen meatballs, and a well-seasoned rolled piece of beef or pork (*braciole,* or *"bragiol"* in dialect). Such abundance! Since it was usually the focal point of the traditional and compulsory Italian family Sunday meal, it had to be.

My grandmother made a large pot of *ragù* twice a week, every week. On the day she made it, she served it over spaghetti or macaroni, and on Sundays, over freshly made ravioli or in lasagna. It remained in the refrigerator all week and Nonna would ladle out small amounts to use in a number of other recipes. When she fried sausage or veal and peppers, in went a cup of sauce. It was the "mayonnaise" for a meatball sandwich. It was the layering for her eggplant Parmesan.

When we left Nonna's house after Sunday dinner, she often sent us home with some of her sauce in a blue-and-white-striped pottery bowl with a kitchen plate as a cover. During the week, we all dipped into that sauce for our own culinary creations. My brother Chuck would carefully lay English muffins on a baking tray, lightly toast them in the oven, and them cover them with the sauce, sprinkle them with cheese and dried oregano, and heat them again. They were "Chuck's pizzas" and were absolutely delicious—I think.

For Italians, *ragù* makes two courses; the sauce is served over pasta for one course and the meat that flavored the sauce is served with a salad or vegetables for a second course. Therefore, although any piece of pork or beef will flavor the sauce, if you want to eat it, choose cuts that will become tender after the long cooking.

1 pound each inexpensive pork and
    beef, preferably some with bones
    attached (e.g., neck, shoulder, shank,
    shoulder chops, spareribs, stewing
    beef)
¼ cup extra-virgin olive oil
1 medium onion, coarsely chopped
    (about 1½ cups chopped)

Salt
½ a hot pepper or ¼ teaspoon hot red-
    pepper flakes (optional)
6 cups canned Italian plum tomatoes,
    seeded but with their juice, finely
    chopped (see pages 21–22)
2 cups water or 1½ cups water and
    ½ cup red wine

Trim any excess fat from the meat, then rinse the meat and pat it dry. Cut it into large pieces—4 to 5 inches long. Heat the oil in a deep pot and brown the meat on all sides; work in batches if your pan will not hold all the meat in one layer. Remove the pieces to a bowl as they are browned; when they are all out of the pan, reduce the heat and stir in the onions, salt, and the hot pepper if you are using it. Cook the onions slowly, moving them around the pan often, until they are translucent; do not let them brown or the sauce will be bitter. Pour in the tomatoes and the water or water and wine. Season with salt, bring to a quick boil, then reduce the heat and return the meat to the pan. Put the cover on askew to avoid too rapid a reduction and adjust the burner so the sauce simmers very slowly. If it does become too thick, add small amounts of warm water. Cook about 2 hours, until the meat is tender and the flavor is delicious! Dip a piece of Italian bread in and taste it to be sure.

Remove the meat from the sauce and serve, or store it separately with a little of the sauce on top. The sauce can be used immediately on pasta or stored for up to 5 days in the refrigerator or 3 months in the freezer.

VARIATION: The recipe can be doubled or tripled with great success.

VARIATION: Even my sons, when they were too young to know it as "*ragù* and pasta" asked for "spaghettimeatball" as though it were one dish. Italians do not always eat meatballs with spaghetti and *ragù* but they are a delicious addition. Use the meatball recipe on page 91 in the soup chapter, but shape them into ten balls of about 1¼ inches round. Add them to the sauce during the last 30 minutes of cooking. You can add them as is (my family's method) or brown them first in a little olive oil. I think adding them "nude" makes them more tender. Sausage is also a common addition, but it should be browned at the same time as the other meat and left in the sauce for the long cooking.

White Sauce

MAKES ABOUT 4½ CUPS

Although a white sauce will pop up here and there in Italian cooking, its starring role is in baked pasta dishes. It elevates them to an almost elegant status. White sauce (*besciamella*) freezes beautifully, so, if you are in the mood, make a large amount; the recipe can easily be doubled or tripled. Freeze it in cup-size plastic freezer bags or containers. A thawed leftover sauce can be refrozen. You will be very happy to have it when you are wondering what to make quickly for a crowd and lasagna comes to mind.

4 tablespoons (½ stick) unsalted butter

⅓ cup flour

4½ cups milk, heated

2 or 3 gratings of nutmeg

Salt and freshly ground black pepper to taste

Melt the butter in a heavy saucepan on medium-low heat. Take the pan off the heat and sprinkle the flour on the melted butter; whisk constantly until you have a smooth paste. Working off the heat will give you better control at preventing lumping. Return the pan to the heat and cook for 6 minutes on low heat, whisking often, to cook away the raw-flour taste. Do not allow the paste to color.

Again remove the pan from the heat and pour in the heated milk, slowly, in a steady stream, whisking well to create a smooth sauce. Return the pan to the heat and bring the sauce to a boil. It will thicken quickly. Stir in the nutmeg, salt, and pepper, turn the heat to low, and cook gently for 30 minutes to blend the flavors, stirring often and thoroughly to prevent it from sticking on the bottom. The sauce will reduce slightly and thicken. The sauce may be used immediately, cooled and refrigerated for 3 days, or frozen for 3 months.

VARIATION: The above recipe is for a very simple, all-purpose white sauce. You can vary the flavor by slowly cooking a few tablespoons each of finely chopped carrots and onions in the butter. Add the flour once the vegetables are soft, and add a sprig or two of fresh thyme after adding the milk. Strain the sauce before using.

Broth

HOMEMADE BROTH

My grandfather owned his own butcher shop, and Saturday was his busiest day, since meat was commonly the centerpiece of the traditional Italian noon meal on Sunday. His day would be spent cutting whole calves into the veal parts, and large sides of beef into roasts and steaks. Down the street, the "chicken man" was doing the same thing with his hens and rabbits. On Monday morning, they would place the bones and nonsalable pieces from their Saturday trimming in their cases for shoppers to take for their Monday *brodo*-making.

It's been a very long time since I've seen such kitchen jewels offered free, but if you develop a good relationship with a market that trims its own meat, you can ask for some. If you are an avid cook, you can collect your own. Save the bones when you remove them from chicken breasts; use chicken carcasses—raw or from a cooked bird—reserve wing tips and vegetable tops and trimmings. Keep these pieces in plastic bags in the freezer, and make a broth when the bags are full. Italians use broth in a number of ways: to make soup, to deglaze a pan, to braise meats and vegetables, and occasionally to poach.

Recipes for broth should be considered merely guidelines; there's a lot of wiggle room here. Perhaps you have a small bunch of scallions on hand, a potato to use up, or are short on carrots. You can use almost anything, but be careful of strong-tasting ingredients such as those from the cabbage family. Eggplant will muddy the broth; too many carrots will make it overly sweet. Lamb and pork would dominate the flavor.

Chicken or Meat Broth

BRODO DI POLLO O BRODO DI CARNE

MAKES ABOUT 3 QUARTS

Italian meat broth cooks a shorter time and is consequently lighter and less concentrated than what the French call "stock." In fact, many fine Italian home cooks use reconstituted bouillon cubes, and Italian cookbooks often call for water, not broth. The point is that if you use a rich, concentrated stock the finished dish will not taste like Italian home cooking.

Use only chicken for the chicken broth, and a combination of chicken and meats or just meat for meat broth. Be sure always to use some veal for the meat broth. Since the broth may be used as part of another recipe, which could be salty, do not salt it while it is cooking.

About 5 pounds meaty chicken bones (backbones, carcasses, necks, wings, giblets), or use a 5-pound chicken

Or 5 pounds (total) chicken and inexpensive meaty beef and veal pieces with bones (beef neck, veal breast, veal shins, etc.)

2 medium carrots, washed, peeled, and cut into 2-inch pieces

3 medium onions, quartered

3 celery stalks, with tops, cut into 2-inch pieces

3 plum tomatoes, canned or fresh

1 bay leaf

Small bunch parsley stems

Put the meat and bones into a 7-to-8-quart stockpot, and add enough warm water just to cover the pieces. Bring to a boil, and then immediately discard the water and rinse the meat and bones under warm running water. This initial quick boil will clean the bones and save you from having to skim continuously.

Return the meat and bones to the pot, add the vegetables, and pour in about 4 quarts of cold water; enough to cover the ingredients by an inch or two. Bring to a boil and add the herbs. Reduce the heat and simmer gently, uncovered, for 2 to 3 hours, or until the broth has a delicate chicken or meat flavor. While the broth is cooking, skim any foam that rises to the top. Do not let the broth boil hard when it has the meat and vegetables in it, or it will become cloudy.

Strain the finished broth through a fine-meshed strainer or washed cheesecloth, and refrigerate until any fat has risen to the top. Spoon off and discard the fat, and your broth is ready to use immediately.

VARIATION: **Brown Broth.** The above is a white broth, light in color. To make a brown broth, slightly richer in flavor, put the meat, bones, and vegetables in a large roasting pan and coat lightly with oil. Roast at 450° F for about 30 minutes, until the ingredients are browned but not blackened. Pour off all the fat and transfer the pieces to the stockpot. Add the herbs, pour in the water, and continue as above. The broth may be stored 3 days in the refrigerator, or frozen for 3 months. Always boil refrigerated or frozen broth before using, to kill any possible bacteria.

Vegetable Broth

MAKES 4 QUARTS

I am sure that vegetable broth was once a standard part of Italian home cooking, since meat was scarce in much of Italy, especially in the south. It was not part of my family's cooking, because my grandfather's shop supplied all the meat we could use. I include it here because I know there is a need for a substitute to meat broth. Many of my sons' friends are vegetarians, and I have friends who follow strict liturgical fast days or simply want to cut down on the meat in their diets.

2 to 4 medium onions, quartered

4 medium carrots, washed, peeled, and cut into 2-inch pieces

4 to 6 medium celery stalks, some with tops, cut into 2-inch pieces

3 plum tomatoes, canned or fresh

Greens from about 6 scallions, washed

2 bay leaves

2 or 3 sprigs fresh thyme, or 1 teaspoon dried

1 small bunch flat-leaf parsley, including stems

4 quarts cold water

Put all of the ingredients in a saucepan with a capacity of at least 8 quarts. Bring the water to a boil, then reduce the heat and simmer for 1 hour. Strain the broth through a fine-mesh strainer or through washed cheesecloth, and use immediately or allow it to cool for storing. The broth may be stored 3 days in the refrigerator, or frozen for 3 to 4 months.

When a recipe calls for broth in addition to a number of other ingredients that will dominate its flavor, I often use canned broth. On the other hand, if I am making a dish in which the broth is the main attraction, such as *pasta in brodo* (clear soup with pasta), I always use my own carefully seasoned broth. I keep cans of unsalted chicken, beef, and vegetable broth on hand. I use the chicken broth straight from the can, but when I want a meat broth, *brodo di carne,* I mix 1 can of chicken broth with 1 can of beef broth, because I find canned beef broth alone is the wrong flavor for Italian dishes. Sometimes a recipe calls for ½ or ¼ cup of broth. Once you have opened a can, you can use what you need and freeze the rest. Thawed broth should always be boiled before use, to kill any possible bacteria. Leftover canned broth can be frozen and thawed again.

Shell Beans

With the exception of a few seasonal offerings, it is rare to find a proliferation of fresh shell beans in the average market. Dried beans, on the other hand, are readily available, and if they haven't been sitting in a bin for too long are of excellent quality. Check their age by their appearance. Young beans will be glossy; older beans dull and wrinkled. Older beans take forever to cook and lose their "beany" flavor. Choose those without cracks, store tightly covered in a dry place, and use within a year.

Having cooked beans on hand is like arriving at a busy checkout counter and being waved to the first place in line. Some canned beans, drained and rinsed, are acceptable for soups, though they cost more and never have a flavor or texture as good as your own. Frozen cooked beans are closer to home-cooked ones. Some markets carry a small variety of frozen beans, but it is easy to freeze your own (see below).

Typical of Italian cooking are cannellini (white kidney beans), for which I often substitute Great Northern beans; *borlotti* (cranberry beans), *lenticchie* (brown lentils), *ceci* (chickpeas or garbanzos), and fava (broad beans).

Dried beans are soaked before cooking in order to reduce their cooking time. Directions usually state, "Cover with cold water by 2 inches and soak overnight." Actually, 4 hours is sufficient for most beans (stubborn fava beans need at least

12). I have seldom used the long-soak method since some astute cook alerted us to the "quick-soak" technique that works just fine. Either way, first wash the beans and go over them carefully to remove any small stones.

For the "quick-soak" method, put the beans in a pot and cover with water by 2 inches. Bring to a boil, boil 2 minutes, then cover and turn off the heat. Let the beans sit for 1 hour, then drain. Do not add any salt to the soaking water or to the beans while they are cooking, because it will toughen the skins and they will not become tender. Once the beans have softened, they can be salted.

COOKING

To cook the beans, pour the soaked beans into a clean pot and cover with fresh water by 3 inches. Bring to a boil, and then reduce the heat so the liquid barely simmers. For about every 1 cup of beans, include large pieces of a celery stalk with its top, one medium onion, 1 tablespoon olive oil, one bay leaf, three fresh sage leaves, and optionally a 1-ounce piece of pancetta and three peeled garlic cloves. Simmer until the beans are tender; you should be able to mash a cooked bean easily with your fingers. Fish the vegetables and pancetta out of the liquid.

Cooking times will vary according to the beans:

Cannellini: 1 to 1½ hours
Borlotti: 45 minutes to 1 hour
Lenticchie: need no presoaking. They will cook in 30 to 35 minutes.
Ceci: 2 to 2½ hours

Fava beans, alas, must be peeled, a necessary, time-consuming chore. Peel after soaking, using your thumbnail or a paring knife to coax apart the skin. Peeled favas can take anywhere from 1 to 3 hours to become tender.

Do not salt the beans until they have become tender, or they never will; 1 cup of dried beans need about 1 teaspoon of salt. Beans will just about double in volume when they are cooked. Store the cooked, cooled beans in their liquid in the refrigerator for 3 days, or in the freezer for about 3 months. If you have cooked a large amount, which I greatly recommend, fill several plastic freezer bags with 1½ cups of beans each and some of the cooking liquid.

Using This Book

Get Ready

Regardless of which recipe you choose to make, be sure to read through the entire Primary Recipe at the beginning of that section. That is the only one that precisely details the techniques you need to know for all the recipes and variations that follow in that section. Then, before you turn on the heat, get out all your ingredients. Do all the washing, peeling, chopping, and measuring that is required. When all the prepared items are lined up next to you, begin to cook. This "putting in place" of the items you need allows you to cook with ease rather than with chaos.

Watch and Taste

My brothers, sister, and I agree we seldom saw Nonna anywhere but in her kitchen. This was not unusual for Italian women of that generation. I spoke with a man whose grandmother's sole pastime was feeding the household. He recalled a day when he was gathered with his large family in front of the television to watch a space landing. His grandmother called from the kitchen that dinner was ready. "We can't come now. John Glenn is just coming down." "Bring him. I cooked plenty!" she answered.

Our grandmothers weren't always stirring when they were in the kitchen, but they were observant. Whether it's a soup or a sauce or a stew, watch it, stir it, check its temperature, make sure the bottom isn't sticking. And for heaven's sake—taste!

Seasoning

The choice and amount of seasoning in each recipe is merely a guide. It should be a matter of taste—yours. There are, however, some basic chemical principles involved in seasoning that influence the success of a dish. The use of salt is one. Salt is not only a seasoning, it is a preservative. That means that it has the ability to seal in the flavor of a food. You will notice that I direct you to season each component of a dish as it is added. That is because I want that ingredient to maintain its individual character—its flavor. Use the salt sparingly, so the final dish will not be overly salty.

Chemistry is also involved in the balance of a dish. Lemon juice will add acid, which will perk up flavor. Salt will temper too much acid. Cream or butter will tame a dish that got away from you with too much acidity or spice.

CHAPTER 2

Soups

My relationship with soup has had a checkered past. Italian immigrants of my grandparents' generation often made an evening meal of soup, especially when they had eaten a substantial lunch. My grandfather went home (upstairs, over his meat market) every noon for a long midday meal. When he closed shop late in the evening, Nonna would feed him soup. I have such a clear, warm vision of Papa sitting at the large oak table in a freshly donned white shirt with his suspenders comfortably dropped from his shoulders, slowly relishing that soup with a bit of bread, perhaps a salad or some cooked vegetables, and a small glass of homemade wine. When we grandchildren spent an evening, Nonna fed us earlier than she did Papa, but it was usually soup—splendidly satisfying soup. My favorite was her version of *Zuppa alla Pavese* (page 89)—chicken broth in which she cooked the tiniest pasta before dropping in an egg that gently poached in the hot broth. Topped with butter and Parmesan cheese, it was and still is my quintessential comfort food.

When I became involved with food professionally and Italian cooking became a discipline rather than supper, I learned that soup (like Nonna's other standard evening meal, pasta) was only the first course in the composition of the cultured Italian meal. Subsequently, for years, I hesitated to consider my grandmother's plebeian practice worthy of my family or friends. My meals were all structured in the Italian manner of at least two courses—soup or pasta first, followed by a meat or fish dish. I felt continental.

Fortunately, distance and perspective play indispensable roles in teaching us to appreciate the traditions of bygone days. Now I am quite content to make a meal of soup.

Soups are a satisfying means to understanding the basics of Italian cooking because they are flexible and forgiving. Once you have mastered the straightforward method of the Primary Recipe, you can try your own combination of ingredients. Suggested possibilities are outlined below.

Liquid

Liquid not only puts the "soup" in the soup but also adds flavor. If the soup has a number of highly flavorful ingredients and will cook a fairly long time, you can use water. Simple Italian soups often call for it. A liquid with flavor, however, will give much more interesting results. Chicken, vegetable, fish, or meat broths—home-made or canned—are most commonly used. Other options are the soaking liquid from dried mushrooms, the tomato juices from canned tomatoes, and the cooking liquid from beans. You can combine liquids, but don't mix so many as to create an unpleasant muddle of tastes.

Starch Additions to the Soups

Many different starches, alone or in combination, find their way into Italian soups. To use more than one starch—pasta *and* beans, for example—measure half the amount suggested for each.

RICE

Use short- or medium-grain rice (*riso*), because it will hold its texture during cooking. Arborio is an excellent soup rice, as are Vialone Nano and Carnaroli. Arborio will be the easiest to find. One-half to 1 cup of rice is the right amount for 6 to 8 cups of broth; it will vary according to the volume of other ingredients. Stir the rice into the boiling broth and cook for 15 to 20 minutes, until the rice is tender but firm to the bite (*al dente*).

Chickpeas, lentils, and fava beans are some of my favorite combinations with rice.

PASTA

Choose either fresh egg pasta (*pasta all'uovo*) or dried semolina pasta (*pasta secca*). Small egg-noodle shapes like the irregularly cut *maltagliati,* or stuffed pasta such as small ravioli (*raviolini*) or tortellini, are classic in soups from the north of Italy, whereas *pasta secca* is usual in the south.

For dried pasta, choose small shapes known collectively as *pastine* (small pasta)—*ditalini, tubetti, stelline, acini*—or break spaghetti or *capellini* into small pieces. Chances are, if the pasta ends in "*-ine,*" "*-ini,*" "*-ette,*" or "*-etti*"—suffixes for "small"—then the pasta is the right size for soup.

Use approximately ½ to 1 cup or 4 to 8 ounces of fresh or dried pasta for 6 to 8 cups of broth, depending on the volume of other ingredients and how thick you want the soup. Stir the pasta into the boiling soup and cook, stirring from time to time, until it is tender. The time will vary depending on the size and whether the pasta is fresh or dried. Tiny shapes and fresh flat pasta take only a minute or two; stuffed pasta and ½-inch *ditalini* and *tubetti* need at least 8 minutes; broken spaghetti, up to 20 minutes depending on its thickness. Taste, not time, is your measure. The pasta should be tender, but firm to the bite (*al dente*). You may see recipes that call for the pasta to be boiled first and then added to the soup, in which case it will absorb less liquid. I calculate the liquid accordingly and cook the pasta in the soup, since it will absorb the other flavors. Pasta can make the broth cloudy, but in the case of these vegetable soups, it would never be noticed. In some recipes for *Brodo Ripieno* (page 87), the pasta should be cooked separately to keep the broth clear.

Pasta marries well with any variety of beans.

GRAINS

Depending on the area of Italy, one or another type of grain may be used to thicken soup. Polenta, yellow cornmeal, is used extensively in northern Italy and less often in the south. Look for a coarse-grained yellow cornmeal; very fine polenta, usually labeled *bergamasca,* is more suitable for baking. I've found some domestic brands of stone-ground cornmeal such as that from Grey's Mill of Adamsville, Rhode Island, to be as good as imported varieties.

Use approximately ½ cup of cornmeal for every 6 to 8 ounces of broth, depending on the volume of other ingredients. To avoid lumping, drizzle the cornmeal slowly—*come neve,* "like snow," is the Italian direction—from one hand into the boiling broth as you stir constantly with the other. Or, if you have had bad experiences with lumping cornmeal, you can moisten the dry grain with cold water or broth and then stir the hot broth into it.

Cook the cornmeal for at least 30 minutes, or until it loses its raw taste. Longer cooking will not harm it. The quick-cooking variety of polenta works just fine, but it is not ready in the 5 minutes suggested on the package. I find it needs at least 20 to lose the raw-cornmeal taste.

Semolina, and the American equivalent, farina, will give the soup body and add a bit of protein. Use 1 tablespoon per cup of broth and, as with cornmeal, mix it into some of the cold liquid before pouring it into the soup to avoid lumping. Semolina cooks in three to five minutes after it reaches a boil but can continue to cook without harm until the soup is finished.

Couscous is widely used in the Italian regions of Sicily and Sardinia. *Fregula,* common to Sardinia, is a slightly larger grain than couscous and is beginning to appear in American specialty markets. A half-cup of either is sufficient for 6 to 8 cups of broth. Stir the grain into the boiling broth and cook for 4 to 5 minutes.

Farro is an ancient grain that has enjoyed a rediscovery in the past few years. It is similar to barley and should be soaked in cold water for 2 hours, then drained before using. Stir about 1 cup of the presoaked farro into 6 to 8 cups of boiling broth, where it can take anywhere from 30 minutes to an hour to become tender.

Grains and beans make a sturdy combination.

SHELL BEANS

Soup recipes in this chapter that call for beans specify fully cooked beans (see page 39). Once they are added, the soup needs only to cook long enough to heat them and marry them with the other flavors.

If you do not have cooked beans on hand and are starting with dried beans (other than lentils, which only need to be washed), give them a quick soak as directed on page 40 and finish their cooking in the soup; the soup will take as long to cook as the beans need to become tender. (Use the cooking times on page 40 as a guide to timing.) You may need to add a cup or two more broth if the soup reduces too much during the longer cooking.

Fresh beans need no precooking. Simply break open the pods, flick out the beans, and add them directly to the soup. Most will cook in less than 30 minutes. Fresh fava beans, unless they are very young and small, should be peeled after they are removed from the pods. A 30-second blanching in boiling water will ease the job of peeling the thin skin, which you can accomplish with your fingernails or a sharp paring knife.

Depending on the volume of other ingredients, 6 cups of broth can manage 2 to 3 cups of cooked beans, 2 to 3 cups of fresh beans (about 3 pounds unshelled weight), and 1 to 1½ cups soaked but uncooked dried beans.

Beans are a traditional Italian combination with rice, cornmeal, or pasta.

BREAD

Some of the frugal Italian kitchen's most time-honored soups are substantial meals because thick slices of yesterday's bread are an ingredient. To make the Italian toast, known variously (according to the Italian region) as *bruschetta, crostini,* or *fettunta,* cut firm-textured Italian bread into ½-inch-thick slices, one for each soup bowl, and one or two extras per person to be served separately. Put the slices directly on an oven rack and toast in a 400° F oven for a total of 5 to 7 minutes or more, until the pieces are lightly brown on both sides, turning halfway through. Rub one side of the toasts with the cut side of a halved, unpeeled garlic clove—if you want a garlic flavor—and drizzle or brush that side with olive oil. You can sprinkle grated cheese on the oiled sides and return them to the oven until the cheese melts. The bread can also be toasted on the grill, if you happen to have it lit, or spread with butter and cooked slowly in a frying pan on top of the stove. The toasts can be made several hours ahead of time, but not the day before, or they might take on an off taste. Slide a slice into the bottom of each soup bowl, and ladle the hot soup on top. Add additional flavor by sprinkling chopped fresh herbs on top before ladling on the soup.

Finishing the Soup

Once soup is cooked, it can be "finished" or enriched in a number of ways. This optional last step will add another dimension. Don't be restricted by the suggested finishes at the end of the recipes. Experiment!

CHEESE

Grated cheeses such as Parmesan, grana padano, and pecorino can either be stirred into the soup right before serving or passed at the table.

HERBS

Choose herbs that are already in the soup. Stir in a few tablespoons of chopped fresh herbs and cook for a minute or two before serving. Herbs can also be mixed into grated cheese and stirred together into the soup.

OLIVE OIL, BUTTER, PESTO

Two or three teaspoons of your very best extra-virgin olive oil drizzled onto each hot bowl of soup will please both the nose and the palate. Make your own flavored oil by briefly heating a few tablespoons of oil over very low heat with some chopped fresh herbs and perhaps some finely chopped garlic. A few tablespoons of butter stirred into the finished soup provide a simple enrichment. A tablespoon of pesto stirred into each steaming bowl is sublime.

Egg yolks give any soup a feeling of importance by transforming it into a *vellutata* (see Italian Soups, below). Use three or four yolks per 8 to 10 cups of finished soup. More will make the soup thicker, which is perfectly acceptable. If grated cheese is to be served with the soup, I like to add some first to the eggs. Measure approximately 2 tablespoons of cheese—Parmesan, grana padano, or pecorino—for each egg yolk, and stir it into the beaten yolks. Herbs add yet another dimension, and 3 tablespoons of finely chopped fresh herbs or 1 tablespoon dried is about right for the three yolks.

Adding the yolks to the hot soup is trickier than determining how to flavor them, since the possibility of making scrambled eggs is very real. When the soup has finished cooking, gradually whisk about 1 cup of the hot broth into the eggs to warm them. Then reverse the procedure by beating the warmed eggs back into the soup pan. Carefully bring the soup to a simmer until it has thickened, but do not allow it to boil, or the eggs will indeed scramble.

Italian Soups

MINESTRA: Literally translated, it means "soup," but on Italian menus the plural, *minestre,* often indicates first courses, *i primi,* whether they are soups, pastas, risotti, or polentas. This is probably because they are all served in the slope-sided dish that is also known as a *minestra.* When it is soup, it is usually qualified as *minestra al',* i.e., soup of something or other. That something or other is most often vegetables.

MINESTRONE: When "*-one*" is added to the end of a word, it indicates that the item is large or important. Properly made, *minestrone* is a big, hearty, important vegetable soup.

ZUPPA: Long a mainstay of Italian home cooking, a *zuppa* is distinguished from other soups in that it is always served with or over toasted bread or croutons. In fact, the Italian equivalent of "It's six of one and half a dozen of the other" is *Se non è zuppa è pan bagnata*—"If it's not soup, it's wet bread."

BRODO: Meaning "broth," *brodo* may be meat-, fish-, or vegetable-flavored. It is the clear liquid base of other soups and braises. When it is served as soup it is almost always *ripieno*—that is, filled with pasta, rice, or small pieces of meat or vegetables.

BRODETTO: In most regions of Italy, this term (literally, "little soup") is reserved for fish soups or stews. The "little" refers to the amount of broth and not the substance of the soup, which is usually substantial. There are some meat *brodetti,* but this type of irregularity in Italian terms is to be expected.

BURIDA, BURRIDA, CACCIUCCO, CIUPPI(N): These are just some of the names of the many regional fish soups of Italy.

CREMA (IN REFERENCE TO SOUP AS OPPOSED TO PASTRY) AND PASSATO: Both terms refer to soups that are made creamy by straining or pureeing. They may or may not contain cream.

VELLUTATA: This term, which literally means "velvety," is correctly reserved for soups that have been thickened with egg yolks. I have occasionally seen it used for pureed soups that are not thickened with eggs, but I suspect that it was used incorrectly.

The Soup Pan

The best pan for making soup is one that is heavy and has good, even heat-conduction properties, such as enameled cast iron or copper. Stainless steel works well, but be sure that it is heavy-gauge and preferably with a bottom that has a sandwich of other metals that conduct heat well. This will prevent the ingredients from sticking or "grabbing." If the soup contains high-acid ingredients such as tomatoes, lemon juice, or wine, avoid unclad cast iron or aluminum; they will react with the acid and turn the ingredients gray. Otherwise, aluminum is a good conductor of heat.

Although all the soups in this chapter can be made in a 4-to-5-quart pan, my favorite pan has a capacity of 6 quarts. It is 10 inches in diameter and has a decidedly snug-fitting lid. If you cut one of the soup recipes in half, use a smaller pan—2 to 3 quarts—since the soup would reduce too quickly in the larger pan.

Serving Size and Temperature

Most of the recipes in this chapter are substantial enough to make a full meal, perhaps accompanied by bread and a salad. If you wish to have any of these soups as a first course, serve a smaller amount and make certain that the course that follows is simple. To make a soup meal more extravagant, set out an *affettato* platter (Italian cured meats such as prosciutto, sweet and spicy salami, *coppacola, mortadella*), a mixed salad, great wedges of cheese, bowls of herb-scented olives, cooked, cooled vegetables or chicken pieces on the bone dressed with olive oil and vinegar, and Italian bread toasted and flavored with herbs and garlic. It will make a colorful, appealing meal.

The recommended servings in this chapter, unless noted otherwise, are slightly less than 2 cups per person. I can barely eat that much, but my sons eat that much, then finish mine. When you have determined your family's appetites, or want to make just one or two servings, use the guides that follow the recipes in each category to increase or decrease the proportions. Don't worry about making too much; leftover soup in the refrigerator is a treasure.

Most Americans expect their soups to be hot or refrigerator-cold. Italians do not. Though they will enjoy a soup that is hot, they are just as pleased to eat one at room temperature—not cold. Most soups will taste even better a day or two after they have been made. Because some starches, especially rice and pasta, will continue to absorb liquid as they sit, a soup that you have made ahead may become too thick for your liking. In that case, add some additional hot broth to it just before serving. You can also make the base of the soup up to the point of adding the starch, then, later, bring that base to a boil and proceed with the starch. Serve it before the starch has time to absorb more liquid.

Tomato Sauce in Place of Tomatoes

Substituting *marinara* sauce in soup that calls for uncooked tomatoes gives the soup an added depth and the cook a ready shortcut, since the sauce has already cooked long enough to develop its flavor. It is a substitution that you can make in many of the soups that call for tomatoes in the vegetable list. I do not do it when I want the fresh flavor of an in-season tomato. Use slightly less than the amount of tomatoes called for, since the sauce does not need to reduce. But a little more or less is not going to make a great difference. It is then only necessary to cook the soup until the sauce is heated before proceeding to the next step.

VEGETABLE-BASED SOUPS

The soups in this section are what Italians would call *minestre* in that they are primarily vegetable. They are not necessarily vegetarian. Many of them have pancetta in the *soffritto* and/or use beef or chicken broth. You can make them vegetarian by eliminating the pancetta and using vegetable broth in place of meat broth. The soups that list meat in the title, however, contain bite-size pieces of meat; they depend on that meat for substance and would not do well without it. Some meat, such as sausage and beef, can remain in the soup for the duration of the cooking time. Chicken, on the other hand, becomes dry and tough if it cooks too long. The best defense is to brown the chicken, remove it, then return it to the soup near the end of the cooking time and let it simmer there just until it is cooked through.

Zucchini Rice Soup

MINESTRA DI ZUCCHINI E RISO

MAKES ABOUT 10½ CUPS

This recipe pays homage to a summer garden, but it is doable any time of year, since zucchini never seems to go out of season. If yellow summer squash is not available, use all zucchini. In summer, I like to serve this soup at room temperature with a generous garnish of fresh basil or a scoop of pesto.

THE START (*SOFFRITTO*)

2 tablespoons extra-virgin olive oil

1 tablespoon unsalted butter

2 large garlic cloves, finely chopped (about 1 tablespoon)

1 large onion, finely chopped (about 1½ cups)

1 large celery stalk, peeled, trimmed, and finely chopped (about ½ cup)

1 small carrot, peeled, trimmed, and finely chopped (about ⅓ cup)

⅓ cup snipped fresh basil, or 3 tablespoons fresh marjoram or oregano

3 tablespoons chopped fresh flat-leaf parsley

Salt and freshly ground black pepper

The ingredients for the start are for a traditional *battuto* (pages 9–10), which means they should be finely, finely chopped and cooked very slowly. Measure the oil and butter into a 6-quart soup pan and set it over medium-low heat. Stir the garlic, onion, celery, and carrot, and the basil and parsley into the warming oil, season with salt and pepper, and cook slowly and gently until the vegetables are tender, aromatic, and translucent, 15 to 20 minutes. (Pages 9–10 in Chapter 1 have a complete description of cooking a *soffritto*.)

When the vegetables have softened, you are ready to add the zucchini and a bit of salt and pepper. Note that each addition of solid ingredients should be seasoned to bring out its flavor—but seasoned lightly, so the soup is not too salty or peppery. Stir the zucchini into the pan and let it cook, turning it over and around with the aromatics, until it just begins to soften, about 5 minutes. Then put in the yellow squash, season, and cook another 5 minutes, or until it begins to soften. Vegetables should be added to the soup in stages, beginning with the firmest or longest-cooking ones and ending with those that need less time. Giving each vegetable a solo introduction into the pan helps it maintain its own character.

Pour the tomatoes into the pan, season them lightly, and stir so they are evenly distributed. Raise the heat to high and cook for about 3 minutes, or until the tomato juices have reduced by at least half, thereby concentrating their flavor.

Cover the ingredients with the broth and bring it to a boil. Stir the rice or pasta into the boiling soup and continue to stir on high heat until the broth boils again; then reduce the heat so that the soup is at a lazy, steady simmer; its surface should be visibly rippling. Stir the soup now and then, to be sure the rice or pasta is not sticking to the bottom or to itself, and simmer until it is cooked, about 20 minutes for rice, 8 to 10 for pasta. Taste a bit of the starch and of the vegetables to be sure they are cooked, and check the seasoning at the same time.

Stir in the butter and cheese, and serve garnished with more basil if you like.

VARIATION: **Rich Zucchini Soup.** Omit the rice or pasta, and finish the soup with three egg yolks blended with ½ cup of freshly grated cheese (page 48). Serve as is, or pour the enriched soup over toasted Italian-bread slices.

VARIATION: **Carrot Rice Soup.** Substitute the same measure—that is, about 7 cups—of diced carrots for the zucchini and yellow squash. Add a dash of lemon juice with the broth, to balance their sweetness. I like the rice, as opposed to the pasta, best with carrots.

THE VEGETABLES

1 pound zucchini, ends trimmed, washed, cut into ½-inch dice (about 3½ cups)

1 pound yellow squash, ends trimmed, washed, cut into ½-inch dice (about 3½ cups)

1 pound fresh, ripe tomatoes, chopped into rough ¼-inch pieces, or 2 cups drained, chopped canned Italian plum tomatoes

THE BROTH

6 cups meat, chicken, or vegetable broth

THE STARCH

1 cup short-grain rice or tiny pasta such as *stelline* or *acini* or orzo

THE FINISH

2 tablespoons unsalted butter, at room temperature

⅔ cup freshly grated Parmesan cheese

½ cup shredded fresh ham (optional)

Venetian Rice and Pea Soup

RISI E BISI

MAKES ABOUT 9 CUPS

Risi e bisi is Venetian dialect for "rice and peas." Venetians say that the soup was created in honor of the April 25 feast day of St. Mark, patron saint of their republic, which lasted a good thousand years and so was well deserving of such an honor. I suspect, however, that the soup's creation was as much about the spring arrival of peas as it was about the saint. Throughout Italy, peas herald the advent of the growing season. A typical Sicilian spring variation follows the recipe.

Italians only use fresh peas to make *risi e bisi*. I see no reason to wait for spring. Frozen tender tiny peas make a fine soup.

GETTING READY

For fresh peas:

About 2½ pounds (weight still in the pod) fresh peas (about 3 cups shelled)

For frozen peas:

6 cups (20 ounces) tender tiny peas, thawed

THE START (*SOFFRITTO*)

4 tablespoons unsalted butter

2 ounces prosciutto or pancetta, finely chopped

1 large onion, finely chopped (about 1½ cups)

3 tablespoons finely chopped flat-leaf parsley

Salt and freshly ground black pepper

THE VEGETABLE

The shelled peas and peeled pods or thawed peas from above

THE BROTH

6 cups meat broth

THE STARCH

1 cup short-grain rice

THE FINISH

3 tablespoons unsalted butter, at room temperature

About 1½ cups freshly grated Parmesan cheese

Remove the peas from the pods. Taste a few, to make sure they are nicely sweet. If you feel that they are not, use this classic chef's trick. Pick out about a quarter of the pods, choosing those that are plumpest and least blemished. There will be a thin membrane along the inside of each pod. Snap the end of the pod in the direction of the inside and pull down gently. The membrane will come away easily; discard it. Wash the peas and peeled pods together.

Melt the butter and cook the *soffritto* ingredients as in the Primary Recipe (page 52). Stir in the peas and, if you are using fresh peas, the pods; season with salt and pepper and cook for about 2 minutes. Add the broth, bring to a boil, and stir in the rice. Reduce the heat, and simmer for about 20 minutes, until the rice is tender. The pea pods should have disintegrated, or at least be tender enough to remain in the soup for eating. Stir in the butter, and wait for it to begin to melt; then serve the soup with a generous grating of Parmesan cheese.

VARIATION: **Sicilian Rice and Pea Soup with Macaroni.** For a Sicilian version of *risi e bisi,* use olive oil in place of the butter in the *soffritto,* and substitute *ditalini* for the rice and pecorino for the Parmesan. A dash of red-pepper flakes added to the *soffritto* wouldn't be objectionable.

VARIATION: **Spinach or Asparagus Rice Soup.** Use 3 cups of shredded spinach or peeled asparagus pieces in place of the peas.

Cauliflower Soup with Broken Spaghetti

MINESTRA DI CAVOLFIORE ALLA ROMANA

MAKES 10 CUPS

I make this soup with regular white cauliflower, but it would be just as good with purple broccoli or the pale green broccoflower, a type of cauliflower that looks like a cross between broccoli and cauliflower. You could also make it with the same amount of broccoli. See variation below to use broccoli rabe.

THE START (*SOFFRITTO*)

3 tablespoons extra-virgin olive oil

4 to 6 large garlic cloves, even more if
    you like, finely chopped

¼ pound pancetta, finely chopped

¼ to ½ teaspoon hot red-pepper flakes

Salt

THE VEGETABLES

1 large head cauliflower (about
    2¾ pounds untrimmed weight,
    1¾ pounds trimmed)

½ pound fresh, ripe tomatoes (about
    1 cup chopped), or 1 cup drained,
    chopped canned plum tomatoes, or
    1 cup tomato sauce

THE BROTH

6 cups meat, chicken, or vegetable broth

THE STARCH

½ pound thin spaghetti, broken into
    pieces about 2 inches long

THE FINISH

½ cup freshly grated Parmesan or
    pecorino cheese

A healthy grinding of black pepper, or a
    splash of hot-pepper oil

Cook the *soffritto* as in the Primary Recipe (page 52). Chop the cauliflower into small pieces, no larger than ½ inch, and when the *soffritto* is ready toss the pieces into the pan, season with salt, and stir over medium heat until the cauliflower is warmed through, about 7 minutes. Pour in the tomatoes or sauce, cover the pan, and cook over low heat until the cauliflower is tender, about 7 minutes. Uncover the pan, raise the heat, and let the tomato juices reduce by half. Pour in the broth, bring to a boil, and stir in the spaghetti. Simmer for about 18 minutes, or until the spaghetti and cauliflower are tender, stirring often so the pasta doesn't stick to the pan or to itself. Taste. Serve with cheese and black pepper.

VARIATION: **Cream of Cauliflower Soup.** For pureed soup, *crema,* omit the spaghetti and simmer the soup until the cauliflower is quite soft. Puree the finished soup in a blender or food processor.

VARIATION: **Broccoli Rabe and Bean Soup.** Broccoli rabe was a popular Italian-American immigrant food, and, growing up, we must have eaten it a hundred different ways. Soup was just one of my favorites.

For the above recipe, you will need approximately 2 pounds of broccoli rabe. The stems of rabe will remain tough after cooking unless they are peeled beforehand. It is actually a destringing motion akin to peeling celery. Use the sharp side of a small paring knife to grab a piece of peel at the bottom of the stalk and pull it toward the top; it will snap off when it reaches the head. Cut the stems and the tops into ½-inch pieces. Drop them into a large pan of salted, boiling water, and boil for 5 minutes to remove the excess bitterness. Drain, and run under cold water to cool. Use in place of cauliflower above. Beans and rabe are one of the most satisfying combinations (use 3 cups of cooked white or cranberry beans). Or substitute 1½ cups of small dried pasta, such as *ditalini,* or 1½ cups of rice for the broken spaghetti; use pecorino cheese and extra-virgin olive oil to finish the soup.

Soup with Porcini and Cornmeal

MINESTRA DI FUNGHI PORCINI E GRANTURCO

MAKES ABOUT 10 CUPS

As soon as the trees take on a hint of fall color and the air becomes a bit crisp, porcini soup creeps into my thoughts. It is a richly flavored, comforting soup, the directions for which should read, "Light a fire, open a full-bodied red wine, and turn the lights down low."

I like to make this soup with *marinara* sauce—it gives it a deep, rich flavor. If you want to try it with tomatoes instead, use the same amount of drained canned tomatoes or of peeled, squeezed fresh ones.

MAKING AHEAD

1½ cups cooked cannellini or other
   medium-size white beans (page 39)

GETTING READY

1 ounce dried porcini mushrooms

2 cups hot water

THE START (*SOFFRITTO*)

3 tablespoons extra-virgin olive oil

3 large garlic cloves, finely chopped

2 medium onions, finely chopped

¼ teaspoon hot red-pepper flakes

Salt

THE VEGETABLE

Mushrooms from above

THE BROTH

Strained porcini juices from above

5 cups meat broth or vegetable broth

1½ cups *marinara* sauce, or 2 cups
   chopped fresh or canned tomatoes

THE STARCH

½ cup coarse-ground yellow cornmeal

The beans from above

THE FINISH

⅓ cup chopped flat-leaf parsley

Freshly grated Parmesan cheese

Soak the mushrooms in the hot water for 20 minutes, or until they are soft. Lift the mushrooms out of the water with a tea strainer or slotted spoon and rinse them under water until you are sure no dirt or grit remains. Rub your fingertips over them; if there is grit you will feel it. Chop the mushrooms into ¼-inch pieces. Strain the soaking juices through a paper coffee filter or a piece of paper towel set in a small strainer, and reserve mushrooms and juices separately.

Cook the *soffritto* as in the Primary Recipe, page 52. Turn up the heat slightly, to a medium temperature, and stir in the mushrooms; sauté for 5 minutes. Pour in the porcini juices, the broth, and the tomatoes or *marinara* sauce, and bring to a boil. Gradually but steadily stir in the cornmeal; if lumping has been a problem for you in the past, then stir about 2 cups of the cool broth into the cornmeal before adding it to the pan. Cook 10 minutes, stirring frequently. Be sure to scrape your spoon around the sides and the bottom of the pan, since cornmeal will stick to the pan if given the opportunity. Add the beans, and simmer the soup for 30 minutes. Taste carefully. Stir in the parsley, and serve with grated cheese.

VARIATION: Add about ¾ pound of fresh mushrooms to the recipe. Wipe them clean, and trim the ends and slice the caps into thick slices. Stir them into the pan along with the porcini, seasoning them lightly with salt. Sauté them until their juices run and their color is slightly brown. The woodsy flavor of the porcini will permeate the more subtle taste of the cultivated mushroom.

VARIATION: **Cream of Mushroom Soup.** Add the fresh mushrooms as in the variation above, but omit the beans and cornmeal. Use four egg yolks beaten with ½ cup of grated Parmesan to thicken the soup. Serve over slices of toasted Italian bread (page 46).

Tuscan Greens Soup

ZUPPA DI CAVOLO NERO

MAKES ABOUT 10½ CUPS

Tuscans often drizzle fresh olive oil in the shape of a C onto each bowl of soup before serving it. The heat of the soup releases the fragrance and flavor of the oil. Some Italians refer to it as *battesimo dell'olio,* baptizing with oil, so perhaps it symbolizes the casting off of bad taste or evil kitchen spirits. All the more reason to do it.

The traditional Italian green for this soup is Tuscan kale, known as *cavolo nero* (black cabbage). It is a somewhat tangy green that develops a subtle sweetness during cooking. Many American grocery stores, and seed catalogues, market it as "Lacinato" or "dinosaur kale." Regular kale may be substituted if your greengrocer has not yet caught up with the Tuscan variety.

MAKING AHEAD

4 cups cooked cannellini or other medium-size white beans (page 39)

GETTING READY

6 to 12 slices of Italian bread (page 46)

THE START (*SOFFRITTO*)

3 tablespoons extra-virgin olive oil

2 ounces pancetta, finely chopped

1 large red or yellow onion, finely chopped

4 large garlic cloves, finely chopped

1 large celery stalk, finely chopped

1 medium carrot, peeled and finely chopped

Salt and freshly ground black pepper

THE VEGETABLES

1 pound *cavolo nero* (dinosaur kale or Lacinato) or regular kale, stems removed, leaves washed and shredded

½ pound fresh, ripe tomatoes (about 1 cup chopped), or 1 cup drained, chopped canned plum tomatoes, or 1 cup tomato sauce

THE BROTH

6 cups unsalted vegetable or meat broth

THE STARCH

Cooked beans from above

THE FINISH

Extra-virgin olive oil

Toasted Italian bread from above

Toast the bread according to the directions on page 47. Cook the *soffritto* as in the Primary Recipe, page 52. Scatter the kale over the *soffritto,* season with salt and pepper, stir it around to distribute the *soffritto* as evenly as possible, and cook over a moderate heat until the greens are wilted, about 7 minutes. Stir in the tomatoes, season, and cook 7 more minutes. Pour in the broth, and bring to a boil. Then reduce the heat, cover the pan, and simmer for 30 minutes. Add the beans to the soup, and cook, covered, for 20 minutes. Slide a piece of the toasted bread, olive-oil side up, into each soup bowl, and ladle the hot soup on top. Drizzle on a C of olive oil and serve.

VARIATION: A small change but one that is quite common to this soup is to add 2 to 3 tablespoons of fennel seed to the *soffritto.*

VARIATION: Any green, such as spinach or escarole or a mixture of two or three different varieties, will produce perfectly splendid soup. Use a total of approximately 7 cups of shredded greens. Season spinach with a bit of nutmeg or a squeeze of lemon, and consider other starches, such as rice or couscous.

Ischian Pasta and Bean Soup

PASTA E FAGIOLI ALL'ISCHITANA

MAKES ABOUT 9½ CUPS

My paternal grandfather, just like many of the Italian immigrants who settled on Providence's Federal Hill, was born on the island of Ischia, off the coast of Naples. Papa, as we called him, arrived in the United States a 13-year-old boy speaking no English and having no skills other than fig-farming. By the time he met and married Nonna, who was also from Ischia, he had worked and saved enough to buy land in the country, a number of Providence buildings, and his own meat market. He and Nonna were able to provide good sustenance for their family. There was no shortage of meat—the Old World symbol of achievement—but Nonna continued to serve rustic foods, such as *pasta e fagioli,* which were reminiscent of her Ischian childhood. We always called it by its dialect name, *pasta fazoo,* and it was a while before I realized that the more elegant sounding *pasta e fagioli* was the same peasant dish.

MAKING AHEAD

3 cups cooked cranberry beans, white
    beans, or *ceci* (see page 39)

THE START (*SOFFRITTO*)

2 tablespoons extra-virgin olive oil

4 ounces pancetta, finely chopped
    (about 1 cup)

¼ teaspoon hot red-pepper flakes

1 large onion, finely chopped (about
    1½ cups)

3 large garlic cloves, finely chopped

2 medium celery stalks, peeled and
    finely chopped (about ⅔ cup)

Salt and freshly ground black pepper

¼ cup torn basil leaves, or 3 tablespoons
    chopped fresh flat-leaf parsley

THE VEGETABLES

2 pounds fresh plum tomatoes, peeled,
    seeded, and chopped, or 4 cups
    lightly drained canned Italian plum
    tomatoes, coarsely chopped

THE BROTH

6 cups meat or vegetable broth

THE STARCH

Beans from above

1½ cups (12 ounces) mixed small pasta—
    such as *ditalini,* elbow, *tubetti*—or
    use all one shape

THE FINISH

Grated Parmesan or grana-padano
    cheese

Cook the *soffritto* as in the Primary Recipe, page 52. Stir the tomatoes into the pan, season with salt, and cook for 8 to 10 minutes over medium-high heat, to reduce their juices slightly. Pour in the broth and bring to a boil. Stir the beans and pasta into the broth, reduce the heat, and simmer until the pasta is tender. Remember to stir occasionally. Let the finished soup sit at least 5 minutes before serving. Serve hot with grated cheese, or, in the summer, try it at room temperature without the cheese.

Squash Soup with Sausage and Tomatoes

MINESTRA DI ZUCCA, SALSICCIA, E POMODORI

MAKES ABOUT 10 CUPS

My aunt Irma, my father's brother's wife, cooked butternut squash with tomatoes as a vegetable side dish. I took it one step further and made it into a soup—and, at the risk of sounding less than humble, a very good one! I like it best when made with *marinara* sauce.

THE START (*SOFFRITTO*)

3 tablespoons extra-virgin olive oil

3 medium onions, finely chopped (about 3¾ cups)

1 small carrot, finely chopped

4 or 5 large garlic cloves, finely chopped

Salt and ½ teaspoon hot red-pepper flakes

3 tablespoons fresh oregano or marjoram or 1 tablespoon dried

THE MEAT

½ pound sweet Italian sausage, casing removed

THE VEGETABLES

1 medium to large butternut squash (about 2 pounds), peeled and cut into ½-inch dice (about 5 cups)

2½ cups *marinara* sauce or 1½ pounds fresh or lightly drained canned plum tomatoes (about 3 cups chopped)

THE BROTH

6 cups unsalted chicken or meat broth

THE STARCH

¾ cup coarse-ground yellow cornmeal

THE FINISH

About 1 cup freshly grated pecorino or Parmesan cheese (optional)

Cook the *soffritto* as in the Primary Recipe, page 52. When the vegetables are meltingly tender, turn up the heat, tear the sausage into pieces, and drop the pieces into the pan. Work quickly to break the meat into bits about the size of shelled walnut halves and cook until it begins to brown.

Stir the squash into the pan; season with salt and red pepper and cook for about 8 minutes, until it is evenly warm. Pour in the sauce or tomatoes, season, cover the pan, and cook over low heat until the squash is just slightly tender, about 5 minutes. Pour in the broth, bring to a boil, and then slowly and steadily stir in the polenta, or, if you are afraid of lumping, stir about 2 cups of the cool broth into the cornmeal before adding it to the pan. Either way, keep stirring as you add the cornmeal to prevent lumping and sticking. Simmer until the squash is tender and the cornmeal is cooked, about 25 minutes. Serve with or without grated cheese.

VARIATION: Four cups of any winter squash can be substituted for the butternut.

VARIATION: **Squash Soup with Rice and Tomatoes.** Omit the sausage from the recipe above and replace the cornmeal with 1 cup of rice. Cook the soup until the rice is tender, about 20 minutes. Serve with cheese.

VARIATION: **Squash Soup with Pancetta and Tomatoes.** Substitute ⅓ pound of finely chopped pancetta for the sausage and cook it with the vegetables in the *soffritto*.

VARIATION: **Cream of Winter Squash and Tomato Soup.** To make this a pureed soup *(crema),* omit the cornmeal and when the squash is tender puree it in a blender or food processor.

Cabbage and Sausage Soup

MINESTRA DI CAVOLO E SALSICCIA

MAKES ABOUT 11 CUPS

This thick and hearty soup will soothe a chilly autumn or winter evening. In this recipe, the sausage is cooked with the aromatics as part of the *soffritto*.

THE START (*SOFFRITTO*)

2 tablespoons extra-virgin olive oil

1½ pounds Italian sweet sausage, casing
  removed

2 medium onions, thinly sliced (about
  3 cups)

3 large garlic cloves, coarsely chopped

Salt

¼ teaspoon hot red-pepper flakes

2 teaspoons fennel seed

THE VEGETABLES

1½ pounds Savoy cabbage or regular
  green cabbage, shredded

2 cups fresh or canned Italian plum
  tomatoes, with juices, chopped

THE BROTH

6 cups unsalted meat broth

3 to 4 tablespoons red-wine vinegar

THE STARCH

1 cup *ditalini* or *tubetti*

Measure the oil into the soup pan and set it over medium heat. Tear the sausage into pieces and drop them into the pan. Work quickly to break the meat into pieces about the size of shelled walnut halves, and cook until it begins to brown. Stir in the onions and garlic, season with the salt and red pepper, and cook gently until the onions are limp. Stir in the fennel seeds and cook for 1 minute to blend flavors.

Use a long, sturdy wooden spoon or fork to stir the cabbage into the onions and sausage so the pieces are nicely distributed. Season lightly, and cook on low heat until the cabbage wilts, about 10 minutes. Keep the heat low enough, and stir the pan frequently, so that the cabbage wilts but does not brown.

When the cabbage is limp, pour in the tomatoes, season, and bring their juices to a boil so they will reduce by about a third. Add the broth and the vinegar, and bring again to a boil. Taste the soup after adding 3 tablespoons of the vinegar, and decide if you want to add more. It should be subtly tangy.

Stir in the pasta, and turn down the heat so the soup simmers. Stir occasionally to prevent the pasta from sticking. When the pasta is cooked *al dente,* 8 to 10 minutes, check the seasonings and serve.

VARIATION: **Sausage, Chicory, or Escarole and Chickpea Soup.** Substitute 1½ pounds of shredded chicory or escarole for the cabbage. Because these lettuces are bitter, they should first be boiled in a large pot of boiling salted water for 3 minutes, then drained and dried, before being added to the soup pan. Substitute chickpeas for the pasta, and serve the soup over toasted Italian bread (page 47) with a drizzle of olive oil.

Chicken Soup with Lemon, Spinach, and Artichokes

MINESTRA DI POLLO, SPINACI, E CARCIOFI

MAKES ABOUT 11 CUPS

Nonna's *minestra di pollo* began with a visit to the chicken man, where she personally selected a live hen. With no ceremony worth recording, the chicken man relieved the bird of its head and sent my grandmother home with the rest. Back in her kitchen, she finished dressing the bird right down to hand-plucking the feathers. The denuded chicken went into the soup pan with water and vegetables. Cooking the whole bird will indeed provide a rich broth, but there is not always the time to do so or the desire to make such a large amount. This quick method makes a lovely, quick soup. You can also use leftover cooked chicken, which you should shred or chop and add to the soup when the pasta is cooked.

GETTING READY

2 large globe artichokes, trimmed and
thinly sliced, or two 9-ounce boxes
frozen artichoke hearts, defrosted
(3½ cups) (see page 368 for artichoke-
trimming directions)

THE START (*SOFFRITTO*)

3 tablespoons extra-virgin olive oil

2 boneless, skinless chicken-breast halves
(about ¾ pound total)

2 large onions, finely chopped

4 large garlic cloves, finely chopped

Zest of 1 large lemon

⅔ cup finely chopped Italian flat-leaf
parsley

2 teaspoons finely chopped fresh thyme

Salt and freshly ground black pepper

THE VEGETABLES

The artichokes from above

½ pound spinach, stems removed, leaves
coarsely chopped (about 4 cups)

THE BROTH

8 cups chicken broth

Juice of 1 large lemon

THE STARCH

1 cup short-grain rice or *ditalini* or
tubetti

THE FINISH

¼ cup chopped Italian flat-leaf parsley

½ cup freshly grated Parmesan cheese

Coarsely ground black pepper

Heat the oil in the soup pan over medium heat, and sauté the chicken breasts on both sides just until they lose their pink color. Push the chicken to the side of the pan and stir the onions, garlic, zest, and herbs into the oil. Do add more oil if the pan is dry. Push the chicken back to the center of the pan and season everything with salt and pepper.

Cook the *soffritto* gently, turning the chicken once, until the onions and garlic are limp and translucent and the chicken is cooked through to the center, 6 to 8 minutes. If you are not sure, cut into it; it will be shredded later. The important thing is not to overcook it at this point, or it will become dry when it is returned to the soup.

Remove the chicken from the pan and add the artichoke hearts to the *soffritto,* season with salt, cover the pan, and cook over low heat about 6 minutes, until the artichokes begin to soften. If the pan seems dry, add a tablespoon or so of warm water. Toss in the spinach, season with salt, and cook just until it wilts, then pour in the broth and lemon juice and bring to a boil. Reduce to a simmer, and cook for 30 minutes.

Raise the heat so the broth boils again, and stir in the rice or pasta. Reduce the heat and simmer the soup until the rice or pasta is tender—20 minutes or 8 to 10 minutes, respectively. Meanwhile, use a knife to shred the chicken into manageable mouthful-size pieces and return it to the pan with the ¼ cup parsley. When the chicken is warm, stir in the Parmesan and black pepper.

VARIATION: Just think of the endless possibilities! Chicken, celery, carrot, and orzo soup. Chicken, asparagus, and pastina soup. Chicken, kale, and bean soup. Follow all the directions exactly, and keep the total amount of vegetables under 3 pounds.

Fennel Soup with Ham

VELLUTATA DI FINOCCHIO E PROSCIUTTO

MAKES ABOUT 10 CUPS

If you do your shopping at an Italian greengrocer, you may find fennel called "anise." Whatever its name, it is a lovely vegetable with a distinctive flavor and a crisp texture that lends itself well to soup.

GETTING READY
3 large fennel bulbs, about 4½ pounds
THE START (*SOFFRITTO*)
2 tablespoons extra-virgin olive oil
1 tablespoon unsalted butter
½ pound boiled ham, roughly cut into
   bite-size pieces
1 large garlic clove, finely chopped
   (about 1 tablespoon)
1 medium onion, finely chopped (about
   1½ cups)
1 large celery stalk, peeled, trimmed,
   and finely chopped

1 small carrot, peeled, trimmed, and
   finely chopped
Salt and freshly ground black pepper
THE VEGETABLE
Fennel slices from above
THE BROTH
6 cups chicken or meat broth
THE STARCH
1 cup pastina or orzo
THE FINISH
3 egg yolks beaten with ½ cup freshly
   grated Parmesan cheese
3 tablespoons of the chopped fennel
   tops from above

Trim the tops and bruised outer layers from each fennel bulb. Slice the bulbs in half, and then cut away the root end and the hard inner core. Slice each half crosswise into thin slices, about ⅛ inch thick. Chop the feathery part of the tops to use for finishing the soup.

Cook the *soffritto* as in the Primary Recipe, page 52. Stir the fennel into the pan, season with salt and pepper, and toss it around with the *soffritto* for 2 minutes. Pour in the broth, and bring it to a boil. Reduce the heat, and let the soup simmer until the fennel is tender but still has some bite. Stir in the pastina or orzo, and simmer until it is cooked.

While this last bit of cooking is going on, beat the eggs with the cheese and a tablespoon of chopped fennel tops. When the soup has finished cooking, dip a ladle into it and scoop out some of the hot broth. Beat it, a little at a time, into the eggs; after you have added about 1 cup, gradually stir the eggs into the soup. Do not let the soup boil, but continue to heat and stir until it begins to thicken. Serve at once, with a sprinkling of more chopped fennel tops.

VARIATION: This is a lovely, less rich soup without the finish of the eggs. Serve simply with freshly grated Parmesan cheese.

VARIATION: **Ham and Celery Soup.** If you are so lucky as to grow your own lovage, or can snip some from a neighbor's garden, try this soup with fresh celery in place of the fennel, and add the chopped lovage to the *soffritto,* saving a bit for the finish.

Tuscan Beef Soup

MINESTRA DI MANZO ALLA TOSCANA

MAKES ABOUT 9½ CUPS

I did not receive the inspiration for this absolutely delicious and satisfying soup in a little Tuscan trattoria. I stumbled on it in Jack Denton Scott's *The Complete Book of Pasta: An Italian Cookbook.* I was drawn to the soup because the combination of chicken livers and tomatoes reminded me of the traditional southern *soffritto,* a sturdy stew made with chicken innards and tomatoes, not to be confused with the aromatic base *soffritto.* My grandmother made it often when I was young, but, like many Italian-Americans, she stopped when the Food and Drug Administration banned the use of chicken lungs, supposedly an essential part of the stew. I played with Scott's recipe and, alas, did not re-create the flavor of Nonna's *soffritto* (perhaps she was right about the lung after all). But I did wind up creating one of my favorite soups.

THE START (*SOFFRITTO*)

1 tablespoon extra-virgin olive oil

3 tablespoons unsalted butter

2 large garlic cloves, finely chopped (2 tablespoons)

1 medium onion, finely chopped (1¼ cups)

Salt and freshly ground black pepper

¾ pound blade steak, chopped into ¼-inch dice (about 1¼ cups)

¼ pound chicken livers, cleaned and finely chopped

3 tablespoons finely chopped flat-leaf parsley

THE VEGETABLES

½ pound ripe tomatoes, peeled and seeded, or ¾ cup lightly drained, canned tomatoes, chopped

1 pound escarole, trimmed and finely shredded

THE BROTH

6 cups chicken or meat broth

THE STARCH

1 cup orzo or pastina such as *acini di pepi*

Cook the *soffritto* as in the Primary Recipe, page 52, making sure that it cooks at least 15 minutes. Scoop the tomatoes into the pan, season with salt, and stir over medium heat for a minute or two, just to release their flavor. Add the escarole to the pan, season with salt, and turn it over and over until it has wilted. Cover the pan, and let the greens stew with the *soffritto* and tomatoes for 15 minutes. Pour on the broth, and bring to a boil. Stir the orzo or pastina into the boiling broth, reduce the heat, and simmer the soup until the starch is cooked.

VARIATION: **Beef and Farro Soup.** This is a perfect place to use that bag of farro that you bought because it was new on the market shelf but you didn't know exactly how to use it. Substitute 1 cup of farro for the pasta. Soak it in cold water for 2 hours, and then drain it. Increase the broth to 8 cups, and plan on simmering the soup 30 minutes to 1 hour, until the farro is cooked.

Creating Your Own

In the preface I mentioned that my grandmother, like most Italians, never cooked from recipes. Nor did she go to the market with a rigid idea of exactly which ingredients she would buy. Actually, when I was growing up, the market came to Nonna, in the form of pushcarts. The vendors would call up and down the street for housewives to come out and see how truly splendid their wares were. If she had soup in mind and was thinking cabbage, but the pushcart held the season's plumpest squash, then squash is what she chose.

You, too, should cook with that flexibility. The Primary Recipe explains how to handle the ingredients. The following is a guide to amounts you will need. It is only a guide; a little more or less, unlike the proverbial too many cooks, will not spoil the soup.

Creating Your Own Vegetable-Based Soups

FOR 2	FOR 4
3 to 4 cups	9 to 10 cups

THE COOKING FAT

2–3 tablespoons cooking fat (oil, unsalted butter, pork fat, or a combination)

THE AROMATICS

Use any or all of them—the amounts can vary according to what flavors you want to emphasize.

1 medium or small onion, finely chopped (about ¾ cup)

1 or 2 large garlic cloves, finely chopped (about 1 tablespoon)

1 small celery stalk, peeled, trimmed, and finely chopped

1 very small carrot, peeled, trimmed, and finely chopped

THE VEGETABLES

Use a single variety or a combination.
12 ounces to 1 pound

THE LIQUID

3 to 5 cups vegetable, meat, or chicken broth, or 2 cups broth and ½ cup tomato sauce or chopped tomatoes with juices

THE STARCH

⅓ to ¾ cup rice or pasta, or 1½ to 2 cups cooked beans, or ½ cup cornmeal

THE FINISH (Optional)

¼ cup grated cheese, plus 1 tablespoon butter or oil; or 1 to 2 egg yolks

---

THE COOKING FAT

3–4 tablespoons cooking fat (oil, unsalted butter, pork fat, or a combination)

THE AROMATICS

Use any or all of them—the amounts can vary according to what flavors you want to emphasize.

1 large or 2 small onions, finely chopped (about 1½ cups)

3 or 4 large garlic cloves, finely chopped (2 to 3 tablespoons)

1 large celery stalk, peeled, trimmed, and finely chopped

1 small carrot, peeled, trimmed, and finely chopped

THE VEGETABLES

Use a single variety or a combination.
1½ to 3 pounds

THE LIQUID

6 to 8 cups vegetable, meat, or chicken broth, or 5 cups broth and 1½ cups tomato sauce or chopped tomatoes with juices

THE STARCH

1 to 1½ cups rice or pasta, or 3 to 4 cups cooked beans, or ¾ cup cornmeal

THE FINISH (Optional)

½ to ⅔ cup grated cheese, plus 2 to 3 tablespoons butter or oil; or 3 to 4 egg yolks

CREAMED SOUPS

Creamed soups in Italian cooking are made creamy by pureeing and may or may not contain cream. The name *crema,* which means "cream," refers to the texture of the soup. Although all vegetables lend themselves nicely to creamed soups, the starchier ones will produce thicker soups. You can always cook a boiling potato with the less starchy vegetables to thicken the puree. A *crema* may be either completely smooth—that is, all the ingredients pureed—or may contain small pieces of vegetables and/or meat. The following two recipes outline how to accomplish each.

Cream of Pepper Soup

CREMA DI PEPERONI

MAKES ABOUT 8 CUPS

Travelers to Florence seeking dining recommendations often find themselves at Cibrèo. Chef-owner Fabio Picchi is a talented if somewhat unconventional restaurateur. This is my interpretation of his cream of yellow pepper soup, a complete puree. It is a pretty soup that I often serve in small cups as a first course before a chichi meal.

Use either yellow or red peppers or a combination of both. Add a drop or two of lemon juice with all red peppers, since they are often sweeter than the yellow. Green peppers are not sweet enough for this soup.

THE START *(SOFFRITTO)*

3 tablespoons extra-virgin olive oil

2 large garlic cloves, smashed and peeled but not chopped

1 large onion, roughly chopped (about 1½ cups)

1 large celery stalk, peeled, cut into ½-inch pieces (about ½ cup)

1 medium carrot, peeled and thinly sliced (about ⅓ cup)

Salt

¼ teaspoon hot red-pepper flakes

Heat the olive oil with the garlic until the garlic is lightly browned. Discard the garlic, and add the onion, celery, and carrot to the oil in the pan. Season with salt and red-pepper flakes, and cook over low heat, stirring often, until the onion is translucent, about 10 minutes.

Stir in the potatoes, season with salt, and cook, stirring occasionally, for 5 minutes, to heat up and begin to cook. Do not brown them. Stir the peppers into the pan, season with salt, cover the pan, and cook for another 5 minutes, so the peppers begin to cook.

Pour the broth into the pan, and bring it to a boil.

Reduce the heat, and simmer the soup for 15 to 20 minutes, until the vegetables are very tender. Puree the soup, in batches, in a blender or a food processor or through a food mill. Or use an immersion blender. For a very fine texture, strain the soup and return it to the cooking pan to reheat. Serve hot with Parmesan cheese and perhaps a drizzle of extra-virgin olive oil.

VARIATION: Start the soup with butter in place of the oil, and finish it with about ¼ cup cream.

VARIATION: In place of the Parmesan cheese, I sometimes float a few rinsed and dried capers with the drizzle of oil on top of each serving.

VARIATION: **Cream of Fennel Soup.** Substitute 2 pounds of chopped fresh fennel for the peppers. Add a few tablespoons of the chopped feathery tops to the onion, carrot, and celery, and save some for sprinkling on top of the finished soup with the grated cheese.

THE VEGETABLES
1 pound boiling potatoes, peeled, cut into 1-inch dice
2 pounds red or yellow peppers, about 4 large, washed; seeds, stems, and ribs removed; then roughly chopped

THE LIQUID
4 cups chicken, meat, or vegetable broth

THE FINISH
Freshly grated Parmesan cheese

Cream of Asparagus Soup

CREMA DI ASPARAGI

MAKES ABOUT 9 CUPS

This finished *crema* contains the tips of the asparagus. The stalks are boiled, then pureed, and used as part of the liquid ingredients. Use either thick or thin asparagus, adjusting the boiling time accordingly.

GETTING READY

2 pounds asparagus

Salt

THE START (*SOFFRITTO*)

3 tablespoons unsalted butter

1 tablespoon vegetable oil

1 small carrot, finely chopped

1 medium onion, finely chopped

Salt and freshly ground black pepper

Zest of 1 small lemon

1 tablespoon chopped fresh thyme,
   or 1 teaspoon dried thyme

THE VEGETABLE

The asparagus tips from above

THE LIQUID

The pureed asparagus from above, plus
   enough chicken or vegetable broth to
   make 6 cups

Juice of 1 small lemon (about 1 tablespoon)

THE FINISH

Grated Parmesan cheese

Rinse the asparagus—there is no need to peel the spears—and then cut the tips from the stalks so the tips are approximately 1½ inches long, and reserve them. Trim a thin sliver from the ends of the stalks to remove any part that is dry. Drop the asparagus stalks into 5 to 6 quarts of rapidly boiling water with 2 tablespoons of salt, and boil until they are very tender, which can take between 6 and 18 minutes, depending on their thickness. Drain them, reserving 1 cup of the cooking water. Puree the stems in a blender or food processor with the cup of water. Do this in batches so the pressure from the heat of the asparagus does not force the top of the machine to blow off. The asparagus can also be passed through a food mill, using the disk with the smallest holes. Pour the puree through a strainer, and set aside to use as part of the liquid for cooking the soup. You should have approximately 3 cups. Slightly more or less will not matter.

Cook the *soffritto* as in the Primary Recipe, page 72. Stir in the asparagus tips, season with salt and pepper, and cook gently for 2 to 3 minutes, until they feel warm to the touch. Pour in the asparagus puree and the broth and the lemon juice and bring to a boil. Reduce the heat, and simmer for 20 minutes. Taste, and adjust the seasoning. Serve with a sprinkling of Parmesan cheese.

VARIATION: **Asparagus Soup with Shrimp.** This is a lovely soup in which to cook shrimp. Use about 1 pound of peeled medium shrimp. When the soup has cooked for 20 minutes and you have tasted it for seasoning, drop the shrimp into the broth, return it to the boil, and then reduce the heat and cover the pan. The shrimp are cooked when they have turned pink and begun to curl, in about 2 minutes' time. Omit the cheese.

VARIATION: **Creamy Asparagus Soup with Rice.** With or without the addition of shrimp, rice makes this *crema* a most substantial offering. After the broth has been added and the soup has returned to the boil, stir in ½ cup of rice. Simmer for 20 minutes, or until the rice is tender. Stir often, because the rice will most definitely want to stick to something. If you are using the shrimp, add them when the rice is tender.

FISH SOUPS

ZUPPE DI PESCE

Just about every region of Italy boasts of its own fish soup, and these range from simple thin soups with a single fish to elaborate stews made with everything the fishmonger had to offer. I just cannot emphasize how important freshness is, so please read about buying and storing fish in Chapter 5, on pages 269–71. You will also find directions there for cleaning fish and shellfish.

The Fish

Fish for soups should be firm-textured and white-fleshed. Strong-flavored and/or oily fish such as mackerel or bluefish will overpower the soup. My favorites are haddock, cod, halibut, and sea bass. Other good choices are hake, orange roughy, and pollack. Use one or a combination of fish, keeping the total weight the same as the recipe calls for. You can leave perfectly scaled skin attached, but I prefer to remove it.

Squid, shrimp, hard-shell clams, and mussels all make delicious fish soups, alone or in combination with each other or with fish. Whenever possible, I buy littlenecks, the smallest, sweetest, and most tender of the Atlantic hard-shell clams. Cherrystone clams are a bit bigger, not quite as sweet and tender, but still a very good choice. If I am forced to buy clams larger than 2½ inches wide, I steam them open separately and chop them up before putting them back into the soup; the directions are on page 77. As for mussels, either cultivated or wild are perfectly fine. It's a bit of a trade-off. Wild mussels have a more robust flavor but are usually covered with barnacles and so require a good deal more scrubbing and trimming.

Small, medium, or large shrimp are the right sizes for soup. The extra-large and jumbo need to be cut into pieces, which are not as attractive as entire bodies. I buy shrimp in their shells and peel them myself. They are less expensive, and I then have the shells for making a simple shrimp broth to use for the soup. I peel shrimp for fish soups because I like to be able to scoop them up with the other ingredients and not have to remove the shells as I eat. You can certainly leave the shells on—and heads, for that matter. I do not devein them.

The Liquid

I can clearly recall the green pushcart that arrived on Wednesdays and Fridays laden with fish complete with their heads. As in most parts of Italy, the flavor of Nonna's fish soup came from having the fish head and frame simmer directly in the soup. Realistically, many people do not have access to a reliable source of fish heads or whole fish. My own fishmonger went out of business a while back, leaving me headless and frameless. Fortunately, my assistant, Karl Schoonover, convinced me to revisit a kitchen hint I had abandoned: bottled clam juice, either mixed with water or used undiluted for a stronger seafood flavor. We tested different brands and decided that Snow's clam juice has the sweetest flavor. Julia Child, always inventive and practical in the kitchen, alerted me to the success of substituting a light chicken broth for fish broth. It takes on the flavor of the fish quite successfully. Some markets sell frozen fish broth, and it can be quite good, but you should ask what fish was used in its making. A strong fish broth—one made with oily fish, for example—can overpower a soup that contains more delicate fish.

In addition to the broth, water, wine, and the juices from tomatoes can be used for liquid.

Timing the Soup

As easy as fish soups are to make, the timing, especially when there is more than one variety of fish, makes them a bit tricky. Fish can quickly overcook and ruin your efforts. If you are unsure how to know when it is done, read page 273 in the fish chapter.

There are two major ways to cook fish in a soup:

1. Slip the fish into simmering broth and cook gently until it tests done. If you are using a variety of fish of different sizes, add the thicker pieces first.
2. When there is enough broth in the pan to cover the fish completely, you can gently submerge the fish, bring the liquid to a boil, cover the pan, and remove it immediately from the heat.

Steaming Clams Open

Put the washed clams in a pan with ½ inch of water. Cover the pan, and heat until the clams steam open. Shake the pan a bit to move the clams around, and check under the cover from time to time to see which have opened. Use tongs to remove those that have opened, and be patient with the more tenacious ones. Some clams open in 2 minutes; others need 10 or 12. When they've all opened, remove them from their shells and chop them into ¼-inch-or-so pieces. Pour the cooking juices into a measuring cup, leaving any sand behind, and use them as part of the liquid component of the recipe.

Fish Soup

ZUPPA DI PESCE

SERVES 6 AVERAGE OR 4 HEARTY EATERS

The base of this *zuppa*—the *soffritto,* tomatoes, and wine—forms the foundation of a number of Italian fish soups. Following the Primary Recipe are suggestions for ways to vary it.

For the fish and shellfish, use any combination that appeals to you, or use all shellfish or just fish fillets. You might consider the proportions of 3 large shrimp, 4 littleneck clams or 3 cherrystone clams, or 4 mussels per person, and a total of 1½ pounds of skinless fish fillets and, if you have it, one fish head.

GETTING READY

10 to 12 slices of Italian bread
　½-inch thick
A total of 3 pounds fish and
　shellfish (see above)
1 teaspoon extra-virgin olive
　oil
2 teaspoons white-wine vine-
　gar or lemon juice
1 tablespoon finely chopped
　flat-leaf parsley
Salt and freshly ground black
　pepper

Make the toast according to the directions on page 47. Scrub the clams or mussels as described on page 272, and peel the shrimp. Wash and dry the shrimp and the fish fillets, and season them with the olive oil, vinegar or lemon juice, parsley, salt, and pepper, and refrigerate.

Heat the oil in a soup pot with the onion, garlic, and seasonings, and cook slowly until the aromatics are soft and golden. Stir in the tomatoes, and season with salt. Turn the heat to medium high so that the tomatoes bubble a bit, and cook them for 5 minutes. Pour in the wine, and let it boil vigorously for 2 minutes. Add the other liquid (and the fish head, if you have it), and once it boils, reduce the heat, cover the pan, and let the base simmer for about 30 minutes. The initial simmering allows the soup to develop a deep, rich flavor, since it will not cook long once the fish is added. For a lighter flavor, cook it less time; but never cook fish broth longer or the flavor will go off. Remove the fish head if you have used it. The base can be made well ahead of time, even a day or two before you need it, and stored, covered, in the refrigerator. Bring it back to a boil before adding the fish.

About 10 minutes before serving time, put the well-scrubbed clams into the boiling base, cover the pot, and boil until they just begin to open; check at about 3 minutes. Then gently coax the fillets into the pan under the clams. Return the broth to the boil, and immediately reduce the heat so the broth barely simmers. Cover the pan and cook for 5 to 8 minutes, depending on the size and thickness of the fish, until it is almost done. Push the tip of a paring knife gently into the center of the fillet, and pull it apart to see what it looks like. There should be just the barest amount of translucency left. Then drop the shrimp into the broth, cover, and cook 2 to 3 more minutes, until all the fish is cooked. At this point the fish should show a willingness to break into large pieces, and the shrimp should be pink and slightly curled. If any clams or mussels have not opened, transfer them to a small pan with a little of the broth, and continue to steam until they do.

Slip a slice of the toast in the bottom of each diner's soup bowl, and sprinkle on a bit of parsley. Break the fish into serving-size pieces—large or small, to your liking—and ladle the seafood and broth on top of the bread. Serve the remaining toasts separately or tucked into the side of each bowl.

VARIATION: Just about every Italian cook has his or her own

THE START (*SOFFRITTO*)

3 tablespoons olive oil

1 large onion, finely chopped (1½ cups)

3 large garlic cloves, finely chopped (2 tablespoons)

Salt

¼ to ½ teaspoon red-pepper flakes

⅓ cup finely chopped parsley, plus more for the finish

THE VEGETABLES

1 pound fresh plum tomatoes, chopped into ½-inch pieces (2 cups of pulp), or 2 cups chopped canned plum tomatoes with their juice, or 2 cups of *marinara* sauce

THE LIQUID

1 cup dry white wine

3 cups clam juice mixed with 1 cup water, or 4 cups Chicken Broth (page 36)

THE FISH

Fillets and shellfish from above

THE FINISH

The toasts from above

About ¼ cup finely chopped flat-leaf parsley

"secret recipe" for the base of fish soup. You should vary it according to your own taste to make your own recipe. Two to three tablespoons of chopped fresh thyme or savory can be added to or substituted for the parsley. Two bay leaves and the zest of an orange will add another dimension. Use a bit more or less onion, garlic, and red pepper. Add thin slices of zucchini or sweet bell peppers to the vegetables. Cook about 1 cup of pitted black olives, and/or three mashed anchovies, and/or 2 tablespoons rinsed and minced capers, or ¼ cup slivered sun-dried tomatoes with the *soffritto*. Use these salty ingredients sparingly, since they will create a stronger-flavored broth.

VARIATION: **Fish Soup with Thin Spaghetti.** Omit the toast and serve the soup over 1 pound of boiled *capellini*.

Squid and Clam Soup

ZUPPA DI CALAMARI E VONGOLE

SERVES 6 AVERAGE OR 4 HEARTY EATERS

The steps for making this soup are exactly the same as those in the Primary Recipe with two simple adjustments: one for timing and one for the amount of liquid. The squid must be cooked in the base for 30 to 40 minutes before it will be tender. Squid is an interesting food; it will be tender if it is cooked very briefly and also if it simmers for a long time. Anything in between will produce something that tastes like an eraser. Since you want the soup base to have the maximum flavor, the long simmer is the way to go.

The adjustment in the amount of broth—1¾ cups as opposed to the 3 cups in the Primary Recipe—is made to accommodate the large amount of liquid the clams will exude.

I like this *zuppa* spicy, but you can cut down on or omit the hot pepper. Or, depending on your taste, you might even want to increase it.

GETTING READY

10 to 12 slices of Italian bread ½-inch
    thick
2 pounds squid
Salt and freshly ground black pepper
18 to 24 littleneck or cherrystone clams

THE START (*SOFFRITTO*)

3 tablespoons extra-virgin olive oil
1 large onion, finely chopped
3 garlic cloves, finely chopped
Salt
⅓ cup sliced pickled green *peperoncini*
¼ to ½ teaspoon hot red-pepper flakes
⅓ cup finely chopped flat-leaf parsley,
    plus more for the finish

THE VEGETABLES

1 pound fresh plum tomatoes, chopped
    into ½-inch pieces (2 cups of pulp),
    or 2 cups chopped canned plum
    tomatoes with their juice, or 2 cups
    marinara sauce

THE LIQUID

¾ cup dry white wine
1 cup Snow's clam juice mixed with ¾
    cup water, or 1¾ cups Chicken Broth
    (page 36)

THE FISH

The squid from above
The clams from above

Make the toast according to the directions on page 47. Clean the squid; see page 273 for instructions. Cut the bodies of the cleaned squid into ½-inch-wide rings and the tentacles into 2-inch pieces. Rinse, dry, and season with salt and pepper. Clean the clams (page 272).

Cook the *soffritto* (page 9). Stir in the tomatoes, season, turn the heat to medium high so that the tomatoes bubble a bit, and cook them for 5 minutes, until their juices are released. Pour on the wine, and let it boil until it is reduced to about ½ cup. Add the broth, and once it boils, stir in the squid. Reduce the heat, cover the pan, and let the base simmer for 30 to 40 minutes, until the squid is tender. Stir the clams into the soup, cover the pan, and raise the heat. Peek in from time to time to check if the clams have opened. I usually remove those that have opened, using a slotted spoon, since some clams are quite stubborn, and I don't want the early bloomers to wither. When all the clams are open, check the seasoning, and serve the soup with the toasted bread tucked into the sides of the bowl. Sprinkle a little parsley on top.

VARIATION: **Squid and Mussel Soup.** Substitute mussels for the clams.

VARIATION: Add 1 tablespoon of fennel seed to the *soffritto*. When the clams or mussels have opened, remove the meat from the shells and return it briefly to the broth to reheat. Serve the soup over fine spaghetti or soft polenta (the recipe on page 200 but without the butter and cheese).

Sette Cose Fa la Zuppa

Soup does seven things. It relieves your hunger, quenches your thirst, fills your stomach, cleans your teeth, makes you sleep, helps you digest, and colors your cheeks.

—SOUTHERN ITALIAN SAYING

Shellfish Soup

ZUPPA DI CROSTACEO

SERVES 6 AVERAGE OR 4 HEARTY EATERS

The flavor of this soup is deliciously intense because the broth comes only from the juices exuded by the shellfish and the tomatoes. For a brothier soup, you can add 1 cup of clam juice and ½ cup of water to the liquid ingredients. If you choose to open the shellfish separately (see page 77), add the juices to the base after the wine has reduced.

GETTING READY

6 to 12 slices of Italian bread ½-inch
    thick
3 dozen mussels or littleneck or cherry-
    stone clams

THE START *(SOFFRITTO)*

¼ cup pancetta, finely chopped
3 tablespoons extra-virgin olive oil
5 garlic cloves, finely chopped
1 large onion, finely chopped
½ cup chopped flat-leaf parsley
2 tablespoons chopped fresh oregano
¼–½ teaspoon hot red-pepper flakes

THE LIQUID

2 cups chopped Italian canned plum
    tomatoes with juice
1 cup dry white wine

THE FISH

The clams or mussels from above

THE FINISH

The cooked pancetta from above
⅓ cup chopped flat-leaf parsley

Make the toast according to the directions on page 47. Follow directions on page 272 for cleaning mussels or clams. Cook the pancetta in the olive oil until it is crispy. Remove it with a slotted spoon, save for the finish, and reserve the fat in the pan. Put the remaining aromatics into the pan and cook the *soffritto*. Add the tomatoes and white wine and bring to a boil. Add the mussels to the tomato base, turn the heat to high, cover the pan, and cook until the mussels open. Spoon into soup bowls, sprinkle on the pancetta and parsley, and tuck toast halves into the sides of the dishes.

VARIATION: Omit the pancetta, and increase the oil to ¼ cup.

La Zuppa L'È Cotta

La zuppa l'è cotta,
La zuppa l'è cotta.
La zuppa l'è pronta. . . .
Venite a mangiar!
Soup's cooked. Soup's cooked. Soup's ready. Come and get it!
—MILITARY MESS BUGLE CALL

Fish and Potato Soup

BRODETTO DI PESCE CON PATATE
ALLA CALABRESE

SERVES 6 AVERAGE OR 4 HEARTY EATERS

Some areas of southern Italy make fish soups without tomatoes. The custom stems from the tradition of serving a Christmas Eve meal consisting of only fish. Some provinces went a step further and said the dishes must be "white." The well-known standard pasta with white clam sauce is part of this tradition. The lack of tomatoes does not mean lack of flavor or possibility of variations.

GETTING READY

3 pounds firm fish fillets, such as striped
    bass, cod, or haddock

1 lemon

1 teaspoon extra-virgin olive oil

1 tablespoon finely chopped flat-leaf
    parsley, plus more for the base and
    the finish

Salt and freshly ground black pepper

THE START (*SOFFRITTO*)

⅓ cup extra-virgin olive oil

2 large onions, coarsely chopped

2 large garlic cloves, coarsely chopped

Salt and freshly ground black pepper

3 tablespoons chopped thyme

¼ cup chopped flat-leaf parsley

Lemon rind from above

THE VEGETABLES

2 pounds boiling potatoes, peeled, cut in
    half, and then into ¼-inch-thick slices

1 cup Italian green olives, pitted and
    sliced (preferably large Sicilian olives)

THE LIQUID

1 cup white wine

4 cups clam juice mixed with 1 cup
    water, or 5 cups Chicken Broth
    (page 36)

THE FISH

The fillets from above

THE FINISH

Grated rind of 1 lemon

Chopped flat-leaf parsley

Wash and dry the fish. Grate the rind of the lemon and set it aside for the soup. Squeeze 2 teaspoons of lemon juice, and use it along with the oil, parsley, salt, and pepper to season the fish as in the Primary Recipe.

    Cook the *soffritto* (page 9). Add the potatoes to the pan, and season lightly with salt and more generously with pepper. The olives will add saltiness, so add just a pinch of salt at this time. Stir the potatoes around the pan to coat them with the oil, and cook them over medium heat—do not fry them—until they are beginning to soften, about 5 minutes. Stir in the olives and cook 2 minutes more.

Pour in the white wine, and raise the heat so the wine boils. Let it boil until it reduces to a few tablespoons, then pour in the broth. Bring that to a boil, and simmer the lot for 15 minutes. The potatoes should be just tender. Lay the fish in the pan and push it gently down so that it is covered with broth as much as possible. As soon as the broth returns to the boil, reduce the heat so the liquid just simmers, cover the pan, and cook until the fish is done, 5 to 10 minutes, depending on the thickness of the fish. Stir in the lemon rind and parsley and serve.

VARIATION: **Fish and Fennel Soup.** By varying the vegetables, you can create entirely new soups. I particularly like to use 2 pounds of trimmed and sliced fennel in place of the potatoes. Omit the olives and lemon rind, and use the chopped fennel tops for the *soffritto* and the finish. Cook the fennel until it is tender before adding the fish. Or use a combination of fennel and red and yellow peppers. Cut the peppers in slivers about the same size as the fennel. Peeling them first is a bother but is worth it in this preparation. The combination of red onions, zucchini, and potatoes all cut into large chunks makes a delightful soup. Finish it with a dash of pesto. Keep the total weight of the vegetables at 2 pounds.

Creating Your Own

The following table will help you to create combinations in proportions to fit your needs. If you like fish soup and plan on making it often, I recommend that you make the tomato base in the Primary Recipe and freeze it small portions. Defrost as many as you need, according to how many people you are serving.

Creating Your Own Fish Soups

FOR 2 3 to 4 cups	FOR 4 9 to 10 cups
THE COOKING FAT 2–3 tablespoons cooking fat (oil, unsalted butter, pork fat, or a combination)	**THE COOKING FAT** 3–4 tablespoons cooking fat (oil, unsalted butter, pork fat, or a combination)
THE AROMATICS Use any or all of them—the amounts can vary according to what flavors you want to emphasize. 1 small onion, finely chopped (about ¾ cup) 1 or 2 large garlic cloves, chopped (about 1 tablespoon) 1 small celery stalk, peeled, trimmed, and finely chopped 1 very small carrot, peeled, trimmed, and finely chopped	**THE AROMATICS** Use any or all of them—the amounts can vary according to what flavors you want to emphasize. 1 large or 2 small onions, finely chopped (about 1½ cups) 3 or 4 large garlic cloves, finely chopped (2 to 3 tablespoons) 1 large celery stalk, peeled, trimmed, and finely chopped 1 small carrot, peeled, trimmed, and finely chopped
WITH TOMATOES 1 cup tomatoes with juices, or 1 cup *marinara* sauce ½ cup dry white wine 1 cup clam juice plus 1 cup water, or 2 cups clam juice, or 2 cups chicken broth	**WITH TOMATOES** 2 cups tomatoes with juices, or 2 cups *marinara* sauce 1 cup dry white wine 3 cups clam juice plus 1 cup water, or 4 cups chicken broth
WITHOUT TOMATOES 1 cup dry white wine 4 cups clam juice plus 1 cup water, or 5 cups chicken broth 1 pound vegetables, trimmed and cut	**WITHOUT TOMATOES** 1 cup dry white wine 4 cups clam juice plus 1 cup water, or 5 cups chicken broth 2 pounds vegetables, trimmed and cut
FISH About ½ pound per person	**FISH** About ½ pound per person

"FILLED" BROTHS

Brodo ripieno (*brodo pieno* in dialect) translates roughly as "full or stuffed broth." The Italian words sound ever so much tastier. These soups begin with a clear broth which is boiled and then "filled" with vegetables, meat, pasta, and/or eggs.

The Broth

Although there is nothing complicated about this category of soups, they do require that you begin with the most flavorful broth—that is, your own homemade one (see page 36). Be sure that it is as clear as possible—meaning that all fat and scum have been removed. If your broth is weak-tasting, reduce it to concentrate the flavor.

I realize that many home cooks do not always have their own broth on hand. But don't abandon all thought of making *brodi ripieni*. You can improve the taste of low-sodium canned broth by poaching a skinless chicken breast on the bone, 1 small carrot, 1 small unpeeled onion, quartered, 1 celery stalk with tops, a few parsley stems, and perhaps a sprig of thyme in the 6 cups of broth. When the chicken is cooked, strain the broth and either cut up the chicken for the soup or save it for tomorrow's sandwich.

Adding Pasta to Broth

When pasta is added to a boiling broth, some of its residual starch can wash off into the broth, thereby making it cloudy. This does not trouble me when I am making homespun *brodi ripieni* such as the ones in this section of the chapter. If you want a more elegant presentation with crystal-clear broth, boil the pasta separately until it is almost tender and then add it to the soup.

Nonna's Chicken and Egg Soup

MINESTRA DI POLLO E UOVA ALLA NONNA

MAKES ABOUT 9 CUPS

This soup of eggs poached in a broth is similar to the classic *Zuppa alla Pavese* (see variation below), but instead of being served over grilled slices of Italian bread it has pastina (tiny pasta) cooked in it. The classic recipe was probably Nonna's inspiration for her soup, even though the ancient Roman city of Pavia in Lombardia, which is credited with creating the soup, is very far from her native Ischia. Indeed, this delicate, nourishing soup in one form or another is found in many regions of Italy.

Nonna always made it with *stelline,* very tiny star-shaped pasta, and I still do. Any tiny pasta will work just fine, but children do seem to love the stars. Poach one to two eggs per person, depending on the appetites.

THE BROTH

6 cups homemade Chicken Broth (page 36)

Salt and freshly ground black pepper

THE FILLING (*RIPIENO*)

1 cup pastina, preferably *stelline*

4 to 8 eggs

Make sure to choose a pan that is wide enough to accommodate the number of eggs you intend to cook. They should remain separated. Bring the broth to a boil, taste for seasoning, and add salt and pepper as needed.

Stir the pasta into the boiling broth, and simmer until the pastina is cooked—5 to 7 minutes, depending on its size. Stir often, since the tiny pieces have a tendency to cling to each other and/or the bottom of the pan when boiled in such a relatively small amount of liquid. Break one egg at a time into a small cup with a handle or into a metal measuring cup, and then carefully slip it into the broth. Work quickly, so that the first egg does not overcook while waiting for the last to be added to the pan.

Reduce the heat so the broth just barely simmers. Cover the pan, and cook gently for about 3 minutes, or until the yolks are set. Turn off the heat, and gently scoop the eggs with the pasta and broth into soup bowls. Place a pat of butter and a sprinkle of cheese on top of each egg. Buttered Italian toast is a worthy accompaniment.

To my taste, the best way to eat this dish is to break the yolks immediately and let them run into the pasta and broth.

VARIATION: **Zuppa alla Pavese.** The traditional recipe for *zuppa alla pavese* directs the cook to break the eggs onto the toast in a bowl and pour the boiling broth over them. The eggs are then barely cooked. I prefer to poach the eggs as follows. Omit the pasta from the recipe above. Butter both sides of ½-inch-thick slices of Italian bread (one or two pieces per person), and gently fry them in a skillet until they are golden on both sides. Place the slices in soup bowls. Bring the 6 cups of broth, either chicken or meat, to a boil, and poach the eggs as in Nonna's recipe above. Scoop the eggs on top of the toast, ladle on the broth, and sprinkle with the cheese. No additional butter is needed, but if you must . . . !

THE FINISH

1 to 2 tablespoons unsalted butter

½ cup freshly grated Parmesan cheese

"Little Rags" Soup

STRACCIATELLA

MAKES ABOUT 7½ CUPS

A favorite with many Italians, this soup is named for little rags because that is what the eggs look like once they have been added to the hot broth. There are a number of regional Italian versions. Some are flavored with lemon juice, some with grated nutmeg. Some versions call for the same measure of cornmeal in place of the breadcrumbs.

THE BROTH

6 cups homemade Chicken or Meat
   Broth (page 36)

Salt and freshly ground black pepper

THE FILLING OR "RAGS"
(*RIPIENO*)

3 large eggs

¼ cup fine dry breadcrumbs or cornmeal

⅓ cup freshly grated Parmesan cheese

A few drops fresh lemon juice (less than
   ¼ teaspoon), or a small grating of
   nutmeg

Dash of salt and freshly ground black
   pepper

THE FINISH

About ½ cup freshly grated Parmesan
   cheese

Chopped flat-leaf parsley, if desired

Bring the broth to a boil, taste for seasoning, and add salt and pepper as needed. Meanwhile, beat the eggs with the breadcrumbs or cornmeal and the cheese. I use a 2-cup glass measure and a small whisk, but a small bowl and a fork are fine. Season with the lemon juice or nutmeg and the salt and pepper. Keeping the broth at a boil, pour the eggs into the pan, letting them fall from the cup or bowl in strands rather than big scoops. Use a wooden spoon to stir the eggs around in the broth, and continue to stir until they form—well, little rags. Simmer gently for 5 minutes, and then turn off the heat and let the soup settle for 5 minutes. Ladle into soup bowls, and sprinkle on the cheese and parsley.

Tiny Meatball and Escarole Soup

BRODO CON POLPETTINI E SCAROLA

Meatball and escarole is the traditional start to holiday meals in many Italian homes. It is a light soup that definitely leaves room for all that follows in those copious festival dinners.

GETTING READY

The tiny meatballs:

1 pound ground veal or beef

¾ cup dry breadcrumbs

¼ cup freshly grated Parmesan cheese

¼ cup finely chopped flat-leaf parsley

2 large eggs

Salt and freshly ground black pepper

4 hard-boiled eggs (boiled no more than
 10 minutes)

1 medium head escarole (about
 1 pound)

THE BROTH

6 cups beef or chicken broth

THE "FILLING"

The meatballs from above

THE FINISH

The egg slices from above

About ½ cup freshly grated Parmesan
 cheese

Mix together the ingredients for the meatballs, and form into balls no larger than 1 inch in diameter. Peel the hard-boiled eggs and cut them into slices approximately ⅛ inch thick. Wash the escarole, and discard any bruised outer leaves. Escarole is a slightly bitter lettuce, and to tame the sharpness, blanch it first. Bring a large pan of salted water to a boil, and drop the escarole in. When the water returns to the boil, cook, uncovered, for 5 minutes. Drain it, rinse under cold water, and then pat it dry. If you enjoy that extra bite, you can add it to the soup raw. Either way, wash it very well and shred it into ¼-inch-wide ribbons before adding it to the soup.

Bring the broth to a boil and drop in the meatballs. Simmer for 15 minutes, then add the escarole. Simmer until the escarole is cooked, about 5 minutes. Divide the egg slices among the soup bowls, and pour on the hot soup. Immediately sprinkle on the cheese.

CHAPTER 3

Pasta, Pasta Sauces, Pizzas, Risotto, Polenta

PASTA

"Not yet assimilated. Still eating spaghetti." That was how social workers described Italian immigrants who preferred their native food to the American diet of meat and potatoes. How times change! A survey taken in January 1999 found that 62 percent of Americans cook pasta at home at least once a week. And why not? Pasta is nutritious, satisfying, and delicious.

My family cooked pasta so often that we never had to think about how to do it. We chose the same large, well-worn aluminum pan, which held just the right amount of water. We added enough salt to the water and didn't cook the pasta until we knew the sauce would be ready. Overcooking pasta or, worse yet, letting cooked pasta sit around waiting to be sauced was criminal! We wouldn't consider rinsing it; that would have removed the surface starch that bound the pasta to the sauce. We weren't aware of the reason—we just knew you didn't do it. Nor did we drown it in sauce; there was just enough to coat each piece.

A perfect plate of pasta is a harmonious marriage of two splendid partners—pasta and sauce. Neither is difficult to prepare. With attention to the simple Italian basics, you can easily produce a dish that will resemble what you may have eaten or dreamed of eating in a cozy Italian trattoria.

Choosing Pasta

My grandmother never cooked "pasta"; she cooked *spaghetti, linguine, capellini, vermicelli, perciatelli, rigatoni, fusilli, pastine, ditalini, tubetti,* or *ziti.* We knew them all by their melodic Italian names; she knew by instinct which one to choose. Before you are ready to cook pasta, you must select it. The choices are splendidly vast. Your main considerations arc shape, composition, and quality.

The choice of pasta shape depends on the sauce, and the goal is to choose a shape that will capture the sauce. Ideally, you should taste both in perfect balance at the same time. Thin, runny sauces work best with long, thin strands such as spaghetti and linguine, because they have something to run along. Creamy and meaty sauces want to grab on to thicker shapes. Chunky sauces appreciate the nooks and crannies that fat, hollow macaroni offer.

When you have selected a sauce to make and are trying to think of what pasta shape will work with it, look to some of the classic combinations, such as Alfredo and fettuccine, white clam sauce and linguine, *carbonara* and spaghetti. Think about the texture and ingredients of the classic sauces and what pasta they dress, and use that thought as a guide.

In addition to shape, you have to consider homemade egg pasta versus packaged, dried pasta. Egg and dried pastas are simply different; one is not better than the other. But each should be paired with a sauce that complements its character. Most factory-made dried pasta, *pasta secca,* is made only from hard semolina flour and water, which makes it the right choice for oil-based sauces, piquant sauces, and full-bodied tomato sauces and, because it will maintain its texture, baked pasta dishes. I use only those imported from Italy, because they are sturdier and have a better flavor than American products. I rely on the following brands: De Cecco, Del Verde, Del Rosa, Martelli, Il Torino, Latini, and Rustichella d'Abruzzo. The costlier brands merit the higher price, because they are shaped with special bronze dies and then dried slowly and so have a better texture. I have had good luck ordering imported pasta online (see pages 27–29).

Homemade pasta is made with soft flour and eggs. Many good cookbooks devoted solely to the art of making pasta are available. If you do not make your own, look for a specialty-food store that makes it by hand or with a machine that rolls the dough into sheets before cutting. Extrusion-style pasta machines swallow eggs and flour and spit out pseudo-pasta paste. Egg pasta must be stretched or it will be gummy. I use egg pasta mainly with delicate sauces and those rich in butter and cream.

Imported Pasta According to Alfredo

One of my favorite stories—perhaps true, maybe not—is that of Alfredo, the owner of the celebrity-filled Roman restaurant, which became internationally famous for its fettuccini Alfredo. The colorful, mustached restaurateur was invited to the St. Louis World's Fair in the 1940s to reproduce his renowned dish. He had his chefs bundle up pounds of flour and dozens of eggs for making the tender pasta. He brought his own butter and cheese. When the chefs prepared the recipe in St. Louis and presented him with a dish for tasting, he exclaimed, "I should have brought the water!"

Pasta Shapes

Don't consider these names and definitions the last word. In spite of an entire museum in Rome devoted to pasta, Italians call things as they see them. And new shapes are being developed all the time. Recently, I saw an Italian box with the term *racchette* on it. I had never heard of the shape and closer inspection showed the pasta to be in the form of tennis rackets! My first reaction was, How foolish. But, when I thought about it, I realized that they would capture sauce the same way that the spoke wheels (*ruote*) do, and be quite the thing for a tennis party.

This is but a sampling of some of the more descriptive Italian names for pasta.

Long Pasta

CAPELLINI: "Fine hair." From *capello,* hair. The "*-ini*" makes it small. Also called ***capelli d'angelo,*** "angel's hair." Very thin round spaghetti most often used in soup and sometimes with very thin sauces. *Capellini* is also baked in sweet pies and cakes.

VERMICELLI: "Little worms." This, like the slightly thinner ***fedelini,*** "the faithful," is round spaghetti that lends itself to a variety of sauces, from simple garlic and oil, to tomato and vegetable and cream sauces.

FUSILLI: A favorite of southern Italians. The name may be dialect for "springs," but the shape is exactly like long corkscrews, so that is what we call them. **Fusilli corti** are short corkscrews. Both are good with meaty *ragù,* spicy tomato sauces, and sauces with ricotta cheese.

LINGUINE: "Tongues." This and the even narrower "sparrow tongues," **linguine di passero,** are most popular in the south of Italy for oil-based sauces and especially with seafood sauces.

FETTUCCINE, TAGLIATELLE, PAPPARDELLE: "Little ribbons," "little cuts," and "gobble-ups." These are three types of egg-pasta ribbons of various widths (fettuccine being the narrowest and *pappardelle* the widest). Usually homemade but also available dried. Fettuccine and *tagliatelle* are most often eaten with rich cream-, cheese-, and/or butter-based sauces. *Pappardelle* are good with the same, but are more often matched with rich meat, mushroom, or game sauces.

Short Pasta

Italians refer to short pasta shapes collectively as "macaroni."

PENNE: "Pens" or "quills." Pointed at both ends like an old-fashioned feather writing-instrument, this is one of the most versatile and therefore frequently used of the short, tubular pasta shapes. Whether simply sauced or baked, it adapts to a wide range of sauces, cream- or tomato-based. **Penne rigate,** "ridged pens," are the same shape as *penne* but with ridges and can be used interchangeably with the smooth version, but are the better choice for cheesy sauces.

ZITI: "Bridegrooms" are fat, tubular pasta that were the shape of choice for southern Italian weddings; hence the name, although some contend that it refers to the fact that the shape is reminiscent of the bridegroom's trouser legs. These tubes may be labeled *ziti corti,* since some companies call very long, hollow macaroni *ziti.*

RIGATONI: "Large lines or furrows," in reference to the pasta's size and ridges. This short, broad, tubular shape is a perfect vehicle for chunky vegetable sauces, meaty sauces, and baked dishes. It is the one most chosen for sauces thickened with fresh ricotta cheese.

Short Pasta Especially For Soups

PASTINE: "Tiny pasta." This is the collective term for very small pasta shapes.

DITALINI: "Little thimbles" are approximately ⅜ inch long, slightly bent, and may be ridged or smooth.

TUBETTI: "Little tubes." These are very short, small tube-shaped pasta. *Tubettini,* "very little tubes," are even shorter. May be either ridged or smooth.

ACINI DI PEPE: "Pepper berries." Very tiny round pasta.

STELLINE: "Little stars." They are especially appealing to children. At least they were to me and mine.

Special Shapes

FARFALLE: "Butterflies"; **FARFALLONI,** "big butterflies"; **FARFALLETTE,** "small butterflies"; **FARFALLINE,** even smaller butterflies. Americans usually refer to them as "bows" or "bow ties." The larger species are best paired with simple sauces such as *marinara* made with butter and fresh tomatoes, or a butter-and-Parmesan-cheese sauce. The babies are for soup.

CONCHIGLIE: "Shells." Ridged, shell-shaped pasta made in many sizes, from tiny ones for soup to large ones that are stuffed and baked. The medium ones, about 1½ inches wide, are good sauced, or sauced and baked.

LUMACHE: "Snails." Ridged pasta that resembles snails without the heads or tails. Made in various sizes, they are good with seafood sauces. The largest are usually stuffed and baked.

ORECCHIETTE: "Little ears." These small, handmade specialties of Apulia are made from semolina and water by pressing a thumb into a pinch of dough. Commercially made ones are available in packages. Though they are good with all vegetable sauces, the Apulian tradition is to boil them with greens and serve them with olive oil, garlic, and perhaps anchovies.

RADIATORI: "Radiators." I would have named these "accordions," because they resemble miniature ones. Their exaggerated ridging will stand up to many sturdy sauces, especially *ragù* and those made creamy with ricotta cheese.

Cooking Pasta

There are no difficult tasks here: just basic principles that assure success.

The Pan and the Water

A light, thin pan, such as aluminum, will allow the water to come quickly to a rapid boil and maintain it. The bottom of the pan should be flat, without dents, so the water gets the maximum amount of heat. It should have a capacity of 6 quarts, but 5 will do. Every pound of pasta needs at least 4 quarts of water to swim about while it is cooking. This generous amount keeps the pieces separated so they can't glom on to each other, and it washes away the excess starch, thus preventing the pasta from becoming gummy or gluey. If you are cooking less, even just ¼ pound, still use a large pan and at least 3 quarts of water. Cooking more than 2 pounds of pasta at one time is inviting disaster.

When the water is boiling rapidly (4 quarts of water will need a minimum of 15 minutes to come to a boil but can take 25, so plan ahead), add salt—and don't skimp! Salt seals in the flavor of the pasta, and you cannot make up for its lack later. I use 2 tablespoons of regular table salt in 4 quarts of water for a pound of pasta. You will need slightly more coarse salt. The water should actually taste salty.

I have never taught a cooking class in which someone did not ask if they should put oil in the water. The quick answer is "no," but there are optional exceptions. Some Italians believe that oil in the water helps pieces of stuffed pasta slide by one another without breaking open. I have never had the problem of bursting ravioli, so I don't do it. But if your stuffed pasta regularly burst open, then give it a try. I add a small amount of oil—a tablespoon to 4 quarts of water—when I am boiling lasagna noodles. The oiled surface makes the partially cooked noodles easier to handle. Other than these instances, oil is not only unnecessary but can interfere with the absorption of the sauce.

Adding the Pasta, Boiling, and Testing

Do not put the pasta in the water until the sauce is finished or just about finished. Try to estimate the time you will need to finish the sauce and the time to cook the pasta; most brands give time guidelines, but remember, they are just guidelines. The sauce will hold until the pasta is cooked; the pasta will not hold for the sauce. If the water is evaporating and you think you need more time, add more water to the pan and bring again to the boil. Drop the pasta into the boiling water, gently coaxing long strands such as spaghetti into the water first with your hands and then with a long wooden fork or tongs so they are totally submerged. Continue to stir intermittently until the water is again boiling and the pasta is swimming freely. Once the water boils, you need only stir from time to time to be sure the pieces are still separated.

Pasta should be cooked uncovered, but the heat of some burners is so low that the water can take forever to return to the boil. In that case, cover the pan, stand right there, and lift the cover occasionally to stir. When the water is again rapidly boiling, remove the cover or, if your burner is truly hopeless, cook the pasta with the cover askew. A tightly covered pot can boil over with a startling and messy eruption.

Test the pasta by tasting a piece. Italians prefer their pasta *al dente*—that is, tender but firm to the bite—literally, "to the tooth (*dente*)." This term is written so often that it must be assumed all readers know just when that point has arrived. Yet students invariably call me over in class and ask, "Is this done?" With thick pieces of dried pasta, *pasta secca,* cut into a piece that has cooked for only 4 or 5 minutes. There will be a white ring in the center. When the pasta is fully cooked, the white will have disappeared and any floury taste will be gone. When you bite into pasta that is ready, your teeth should easily penetrate the outside and then meet a bit of lazy resistance at the center. The amount of resistance varies from Italian to Italian, and you must be the final judge of what you like. Cooking it a bit more or less will not ruin the dish, but very soft *pasta secca* is not an Italian taste. Egg pasta, on the other hand, tastes best when it is on the more tender side. Egg and stuffed pastas will float to the top of the water to signal that they are ready or almost ready.

Draining and Saucing

When you have determined that the pasta is almost cooked, scoop out 2 or 3 cups of the cooking water from the pan. Pour some into the serving bowl to warm it, discarding it just before adding the pasta. Keep more of the water nearby, in case you have to stretch or thin the sauce to coat the pasta.

Drain the pasta either by emptying it into a footed colander set in the sink or by scooping it up with a pasta strainer. Do not rinse the pasta or drain it completely dry. The bit of residual starch will help bind the pasta to the sauce, and the bit of water clinging to the pieces will keep them from sticking together. Toss immediately with the sauce, using tongs or two long wooden forks. Serve boiled pasta as soon as it is sauced.

Amount to Cook

In the traditional Italian meal, pasta is a first course. But many of us are happy to make it our only course. The recipes in this chapter are suitable for either. As a main course, I usually cook 1 pound of pasta for four or five people with average appetites. I seldom eat a whole ¼ pound myself, but my grown sons can eat at least ⅓ pound each. To serve six to eight people, use 1½ to 1¾ pounds of pasta and increase all the sauce ingredients proportionately. As a first course, 1 pound will serve six to eight, depending on how rich the dish is or how substantial in terms of other ingredients.

Italian Pasta Terminology

The following terms are especially helpful in Italian restaurants.

PASTA SECCA: "Dried pasta." This is commercial pasta that is sold in boxes or bags. It is made by machine and contains only hard-grained semolina flour and water. The dough is cut into any number of shapes, again by machine, and dried.

PASTA ALL'UOVO: "Pasta made from eggs," is how Italians distinguish this product from *pasta secca*. Egg pasta is usually made at home, in which case it is also called *pasta fatto in casa* (homemade pasta). It is made with soft white flour and eggs and is either cooked immediately or dried and stored, in which case it is still not *pasta secca*. Americans often refer to egg pasta as "fresh pasta," an unfortunate term, because the implication is that "fresh" is better than dried, and that is not the case. They are different, just as rice is different from pasta, and Italians appreciate and use both.

PASTA ASCIUTTA: Literally "dried pasta." This term is used to alert the diner that the pasta is served with a sauce. The reference to "dry" indicates that it is not served in soup. Both *pasta secca* and *pasta all'uovo* can be served as *pasta asciutta*—that is, sauced.

PASTA IN BRODO: This is the name given to any pasta that is served in a soup. Both *pasta secca* and *pasta all'uovo* can be served *in brodo*.

MACCHERONI: Theoretically the name used for short, tubular *pasta secca,* but if you share my southern Italian heritage then you know that if it is pasta we called it macaroni.

Pasta Sauces

The second half of the pasta marriage is the sauce, and the possibilities are endless. The recipes in this chapter are primarily for sauces that you can assemble quickly from your cupboard or from an irresistible display at the farmers' market. They are the ones I find most gratifying and practical to make. Most can be ready in the time it takes to boil the water and cook the pasta. The Italians have a word for them—those little sauces that can be put together quickly and easily—*sughetti.* The name itself suggests the spontaneity of making something from whatever is on hand. Whereas *sugo* is a definite sauce, the diminutive *sughetto* has the sense of "This won't take long—I'll make a little sauce and we'll eat!"

The Pan

Sauces can be cooked in saucepans or in frying pans. A wide frying or sauté pan will reduce the sauce more quickly than the deep saucepan, so you have to watch it a bit more closely. When recipes call for the pasta to be drained when it is just a hair shy of *al dente* and finished over the heat in the pan with the sauce, a frying or sauté pan is the right choice, and it should be large enough to hold both sauce and pasta. A 14-inch (measured across the top) pan will give you plenty of room for a pound of pasta. Twelve inches is large enough if there is not a large volume of sauce and if you toss carefully. I do have two unconventional favorite pans: a 12-inch wok (Joyce Chen Peking Pan) and a 14-inch round Mexican earthenware baking pan. Both have deep, sloping sides that allow a good deal of enthusiastic tossing without worrying about whether my dinner will wind up on the stovetop. They conduct heat gently, evenly, and steadily and will readily hold pasta and sauce for eight people. When I need a cover, I use a 10-inch pan lid, which fits down snugly on top of the ingredients. The Mexican dish is attractive enough to bring to the table, and perfect for baked pasta.

If you increase the recipe to serve six to eight people, a standard 12-to-14-inch frying pan is large enough to make the sauce but cannot accommodate the pasta as well. In that case, pour the drained pasta directly into a serving bowl and pour the sauce over it. If you decrease the recipe to make one or two servings, use an 8-to-10-inch frying pan or the deeper saucepan, since a larger frying pan would evaporate the liquid too far, too fast, leaving you with an insufficient amount of sauce for the pasta.

The Sauce Components

As with so many Italian dishes, pasta sauces usually begin with cooking aromatics, as discussed on pages 9–10. This may simply be olive oil and a bit of garlic, or a generous number of aromatics. Whatever is there will influence the final flavor of the dish, so it should be chosen with a purpose in mind. Anchovies, sun-dried tomatoes, and capers, for example, will add piquancy; carrots will add a bit of sweetness; pork products will add a meaty flavor.

The Cooking Fat

Your first decision is the cooking fat. It really is a matter of what you like. In general, piquant sauces, such as those with a good bit of capers, olives, garlic, or anchovies, are best begun with olive oil. Sauces that are predominantly cream taste best with unsalted butter as the base.

Depending on what other ingredients are added, the sauce for a pound of pasta will begin with 2 to 8 tablespoons of fat. The larger amount is necessary when the sauce has no other liquid in it and the fat must coat the pasta. The simple southern dish of *spaghetti all'aglio e olio,* for example, has only oil, garlic, and hot pepper, so it needs 6 to 8 tablespoons of olive oil. The same amount of butter is used for the delicate dish of northern Italy, *fettuccine al burro,* where butter and Parmesan cheese are the sole ingredients. *Marinara* sauce, on the other hand, has 4 cups of tomatoes, so 2 to 3 tablespoons of oil or butter are sufficient, since the juice from the tomatoes provides enough sauce. Some vegetables, such as broccoli and cauliflower, will release no juices and so will require a larger amount of fat, whereas watery zucchini and mushrooms will require less. Even if the amount of liquid is large, you can still use a higher proportion of fat, up to 8 tablespoons per pound of pasta, if you want its flavor to be pronounced. So don't expect an exact formula here—remember that Italian cooking is spontaneous. What you want to avoid is a sauce that doesn't have enough liquid or fat to coat the pasta.

The Main Ingredient

Once the aromatics have softened and released their flavors, you will add the main ingredient, the distinguishing flavor. The Italian verb for this step is *insaporire,* to flavor. The choices are as wide as what your refrigerator, markets, and gardens have to offer. Vegetables, fish, meat, cheese, and legumes are all possibilities, but not all together. The Italian ideal is simplicity. If you have just harvested an exquisite crop of arugula or spotted a fresh shipment of porcini mushrooms, then they are what you want to taste. Too many other ingredients will mask their flavors.

Pasta is also a great opportunity to use leftovers. Last night's cooked vegetables tossed into a freshly made *soffritto* can make a delicious sauce.

The Liquid

When the sauce is lean—that is, does not use a large amount of butter or oil at the start—you will need to add a liquid. Tomatoes are a good source, and when used for this purpose they should include their juices. Heavy cream makes a lovely, rich sauce. Watery vegetables release juices, and some can be cooked, pureed, and used as the liquid, in which case the sauce tastes deceptively rich. Lemon juice, wine, and broth are all possibilities, as is some of the hot water from the boiling pasta.

If you have created your own sauce and the liquid appears too voluminous, turn up the heat and reduce it. If there doesn't seem to be enough, use some of the pasta-cooking water to stretch it. Use the pasta water, not other hot or boiling water, since its residual starch will add a bit of flavor and thickening power.

The Finish

The finish is what you stir into the cooked sauce or toss on top of the plated pasta. Grated cheese (page 23) is one of the simplest yet most satisfying finishes. Sprinkle a little on top of each serving, and pass some extra at the table. When the dish will benefit from the flavor and texture of melted cheese, toss the cheese into the pan with the sauce at the same time as the pasta. In the case of *grana* (hard grating cheese), turn off the heat before adding it, since the fine pieces can grab on to the bottom of the pan and quickly become stringy.

Fresh butter and oil are simple additions that add a lovely finish. In most cases you will use the one that began the dish, but it is not compulsory. Interesting nuances are achieved by alternating the fat in the start with that in the finish. When butter is added to a sauce at the same time as the pasta is added, melt it first so it will coat evenly and quickly. A fresh splash of olive oil can be added to the sauce, or drizzled from the bottle on top of the sauced pasta in a serving bowl or on top of each plate of pasta. Heavy cream—even a small amount—stirred into the sauce provides a smooth, rich finish.

Fresh herbs, especially whole small basil, sage, or parsley leaves, are a fine finish. Toss them into the sauce at the same time as the pasta, so the heat wilts them slightly.

A Note on Sauce Amounts

In classic Italian cooking, the sauce adequately coats the pasta but does not overwhelm it. Pasta literally drowning in sauce is an unfortunate characteristic of many Italian-American restaurants and is not at all Italian. Good pasta has flavor and texture, and it is a shame to bury it in sauce. But this is *your* dinner—if you want more, increase the sauce amount by a third or so.

Working Ahead

Once made, sauces for pasta, unless otherwise noted, will hold beautifully. Most can be made hours ahead of time, and many even 2 or 3 days before they are to be served. Do not add the finish ingredients until the sauce is reheated and ready for the pasta to be added.

PASTA DISHES WITH TOMATO SAUCE

Tomato sauces, naturally, are red, and to many people "red sauce" means that ubiquitous thick, garlicky Italian-American tomato *ragù* of southern Italian heritage as opposed to the lighter "white" sauces associated with northern Italy. Both northern and southern Italy claim many classic sauces that include tomatoes. Some are long-cooking and rich with meat; others are a mere flash in the pan of a lush ripe tomato, a pat of butter, and a few leaves of basil; some are spicy, others delicate. Italian tomato sauces have names that reflect their regions, their origins, their creators, or perhaps their legends.

Penne with Marinara

PENNE AL MARINARA

FOR 1 POUND PASTA TO SERVE 4 OR 5

My family always made *marinara* with olive oil, and I love the taste of it. Cooking classes with Lorenza de' Medici in Tuscany showed me how good it is with butter—so now I do it both ways. Made with butter, it will have a richer, creamier flavor.

The standard can of tomatoes measures 1 pound 12 ounces and holds 3 cups of tomatoes. Sometimes you find excellent Italian brands packed in 35-ounce cans, which yield 4 cups of tomatoes. Don't angst. Add another tablespoon of butter or oil and a little more seasoning and be happy to have the extra cup of sauce on hand.

THE PASTA: Penne and spaghetti are my favorite choices.

THE PASTA

At least 4 quarts water

2 tablespoons salt

1 pound penne or spaghetti

THE START (*SOFFRITTO*)

3 tablespoons extra-virgin
olive oil or unsalted butter

2 large garlic cloves, thinly
sliced

Small pinch hot red-pepper
flakes, or ¼ teaspoon hot
paprika

THE MAIN INGREDIENT
AND LIQUID

About 3 cups peeled or
unpeeled, fresh or canned

Put the water in a large pan, and when the sauce is almost finished, bring the water to a boil, add the salt and pasta, cook until *al dente* (see pages 98–100).

Choose a wide, nonreactive skillet at least 2 inches deep, or a deep nonreactive saucepan. Put the oil or butter into the skillet, and set it over medium-low heat. Add the garlic and cook, stirring often, until it is golden in color and softened; do not allow it to brown, or it will become bitter. Add the pepper flakes or paprika and stir for 15 seconds, then pour in the tomatoes with their juice and bring to a boil. Reduce the heat to low, season with about ½ teaspoon salt and the torn basil, and simmer 20 to 25 minutes. The sauce will have thickened, and you may notice small pools of orange where the oil has separated from the tomatoes. Stir in the 2 tablespoons of basil, taste carefully and adjust the seasoning if necessary. You may want a little more salt. Whether or not you need the pinch of sugar will depend on your tomatoes. If the sauce lacks the natural sweetness of perfectly ripe, fresh tomatoes, then add the sugar.

Remove about 2 cups of pasta-boiling water and pour it into a pasta bowl to warm it. Drain the pasta when it is *al dente* and immediately transfer it to the drained warm pasta bowl. Pour on the sauce and serve at once; pass grated Parmesan cheese separately if desired.

tomatoes, with their juices, coarsely broken up with your hands or chopped into medium-size pieces (pages 20–22)

Salt

Small pinch sugar if necessary

About ¼ cup basil leaves torn into small pieces, plus 2 tablespoons for the finish

THE FINISH

The 2 tablespoons of torn basil from above

Parmesan cheese

VARIATION: Fresh basil is the typical Neapolitan flavoring for this sauce, which is made when both tomatoes and basil are at their best. If you cannot find fresh or if the market price is outrageous, substitute a teaspoon or so of dried oregano. This is precisely what Italian immigrants did, and the taste of oregano-flavored sauce became almost synonymous with pizza sauce.

Tip for Cooking Fresh Tomatoes

Sometimes fresh tomatoes are a bit stubborn about releasing their juices into the pan. If so, just cover the pan for 3 or 4 minutes, or until the juices run and bubble.

To Peel and Seed or Not

If I am making a *marinara* sauce to be used right away, or stored and simply reheated, I do not peel or seed the tomatoes. The skin and seeds are hardly detectable. If, on the other hand, I am making a quantity for the freezer that I may later use in long-cooking recipes, I peel the tomatoes and always remove the seeds, which can become bitter when cooked for a long time.

Spaghetti with Harlot's Sauce

SPAGHETTI PUTTANESCA

SERVES 4 OR 5

Perhaps no Italian quick sauce quite stimulates the imagination and the appetite like *puttanesca*. Supposedly named for Neapolitan "women of the night," who would throw the sauce together between tricks, *puttanesca* is open to many interpretations and variations.

THE PASTA: Spaghetti is the traditional shape for *puttanesca* sauce.

THE PASTA

At least 4 quarts water

2 tablespoons salt

1 pound spaghetti or spaghettini

THE START (*SOFFRITTO*)

6 tablespoons extra-virgin olive oil

3 large garlic cloves, crushed and peeled

4 anchovy fillets, rinsed

2 tablespoons capers, or more, depending on how much you love them,
  rinsed
½ to 1 small hot red pepper, seeds
  removed, minced, or ¼ to ½ teaspoon hot red-pepper flakes or
  paprika, or to taste

THE MAIN INGREDIENT AND
  LIQUID

3 cups peeled or unpeeled, fresh or
  canned tomatoes, with their juices,
  coarsely broken or chopped into
  medium-size pieces, or 2¼ cups *marinara* sauce

Salt, only if needed
⅓ cup pitted and quartered brine-cured
  black olives (preferably Gaeta,
  page 15)
2 tablespoons chopped fresh oregano,
  or 3 teaspoons dried
Small pinch sugar if necessary

THE FINISH

About ¼ cup flat-leaf parsley, either
  chopped or left in whole leaves
Freshly grated pecorino cheese

Put the water in a large pan, and when the sauce is almost finished, cook the pasta according to the directions on pages 98–100.

Heat the oil with the garlic in a 12-to-14-inch sauté pan over medium heat. As the garlic cooks, push it into the oil with the back of a wooden spoon to release its flavor. When it is lightly brown on all sides, discard it. Put the anchovies in the pan, and mash them into the oil. When they have melted, usually in just a minute, stir in the capers and pepper, pepper flakes, or paprika, and cook just a minute or two to blend the flavors.

Pour in the tomatoes, season with a small pinch of salt if you wish, and turn the heat up a bit so they bubble and their juices run. Stir in the olives and oregano, and simmer for 20 to 25 minutes, until the sauce is thickened and the oil separates from the tomatoes. Or pour in the *marinara* sauce, bring to a boil, then reduce the heat, add the olives and oregano, and simmer 2 to 3 minutes to heat and blend flavors. Taste and correct the seasoning if necessary, adding the sugar if the sauce needs sweetening.

Drain the pasta when it is just shy of *al dente,* and toss it in the pan with the sauce. Stir in the parsley; if the sauce does not completely coat the pasta, use some of the reserved cooking water to stretch it. Toss until the pasta is perfectly *al dente,* and then transfer to the drained warm pasta bowl. Serve with the grated cheese passed separately.

VARIATION: I don't think that exact proportions should restrict a *puttanesca* sauce. Make it according to your taste. Increase the garlic, or mince it and leave it in the sauce, for a stronger flavor. Decrease or increase the anchovies and/or capers, or eliminate them. Add a bit of basil or some sliced sun-dried tomatoes or even raisins to make your own version. Just be careful with salt, since the ingredients themselves are already salty. Instead of the cheese, serve the pasta with breadcrumbs fried in olive oil (page 17).

VARIATION: **Spaghetti with Anchovy Sauce.** To make a decidedly anchovy sauce, replace 4 tablespoons of the oil with 4 tablespoons of butter and increase the number of anchovies to at least eight fillets. Keep the oregano, or substitute ⅓ cup snipped fresh basil. I prefer it without the olives but with the capers.

Thick Spaghetti in the Style of Amatrice

SPAGHETTI AMATRICIANA

SERVES 4 OR 5

Amatrice is located northeast of Rome, and if it is famous for nothing else it should be remembered for this sauce, which is simplicity itself. What distinguishes this sauce from other simple tomato-based sauces is the addition of pork to the aromatics. The classic dish uses *guanciale,* cured pig's cheeks and jowls, which I have never encountered in an American market. Italians, here and in Italy, commonly substitute pancetta or prosciutto. Many Americans substitute bacon, and though that may not be a classic *amatriciana,* it makes a fine-tasting Italian sauce.

THE PASTA: Thick spaghetti, known in Amatrice as *bucatini* and elsewhere as *perciatelli,* is the traditional pasta and the best long shape to use. *Penne* and *fusilli* are good choices for short pasta.

THE PASTA

At least 4 quarts water

2 tablespoons salt

1 pound *bucatini, perciatelli,* or thick
    spaghetti

THE START (*SOFFRITTO*)

4 tablespoons extra-virgin olive oil

¼ pound pancetta or prosciutto,
    finely diced

1 medium onion, diced

Salt

½ small hot red pepper, seeds removed,
    minced, or ¼ teaspoon hot red-
    pepper flakes or hot paprika,
    or to taste

THE MAIN INGREDIENT AND
LIQUID

3 cups peeled or unpeeled, fresh or
    canned tomatoes, with their juices,
    coarsely broken or chopped into
    medium-size pieces, or 2¼ cups
    marinara sauce

THE FINISH

At least ⅔ cup freshly grated pecorino
    cheese

Put the water in a large pan, and when the sauce is almost finished, cook the pasta according to the directions on pages 98–100.

Heat the olive oil, pancetta or prosciutto, and onion in a 12-to-14-inch sauté pan over medium heat. Season with a very small pinch of salt, and stir in the hot pepper or paprika. Cook slowly until the onion is translucent. Stir in the tomatoes, season, bring to a boil, then reduce the heat and simmer gently for 20 to 25 minutes; or pour in the *marinara* sauce, bring to a boil, then reduce the heat and simmer 2 to 3 minutes to heat and blend flavors.

Remove and reserve some of the pasta-boiling water to heat the serving bowl, drain, and toss the pasta in the sauce. Turn off the heat and sprinkle on the cheese.

VARIATION: **Pasta Arrabiata.** This Roman specialty is very similar to the recipe above but is spicier. The name means "angry" or "furious," and the degree of ire will depend on how much hot pepper you use. Using the recipe above, substitute three minced garlic cloves for the onion, and increase the hot red pepper to at least a whole one or the red-pepper flakes or paprika to ½ teaspoon or more. Finish the sauce by stirring in ¼ cup of snipped basil. *Arrabiata* is traditionally served with short macaroni such as *penne,* and topped with pecorino cheese.

Linguine with Tuna and Pea Sauce

LINGUINE CON TONNO E PISELLI

SERVES 4 OR 5

Adding fish to simple tomato-based sauces has sustained more than a few fishermen in every coastal town of Italy. Using fish from a can was surely pure inventiveness on the part of the Italian housewife when the catch was small. If you can find it, use Italian tuna canned in olive oil; otherwise, use any good-quality tuna packed in oil.

THE PASTA: Choose a long pasta, such as the flat linguine or the flat *spaghetti alla chitarra* from Abruzzi.

THE PASTA

At least 4 quarts water

2 tablespoons salt

1 pound linguine

THE START (*SOFFRITTO*)

4 tablespoons extra-virgin olive oil (¼ cup)

1 medium onion, diced

Salt

½ to 1 small hot red pepper, seeds removed, minced, or ¼ to ½ teaspoon hot red-pepper flakes or hot paprika, or to taste

½ cup chopped flat-leaf parsley, plus 3 tablespoons for the finish

THE FISH/VEGETABLES/ LIQUID

Two 6-ounce cans tuna fish packed in oil, drained

3 cups peeled or unpeeled, fresh or canned tomatoes, with their juices, coarsely broken or chopped into medium-size pieces, or 2¼ cups *marinara* sauce

1 cup tender fresh peas, blanched for 1 minute, or frozen tender tiny peas, thawed

THE FINISH

The 3 tablespoons chopped parsley from above

1 to 2 tablespoons extra-virgin olive oil

Put the water in a large pan, and when the sauce is almost finished, cook the pasta according to the directions on pages 98–100.

Heat the olive oil in a 12-to-14-inch sauté pan over medium heat. Add the onion to the warming oil, season with salt, and cook until the pieces are soft and translucent. Stir in the pepper, pepper flakes, or paprika and the ½ cup parsley and cook for a minute more, to blend the flavors. Empty the tuna into the pan, and break it up into small chunks with a fork. Stir in the tomatoes, and season with salt. Bring the juices to a boil, then reduce the heat and simmer gently for 15 minutes. Add the peas, and continue to cook another 5 minutes. Or add the *marinara* and the peas together, and simmer just until they are heated.

Reserve some of the boiling water, drain, and toss the pasta in the sauce. Transfer the pasta to the drained, warm pasta bowl, sprinkle on the 3 tablespoons of parsley, drizzle on the olive oil, toss together, and serve.

VARIATION: Omit the peas and add three or four rinsed and chopped anchovies (or more, depending on how much you like them) to the pan with the tuna. Rinsed capers and/or black olives are a nice addition with the anchovies.

VARIATION: **Linguine with Shrimp, Tomatoes, and Peas.** Substitute 1 pound of small peeled shrimp for the tuna. When the onion is soft, sauté the shrimp a minute or two, until they are cooked; they will turn pink, and their tails will curl slightly. Remove them with a slotted spoon and put the tomatoes in the pan. Cook as above, adding the peas when the sauce has about 5 minutes of cooking left. Return the shrimp to the pan just long enough to reheat them.

> The difference between the king and me is that the king eats as much pasta as he likes, whereas I eat as much pasta as I've got.
> —CALABRIAN SAYING

Rigatoni with Eggplant Sauce

RIGATONI CON SALSA DI MELANZANE

This recipe takes slightly longer to prepare than the truly quick *sughetti,* since the eggplant must first be salted and drained to remove any bitter juices and then cooked in batches until it is soft. If you are fortunate enough to have small eggplant that you have just picked from the garden, then omit the salting and draining.

THE PASTA: I like this eggplant sauce with short fat tubular pasta such as *rigatoni* or *ziti* or a thick spaghetti such as *perciatelli.*

GETTING READY

1 pound eggplant

Salt

THE PASTA

At least 4 quarts water

2 tablespoons salt

1 pound short fat tubular pasta

THE VEGETABLES/LIQUID

At least ¼ cup extra-virgin olive oil

The eggplant from above

Salt and freshly ground black pepper

¼ cup sliced black olives such as Gaeta

⅓ cup chopped Italian flat-leaf parsley

3 cups peeled or unpeeled, fresh or
    canned tomatoes, with their juices,
    coarsely broken or chopped into
    medium-size pieces, or 2¼ cups
    marinara or *ragù* sauce

THE FINISH

Freshly grated pecorino cheese for
    passing

Put the water in a large pan, and when the sauce is almost finished, cook the pasta according to the directions on pages 98–100.

Wash and trim the eggplant (do not peel it), and cut it into ½-inch cubes. Scatter the cubes in a colander, and lightly salt each layer. Place a plate on top of the eggplant and a heavy weight on top of the plate. Drain for 45 minutes. Rinse, and pat the eggplant with paper towels until thoroughly dry.

Heat ¼ cup olive oil in a large sauté pan over medium-high heat until it is so hot that the eggplant sizzles when added. Cook the eggplant in batches so as not to crowd the pan. Season each batch with salt and pepper, and cook, stirring often, until it is soft but still retains its shape, about 3 minutes. Add more oil if all of it is absorbed before the eggplant is cooked. Return all the cooked eggplant to the pan.

Stir the olives and parsley into the pan, and cook with the eggplant for about a minute. Pour in the tomatoes, season with salt, bring to a boil, then reduce the heat and simmer gently for about 20 minutes. Or, if you are using the *marinara* or *ragù* sauce, pour it into the pan and bring it to a boil, reduce the heat, and simmer for a few minutes to blend the flavors. Taste for salt and pepper.

Remove 2 cups of the pasta boiling water and pour it into a serving bowl. Drain the macaroni, pour the water out of the serving bowl, and transfer the pasta to the warmed bowl. Pour on the sauce, toss together, and immediately serve with grated cheese.

VARIATION: **Rigatoni with Eggplant, Peppers, and Anchovies.** Stir any or all of the following into the pan when the eggplant is cooked: two roasted and thinly sliced red peppers, four to eight minced anchovy fillets, and about 1½ tablespoons capers.

Mock Bolognese Ragù

RAGÙ ALLA BOLOGNESE FINTO

MAKES ABOUT 6 CUPS

The classic *ragù alla bolognese* calls for very finely chopped pieces of beef—not hamburger—and it cooks for a good 3 to 4 hours. The first time I made it was in a restaurant kitchen in Bologna during a TV shoot for *Good Morning America*. We were on a tight, fast-paced schedule, and I was anxious to get it on the table before the "talent" arrived for filming. I asked the chef repeatedly if it was *pronto,* trying to communicate the point that this was "television not taste-vision." I remember well his annoyance, not only at my impatience, but at my obvious lack of understanding of the nuances that develop with long, lazy simmering. He knew someone would taste it. (Truthfully, I think he was primarily annoyed at having to tolerate an American woman in his kitchen. But that was long ago.)

When the sauce was finished, I understood why it is not to be rushed, and I religiously made it his way for my sons, who named it their most favorite dish. One hurried night, however, when I had hamburger and *marinara* sauce but little time on hand, I made this quick version, and though I won't tell you that it tastes exactly like the traditional sauce, it is very, very good. The real version is in the variation, and worth the time when you have it.

The proportions below are enough for 2 pounds of pasta. I always make this much, because I love having it in the freezer. You could cut the recipe in half, but I really suggest you double it instead.

MAKING AHEAD

3 cups *marinara* sauce

THE START (*SOFFRITTO*)

3 tablespoons unsalted butter

1 tablespoon extra-virgin olive oil

1 medium onion, finely chopped (about 1 cup)

2 medium garlic cloves, finely chopped (about 1 tablespoon)

1 small carrot, finely chopped (about
   ¼ cup)
1 celery stalk, finely chopped (about
   ½ cup)
Salt and freshly ground black pepper

THE MEAT
1 pound ground beef

THE LIQUID
¾ cup dry red wine
The *marinara* sauce from above
½ cup heavy cream or whole milk

THE FINISH
Freshly grated Parmesan cheese

Melt the butter with the olive oil in a 12-to-14-inch sauté pan on medium-low heat. Stir the onion, garlic, carrot, and celery into the warming oil, season with salt and pepper, and cook gently until the onion is soft and translucent. Turn the heat up slightly and add the beef to the pan. Sauté it, breaking it up into small pieces with the back of a wooden spoon or spatula, until it is no longer pink. Season lightly with salt and pepper, and then pour on the wine. Turn the heat to high, and boil the wine until it has reduced to a tablespoon or two. Immediately add the *marinara* to the pan, and once it boils, reduce the heat and simmer the ragù for 5 minutes. More time will not hurt it.

Increase the heat, and pour in a third of the cream. Let it reduce to a few tablespoons, and then add another third. Reduce it again to a few tablespoons, and then add the rest of the cream and reduce it again. The cream should just coat the other ingredients.

Toss the sauce into hot pasta and serve with grated cheese.

VARIATION: **Traditional Ragù alla Bolognese.** Use 1 pound of lean beef chuck diced into ⅛-inch pieces in place of the hamburger, and 4 cups of chopped canned tomatoes with their juices instead of the *marinara* sauce. Keep the other ingredients the same, but simmer the sauce for 3 or 4 hours, adding small amounts of milk from time to time. The meat should be tender when the sauce is finished.

> No man is alone while eating spaghetti—
> it requires too much attention.
> —CHRISTOPHER MORLEY

Ziti with Sausage and Peppers

ZITI ALLA NONNA

SERVES 4 OR 5

Perhaps no combination of foods reminds me of my grand-mother's kitchen more than sausage and peppers. She would cook them together for a main course and then tuck the leftovers inside Italian rolls for sandwiches. Sometimes she stirred them into scrambled eggs, or made *sugo alla Nonna*.

THE PASTA: Nonna used *ziti* with this sauce, but you can use any large, hollow macaroni.

MAKING AHEAD
3 roasted red bell peppers (page 397)

THE PASTA
At least 4 quarts water
2 tablespoons salt
1 pound short macaroni, such as *ziti* or *penne*, or thick spaghetti, such as *perciatelli*

THE START (*SOFFRITTO*)
2 tablespoons extra-virgin olive oil
1 pound Italian sweet sausage, casing removed
Salt
½ to 1 small hot pepper, or ¼ to ½ teaspoon hot red-pepper flakes or hot or sweet paprika

¼ cup torn basil leaves, plus ½ cup small whole leaves for the finish, or use 2 teaspoons dried oregano for cooking

THE VEGETABLES/LIQUID
The peppers from above
3 cups peeled or unpeeled, fresh or canned tomatoes, with their juices, coarsely broken or chopped into medium-size pieces, or 2¼ cups *marinara* or *ragù* sauce (pages 30 and 33)

THE FINISH
The ½ cup basil leaves from above
About 1 cup freshly grated Parmesan or pecorino cheese

Cut the roasted peppers into pieces approximately 2½ inches long and ¾ inch wide.

Put the water in a large pan, and when the sauce is almost finished, cook the pasta according to the directions on pages 98–100.

Heat the olive oil in a 12-to-14-inch sauté pan over medium heat. Break the sausage into pieces, and drop into the pan. Continue to break it up into small pieces as it cooks. When it has lost its pink color, season it with salt, hot pepper or paprika, and basil, and stir together for a minute or two. Add the roasted peppers, season, and cook for 30 seconds, then stir in the tomatoes, season, bring to a boil, reduce the heat, and simmer gently for about 20 minutes. Or pour in the *marinara* or *ragù* sauce and simmer for a few minutes to blend the flavors.

Remove at least 2 cups of the pasta-boiling water and pour it into a serving bowl. Drain the macaroni, pour the water out of the serving bowl, and transfer the pasta to the warmed bowl. Pour on the sauce and the fresh basil leaves and toss together. Serve immediately with grated cheese.

VARIATION: If you prefer large pieces of sausage rather than the crumbled pieces, cook the whole sausage separately—pricked on all sides with a fork—by putting it in a small sauté pan with a few tablespoons of water. The water will evaporate, and the sausage fat will seep out. Cook the sausage in its own juices until it is cooked, 10 to 15 minutes. Slice it into thin rounds, and stir them into the sauce once the tomatoes have cooked.

VARIATION: **Ziti with Sausage and Mushrooms.** For a mushroom sauce, substitute ¾ pound of cleaned, trimmed, and coarsely chopped mushrooms for the peppers. Before browning the sausage, cook ½ cup of minced onion in the oil until translucent, add the sausage, and sauté until it just loses its pink color. Stir in the mushrooms, and cook until their juices run and evaporate. Use ⅓ cup parsley and 2 tablespoons fresh oregano in place of the basil. I often use ¼ pound of minced pancetta in place of the sausage and increase the mushrooms to a pound.

Creating Your Own

You will see that the guide below gives you a wide range in the amount of fat you use to begin the sauce. You only need to use the minimum amount required to sauté the aromatics without burning them. The larger amount should be used when you want the butter or oil to contribute predominantly to the flavor of the finished sauce.

Creating Your Own Pasta with Tomato Sauces

FOR 2 OR 3	FOR 4 OR 5
1/2 pound pasta	1 pound pasta

THE COOKING FAT

2–4 tablespoons cooking fat (oil, butter, pork fat, or a combination)

THE AROMATICS

These are some of the usual choices for tomato sauces. Choose what you like, and vary the amounts according to what flavors you want to emphasize.

1 onion, small or medium, finely chopped (about $\frac{3}{4}$ cup)

1 or 2 large garlic cloves, finely chopped

1 small celery stalk, peeled, trimmed, and finely chopped

1 or 2 anchovies

$\frac{1}{2}$ to $1\frac{1}{2}$ tablespoons capers

Minced parsley, oregano, marjoram, or snipped basil, to your liking.

A pinch to $\frac{1}{4}$ teaspoon hot red-pepper flakes or paprika, or $\frac{1}{2}$ small hot red pepper

THE VEGETABLES/MEAT/FISH

A total of $\frac{1}{2}$ to 1 pound

TOMATOES

$1\frac{1}{2}$ cups chopped fresh or canned tomatoes with their juices, or $1\frac{1}{4}$ cups *marinara* or *ragù* sauce

OPTIONAL LIQUID ADDITIONS

$\frac{1}{4}$ to $\frac{1}{2}$ cup dry red or white wine

$\frac{1}{4}$ to $\frac{1}{2}$ cup heavy cream

THE COOKING FAT

2–6 tablespoons cooking fat (oil, butter, pork fat, or a combination)

THE AROMATICS

These are some of the usual choices for tomato sauces. Choose what you like, and vary the amounts according to what flavors you want to emphasize.

1 or 2 onions, medium or large, finely chopped (about $1\frac{1}{2}$ cups)

3 to 4 large garlic cloves, finely chopped (2 to 3 tablespoons)

1 large celery stalk, peeled, trimmed, and finely chopped

1 to 6 anchovies

1 to 3 tablespoons capers

Minced parsley, oregano, marjoram, or snipped basil, to your liking.

$\frac{1}{4}$ to $\frac{1}{2}$ teaspoon hot red-pepper flakes or paprika, or 1 small hot red pepper

THE VEGETABLES/MEAT/FISH

A total of $\frac{3}{4}$ to $1\frac{1}{2}$ pounds

TOMATOES

3 cups chopped fresh or canned tomatoes with their juices, or $2\frac{1}{4}$ cups *marinara* or *ragù* sauce

OPTIONAL LIQUID ADDITIONS

$\frac{1}{4}$ to 1 cup dry red or white wine

$\frac{1}{2}$ to 1 cup heavy cream

VEGETABLE-BASED SAUCES

When the author Luigi Barzini wrote, "Italian cooking is the shortest distance from garden to table," he may well have been imagining vegetable-based sauces. Collectively they are called *salse ortolane,* garden sauces, largely by those who are fortunate enough to have vegetable patches in their backyards. Produce stands and supermarkets also offer a satisfying selection of in-season vegetables that are worthy of your garden sauces.

By all means use leftover cooked vegetables when you have them. Perfectly delicious pasta sauces can be made from such treasures as last night's steamed broccoli, chopped up and cooked in olive oil with a little garlic and some black olives, or yesterday's roasted peppers, tossed with fresh basil and melted butter.

Vegetable Size and Texture

A vegetable-based sauce is meant to be just that—a sauce—not a side serving of a vegetable that happened to land on top of a plate of spaghetti. Cut the vegetables into pieces that are small enough to be picked up with a mouthful of pasta. Although you don't want the vegetables to be mushy, do cook them until they are tender, so their texture is not a startling contrast to that of the pasta.

The following recipes for vegetable sauces are divided into two sections according to whether the vegetables are cooked by sautéing or by parboiling.

Sauté Method

For this method, the trimmed and cut vegetables are sautéed until cooked directly in the pan that will hold the sauce. This is the best way to handle tender produce.

Macaroni with Zucchini Sauce

MACCHERONI CON ZUCCHINI

SERVES 4 OR 5

Zucchini that is grated before being cooked exudes a good amount of juice, which provides the liquid base for a sauce. The fine strands also develop a creamy, saucelike texture that coats pasta beautifully. Use the large holes of a box grater, a vegetable mill, or the grating blade of a food processor to grate the vegetable.

THE PASTA: I have successfully married this sauce with various short spiral pastas, such as *cellentani, tortiglione,* or *fusilli corti,* or with special shapes that have holes or grooves, such as *ruote* or *radiatori.*

THE PASTA

At least 4 quarts water

2 tablespoons salt

1 pound short spiral or
grooved macaroni

THE START (*SOFFRITTO*)

4 tablespoons unsalted butter

2 tablespoons extra-virgin
olive oil
Or all butter or all olive oil,
using a total of 6 to 8
tablespoons for the start

3 large garlic cloves, minced
(about 2 tablespoons)

1 large onion, finely chopped
(about 1½ cups)

Put the water in a large pan, and when the sauce is almost finished, cook the pasta according to the directions on pages 98–100.

Heat the butter and oil in a 12-to-14-inch sauté pan. Stir the garlic, onion, celery, and carrot around in the warming oil, season with salt and pepper, and cook gently over medium-low heat until the vegetables are well softened but not browned. Stir in the zucchini, season with salt and pepper, and turn the heat to medium high. Cook, tossing often, until the zucchini is tender and wilted, 7 to 8 minutes. Pour in the wine or lemon juice, and reduce by half.

Remove about 2 cups of the pasta-boiling water, and pour some into a pasta bowl to heat; keep some nearby in case you need it to thin the sauce enough to coat the pasta. Drain the macaroni when it is *al dente,* and transfer it to the warmed bowl. Pour on the sauce and the melted butter, and sprinkle on the basil leaves and the cheese. Toss together well and serve.

VARIATION: **Macaroni with Zucchini and Yellow Squash.** Use ½ pound each of zucchini and yellow squash.
VARIATION: **Macaroni with Sausage or Ground Meat and Zucchini.** Reduce the oil or butter in the *soffritto* to a total of 4 tablespoons, and add 6 ounces (about two) sausages, removed from the casing and crumbled, or 6 ounces ground beef. Or use 6 ounces ground lamb, and substitute three large minced shallots for the garlic.
VARIATION: **Macaroni with Zucchini and Tomatoes.** Reduce the zucchini to ½ pound, and add ½ pound of peeled, seeded, juiced and chopped fresh tomatoes (about 1 cup). Make this change with or without the sausage.
VARIATION: **Creamy Macaroni with Zucchini.** Add about ¼ cup of heavy cream or a soft cheese, such as mascarpone or fresh ricotta, to the pan once the wine has reduced.

1 celery stalk, trimmed and finely chopped (about ⅓ cup)
1 medium carrot, peeled, trimmed, and finely chopped (about ½ cup)
Salt and freshly ground black pepper
THE VEGETABLE
1 pound zucchini, washed, ends trimmed and grated (about 4 cups)
THE LIQUID
¼ cup dry white wine, or 2 tablespoons fresh lemon juice
THE FINISH
2 tablespoons unsalted butter, melted
½ to ¾ cup whole small basil leaves, or larger ones torn in small pieces, or the same amount of whole Italian parsley leaves
¾ cup freshly grated Parmesan or pecorino cheese, or a combination

Guai e maccarun se mangano crud.
Problems and macaroni have to be eaten [resolved] while they are hot.
—NEAPOLITAN SAYING

Pasta with Seasonal Greens

PASTA DI STAGIONE

SERVES 4 OR 5

My son Andrew, who is in his early twenties, telephoned me recently to announce that he and his brother, Brad, had just harvested their first crop of seasonal greens. They live in Boston, with only the small patch of land a city dwelling can offer, and this was their first gardening experience. I was proud and tickled to find that, even though their Italian genes have been diluted with a good bit of Irish, English, and Scots, the Italian penchant for growing one's own food in any available space seems to have passed on to them.

Any young green can be used for this recipe, alone or in combination. Some greens, such as turnip and mustard greens, are slightly bitter when they are young, much more so when they are old. I personally enjoy the sharp taste of these young greens, but if you do not, then choose milder greens or blanch the bitter ones before sautéing them. If you don't have a gardener son or a local farm, baby spinach or a mesclun mix from the market can be substituted.

THE PASTA: Especially good with spaghetti, linguine, *ziti, orecchiette,* or *cavatelli.*

GETTING READY

1½ to 2½ pounds fresh young greens, either a single variety or a combination of Swiss chard, kale, collards, spinach, mustard greens, and turnip greens, or 2½ pounds mesclun mix. Some greens will reduce more than others, so you may want to refer to page 342 for a guide.

THE PASTA

At least 4 quarts water

2 tablespoons salt

1 pound spaghetti, linguine, *ziti, orecchiette,* or *cavatelli*

THE START (*SOFFRITTO*)

6 tablespoons extra-virgin olive oil

5 large garlic cloves, minced

1 small fresh hot red pepper, seeds
    removed and minced, or ¼ to ½ tea-
    spoon hot red-pepper flakes
½ cup pignoli nuts
THE VEGETABLES
The greens from above
Salt

THE FINISH
2 tablespoons extra-virgin olive oil
¼ cup freshly grated Parmesan or
    pecorino cheese or sautéed bread-
    crumbs (page 17) (optional)

Discard any bruised leaves and tough stems. Fill the kitchen sink with cold water and drop in the trimmed greens. Swish them around for a moment, and then lift them out of the water. Drain the sink, wash away any sand left in the bottom, and then repeat the process until no sand remains. Pat the greens dry with a towel, or spin in a salad spinner.

Coarsely chop the greens into pieces no more than 2 inches large.

Put the water in a large pan, and when the sauce is almost finished, cook the pasta according to the directions on pages 98–100.

Heat the olive oil in a 12-to-14-inch sauté pan or wok, and stir the garlic and red pepper into the warming oil. The larger-size pan will make wilting the greens less cumbersome. Cook gently until the garlic is soft but not browned. Toss in the pignoli nuts, and stir around until they are slightly colored, no more than a minute or two. Add as many of the greens as will fit into the pan without spilling over, season with salt, and cover the pan. When they have wilted sufficiently to make room for more greens, uncover the pan and add more. Season, and toss them round with the partially wilted ones. Re-cover the pan, and repeat until you have succeeded in fitting all the greens into the pan. Cook until the greens are tender, but do not let them dry out: the water they exude will coat the pasta. Taste, and correct the seasoning. Toss the cooked and drained pasta and the 2 tablespoons of finishing olive oil into the greens. Turn off the heat, and toss in the cheese or the breadcrumbs if you are using them. Transfer to the warmed pasta bowl and serve immediately.

VARIATION: Pasta with Greens and Pancetta or Prosciutto. Reduce the olive oil to 4 tablespoons (¼ cup), and add ¼ pound of finely chopped pancetta or prosciutto to the start. Keep everything else the same.

VARIATION: I did not suggest this to Andrew, because he has never liked to mix sweet with savory, but ⅓ cup dark raisins added with the pignoli nuts gives a nice flavor to the dish, as does an anchovy or two mashed into the oil as it warms.

VARIATION: **Pasta with Greens and Beans.** For a most substantial meal, add 2 cups of cooked white beans to the greens once they are tender. Heat until the beans are warm before tossing in short tubular pasta and grated cheese.

VARIATION: **Creamy Pasta with Seasonal Greens.** Make this a cheese sauce by reducing the oil in the start to 4 tablespoons (¼ cup) and eliminating it altogether from the finish. Scoop ½ pound of fresh ricotta or soft goat cheese into a pasta serving bowl. Stir 3 tablespoons of the pasta-boiling water into the cheese to loosen it. Toss the cooked pasta and the sauce together well with the cheese.

Penne with Ham and Fennel Sauce

PENNE CON PROSCIUTTO E FINOCCHIO

SERVES 4 OR 5

Not so many years ago, I had to rely on my Italian greengrocer when I had a craving for fresh fennel. Today, it is quite common in many supermarkets, although I find that most checkout clerks still hold it up with a curious look while asking a neighboring worker what to punch in for pricing. Grocery stores sometimes label it "anise," and before this lovely vegetable became popular, Italian markets always listed it so.

THE PASTA: I like it best with ridged *penne,* especially the smaller *pennette,* or with *ziti.*

GETTING READY
1 large fennel bulb or 2 medium (about
2 pounds)

THE PASTA
At least 4 quarts water
2 tablespoons salt
1 pound ridged *penne* or *ziti*

3 tablespoons unsalted butter

3 tablespoons extra-virgin olive oil

3 large garlic cloves, minced

¼ pound prosciutto or boiled ham,
   finely chopped

Small pinch salt and freshly ground black
   pepper

Zest of 1 small lemon

⅓ cup finely chopped Italian flat-leaf
   parsley and/or fennel greens from
   above

THE VEGETABLE

The fennel from above

2 teaspoons lemon juice

THE FINISH

3 tablespoons melted unsalted butter

⅔ cup freshly grated Parmesan cheese

Trim the fennel by slicing away about ¼ inch from the bottom of each bulb and cutting the stalks off where they meet the tops of the bulbs. If your fennel came with feathery green tops, chop and use them in the sauce. Remove any bruised outer layers from each fennel bulb. Wash the fennel in cold water and pat dry (don't forget the feathery tops), and then slice the bulbs into quarters and cut away the tough lower part of the center core. Slice the quarters crosswise into ¼-inch-wide strips. You should have 3 to 4 cups of sliced fennel.

Put the water in a large pan, and when the sauce is almost finished, cook the pasta according to the directions on pages 98–100.

Heat the butter, olive oil, and garlic in a 12-to-14-inch sauté pan over medium-low heat until the garlic is slightly golden. Add the prosciutto or boiled ham, and stir until it is warm. Season lightly with salt and pepper, and stir in the zest and parsley and fennel greens if you have them. Let the ingredients cook gently for 2 minutes.

Toss the fennel into the pan, stir it around to coat with the oil, and then pour on the lemon juice and ¼ cup of warm water. Cover the pan, and cook over low heat until the fennel is tender, about 15 minutes. Peek under the lid from time to time, and if the pan seems dry, add a few more tablespoons of water.

Drain the pasta and toss it with the fennel and the melted butter. Turn off the heat, and toss in the Parmesan cheese.

VARIATION: **Pasta with Creamy Fennel Sauce.** To make a creamy sauce, cook the fennel covered with the lemon juice and water until it is tender, and then add 1 cup of heavy cream in three stages over high heat and cook until it is reduced to ½ cup. Omit the butter from the finish.

VARIATION: **Pasta with Radicchio Sauce.** Radicchio makes a lovely pasta sauce. Substitute three heads (about 1 pound) for the fennel. Trim away the root end, wash and dry the leaves, and cut them into narrow ¼-inch strips. Instead of the lemon juice, use ½ cup dry white wine, and reduce it to a few tablespoons. For the pasta, choose a long, narrow noodle.

Parboil Method

The vegetable sauce recipes in this section differ from the preceding ones in that the vegetables are blanched (i.e. parboiled) first and then briefly sautéed with the other sauce ingredients. This is the best method to use when vegetables are hard and require a long time to cook or when they are slightly bitter. Remove the vegetables from the boiling water with a strainer or slotted spoon as soon as they are tender and use the same water to cook the pasta.

If something is just about perfect, the Italians say it is *Come il cacio sui maccheroni,* i.e., "like cheese on macaroni." To arrive at just the right time is *Arrivare come il cacio sui maccheroni,* "to arrive like cheese on macaroni."

Macaroni with Broccoli Rabe

MACHERONI CON BROCCOLI DI RAPA

SERVES 4 OR 5

Broccoli rabe is parboiled in order to remove its excess bitterness. I always peel the stems of rabe before cooking. (Nonna said, "Peeling makes rabe behave better.") Peeling the stems is as simple as destringing celery, and the more tender results are worth the few extra minutes of time. You could also discard the stems and use twice as many tops, but it would be a shame.

THE PASTA: Use a short pasta such as shells, small ridged *ruote,* or *orecchiette.* Fresh, frozen, or dried *cavatelli* are also a good choice. I especially like the ones made with ricotta cheese with this sauce.

GETTING READY

At least 4 quarts water

1 pound broccoli rabe

2 tablespoons salt

Put the water on the heat, and while it is coming to a boil, prepare the broccoli rabe. Trim off and discard a thin slice from the ends of the stalks. Peel the stems by pinching the outside layer between the sharp side of a paring knife and your finger and pulling toward the top. Continue around the rest of the stem. Rinse the rabe in cold water, and cut the stems and flowers into 1-inch pieces. Pour the salt into the boiling water, and then stir in the rabe. Boil for 5 minutes, remove all the pieces with a slotted spoon or strainer, and drop them into ice water, or run under very cold water to stop the cooking. Pat dry. Keep the water on the heat, and cover it with a lid to prevent it from evaporating while the sauce is cooking.

THE PASTA

The boiling water from above

1 pound short macaroni such
    as shells, small ridged
    ruote, or *orecchiette*

THE START (*SOFFRITTO*)

5 tablespoons extra-virgin
    olive oil

5 large garlic cloves, peeled
    but uncut

½ small fresh hot red pepper,
    seeds removed and
    minced, or ¼ to ½ tea-
    spoon hot red-pepper
    flakes

THE VEGETABLES

½ cup brine-cured black
    olives such as Gaeta, pitted
    and cut into slivers

The broccoli from above

THE FINISH

2 tablespoons extra-
    virgin olive oil

Freshly grated
    pecorino cheese

Once the rabe is cooked, the sauce cooks very quickly, so, if you are ready to eat, boil the pasta in the boiling water that you used for the broccoli, according to the directions on pages 98–100.

Heat the oil with the garlic in a 12-to-14-inch sauté pan over medium heat. As the garlic cooks, push it into the oil with the back of a wooden spoon to release its flavor. When it is lightly brown on all sides, discard it and add the red pepper to the pan. Stir it around the pan for a few seconds to release its flavor, then add the olives to the oil. Cook another few seconds, and then toss the rabe into the pan.

Drain the pasta, and toss it into the pan with the broccoli. Add the 2 tablespoons of olive oil, and remove from the heat. Serve with the grated cheese.

VARIATION: For a more pronounced garlic flavor, mince the cloves and leave them in the sauce.

VARIATION: Italians often eat this as a fast-day dish and substitute toasted breadcrumbs (page 17) for the cheese.

VARIATION: Pasta with Broccoli Rabe and Anchovies. The pleasant, subtle bitterness of broccoli rabe lends itself to strong and/or piquant flavors. Anchovies are a delicious addition. Mash three to five rinsed anchovy fillets into the oil once the garlic is cooked. Add about ¼ cup of slivered sun-dried tomatoes to the pan with the olives.

VARIATION: Pasta with Broccoletti. Broccoletti looks like broccoli rabe but is not at all bitter, and its stems are tender enough to make peeling unnecessary. Although it can be used for a sauce as above, its gentler flavor does best with gentler ingredients. Substitute 5 tablespoons of butter for the start and 2 tablespoons of melted butter for the finish. Keep the garlic, or use shallots or onions instead and leave them in the sauce. Omit the red pepper and the olives, and use Parmesan in place of the pecorino.

Ziti with Cauliflower Sauce

ZITI CON CAVOLFIORE

The cauliflower is parboiled not only to mellow its flavor but also to hasten the cooking time: it will become tender faster in boiling water than it would in the sauté pan. This classic Italian recipe can be made subtle with just a hint of garlic, hot pepper, and anchovy or blatantly robust with a fistful of garlic, an explosion of pepper, and a sea of anchovies. Adjust it according to your taste, but I will tell you that I usually prefer this with the full complement. It is my recipe of choice when I want a full, gutsy dish.

THE PASTA: You will definitely want to use a short tubular pasta such as *ziti* so the sauce can seep inside.

GETTING READY

At least 4 quarts water

1 large head cauliflower (about
2 pounds)

2 tablespoons salt

THE PASTA

The boiling water from above

1 pound short tubular macaroni such
as *ziti*

THE START (*SOFFRITTO*)

6 to 8 tablespoons extra-virgin olive oil

6 or more large garlic cloves, minced

½ to 1 small fresh hot red pepper, seeds
removed and minced, or ¼ to ½ teaspoon hot red-pepper flakes

6 to 8 anchovy fillets, rinsed and minced

THE VEGETABLES

The cauliflower from above

THE FINISH

½ cup sautéed breadcrumbs (page 17) or
freshly grated pecorino cheese

Put the water on to boil. To use the same pan for boiling the cauliflower and then the pasta, you will need one with a capacity of at least 6 quarts to accommodate the 4 quarts of water and the head of cauliflower. If you are using a smaller pan, begin with 3 quarts of water and add another quart once the cauliflower is out of the pan. While the water is coming to a boil, remove the green leaves that hug the cauliflower head. Trim away the end of the stem and cut a cross deep into the core to hasten the cooking. Wash the head in cold water, and when the water is boiling, pour in the salt and gently slip the cauliflower, upside down, into the pan and boil until well tender, 12 to 20 minutes. Lift it out carefully and rinse in cold water to stop the cooking. Pat the head dry, and then chop it into small pieces, ¼ inch or less. Keep the water on the heat, and cover it with a lid to prevent it from evaporating.

Add the pasta to the reserved boiling water and cook pasta (see pages 98–100).

Meanwhile, make the sauce. Heat the oil, garlic, and hot pepper until the garlic is golden. Stir in the anchovies, cook a minute to blend the flavor into the oil, and then add the cauliflower to the pan. Cook about 6 minutes, until the cauliflower is warm and has absorbed the other flavors. Drain the pasta, and toss it into the pan with the cauliflower. Serve immediately topped with the breadcrumbs or grated cheese.

VARIATION: **Ziti with Cauliflower and Black Olives.** Adding ½ cup of slivered black olives to the *soffritto* wouldn't hurt.

VARIATION: **Penne with Asparagus and Lemon.** Use 1 pound of asparagus in place of the cauliflower, and use *penne* for the pasta. Separate the asparagus tips from the stalks and peel the stalks. Cut into 1-inch pieces, and boil the tips and stalks separately until just tender, then drain and cool. Put the stalks into the *soffritto,* and add a teaspoon or two of lemon juice and a bit of grated lemon zest with them. Cook them for 4 to 5 minutes, and then add the tips and heat just until they are warm. For a subtler dish, eliminate the anchovies.

Macaroni with Outlaw's Broccoli Sauce

MACCHERONI DI BRIGANT

SERVES 4 OR 5

Certain stories are part of Italian lore, such as the one about the bandit Treschioppi, who allowed a coach to evade his plunder because he was too busy cleaning up a plate of this Calabrian specialty, or the highwayman Carmine Crocco, who longed for this dish from prison. I see no reason, however, that brigands should have a corner on such an appealing recipe.

THE PASTA: The classic recipe calls for a combination of three shapes of short macaroni. Choose sizes that are similar, so they will cook at the same time. Of course, the sauce is just as good with one shape of macaroni or with thick spaghetti.

GETTING READY

At least 4 quarts water

1 pound broccoli

2 tablespoons salt

THE PASTA

The boiling water from above

1 pound short macaroni, preferably a
　　combination of 3 shapes

THE START (*SOFFRITTO*)

8 tablespoons extra-virgin olive oil

3 large garlic cloves, crushed

⅓ cup pignoli nuts

¼ cup raisins

THE VEGETABLES

2 pounds fresh Italian plum tomatoes,
　　peeled, seeded, juiced, and sliced into
　　narrow strips

The broccoli from above

THE FINISH

½ cup whole flat-leaf parsley leaves

Freshly grated pecorino cheese
　　(optional)

Put the water on the heat, and while it is coming to a boil, prepare the broccoli. Trim off and discard a thin slice from the ends of the stalks. Peel the stems, and then rinse the broccoli in cold water. Separate the heads from the stalks, and break or cut the heads into ½-inch flowerets. Cut the stalks into ½-inch pieces.

When the water is boiling, add the salt, and when it returns to the boil, drop in the stalk pieces. Boil for 2 minutes, then add the flowerets. Boil for 3 to 5 more minutes, or until all the pieces are just tender. Remove them with a slotted spoon or strainer, and drop into ice water or run under very cold water to stop the cooking. Drain and pat dry. Keep the water on the heat, and cover it with a lid to prevent it from evaporating.

Once the broccoli is cooked, the sauce cooks very quickly, so, if you are ready to eat, boil the pasta in the boiling water that you used for the broccoli (see pages 98–100).

Meanwhile, make the sauce. Heat the oil with the garlic in a 12-to-14-inch sauté pan over medium heat. As the garlic cooks, push it into the oil with the back of a wooden spoon to release its flavor. When it is lightly brown on all sides, add the pignoli and raisins to the pan. Stir them around the pan for a few seconds to release their flavors. Toss the tomatoes into the pan, and sauté over medium-high heat for about 6 minutes, until they have begun to soften and release their juices. Toss the broccoli into the pan just before draining the pasta, so it only reheats and does not overcook. Drain the pasta, and toss it into the sauce with the parsley. Serve with the grated cheese if desired.

Pasta with Springtime Sauce

PASTA PRIMAVERA

SERVES 4 OR 5

Pasta primavera is an Italian salute to spring. One of the most favored of sauces, it is also one of the simplest. What blooms in the Italian spring garden, alas, does not bloom in mine. I do try to choose vegetables that have just been harvested at the local farm, but I become impatient and then add a few ingredients from the supermarket that were the results of somebody's spring somewhere. For a classic *primavera*, choose the youngest and smallest of whatever spring vegetables appear locally; otherwise, vary the vegetables according to what your garden or market offers as the season unfolds.

THE PASTA: Even with a riot of vegetables, a *primavera* is a delicate sauce that is at its best with egg pasta. Long ribbons of fettuccine are what I use.

GETTING READY

At least 4 quarts water

2 tablespoons salt

½ pound asparagus, trimmed, peeled, and cut into thin diagonal slices

3 small carrots, peeled and cut into thin diagonal pieces

½ cup fresh peas

THE PASTA

The boiling water from above

1 pound fettuccine

THE VEGETABLES

1 tablespoon vegetable oil

The cooked asparagus, carrots, and peas from above

3 tablespoons chopped flat-leaf parsley

THE FINISH

6 tablespoons unsalted butter, melted

½ cup freshly grated Parmesan cheese

Parboil the asparagus in the boiling salted water for 2 minutes, remove, cool in ice water, drain, and pat dry. Repeat the same steps with the carrots, cooking them 3 minutes, or until tender, and then the peas, which should cook in 1 minute.

Once the vegetables are boiled, the dish goes together very quickly, especially since egg pasta cooks so quickly. So be sure that the finish ingredients are ready and the table is set before continuing.

Pour some of the boiling water into a serving bowl to warm it. Stir the pasta into the remaining boiling water, and at the same time heat the vegetable oil in a large sauté pan. Toss the vegetables and parsley around in the oil until the vegetables are warm. then drain the pasta and transfer it to the warm drained bowl. Pour on the melted butter, the vegetables, and the cheese. Toss well and serve.

Creating Your Own

Vegetable-based sauces will begin with a relatively large amount of oil or butter unless the recipe also calls for a substantial amount of liquid such as broth or tomato juices. Remember that tomatoes can be used only as a vegetable, in which case their juices should be squeezed out.

Before determining the amount of vegetables you need, take into consideration how much they will shrink during cooking. Two pounds of cooked spinach, for example, is not equal to 2 pounds of cooked broccoli. And, don't overlook those leftover cooked vegetables from last night's dinner! They are fine starting points for sauces.

Creating Your Own Pasta with Vegetable-Based Sauces

FOR 2 OR 3 ½ pound pasta	FOR 4 TO 5 1 pound pasta
THE COOKING FAT	THE COOKING FAT
3 to 4 tablespoons cooking fat (oil, unsalted butter, pork fat, or a combination)	6 to 8 tablespoons (½ cup) cooking fat (oil, unsalted butter, pork fat, or a combination)
THE AROMATIC START	THE AROMATIC START
The choice, the combination, and the amounts can vary according to what flavors you want to emphasize.	The choice, the combination, and the amounts can vary according to what flavors you want to emphasize.
1 small onion, finely chopped (about ¾ cup)	1 large or 2 medium onions, finely chopped (about 1½ cups)
1 or 2 large garlic cloves, finely chopped (about 1 tablespoon)	3 to 4 large garlic cloves, finely chopped (2 to 3 tablespoons)
1 small celery stalk, peeled, trimmed, and finely chopped	1 large celery stalk, peeled, trimmed, and finely chopped
1 or 2 anchovies	1 to 6 anchovies
½ to 1½ tablespoons capers	1 to 3 tablespoons capers
Minced parsley, oregano, marjoram, or snipped basil to your liking.	Minced parsley, oregano, marjoram, or snipped basil to your liking.

FOR 2 OR 3	FOR 4 TO 5
½ pound pasta	1 pound pasta

FOR 2 OR 3	FOR 4 TO 5
A pinch to ¼ teaspoon hot red-pepper flakes or paprika, or ½ small hot red pepper	¼ to ½ teaspoon hot red-pepper flakes or paprika, or 1 small hot red pepper
THE VEGETABLES	THE VEGETABLES
A total of ½ to 1¼ pounds. Use the larger measure for vegetables that shrink greatly when they are cooked.	A total of ¾ to 2½ pounds. Use the larger measure for vegetables that shrink greatly when they are cooked.
OPTIONAL LIQUID ADDITIONS	OPTIONAL LIQUID ADDITIONS
¼ to ½ cup dry red or white wine	¼ to 1 cup dry red or white wine
¼ to ½ cup heavy cream	½ to 1 cup heavy cream

BROTH-BASED PASTA SAUCES

The most common broth-based pasta sauces have seafood as the main ingredient—spaghetti with white clam sauce being the most familiar. As with all sauces, the principle is to have just enough sauce to coat the pasta and not leave a puddle in the bottom of the plate. This is especially important with broth-based sauces, since too much liquid will make the finished dish more like a soup, *pasta in brodo,* than a sauced pasta, *pasta asciutta.* The best way to prevent this is to finish cooking the pasta in the pan with the sauce, where it will absorb the liquid as it continues to cook and the heat will allow you to reduce the sauce to a coating consistency.

Linguine with Shrimp Sauce

LINGUINE CON GAMBERETTI

SERVES 4 OR 5

I especially like this dish with small gulf or Maine shrimp, and if you stumble on either, it is reason enough to plan this pasta for dinner. Any shrimp will be good, but make sure that they are small enough to be eaten in one mouthful. This recipe begins by making a quick and easy broth with the shrimp shells.

THE PASTA: Long, narrow, flat noodles such as linguine or the thinner *linguine di passero* will provide the maximum surface for collecting the flavorful broth. Otherwise, use thin spaghetti such as spaghettini or *capellini.*

GETTING READY

1 pound small shrimp, with
   their shells

1¾ cups water

Just a pinch of salt

THE PASTA

At least 4 quarts water

2 tablespoons salt

1 pound *linguine di passero,*
   linguine, or *capellini*

Rinse and pat the shrimp dry. Peel them, and put the shells in a small saucepan. Pour in the water, season with the salt, and bring the water to a boil. Cover the pan, and simmer for 15 minutes, then strain, pushing firmly on the shells to extract as much flavor as possible. You should have about 1⅓ cups. If you have more, pour it back into the saucepan, without the shells, and boil it to reduce. If you have too little, wait until the pasta has cooked and add some of the pasta water to the pan.

Put the water in a large pan, and when the sauce is almost finished, cook the pasta according to the directions on pages 98–100.

Heat 3 tablespoons of the oil in a 12-to-14-inch sauté pan. When the oil is hot, stir in the shrimp and sauté, stirring frequently, until they just turn pink and opaque, not completely cooked, and immediately remove them from the pan with a slotted spoon. The shrimp will go back into the pan after the sauce is made, so if they cook too long here, they will be overcooked at the end.

Reduce the heat, and add the remaining 3 tablespoons of oil to the pan. Toss in the garlic, and cook gently over low heat just until it begins to soften. Stir in the *peperoncini,* lemon zest, and oregano. Cook gently for 2 minutes, just to blend the flavors. Pour in the wine, broth, and lemon juice, and raise the heat so the liquid comes to a lively simmer. It should take about 10 minutes for the sauce to reduce by about half to just over a cup. Don't measure; eyeball it. Taste the sauce at this point, keeping in mind that it will further reduce when the pasta is added; it should have a good hint of acid. If it does not, add more lemon and taste again. Correct the salt and pepper. Return the shrimp to the pan.

Remove about 2 cups of the pasta-boiling water, and pour some into a pasta bowl to heat; keep some nearby in case you need it to loosen the sauce. Drain the pasta when it is just shy of *al dente,* and toss it into the pan with the sauce. If the liquid in the pan has reduced too much to coat the pasta and finish the cooking, then add some of the pasta water; if there appears to be too much liquid, wait. The pasta will absorb some, and boiling will reduce the rest. Turn the heat up and stir the pasta around until the sauce has reduced and the pasta and shrimp are completely cooked—a minute or two.

Transfer to the drained warm pasta bowl, sprinkle with the parsley, and serve immediately.

VARIATION: **Linguine with Shrimp and Capers.** Add a tablespoon or two of rinsed capers to the pan with the *peperoncini,* zest, and oregano.

VARIATION: **Linguine with Shrimp and Fennel.** Instead of *peperoncini* and oregano, use 1 cup of thinly sliced fresh

THE START (*SOFFRITTO*)

6 tablespoons extra-virgin olive oil

The shrimp from above

2 large garlic cloves, minced (about 1 rounded tablespoon)

Salt

3 to 6 tablespoons thinly sliced pickled *peperoncini* (page 14)

Zest of 1 small lemon

3 tablespoons chopped fresh oregano

THE LIQUID

¼ cup white wine

1⅓ cups shrimp broth from above

Juice of 1 small lemon, about 2 tablespoons

THE FINISH

Chopped flat-leaf parsley

fennel and 3 tablespoons of chopped fennel tops. Sauté the shrimp in the 3 table-spoons of olive oil, and when they are removed, use 3 tablespoons of butter instead of more oil. When the garlic is soft, stir the fennel, zest, and tops into the pan, and cook slowly with the cover on until the fennel is tender. Substitute ½ cup of heavy cream for the lemon juice.

VARIATION: **Linguine with Shrimp and Tomatoes.** Add 1 cup peeled, seeded, juiced, and chopped fresh tomatoes to the pan after the aromatics have cooked.

VARIATION: **Linguine with Creamy Shrimp Sauce.** For a lush cream sauce, use 3 tablespoons of butter, instead of the olive oil, to sauté the shrimp as above. Set them aside, and do not add more fat to the pan. Pour the shrimp broth into the pan, bring to a boil, and scrape the pan to deglaze. When the broth is reduced by half, pour in 1½ cups of heavy cream, and reduce again by half. Stir in a tablespoon or two of lemon juice (taste to see what you need) and, if desired, a couple of tablespoons of snipped basil. Return the shrimp to the pan briefly to heat, and serve with fettuccine or *tagliatelle*. I like to toss in about ¾ cup blanched asparagus spears at the end with the shrimp. A pound of bay scallops is lovely cooked this way, but I recommend that you do it only with fish broth, since bottled clam juice is too strong and chicken broth too weak.

Roy's Spaghetti with White Clam Sauce

SPAGHETTI CON VONGOLE ALLA ROY

SERVES 4 OR 5

I was quite happy when I learned that my fiancé liked to cook, but I blanched when he reached into the cupboard to prepare his ver-sion of one of my grandmother's best dishes, pasta with white clam sauce. Canned clams? Not just any canned clams; according to Roy, they must be the Geisha or Cora brand of whole baby clams. They are from Thailand and are very small, tender, and sweet. And butter in place of olive oil? And cheese! All I can tell you is that it is delicious.

Of course, if you find very tiny clams such as Manila or really small littlenecks, you can try Nonna's recipe, following the variation below.

THE PASTA: Roy prefers the very fine *capellini,* but any long, narrow pasta, such as linguine or the thinner *linguine di passero,* or thin spaghetti such as spaghettini, is very good with this sauce.

THE PASTA
At least 4 quarts water
2 tablespoons salt
1 pound *capellini* or *linguine di passero*
THE START (*SOFFRITTO*)
6 tablespoons unsalted butter
3 tablespoons fennel seed
½ teaspoon hot red-pepper flakes
 (optional)
THE LIQUID
¼ cup dry white wine (optional)
1⅓ cups clam juice drained from the two
 10-ounce cans baby clams, below
3 tablespoons lemon juice

THE CLAMS
2 cups whole baby clams (two 10-ounce
 cans baby clams)
THE FINISH
Grated Parmesan cheese

Put the water in a large pan, and when the sauce is almost finished, cook the pasta according to the directions on pages 98–100, removing it when it is just shy of *al dente.*

Meanwhile, melt the butter in a 12-to-14-inch sauté pan. Do not let it bubble or color. When it is melted, crush the fennel seed and red pepper between your palms and drop them into the pan. Cook, giving the spices a stir or two for 2 minutes, then pour in the wine, clam broth, and lemon juice, and reduce by half. Taste, and correct the seasoning.

Remove 1 cup of the pasta-boiling water and keep it nearby. Stir the clams into the sauce, and then drain the pasta and toss it into the pan. Add some of the pasta water if necessary. Simmer just until the pasta is cooked and the clams are warm. Remove from the heat, and serve with Parmesan cheese.

VARIATION: **Spaghetti with Pernod-Flavored White Clam Sauce.** Before it was banned in the United States for being habit-forming, anise-flavored absinthe would have been delicious in place of the white wine. You can, however, use French Pernod for the same boost to the fennel-seed flavor.

VARIATION: **Spaghetti with Fresh Clam Sauce.** To make Nonna's clam sauce with fresh clams, choose two dozen small hard-shelled clams, no larger than 1½ inches across. Wash them well, several times, to remove all the sand and excess saltiness. Pour 6 to 8 tablespoons olive oil into a 12-inch frying pan, and add 2 or 3 cloves of coarsely chopped garlic and a pinch of red-pepper flakes. Cook gently until the garlic is golden, and then put the clams in the pan, pour on ¼ cup dry white wine, cover the pan, and cook until the clams have opened. Scoop the clams out with a slotted spoon; save the juices in the pan. Remove the clams from their shells, keeping a few per diner in their shells for garnish. Return the clams to the sauce at the same time that you toss in the cooked pasta and 3 tablespoons of minced parsley.

VARIATION: Pasta with clam sauce is best when it is a simple dish with few ingredients. You can, however, vary the herbs: try oregano in place of the fennel or parsley, or stir ¼ cup of diced tomatoes into the pan with the oil.

Everything you see I owe to spaghetti.

—SOPHIA LOREN

Creating Your Own

The aromatics for seafood sauces should be kept simple, so they do not overwhelm the flavor of the fish. Choose two or three complementary flavors.

Creating Your Own Pasta with Broth-Based Sauces

FOR 2 OR 3 ½ pound pasta	FOR 4 TO 5 1 pound of pasta
THE COOKING FAT 3 to 4 tablespoons olive oil or unsalted butter or a combination	THE COOKING FAT 6 to 8 tablespoons olive oil or unsalted butter or a combination

THE AROMATIC START
    choose from:
1 small onion, finely chopped
    (about ¾ cup)
1 or 2 large garlic cloves, finely chopped
½ to 1½ tablespoons capers
Minced parsley, oregano, marjoram, or
    snipped basil to your liking.
A pinch to ¼ teaspoon hot red-pepper
    flakes or paprika, or ½ small hot red
    pepper
	THE AROMATIC START
	    choose from:
	1 medium onion, finely chopped
	    (about 1 cup)
	3 to 4 large garlic cloves, finely chopped
	    (2 to 3 tablespoons)
	1 to 3 tablespoons capers
	Minced parsley, oregano, marjoram,
	    or snipped basil to your liking.
	¼ to ½ teaspoon hot red-pepper flakes
	    or paprika, or 1 small hot red pepper

THE FISH OR SEAFOOD ½ pound	THE FISH OR SEAFOOD ¾ to 1 pound

THE TOMATOES (Optional)
¼ to ½ cup peeled, seeded, juiced,
    and chopped
	THE TOMATOES (Optional)
	½ to 1 cup peeled, seeded, juiced,
	    and chopped

THE BROTH ⅔ to ¾ cup	THE BROTH 1⅓ to 1½ cups

OPTIONAL LIQUID ADDITIONS—
    added and reduced by half
¼ to ½ cup dry white wine
1 to 2 tablespoons lemon juice
2 to 4 tablespoons heavy cream
	OPTIONAL LIQUID ADDITIONS—
	    added and reduced by half
	¼ to 1 cup dry white wine
	2 to 3 tablespoons lemon juice
	¼ to ½ cup heavy cream

CREAM SAUCES FOR PASTA

Italian cream sauces are responsible for some of Italy's best-loved pasta dishes. Such classic recipes as fettuccine Alfredo and *paglia e fieno* owe their renown to cream. They are easy to make and elegantly delicious. The simplest cream sauces are no more than a few tablespoons of melted butter to which cream is added and reduced. Cream sauces become "pink sauces" with the addition of a bit of tomato, which lends more than just color. The acid of the tomato balances the richness of the cream.

Cream sauces taste best when they are begun with butter and finished with Parmesan cheese. A small grating of fresh nutmeg—small so as not to be truly tasted—will enhance the flavor of the cream.

Adding the Cream

The cream can be added to the pan all at once or in two or three pourings. When I am in a hurry, I like to add it in stages, because it will reduce more quickly than if I pour it in all at once. When I make sauces in which cream is the only liquid, I always measure out more than the recipe calls for. Then, if the sauce is too thick to coat the pasta, I add small amounts of the extra cream or a few tablespoons of pasta-boiling water to thin it.

Fettuccine with Pink Cream Sauce

SERVES 4 OR 5

A comforting, luscious indulgence!

THE PASTA: It is hard to imagine what this sauce wouldn't be good on, but it does have freshly made fettuccine or *tagliatelle* written all over it. I have also relished it with tortellini, cheese ravioli, and packaged egg noodles, as well as *penne*.

Put the water in a large pan, and when the sauce is almost finished, cook the pasta according to the directions on pages 98–100.

Melt the butter in a 12-to-14-inch sauté pan. Since the rich flavor of the finished cream sauce relies on a delicate butter flavor, it is important not to let the butter take on any color, which would change its taste. Pour in the cream, and raise the heat so that it bubbles lightly. Simmer until it has reduced by about a third—don't measure, just guesstimate; it should be thick enough to coat hesitantly the back of a wooden spoon. Stir often while the cream is reducing, making sure to circle the bottom of the pan, so the cream does not stick there.

Stir in the tomatoes, season with salt, pepper, and nutmeg, and cook for a minute or two to blend the flavors.

Remove about 2 cups of the pasta-boiling water, and pour some into a pasta bowl to heat it; keep some nearby, in case you

THE PASTA
At least 4 quarts water
2 tablespoons salt
1 pound fettuccine or *tagliatelle,* homemade or dried
THE START
4 tablespoons unsalted butter
THE LIQUID
1½ cups heavy cream
¼ cup finely chopped or pureed peeled tomatoes
Salt and freshly ground black pepper
Small grating of fresh nutmeg

THE FINISH

1 cup shredded prosciutto

3 tablespoons chopped flat-
leaf parsley

¼ cup freshly grated Parmesan cheese

need it to loosen the sauce. Drain the pasta, and transfer it to the pan with the sauce.

Scatter on the prosciutto and parsley, and toss together well. Keep over the heat just long enough so the cream has reduced to coat the pasta. If it is too thick, add more cream or a few tablespoons of pasta water. Turn off the heat, and mix in the Parmesan. Transfer to the drained warm pasta bowl, and serve immediately, with additional grated cheese passed at the table.

VARIATION: **Fettuccine with Pink Cream Sauce and Peas or Asparagus.** Toss either ½ cup of tiny cooked peas or ¾ cup cooked asparagus tips, or some of both, into the pasta with the prosciutto. Or use just the vegetables, and omit the prosciutto. You can also omit the tomato, but replace the liquid with ¼ cup more cream.

Fettuccine with Cream Sauce and Prosciutto, Mushrooms, and Peas

FETTUCCINE AL SALSA DI PANNA CON
PROSCIUTTO, FUNGHI, E PISELLI

SERVES 4 OR 5

This recipe combines the same basic flavors as the preceding one, but here the prosciutto is lightly cooked and vegetables are sautéed before the cream is reduced. This dish makes a particularly lovely first course before a main course of spring lamb, in which case the same proportions will serve six to eight people.

THE PASTA: Freshly made or packaged fettuccine or *tagliatelle* or *penne*. It is also good with stuffed pasta such as tortellini and ravioli.

THE PASTA

At least 4 quarts water

2 tablespoons salt

1 pound fettuccine or *tagliatelle*, homemade or dried

THE START

4 tablespoons unsalted butter

2 ounces thin prosciutto, cut into strips ¼ inch wide by about 2 inches long

THE VEGETABLES

½ pound mushrooms, trimmed, wiped clean, and thinly sliced

Salt and freshly ground black pepper

Dash lemon juice

½ pound tiny fresh peas, blanched 1 minute, or same amount frozen tender tiny peas, thawed

THE LIQUID

1 to 1½ cups heavy cream

Small grating of fresh nutmeg

THE FINISH

⅔ cup freshly grated Parmesan cheese

Put the water in a large pan, and when the sauce is almost finished, cook the pasta according to the directions on pages 98–100.

Melt the butter in a 12-to-14-inch sauté pan over medium-low heat. Stir the prosciutto around in the melted butter until it is warmed but not crisp. Toss in the mushrooms, season lightly with salt and pepper and the lemon juice, and cook over medium heat until they release their juices and begin to color. Stir in the peas, and cook until they are warm. Pour in the cream, season with nutmeg, salt, and a good amount of pepper, and reduce by about a third as in the Primary Recipe.

Drain the pasta, and toss with the sauce as in the Primary Recipe. Taste for seasoning, turn off the heat, and toss in the grated cheese. Serve immediately, passing additional cheese, if desired.

VARIATION: Stir 1 pound fresh, ripe tomatoes, peeled, seeded, juiced, and chopped into ¼-inch pieces (about 1 cup), into the pan after the mushrooms have cooked. Cook 5 minutes, or until the tomatoes are warm, before adding the cream.

VARIATION: Creamy Fettuccine with Asparagus. Substitute 1 pound of asparagus for the mushrooms and peas. Cut and parboil it first according to the directions on page 343, reserving the water to boil the pasta.

Penne with Pink Vodka Sauce

PENNE CON SALSA ROSA DI VODKA

SERVES 4 OR 5

Trendy and rather chic, vodka sauce is just a good old-fashioned Italian pink sauce with some added spirits. There is a similar classic Italian sauce that uses Armagnac, and I imagine the vodka was a thrifty chef's attempt to keep costs down.

In this recipe for "pink sauce," the juices of the tomatoes are used as well as the pulp, so less cream is needed.

THE PASTA: The "new classic" combination is *penne* with vodka sauce, but I have enjoyed it with other short dried pasta such as the snail-shaped *lumache* and shell-shaped *conchiglie*. It is also good with long egg noodles and tortellini.

THE PASTA

At least 4 quarts water

2 tablespoons salt

1 pound *penne, conchiglie,* or *lumache*

THE START (*SOFFRITTO*)

4 tablespoons unsalted butter

3 medium to large shallots, minced
(about ¼ cup), or ½ small onion,
minced

Salt

1 small fresh hot red pepper, seeds
removed and minced, or ¼ to ½ teaspoon hot red-pepper flakes or
paprika

THE LIQUID

6 tablespoons vodka

1 pound fresh tomatoes, peeled but with
their juices, or 1½ cups canned Italian
plum tomatoes with their juices,
chopped, or 1⅓ cups *marinara* sauce

1 to 1¼ cups heavy cream

Put the water in a large pan, and when the sauce is almost finished, cook the pasta according to the directions on pages 98–100.

Melt the butter in a 12-to-14-inch sauté pan, and gently cook the shallots or onions, seasoned with salt and red pepper, until they are tender but not brown. Turn the heat up to high, and carefully pour in the vodka—carefully because the alcohol will flame if it splashes on the fire. Boil until the vodka has reduced by half, and then stir in the tomatoes or *marinara* sauce. Season, simmer until the sauce has reduced by about a third, and then, while it is still simmering, stir in the cream and reduce again by about a third.

Drain the pasta, and toss it into the pan with the sauce as in the Primary Recipe. Serve immediately.

Creamy Fettuccine
with Chicken and Spinach

FETTUCCINE CON SUGO DI PANNA CON POLLO
E SPINACI

SERVES 4 OR 5

I created this dish for my sons one evening when they arrived home unexpectedly from college. I was planning on having sautéed chicken and boiled spinach for my dinner, but since I needed to stretch the ingredients and they love pasta, I turned the chicken and spinach into this recipe. We immediately added it to our list of pasta favorites.

THE PASTA: We like it best with fettuccine or *tagliatelle*.

THE PASTA

At least 4 quarts water

2 tablespoons salt

1 pound fettuccine or *tagliatelle*

THE START

4 tablespoons unsalted butter

1 pound boneless chicken-breast halves,
   cut diagonally into strips 1 inch long
   by ½ inch wide

Salt and freshly ground black pepper

THE VEGETABLES

10 ounces fresh spinach, stemmed and
   coarsely chopped

Freshly grated nutmeg

¾ cup finely chopped fresh or lightly
   drained canned tomatoes

THE LIQUID

1 to 1¼ cups heavy cream

THE FINISH

⅓ cup freshly grated Parmesan cheese,
   plus extra for passing

Put the water in a large pan, and when the sauce is almost finished, cook the pasta according to the directions on pages 98–100.

Meanwhile, melt the butter in a 12-to-14-inch sauté pan over moderately high heat. Toss in the chicken, and sauté until just cooked through, 1 to 2 minutes. Season with salt and pepper, and with a slotted spoon transfer the chicken to a plate.

Drop the spinach into the pan, season with salt, pepper, and nutmeg, and cook over moderately high heat until wilted, about 2 minutes. Add the tomatoes, bring to a boil, season lightly, and cook, stirring, until heated through, about 5 minutes.

Stir in 1 cup of the cream, and reduce by a third. Taste, and correct seasoning. Return the chicken to the pan, and stir over medium heat until warmed through.

Drain the pasta, and toss it in the pan with the sauce as in the Primary Recipe. Remove from the heat, and toss in the Parmesan cheese. Serve immediately, with additional Parmesan on the side.

VARIATION: **Creamy Fettuccine with Shrimp or Crab and Spinach.** This is a splendid place for seafood. Try 1 pound of crabmeat or peeled medium shrimp in place of the chicken, and omit the cheese.

Creating Your Own Pasta with Cream Sauces

FOR 2 OR 3	FOR 4 OR 5
½ pound pasta	1 pound pasta
THE COOKING FAT	THE COOKING FAT
2 tablespoons butter	4 tablespoons butter
THE VEGETABLES, MEAT, SEAFOOD, PROSCIUTTO	THE VEGETABLES, MEAT, SEAFOOD, PROSCIUTTO
A total of ½ to 1 pound	A total of ¾ to 1½ pounds
THE TOMATOES	THE TOMATOES
2 tablespoons to ½ cup peeled, chopped fresh, or lightly drained canned	½ to 1½ cups peeled, chopped fresh, or lightly drained canned
CREAM	CREAM
½ cup	1 cup to 1½ cups

CHEESE SAUCES FOR PASTA

Italy produces many superb cheeses that, when melted, make delicious pasta sauces. The choice can be as simple as a small scoop of fresh ricotta or as lush as a creamy mixture of three or four rich cheeses. The flavor of the finished dish will depend greatly on the quality of the cheese. Pages 23–27 give a brief description of what to look for when making your selections.

The recipes in this section are divided into two categories according to method. In the first, the cheese or cheeses are melted over heat; in the second the pasta and sauce are tossed into unmelted cheese.

Method 1—Heating the Cheese

The best cheeses for this method are those that are creamy and have a high moisture content. To prevent the cheese from becoming tough and rubbery, keep the heat low. The sauce should be used as soon as possible once the cheese has melted, since long cooking will evaporate the cheese's moisture and leave you with a rubbery glob. If your sauce seems to be in danger of turning to rubber or of separating, stir in a few tablespoons of the boiling pasta water.

Spaghetti with Gorgonzola and Tomato Sauce

SPAGHETTI CON SUGO DI GORGONZOLA E POMODORI

SERVES 4 OR 5

The distinctive full flavor of this sauce depends on the Gorgonzola, so look for a real one imported from Italy. If you are fortunate enough to have a choice between sweet Gorgonzola and the sharper mountain variety, choose the sweet one for this recipe. It is not sweet, but milder than the mountain. You can substitute other Italian melting cheeses, but make sure they are flavorful and creamy and melt well. Soft goat cheeses would be a good choice.

THE PASTA: The sauce is good with any sturdy dried pasta such as spaghetti, *perciatelli,* or *penne.*

Put the water in a large pan, and when the sauce is almost finished, cook the pasta according to the directions on pages 98–100.

Meanwhile, over medium heat, in a 12-to-14-inch sauté pan, cook the olive oil and garlic until the garlic is slightly golden.

THE PASTA

At least 4 quarts water

2 tablespoons salt

1 pound spaghetti, *perciatelli,*
  or *penne*

THE START (*SOFFRITTO*)

¼ cup extra-virgin olive oil

3 large garlic cloves, minced
  (about 2 tablespoons)

THE VEGETABLES

1½ pounds ripe tomatoes, coarsely chopped (about 3 cups)

Salt and freshly ground black pepper

¼ cup chopped Italian flat-leaf parsley

¼ cup torn fresh basil leaves

THE LIQUID

½ cup dry white wine

THE FINISH

½ pound Italian Gorgonzola cheese, broken into walnut-size pieces

About 16 medium basil leaves

¼ cup freshly grated Parmesan cheese

Pour in the tomatoes, season with salt and pepper, and turn the heat to high so that the tomatoes will cook briskly and begin to give up their juices, which will take only a few moments. Do not let the juices evaporate. Stir in the herbs and cook for 30 seconds, then pour in the wine and cook to reduce the liquid by half, 8 to 10 minutes. Be sure that there is at least ½ cup of liquid left in the pan; if there is not, pour in some of the hot pasta water.

When the pasta is just about ready to be drained, reduce the heat to low, and stir the Gorgonzola and basil leaves evenly into the sauce. Turn the heat off as soon as the cheese has melted. If you want to prepare the sauce ahead of time, make the sauce up to the point of adding the cheese and remove it from the flame. When the pasta is just about cooked, reheat the base and stir in the cheese and seasonings.

Remove about 2 cups of the pasta-boiling water, and pour some into a pasta bowl to heat it; keep some nearby in case you need it to loosen the sauce. Drain the spaghetti, and turn it into the pan with the sauce. Toss together until the Gorgonzola has melted. Serve immediately with a sprinkling of Parmesan.

Pasta with Four Cheese Sauce

PASTA CON SUGO AI QUATTRO FORMAGGI

This dish is a bit of an investment. Italian Fontina and Italian Gorgonzola are expensive cheeses. But you don't need much of them, and they will make a far tastier sauce than domestic brands. See variations below for other cheese suggestions.

I like to make this sauce in a pan that is large enough to hold the cooked pasta and attractive enough to bring to the table. Since there is so much cheese, I cook this sauce over a flame tamer so the heat will remain very low. The dish then can go from the stove to waiting diners immediately, avoiding the possibility that the cheeses cool and become stiff.

This is a delicious and very rich dish that I prefer in small portions as a first course, in which case it will feed six to eight people.

THE PASTA: The sauce is delicious either with egg pasta such as fettuccine, *tagliatelle,* or the wider *pappardelle,* or with short dried pasta such as *lumache* or *conchiglie.*

THE PASTA

At least 4 quarts water

2 tablespoons salt

1 pound egg pasta or dried pasta

THE START (*SOFFRITTO*)

2 tablespoons unsalted butter

1 cup heavy cream

Salt and freshly ground black pepper

THE CHEESES

¼ pound Fontina, chopped into ¼-inch
   or smaller pieces

¼ pound fresh mozzarella, grated

¼ pound Gorgonzola, crumbled into
   small pieces

1 cup freshly grated Parmesan cheese

Put the water in a large pan, and when the sauce is almost finished, cook the pasta according to the directions on pages 98–100. Neither the sauce nor the egg pasta will take long to cook, so pay attention to your timing.

Meanwhile, melt the butter with the cream in a pan that will accommodate all the pasta and sauce. Bring the cream to a slow boil, and then simmer until it has reduced by about a third, or enough so that it lightly coats the back of a wooden spoon, 2 to 3 minutes. Season with salt and pepper. If you are not ready to cook the pasta and serve the dish at this point, turn off the heat, and reheat the cream when you are.

Place a flame tamer on the burner under the pan, and then stir the Fontina, mozzarella, and Gorgonzola into the cream and cook over low heat, stirring almost constantly, until the cheese has melted. Stir the Parmesan cheese into the sauce just before draining the pasta (which should be fully cooked). Toss the sauce and pasta together quickly but well, and serve immediately.

VARIATION: Omit the heavy cream, and increase the butter to 6 tablespoons. Once the butter is melted, and you are ready to finish the dish, stir in the cheeses.

VARIATION: The dish will taste quite different depending on what cheeses you use. You can of course use just two or three cheeses, or as many as five. Keep the total weight of cheese under 1 pound. Asiago, ricotta, Emmenthaler (Swiss), taleggio, and caciocavallo are all possibilities. Try to balance strong and mild cheeses. See pages 23–27 for flavors and melting qualities of Italian cheeses.

VARIATION: **Pasta with Four Cheese Pink Sauce.** Stir ½ cup of peeled, seeded, juiced, and chopped tomatoes into the butter before adding the cream. Cook until the tomatoes begin to soften and break down, and then proceed with the cream and the cheeses.

Method 2—Unheated Cheese

The sauces made according to this method do not subject the cheese to the heat of the stove. Instead, hot pasta and/or other sauce ingredients are poured over the cheese to melt it. The great benefit of this method is that the cheese can be mixed with other ingredients well ahead of time. In many cases this means that you can make the base in the morning and leave nothing more than the boiling of pasta to do at the last moment. Cheese sauces of this type are a staple of southern Italy where the days are hot and the tempered sauces refreshing.

Pasta "Soon Soon"

PASTA SCIUÉ SCIUÉ

SERVES 4 OR 5

One of the simplest of Neapolitan recipes, its name roughly translates from the regional dialect to "sauce—soon, soon." This dish is at its best with ripe fresh tomatoes. In fact, many Neapolitans don't even cook them; they toss them in a bowl with the oil, basil, salt, and mozzarella and then pour the hot pasta and cheese over them.

I do not peel the tomatoes, but if the skins bother you, follow the method on page 20.

THE PASTA: Use long or short dried pasta such as *penne, pennette,* or spaghetti.

Grate or finely chop the mozzarella, and scatter it over the bottom of a pasta-serving bowl. Season it with salt.

Bring the water to a boil in a large pan. The sauce goes very quickly, so you can add the salt and pasta to the water as soon as it boils and cook according to the directions on pages 98–100.

GETTING READY

½ pound fresh mozzarella

Salt

THE PASTA

At least 4 quarts water

2 tablespoons salt

1 pound *penne, pennette,* or
    spaghetti

THE VEGETABLES

6 tablespoons extra-virgin
    olive oil

2 pounds ripe fresh plum or
    round tomatoes, coarsely
    chopped (about 4 cups)

½ cup loosely torn basil leaves

Salt and freshly ground black
    pepper

THE FINISH

¼ cup torn basil leaves

Freshly grated Parmesan
    cheese

Heat the oil, and toss in the tomatoes. Season with basil, salt, and pepper and cook about 5 minutes; the tomatoes should soften but retain their shape. Pour the tomatoes, the drained hot pasta, the ¼ cup basil, and the Parmesan into the bowl with the mozzarella and toss well.

VARIATION: **Pasta with Arugula or Spinach, Tomatoes, and Mozzarella.** Add about ½ pound fresh arugula or small spinach leaves to the recipe. Trim away the stems, wash and dry the greens well, and chop coarsely if they are larger than 1½ inches. Toss them into the olive oil, season with salt and pepper, and wilt before adding the tomatoes. Or put them uncooked into the bowl with the mozzarella, and let the heat of the pasta wilt them. Two minced garlic cloves and a dash of hot red-pepper flakes or paprika cooked in the oil will add a nice zest.

VARIATION: **Pasta with Provola, Pancetta, and Tomatoes.** Any of the string cheeses listed on page 25 can be substituted for the mozzarella. When I use a smoked cheese, such as smoked provola, I like to add a little pancetta. Reduce the olive oil to 3 tablespoons, and cook 2 ounces of finely chopped pancetta in the oil until it is crisp. Continue with the recipe as above, with or without some arugula.

Spaghetti with Bacon, Eggs, and Tomato Sauce

SPAGHETTI CARBONARA CON POMODORI

SERVES 4 OR 5

I have taken a few liberties with this classic Roman dish. The original recipe calls for pancetta or *guanciale* (pig's jowl and cheek), but I like it as well with American bacon. Be sure to choose a good-quality, lean brand. I also added chopped tomatoes, because I like the way they cut the creaminess of the dish.

Note that this recipe uses raw eggs and relies on the heat of the hot pasta to raise the temperature to a degree at which all harmful bacteria will be killed. If you are hesitant to use raw eggs, you can try using pasteurized liquid eggs.

THE PASTA: The traditional pasta for this recipe is spaghetti. It is what I always use, because the large amount of surface area provides the most heat to the egg-cheese mixture and the most flavor to you.

GETTING READY
3 large eggs
1 cup freshly grated Parmesan cheese or
    a combination of Parmesan and
    pecorino cheese
Freshly ground black pepper
THE PASTA
At least 4 quarts water
2 tablespoons salt
1 pound spaghetti

THE START (*SOFFRITTO*)
3 tablespoons extra-virgin olive oil
1/3 pound bacon or pancetta, cut into
    1/8-inch-wide strips
2 large garlic cloves, minced
THE VEGETABLES
2 cups finely chopped fresh or canned
    tomatoes
1/4 cup chopped flat-leaf parsley
Salt
THE LIQUID
1/4 cup dry white wine

Break the eggs into a shallow pasta-serving bowl, and beat in the cheese and pepper. Cover with plastic wrap; if you are cooking the pasta immediately, keep at room temperature; otherwise, refrigerate.

Bring the water to a boil in a large pan, and when the sauce is almost finished, cook the pasta according to the directions on pages 98–100.

Pour the oil into a 10-to-12-inch sauté pan, and add the bacon and garlic to the warming oil. Cook over medium heat until the bacon is just beginning to crisp and the garlic is golden. If there is more than 6 to 8 tablespoons of fat in the pan, spoon off the excess. Stir in the tomatoes and parsley, season lightly with salt, and cook a few minutes, until the tomato juices are released. Pour in the wine, and raise the heat to high to allow the liquid to boil and reduce by about one-third.

Toss the hot spaghetti into the bowl with the eggs, and immediately pour the sauce on top. Toss together well, and serve immediately with additional cheese.

VARIATION: Replace the bacon with ½ pound crumbled Italian sausage.

VARIATION: **Spaghetti with Chicken Livers.** In Elizabeth David's book *An Omelette and a Glass of Wine,* she wrote about a remote, nameless Tuscan restaurant, the whereabouts of which she could only describe as "lost among the trees." She was more exact about the deliciousness of the chicken-liver variation of the recipe above. This is my version of her memory. Beat the eggs and cheese as above. Replace the pancetta or bacon with shredded prosciutto, and when the garlic is golden, sauté ¼ pound of cleaned and chopped chicken livers in the same pan. Season them with salt, pepper, and a tablespoon of lemon juice or the finely grated rind of the lemon. When the livers are cooked, in about 3 minutes, toss them into the eggs with the hot pasta. The tomatoes are not needed, but the parsley is good.

Fusilli with Swiss Chard, Walnuts, and Ricotta Cheese Sauce

FUSILLI CON PUMATE E VERDURE

SERVES 4 OR 5

As in the Primary Recipe for Method 2, this sauce is made by adding hot pasta to uncooked cheese, but here the cheese—ricotta—is a soft and creamy one. When that is the case—as with mascarpone and soft goat cheese as well as ricotta—add some of the pasta-boiling water to the cheese before tossing in the pasta, so the cheese will better coat the pasta.

This dish can be prepared with any fresh leafy green you find in your marketplace or garden. Try beet greens, kale, red chard, spinach, or even romaine, radicchio, chicory, or escarole.

THE PASTA: A short pasta with nooks and crannies to hold the sauce will provide the most satisfaction. Look for *fusilli corti* or *gemelli*.

GETTING READY

2 bunches Swiss chard (about 1½ pounds)

1 tablespoon extra-virgin olive oil

⅔ cup coarsely chopped walnuts

1 cup fresh ricotta cheese

THE PASTA

At least 4 quarts water

2 tablespoons salt

1 pound short pasta, such as *fusilli corti* or *gemelli*

THE START (*SOFFRITTO*)

¼ cup extra-virgin olive oil

2 tablespoons unsalted butter

2 medium garlic cloves, minced (about 1 tablespoon)

¼ cup oil-packed sun-dried tomatoes, drained and cut into narrow slivers

Salt

1 small fresh hot red pepper, seeds removed and minced, or ¼ to ½ teaspoon hot red-pepper flakes or paprika

THE VEGETABLES

Swiss chard from above

THE FINISH

Freshly grated pecorino cheese

Wash the chard and shake off the excess water. Discard any tough parts of the stems, and slice the tender parts into ½-inch pieces. Coarsely chop the leaves.

Heat the oil in a small sauté pan, and lightly brown the walnuts. Remove them with a slotted spoon, and save for later. Scoop the ricotta into a pasta-serving bowl.

Put the water in a large pan, and when the sauce is almost finished, cook the pasta according to the directions on pages 98–100.

Meanwhile, heat the oil and butter in a 12-to-14-inch sauté pan. A 14-inch pan will better accommodate the Swiss chard. Stir the garlic, sun-dried tomatoes, salt, and red-pepper flakes or paprika into the pan, and cook gently until the garlic is golden.

Toss in the chard, season with salt, and sauté, stirring frequently, until the leaves are limp and tender and any excess liquid is reduced to no more than 2 tablespoons, about 6 minutes.

Remove 3 tablespoons of the pasta-boiling water, and stir it into the ricotta to loosen it. Drain the pasta, and toss it over the ricotta with the chard and walnuts. Toss together until the ingredients are evenly mixed. Serve with grated cheese.

VARIATION: **Macaroni with Broccoli, Sausage, and Ricotta.** Substitute 1 pound of broccoli, trimmed and blanched, for the chard. Keep everything else the same, or omit the butter and add ½ pound of sausage to the start. Try with different vegetables and different seasonings.

VARIATION: **Macaroni with Swiss Chard and Goat Cheese.** Use ½ pound of soft goat cheese in place of the ricotta.

Creating Your Own

I don't ever think about creating a cheese sauce per se. It comes to mind instead when I have made a sauce and want to add another dimension, or smooth it out, or use up some lovely leftover pieces of cheese. I also use ricotta cheese in place of cream in cream sauces when I want a less rich sauce. Use ½ to 1 cup of cheese for a pound of pasta as an enrichment.

BAKED PASTA

When you grow up in an Italian family, you always know where you will be on Sundays. We would troop to my grandparents' house along with all my aunts, uncles, and cousins for a substantial noonday meal. My aunt Irma, the uncontested best baker of the family, would bring plates of *wandi* and biscotti, or a golden rice pie. My family was responsible for the bread, and we stopped at the nearby bakery, where fat, crusty, still-warm loaves were shuffled into crisp white bags and then into our eager hands.

We were a large group, which is probably why Nonna so often began the meal with baked pasta, usually lasagna. It fed fifteen of us, and I remember there were leftovers. After dinner she would leave the dish on the counter, and throughout the afternoon, we kids would periodically amble into the kitchen to whittle away at the remains.

Baked pasta dishes invite more creative variations than I could ever imagine. They lend themselves easily to doubling, even tripling, and, once assembled, will wait for you to be ready to bake them. They are impressive presentations. It is no wonder that, in one form or another, recipes for baked pastas are part of each Italian region's celebratory foods. Lasagna is perhaps the best known, but there are also *timballi, timpani,* and *pasticci* (see box) to woo you to celebrate. This section has recipes for the two most common and quickest baked dishes—pasticci and lasagna.

Baked Pasta Terms

TIMBALLO: From the same word derivation as "drum," a *timballo* is a baked dish of layered ingredients. The filling is usually baked in a drum-shaped mold that may be lined with pastry crust, cooked pasta, rice, *crespelle* (crêpes), or simply breadcrumbs. The layered ingredients—meat, vegetables, fish, or more pasta—are moistened with tomato and/or white sauce, baked, and then unmolded. There are numerous dialect and regional names for these baked dishes. The *timpano,* which was the centerpiece of the dinner in Stanley Tucci's exquisite movie, *Big Night,* is a traditional pastry-lined Calabrian *timballo.*

PASTICCIO: Much the same as a *timballo* in concept, except that a *pasticcio* is baked and served from a dish and not formed in a mold. *Che pasticcio!* means "What a mess," so my theory is that the dish was named when a nervous bride attempted to make her mother-in-law's famous *timballo* for her new husband and failed.

LASAGNE: Wide, flat noodles that are typically layered with various fillings, one or two sauces, and cheese and baked. *Lasagna* is the singular form of *lasagne* and means a single noodle, but that is what Americans call the entire dish.

SAUCES FOR BAKED PASTAS

Baked pastas rely on sauce, sometimes two or three sauces, as a binder. *Ragù, marinara,* and white sauce—alone or in combination—are all traditionally used. You can also use any of the tomato-based sauces on pages 106–120. Choose a sauce with the filling in mind. Light tomato sauces go well with vegetables; sturdy *ragù* is a good choice for robust fillings.

The recipes below may give you a choice of white sauce or ricotta. The decision is one of taste. White sauce will give a creamier, perhaps more elegant taste. Ricotta, so prevalent in baked dishes from southern Italy, will seem more rustic. When ricotta cheese is used as a sauce, it should first be beaten with an egg or two. Without the egg, it is a fine-tasting cheese but will not spread and coat the pasta as a sauce will.

You will find it easiest to work if your sauces are at room temperature. If the white sauce has been refrigerated or frozen, warm it over low heat first so it will spread easily. It should be the consistency of thick cream. If, after warming, it is not, use enough milk (or cream) to thin it.

FILLINGS FOR BAKED PASTA

For the filling, use any agreeable combination that marries well with the sauce and cheese. Try to imagine the foods together on your dinner plate. Since the fillings are usually cooked first, baked pasta is a good way to use leftovers. Thin slices of leftover meatballs or sausages, pieces of roasted chicken, sautéed broccoli, or boiled asparagus can all find a new home in a dish of baked pasta. On the other hand, a simple layering of tomato sauce, cheese, and pasta makes a delicious dish.

The best cheeses for baked pastas are those that will melt and spread during baking. (See "Cheese," pages 25–26.) Fontina, provolone, mozzarella, scamorza—alone or in combination—are classic choices. Although melting cheeses are not necessary, they are a definite enhancement. But don't overdo it. The results should be something much more delicate than those plate-to-mouth tightropes that epitomize the baked pasta dishes at mediocre Italian-American restaurants. Many delicious recipes call for no more than a healthy amount of freshly grated Parmesan or pecorino.

MAKING AHEAD

Once assembled, *pasticci* and lasagna can be held for 4 to 5 hours before baking. It is not necessary to refrigerate them, but if you do, either bring them to room temperature before baking, or add 10 minutes to the baking time.

Pasticci

Although *pasticci* are part of quick Italian home cooking, there is no reason why you cannot make them for an elegant meal by choosing a nice dish, preferably a shallow earthenware dish, and lighting the candles. Because the recipes can be doubled or tripled with ease and assembled well ahead of baking, they provide lovely solutions for large dinner parties. If you do triple the recipe, use two pots to cook the pasta, or cook it in stages to control its texture.

THE PASTA FOR *PASTICCI*

Because it is cooked twice—boiled, then baked—the pasta for *pasticci* must be sturdy, and that means a good imported dried durum wheat pasta (*pasta secca*). Although long spaghetti-type pasta will work in the recipes, I prefer to use short macaroni types because they are easier to serve, look more appealing, and capture the sauce and filling in their crevices. *Penne, ziti,* shells, bow ties (butterflies), and rigatoni are some of the possibilities.

Baked Pasta with Mushrooms and Ham

PASTICCIO DI GAIOLE

SERVES 6 TO 8

On a visit to Gaiole in Chianti, I was invited to dinner at a hilltop villa embraced by stately cypress trees. The long, curving stone driveway was candlelit, and I thought the welcoming beauty was sufficient to warm my evening. My senses were more than sated when I entered the foyer and saw and smelled through to the kitchen, where this pasta was bubbling away in an open wood-fired brick oven.

MAKING AHEAD

1 recipe (about 4½ cups)
   White Sauce (page 35)
2 tablespoons unsalted butter

Preheat the oven to 375° F and set the rack in the middle of the oven. Use 2 tablespoons butter to coat the bottom and sides of a shallow ovenproof dish. I like to use an earthenware dish that is attractive enough to bring to the table, but any baking dish that is about 2 inches deep and will hold at least 12 cups is fine.

Melt 3 tablespoons of butter in a medium sauté pan, and toss in the mushrooms. Season with salt and pepper, and cook until the mushrooms are lightly colored, and have released and then reabsorbed their juices. Set aside.

Cook the pasta according to the directions on pages 98–100, but drain it about 2 minutes before it is fully cooked. It should be tender but not quite *al dente*. I begin to taste it after 6 to 8 minutes, depending on the size. It is best to cook the pasta when the sauce is ready, so you can mix it immediately and keep it from sticking together. If you can't, then rinse the drained pasta briefly under cold running water and coat with a tablespoon of oil.

Meanwhile, scoop the white sauce into a small saucepan and bring slowly to a boil, being sure to stir often and all the way to the bottom of the pan to prevent scorching. When it boils, whisk in the heavy cream, and continue to boil gently until it reduces slightly; it should be thick enough to coat a spoon. Check the seasoning, and add salt and pepper if necessary. Keep warm.

When the pasta is ready, drain it, return it to its cooking pot, and immediately stir in the white sauce. Spread one-third of the pasta over the bottom of the prepared dish, and sprinkle on half the mushrooms, half the prosciutto, and almost half the Parmesan cheese (reserve about 3 tablespoons of the cheese for the top). Cover this with another third of the pasta, the remaining mushrooms and prosciutto, and all but the 3 tablespoons of cheese. Spread the rest of the pasta on top, sprinkle on the remaining cheese, and dot the top with pieces of the butter.

Baked pasta dishes can be held at this point for 4 to 5 hours. It is not necessary to refrigerate, but if you do, either bring the dish to room temperature before baking or add 10 minutes to the baking time. Bake, uncovered, 25 to 30 minutes, until the pasta is bubbling, tender, and slightly brown around the edges.

VARIATION: **Baked Pasta with Asparagus or Fennel.** Substitute 1 pound of trimmed and blanched asparagus, cut into 2-inch-long pieces (page 343), for the mushrooms. Or substitute about 2 pounds of fennel, using the directions—substituting butter for the olive oil—for the braised fennel in the pasta recipe on page 127. In any of the above recipes, you could use boiled ham in place of the prosciutto.

GETTING READY

3 tablespoons unsalted butter

1¼ pound mushrooms, any single variety or in combination, trimmed, cleaned, and thinly sliced

Salt and freshly ground black pepper

THE PASTA

At least 4 quarts water

2 tablespoons salt

1 pound *penne*

THE SAUCE

The white sauce from above

1 cup heavy cream

Salt and freshly ground black pepper

THE FILLING

6 ounces prosciutto, shredded or cut into pieces about ⅛ inch wide and 3 inches long

The mushrooms from above

1 cup freshly grated Parmesan cheese

THE FINISH

2 tablespoons unsalted butter, cut into small pieces

VARIATION: **Baked Pasta with Fresh and Dried Mushrooms.** Combining dried porcini mushrooms with the fresh will give a rich, woodsy flavor to the dish. Soak 1 ounce of dried mushrooms in ½ cup of warm water for 30 minutes. Strain the juices well to remove all sand, and add them to the white sauce before adding the cream. Reduce the sauce slightly, and then stir in the cream. Rinse the soaked mushrooms under running water to rid them of dirt, dry, and chop finely. Sauté them in the butter for 5 minutes before adding the fresh mushrooms.

Baked Pasta with Sausage and Peppers

PASTICCIO DI SALSICCE E PEPERONI

SERVES 6 TO 8

The initial preparation of this dish is exactly the same as making my grandmother's sausage-and-pepper sauce on page 118. It demonstrates how you can turn quick pan sauces into baked pasta dishes by adding white sauce or ricotta cheese, or just more tomato sauce and a bit of melting cheese.

THE PASTA: I like this best with large pasta such as *ziti* or *rigatoni*.

MAKING AHEAD

3 to 3½ cups *marinara* or *ragù* sauce
  (pages 30 and 33), or 3 cups chopped
  canned tomatoes with their juices
1 cup warm White Sauce (page 35), or
  1 cup whole-milk ricotta cheese
  beaten with 1 egg

GETTING READY

3 roasted red peppers, cut in strips (see
  page 397)
2 tablespoons olive oil for coating the
  baking dish

THE PASTA

At least 4 quarts water

2 tablespoons salt

1 pound short macaroni, such as *ziti*
   or *rigatoni*

THE START (*SOFFRITTO*)

2 tablespoons extra-virgin olive oil

1 pound Italian sweet sausage, casing
   removed

Salt

½ to 1 small hot pepper, or ¼ to
   ½ teaspoon hot red-pepper flakes
   or paprika

¼ cup torn basil leaves

THE SAUCES

The tomato sauce from above

The warm White Sauce or the ricotta
   sauce from above

THE FILLING

½ pound grated mozzarella

The peppers from above

½ cup small whole basil leaves

1 cup freshly grated Parmesan or
   pecorino cheese

Put the water in a large pan, and when the sauce and filling are ready, cook the pasta as in the Primary Recipe, page 167.

Preheat the oven to 375° F and set the rack in the middle of the oven. Coat the bottom and sides of a shallow, ovenproof dish with the olive oil.

Meanwhile, heat 2 tablespoons olive oil in a 12-inch sauté pan. Break the sausage into pieces, and drop it into the pan. Continue to break it up with a fork or wooden spoon as it cooks, until the pieces are pea-size. When it has lost its pink color, season it with salt, red pepper, and basil, then pour in 2½ cups of the tomato sauce, reserving ½ cup for the top of the dish. Cook just until heated through. If you are using canned tomatoes instead of sauce, add them to the sausage and simmer for 15 to 20 minutes, until the sauce is slightly thickened.

Stir the tomato-sauce mixture and the white sauce or ricotta into the cooked, drained pasta.

Scoop one-third of the pasta into the prepared baking dish. Scatter half the mozzarella, half the peppers, half the whole basil leaves, and one-third the grated cheese on top. Cover with another of pasta, the remaining mozzarella, peppers, and basil, and another third of cheese. Cover with all the remaining pasta, and drizzle the reserved ½ cup of tomato sauce on top. Sprinkle on the rest of the cheese, and bake for 30 to 35 minutes, or until the cheese has melted and the pasta is tender.

VARIATION: **Baked Vegetable Pasta.** Make this a vegetable *pasticcio* by omitting the sausage and using a pound of sliced mushrooms, or ¾ pound of sliced mushrooms and a cup of quickly blanched fresh or frozen peas. Increase the oil to 3 tablespoons, or to 2 tablespoons butter and 1 tablespoon olive oil, and cook three thinly sliced garlic cloves in it. Sauté the sliced mushrooms, and when they are nearly cooked, toss in the peas, and then add the tomato sauce or the tomatoes and continue as above. I like to use white sauce with this particular combination.

VARIATION: **Baked Pasta with Meatballs, Chicken Livers, and Peas.** Substitute 2 cups of cooked peas for the roasted peppers. Make several tiny meatballs as in the recipe on page 91, sautéing them until they are cooked through. Sauté ½ cup of minced onions in the 2 tablespoons of olive oil until they are tender before cooking the sausage. When the sausage is just about browned, add ½ pound of trimmed and diced chicken livers, and sauté about 2 minutes until they are cooked. Layer the pasta, cheese, meatballs, peas, sausage, chicken livers, and sauce as in the Primary Recipe.

Baked Pasta with Eggplant

PASTICCIO CON MELANZANE

SERVES 6 TO 8

With the exception of the eggplant, all the ingredients for this *pasticcio* are always in my pantry, so I am able to throw together what appears to be a fairly elaborate dish. I once had to improvise a dinner for eight unexpected guests after being at an all-day auction. I was home by five, and two *pasticci* were on the table at seven-thirty.

THE PASTA: I have eaten eggplant *pasticci* in Italy made with spaghetti, and because the eggplant forms such an even filling, it is good here, as is *penne*.

MAKING AHEAD

1 cup warm White Sauce (page 35), or
    1 cup whole-milk ricotta cheese
    beaten with 1 egg

3 to 3½ cups *marinara* or *ragù* (pages 30,
    33)

GETTING READY

1 large eggplant (1 pound)

About 2 tablespoons extra-virgin olive
    oil

THE PASTA

At least 4 quarts water

2 tablespoons salt

1 pound *penne, ziti,* or spaghetti

THE SAUCES

The warm White Sauce or ricotta sauce
    from above

The tomato sauce from above

THE FILLING

The eggplant from above

⅓ cup whole basil leaves or coarsely
    chopped flat-leaf parsley

¾ cup freshly grated pecorino or Parme-
    san cheese

8 ounces scamorza or mozzarella cheese,
    coarsely grated or chopped

Wash the eggplant, peel it if desired, and cut it crosswise into ½-inch thick slices. Layer it in a colander with salt, weight it, and let drain for 45 minutes. Rinse and pat dry. Preheat the oven to 375° F. Place the eggplant on a baking sheet in one layer, brush both sides with olive oil, and roast for 8 to 10 minutes, or until tender.

Warm the white sauce if it is cold.

Pour the water for the pasta into a pan and bring to a boil. Cook the pasta according to the Primary Recipe, and immediately stir the white sauce or ricotta and all but ½ cup of the tomato sauce into the cooked and drained pasta. If you are using the parsley, stir that in also.

Spread a third of the pasta in the bottom of an oiled baking dish. Cover with half of the eggplant, a third of the pecorino, and half the scamorza. Scatter the basil leaves on top. Spoon on another layer of pasta, the rest of the eggplant, a third more of the pecorino, and the rest of the scamorza. Spread on the remaining pasta, and drizzle the top with the reserved tomato sauce and the remaining pecorino. Bake about 30 to 35 minutes, until the pasta is tender and the cheese is melted.

VARIATION: **Baked Pasta with Zucchini.** Cook 1½ pounds of zucchini as above, cutting the squash into long, thin pieces before roasting. Use mozzarella and Parmesan for the cheeses.

VARIATION: **Baked Pasta with Leftover Vegetables.** Use about 3 cups of leftover roasted, grilled, or boiled vegetables in place of the eggplant. If you have cooked sausage or meatballs, cut them into thin slices, and either substitute them for the vegetables or use them all together.

Creating Your Own

If you double the recipe for six to eight people, it will be copious enough to feed a group of twelve to sixteen people. Cook a double recipe in two dishes, so the pasta is not too deeply layered.

Creating Your Own Pasticci

FOR 3 OR 4	FOR 6 TO 8
For a shallow baking dish with at least a 6-cup capacity	For a shallow baking dish with at least a 12-cup capacity
$\frac{1}{2}$ pound pasta	1 pound pasta

THE SAUCE	**THE SAUCE**
A total of 2 to 2$\frac{1}{4}$ cups of tomato, white sauce, ricotta beaten with 2 tablespoons of pasta-boiling water, or a combination.	A total of 4 to 4$\frac{1}{2}$ cups of tomato, white sauce, ricotta beaten with 2 tablespoons of pasta-boiling water, or a combination.
THE FILLING	**THE FILLING**
Use a total of 1$\frac{1}{2}$ to 2 cups (vegetables, meat, fish, or a combination)	Use a total of 2$\frac{1}{2}$ to 4 cups (vegetables, meat, fish, or a combination)
THE CHEESE	**THE CHEESE**
You can use simply a grating cheese such as Parmesan or pecorino, or a combination of grating cheese and a melting cheese such as mozzarella.	You can use simply a grating cheese such as Parmesan and pecorino, or a combination of grating cheese and a melting cheese such as mozzarella.
$\frac{1}{2}$ to $\frac{3}{4}$ cup grating cheese	1 to 1$\frac{1}{2}$ cups grating cheese
About $\frac{1}{4}$ pound melting cheese	About $\frac{1}{2}$ pound melting cheese

Lasagna
LASAGNE

When most people hear "lasagna" they probably think of classic Neapolitan *lasagne di carnevale,* made with *ragù,* three cheeses, sausage, meatballs, and sliced hard-boiled eggs. That's what I grew up on, and I was well into my thirties and in cooking classes with Marcella Hazan in Bologna before I realized that there was any other type. From then on, the possibilities for this perfect large-group dish became endless. The Neapolitan version will always have a home in my kitchen, but I have found room for numerous others.

THE PASTA FOR LASAGNA

The recipes that follow are written for the ready-to-bake, no-boil variety of lasagna pasta. I have come to rely on it for a speedy meal. Since these packaged dried lasagna noodles need no preboiling, dinner can be ready so quickly that it would make my Nonna pull at her eye in an Italian gesture of disbelief. And because they are so thin, the layers of filling and pasta melt together beautifully.

You can substitute the traditional packaged curly-edged lasagna (imported from Italy, please) or fresh pasta sheets, but you will need less sauce than called for in the recipes below (see "Creating Your Own Lasagna," page 181).

To precook traditional noodles, boil four or five pieces at a time in 5 quarts of boiling salted water with 1½ tablespoons of oil. Packaged dried noodles are ready as soon as they begin to bend, about 6 minutes, and fresh noodles are ready as soon as the water returns to the boil and the noodles float to the top. Scoop the noodles out of the water and immediately dip them into cold water to stop the cooking. Lay them flat and separated on damp towels and cover with a damp towel.

It is also possible to use traditional need-to-be boiled noodles without pre-cooking them. Layer the dry noodles with the ingredients and sauce required, then pour one cup of boiling water around the edges of the assembled lasagna. Cover the pan with foil, bake for one hour, uncover, and continue to bake for 30 minutes or until the top is golden and the noodles are tender.

Lasagna for Carnival

LASAGNE DI CARNEVALE

SERVES 8 TO 10

Although the name "carnival" suggests a dish reserved for a special holiday—the celebration preceding Lent—this baked pasta was the common beginning to most Sunday meals for Italian-Americans. It also showed up before the Thanksgiving turkey and Easter lamb. I make *lasagne di carnevale* with four layers because the filling is copious; I use three layers for the other lasagnas.

MAKING AHEAD

About 4 cups *ragù* made with
½ pound Italian sausage
and meatballs (variation,
page 34)

GETTING READY

The *ragù* from above

1 cup water

1 pound ricotta cheese
(2 cups)

THE PASTA

¾ pound ready-to-bake
lasagne

THE FILLING

The sausage and meatball
slices from above

3 hard-boiled eggs, peeled
and cut into thin slices

Preheat the oven to 375° F and position the rack in the middle of the oven. Brush the bottom and sides of a rectangular approximately 9-by-13-by-2-inch baking pan with olive oil. The pan can be enameled cast iron, terra-cotta, ceramic, metal, or glass. Traditional lasagna pans usually have swing-up handles at each end, which are much appreciated when the lasagna is plentiful and heavy. Remove the sausages and meatballs from the sauce and cut them into thin slices.

Stir the water into the *ragù* and spread a thin layer—about 1 cup—of the sauce on the bottom of the oiled pan. *Ragù* is a thick sauce, and the water is there to provide moisture for the no-boil lasagne to absorb and soften. It is not necessary to add it for traditional boil-first pasta. Scoop the ricotta into a bowl and beat with a fork to loosen. Beat in, a few tablespoons at a time, enough of the sauce to make the cheese smooth and spreadable.

Cover the sauce with a layer of pasta, overlapping the edges slightly if necessary. The sheets should completely cover the bottom of the pan. Spread a third of the remaining sauce over the pasta, and lay a third each of the sausage, meatballs, and eggs evenly on top. Then scatter a third of the mozzarella and ¼ cup of the Parmesan cheese on top of that. Drop spoonfuls of the ricotta—a third of the total amount—uniformly spaced over the other cheeses. Then use the back of the spoon to spread it as much as possible. Don't fret; it never wants to spread easily, but the heat of the oven will homogenize everything nicely. Place another layer of pasta on top, and press it down lightly to smooth out the ingredients below. Cover with ¾ cup of *ragù* and another third of sausage, meatballs, eggs, cheeses, and ricotta, and then another layer of pasta, followed by ¾ cup more sauce and the remaining meat, eggs, mozzarella, and ricotta. Press on the top layer of noodles, and evenly spread the remaining sauce on top, sprinkled with the last of the grated cheese.

Once assembled, lasagna will wait for you. Cover it with plastic wrap or aluminum foil, and let sit at room temperature for a few hours, or refrigerate overnight. Bring it back to room temperature before baking.

Bake for 40 minutes to an hour, until the lasagna is bubbling and lightly brown at the edges. Push the tip of a small sharp knife or a skewer into the lasagna all the way to the bottom of the pan; the pasta should be tender and offer no resistance. Let it rest for 10 minutes before cutting.

¾ pound mozzarella cheese, grated or finely chopped

1¼ cups freshly grated Parmesan or grana-padano cheese

VARIATION: The above recipe assumes that you have made *ragù* with meatballs and sausage. If you have the *ragù* but no meat, make the recipe for meatballs on page 91, and form them into marble-size balls. Fry them in olive oil until cooked through. Leave the tiny meatballs (*polpettine*) whole. Fry sausages as well, and slice them as above.

VARIATION: *Ragù* is the traditional sauce, but *marinara* makes a lovely lasagna. In that case, make the meatballs as in the variation above, and omit the sausage.

Lasagna with Spinach and Mushrooms

LASAGNE CON SPINACI E FUNGHI

SERVES 6 TO 8

This is another family favorite, and when the boys are coming home with a group of friends, I increase the ingredients by a third and bake it in a 12-by-16-inch pan. See "Creating Your Own Lasagna" (page 181) for the amount of ingredients necessary for this larger pan.

THE PASTA: No-boil or traditional lasagna noodles (see page 173).

FROM THE PANTRY

About 5½ cups *marinara* sauce (page 30)

FILLING

5 tablespoons extra-virgin olive oil

1 pound mushrooms, wiped clean, stems trimmed, and caps sliced

Salt and freshly ground black pepper to taste

1 pound fresh spinach, washed, stems removed, and leaves coarsely chopped

Pinch freshly grated nutmeg

¾ pound mozzarella cheese, grated or finely chopped

1 cup freshly grated Parmesan cheese

2 cups ricotta cheese, beaten with 1 large egg

THE SAUCE

The *marinara* sauce from above

THE PASTA

½ pound ready-to-bake lasagne

Preheat the oven to 400° F. Brush with oil or coat with butter a rectangular baking pan approximately 9 by 13 by 2 inches.

Heat the oil in a 12-to-14-inch sauté pan, and when it is hot, toss in the mushrooms. Season with salt and pepper, and sauté over medium-high heat until they release their juices. Reduce the heat, and cook until the mushrooms are lightly browned and their juices have been reabsorbed. Drop in the spinach, season with salt, pepper, and nutmeg, and cook just until the leaves are wilted. If you are using the smaller pan, add the spinach in stages, waiting for the first batch to shrink before adding more. Remove the pan from the heat.

Spread about 1 cup of the tomato sauce in the bottom of the baking pan. Cover it with a layer of lasagne, placed side by side, and overlapping only slightly if necessary. Coat the pasta with another cup of tomato sauce, and scatter half the spinach and mushrooms evenly over the top. Spread half the mozzarella and half the ricotta over the vegetables, and sprinkle on ¼ cup of the Parmesan. Repeat this sequence with another layer of pasta, 1 cup of tomato sauce, the rest of the spinach, mushrooms, mozzarella, and ricotta, and ¼ cup Parmesan. Add a third layer of lasagna noodles, and drizzle the rest of the tomato sauce over the top. Be sure that the pasta is completely covered with sauce, or the top sheets will not soften. Sprinkle on the remaining Parmesan. Bake uncovered for 30 to 40 minutes, or until the lasagne is tender and the cheese is golden. Let rest 10 minutes before cutting.

VARIATION: **Lasagna with Spinach and Artichoke Hearts.** Replace the oil with unsalted butter, and substitute Fontina cheese for the mozzarella. Instead of the mushrooms, use about 3 cups of thinly sliced artichoke hearts, sautéed briefly in a small amount of butter.

VARIATION: Substitute 1½ cups warm white sauce (page 35) thinned with ½ cup milk for the ricotta and egg. The white sauce is particularly good with the artichoke variation above.

Lasagna with Butternut Squash and Smoked Provolone

LASAGNE CON ZUCCA E PROVOLONE AFFUMICATO

SERVES 6 TO 8

This lasagna may appear a bit complicated, but in fact the squash and the caramelized onions can be prepared up to 3 days ahead and kept ready in the refrigerator.

THE PASTA: No-boil or traditional lasagna noodles (see page 173).

MAKING AHEAD

5½ cups *marinara* sauce

2 recipes (3 pounds) Roasted and
   Mashed Butternut Squash (page 395)

1 recipe Caramelized Onions (page 371)

THE SAUCE

The *marinara* sauce from above

THE PASTA

½ pound ready-to-bake lasagne

THE FILLING

The squash from above

The onions from above

½ cup fresh basil leaves

THE CHEESE

¾ pound smoked provolone cheese,
   thinly sliced

1½ cups grated Parmesan cheese

If the squash and onions have been refrigerated, bring them to room temperature.

Preheat the oven to 400° F. Generously butter a rectangular baking pan approximately 9 by 13 by 2 inches.

Spread 1 cup of the tomato sauce in the bottom of the pan, and cover with a layer of lasagne. Coat with another cup of sauce and half the squash—drop the squash by large spoonfuls, and then spread it as evenly as possible over the entire pan. Scatter half the onions evenly over the squash, and lay half the provolone evenly over the onions. Sprinkle with ¼ cup of Parmesan and half the basil leaves. Drizzle on another cup of tomato sauce, and cover with noodles. Then layer as above, 1 cup sauce, the rest of the squash, onions, basil, ¼ cup Parmesan, and the rest of the basil. Cover with noodles and the last 1½ cups of sauce. Sprinkle on the remaining Parmesan, and bake 30 to 40 minutes, or until the noodles are tender. Let rest 10 minutes before serving.

VARIATION: Use thin slices of grilled or roasted butternut squash or zucchini in place of the mashed.

VARIATION: Substitute mozzarella, or a combination of mozzarella and Fontina, for the provolone.

Leek and Shrimp Lasagna

LASAGNE CON PORRI E GAMBERETTI

SERVES 6 TO 8

One rather hectic day of shooting a segment for cable television in my kitchen, my assistant, Virginia Koster, arrived with this lasagna, which she had created, all ready to bake. Virginia loves to feed people, and her intent was to make sure we had something to eat. I told her she had just provided a sterling addition to the pasta chapter.

This rich, elegant dish makes a lovely meal. A smaller serving is a perfect beginning to a simple fish entrée.

THE PASTA: No-boil or traditional lasagna noodles (see page 173.)

MAKING AHEAD

4¼ cups warm White Sauce (page 35) plus ½ cup milk, or enough to make it the consistency of heavy cream

1 recipe Braised Leeks and Onions (page 366)

GETTING READY

Butter for baking dish

THE PASTA

½ pound ready-to-bake lasagne

THE SAUCES

The warm white sauce from above

1 pound (2 cups) whole-milk ricotta beaten with 1 egg and 1 teaspoon fresh thyme

THE FILLING

The cooked leeks and onions from above

¾ pound medium shrimp, cooked, peeled, and sliced in half lengthwise

½ cup torn fresh basil leaves plus 8–10 whole leaves for garnishing

⅔ cup freshly grated Parmesan cheese

½ pound scamorza or mozzarella cheese, coarsely grated

Freshly ground black pepper

Preheat the oven to 400° F. Generously butter an approximately 9-by-13-by-2-inch rectangular baking pan. Spread 1 cup of the white sauce on the bottom of the pan. Cover the sauce with a layer of lasagne, and smooth half the ricotta on top of the lasagne. Scatter half the leeks and onions, half the shrimp, half the torn basil, and one-third of the Parmesan and scamorza evenly over the pasta. Season with pepper. Spread on another cup of white sauce, cover with noodles, and the remaining ricotta, leeks, onions, shrimp, and torn basil. Scatter on one-third more of the Parmesan and of the scamorza, and season with pepper. Drizzle on another cup of white sauce, cover with pasta, and spread the remaining white sauce evenly over the top. Scatter the last of the Parmesan and scamorza over the sauce, and distribute the whole basil leaves evenly over the top. Bake 30 to 40 minutes, or until the noodles are tender and the top is lightly browned. Let rest 10 minutes before cutting.

VARIATION: Use 1½ cups of *marinara* sauce in place of the ricotta.

VARIATION: **Lemony Vegetable Lasagna.** Substitute any cooked vegetable or combination of vegetables for the shrimp. Asparagus tips are lovely. In fact, they are delicious used with the shrimp. Or cook one thinly sliced small bulb of fennel with the onions and leeks, and use alone or with the shrimp.

Creating Your Own

To cut the recipe in half to serve three or four people, use an 8-inch square pan. Some brands of ready-to-bake lasagna noodles are packaged with several 8-inch aluminum pans. Alternately, make the full recipe and build it in two 8-inch pans; freeze one for another meal. On the other hand, if you double the recipe, use two 9-by-13-inch pans, so the pasta is not too deeply layered.

Creating Your Own Lasagna

FOR 3 OR 4	FOR 6 TO 8

THE PASTA

¼ pound of ready-to-bake is sufficient for 3 layers. If you use traditional dried noodles or freshly made ones, you may need up to ½ pound.

THE FILLING (Meat, Vegetables, Fish)

Use a total of 1 to 3 cups of filling.

THE CHEESE

Keep the total weight of melting cheeses to about ½ pound. Use ½ to ¾ cup grating cheese.

THE SAUCE

For ready-to-bake lasagne, use about 3 cups of sauce. The dry pasta must have some extra liquid to absorb. Traditional and fresh noodles can be made with as little as 2 cups.

THE PASTA

½ pound of ready-to-bake is sufficient for 3 layers. If you use traditional dried noodles or freshly made ones, you may need up to ¾ pound.

THE FILLING (Meat, Vegetables, Fish)

Use as little as 2 cups or as much as 6 cups. More than 3 cups per layer of filling seems extravagant.

THE CHEESE

Keep the total weight of melting cheeses to about ¾ pound; ½ pound is a good starting point. Use 1 to 1½ cups of grating cheese.

THE SAUCE

For ready-to-bake lasagne, use about 5½ cups of sauce. The dry pasta must have some extra liquid to absorb. Traditional and fresh noodles can be made with as little as 3 cups.

PROPORTIONS FOR A 12-BY-16-INCH PAN FOR 10 TO 14 PEOPLE

THE PASTA

14 ounces of ready-to-bake is sufficient for 3 layers. If you use traditional dried noodles or freshly made ones, you may need up to 1 pound.

THE FILLING (Meat, Vegetables, Fish)

Use as little as 3 cups or as much as 9 cups.

THE CHEESE

Keep the total weight of melting cheeses to about 1½ pounds. Use 1⅓ to 2 cups of grating cheese.

THE SAUCE

For ready-to-bake lasagne, use about 7½ cups of sauce. The dry pasta must have some extra liquid to absorb. Traditional and fresh noodles can be made with as little as 4 cups.

My brother Tom recently renovated a charming cottage in southern Connecticut and designed his kitchen around a dome-shaped, wood-fired brick oven. He uses it for everything, even cooked an entire Thanksgiving dinner in it. At large pizza parties, he lines the counter with a host of puffy dough balls and a multitude of bowls filled with chopped, shredded, and sliced topping ingredients and sincerely hopes that a guest will request a combination that is totally new to him. They are fun nights. Tom is fun. Pizza is fun—and easy.

Some historians estimate that brick ovens have been firing up in Italy since 500 B.C. and producing flatbreads of one form or another. In my grandfather's day, it was quite common for Italian families, here and abroad, to build small bell-shaped brick ovens in their backyards to bake pizza and bread. The building of these home ovens may have waned for a while, but the "pie's" magnetism did not. You will find no recipes for homemade pizza in Italian cookbooks written around the 1950s, but, thanks to restaurants and take-outs, pizza consumption grew so that today it is consumed yearly by over three billion hungry American diners—the undisputed, preferred fuel of teenagers. And the home brick oven has been saved from extinction. More and more people are building or installing them—inside and out—to experience the joy of homemade pizza. When Tom was shopping for his oven, he found that there were numerous companies that offered such appliances for the home cook.

For those who are not quite ready to tear out their kitchen walls and install a brick oven, there are pizza stones in all shapes and sizes, and pizza pans with and without perforated bottoms. Pizza peels and pizza wheels crowd the shelves of kitchen-supply stores. Homemade pizza is on the rise and so easy to make that children can do it. You can do it. And, oh, the difference!

Pizza Pieces

The first true commercial pizzeria, Antica Pizzeria Port'Alba, was opened in Naples, Italy, in 1830. It is still in business today, located at Via Port'Alba 18.

In 1889, a Neapolitan *pizzaiolo* (pizza-maker), Rafaele Esposito, created a special patriotic pizza for the visiting King Umberto I and his consort, Queen

Margherita. He emulated the colors of the Italian flag by using tomatoes for the red, mozzarella for the white, and basil for the green, and named it *pizza Margherita* in the queen's honor. Since the queen did not want to be seen in a humble pizzeria, Rafaele delivered it to her. The first pizza delivery! Some two hundred years later, Rafaele's Pizzeria di Pietro e Basta Cosi, now called Pizzeria Brandi, is still in existence, with the original royal thank-you note signed by the "head of the table of the royal household" proudly displayed.

Pizza came to America along with spaghetti and meatballs and the Italian immigrants. Gennaro Lombardi opened the first Stateside pizzeria in New York City in 1895. It was not, however, an immediate smash hit. It took over twenty years for the simple tomato pie to catch on.

The Tools

You can purchase a pizza or bread-baking stone at a kitchen-supply store, or unglazed stone (quarry) tiles at a tile shop. In the case of the baking stone, choose the largest one that will fit in your oven. Stones are made either round or square. I prefer the square, because the extra surface saves my pizza from spilling over onto the oven floor when I shuffle it in with too much exuberance. In the case of the tiles, buy the largest squares you can find, and enough of them to cover most of your oven rack. Move them around at the tile shop to find ones that will abut one another fairly snugly.

You can also make a very good pizza in a pizza pan. It should be thin with a slight raised edge if you like to put sauce on your pie (not all pizzas have sauce). Black steel pans are the most effective because the bottoms quickly absorb the heat and produce a crisp crust. Large, thin black rectangular pans, usually sold in restaurant-supply houses, are handy for making large pies to be cut into small squares. Pans with perforated bottoms are designed primarily for the outdoor grill, but I have friends who use them in the oven and swear by them.

If you plan to use a stone or tiles, you should have a wooden pizza board called a pizza or baker's peel that will accommodate a 14-to-15-inch pizza. They are inexpensive and make sliding a pizza into the oven very easy. You could also use a flat, rimless cookie sheet, but where's the drama? As long as you're shopping, you might as well pick up a pizza wheel for slicing *alla pizzeria*. Otherwise, use a large chef's knife.

Pizza Dough

PASTA PER PIZZA

MAKES 2 MEDIUM (10-TO-12-INCH) ROUND PIZZAS
OR 4 SMALL (6-TO-8-INCH) ROUND PIZZAS
OR 1 LARGE RECTANGULAR PIZZA (12 BY 17 INCHES)

Pizza dough is bread dough that must rise before being rolled out very thin. How thin is up to you, but keep in mind that, if you make it thicker than the recipe indicates, you will have a smaller yield.

AHEAD-OF-TIME NOTE: Once made and risen, the dough can be frozen. Divide it into pieces according to the number of pizzas you intend to make, tuck each in its own plastic bag, and refrigerate overnight or freeze for up to 1 month. If you have enough freezer space, you can spread the dough into a pizza pan and freeze the entire pan, and then defrost it before covering with the topping.

1 cup warm water (110° F)

1 package dry yeast

3¼ to 3½ cups flour, plus more
   for rolling

1 teaspoon salt

Oil for coating the rising bowl

Stir ¼ cup of the water and the yeast together in a small cup or bowl until the yeast is dissolved. Let sit for 5 minutes to be sure the yeast is active

BY HAND: Pour 3 cups of the flour onto the kitchen counter, and mix in the salt. Make a well in the center, and pour in the dissolved yeast and the remaining water. Use a fork to work the flour gradually from the sides of the well into the pool in the center, until the water is completely absorbed. (If you fear the dike will break, you can complete this initial step in a bowl and then transfer the mass to a floured counter.) Gather the dough into a ball, and knead for 10 minutes, adding more flour if the dough is too sticky to handle. When the kneading is finished, the dough should be smooth, and when you poke your finger into it, no dough should cling to it.

BY MACHINE: Put 2 cups of the flour into the bowl of a food processor or of a heavy-duty mixer. Use the processor's dough blade, or the mixer's paddle, and mix in the salt. With the machine running, pour in the dissolved yeast and the remaining water and process for 10 seconds, or until the dough begins to pull together. If you are using the mixer, switch to the dough hook. Add 1 more cup of flour, and knead in the processor for 40 seconds or in the mixer for 5 minutes. Poke the dough with your finger to make sure that it does not stick. Add more flour and process longer if it does.

When the dough is nice and smooth, pat it into a ball, put it into a lightly oiled bowl, and turn it over to coat evenly. If you are accustomed to baking breads and dough and like them to rise in a floured bowl instead of an oiled one, that is also fine. Cover the bowl with a kitchen towel, and leave it to rise in a warm spot until it has doubled in bulk, about 2 hours.

Punch the dough down; divide it in half for two pizzas or in thirds or quarters for three or four smaller ones. Let it relax, under a towel, about 10 minutes. It is then ready to be stretched, as directed in the Primary Recipe on page 187. If you are not ready to proceed, let the dough rest in the refrigerator for 2 or 3 hours and bring back to room temperature before rolling and stretching.

Toppings

Pizza toppings are positively a matter of personal preference. There are classic Italian combinations, but Americans have their own ideas. If you have ever stood in a pizza line, you have probably heard a string of directions such as "everything but anchovies," "just anchovies," "extra sauce," "no sauce," "peppers, onions, and mushrooms—on one half only," and so forth. Make it with the items you like; just don't put too much on, or your pizza will be a soggy muddle.

TOMATOES AND TOMATO SAUCE

Not all pizzas have tomatoes, but when yours does you can use ripe fresh or canned plum tomatoes. Chopped fresh tomatoes can be of any variety and will "melt" into the pizza best if they are peeled. Squeeze out the juices, and chop them into pieces of any size that you would like. Drained canned plum tomatoes are delicious on pizza; cut or crush them into the size you want. Small pieces can be scattered to cover most of the crust and, when the pizza is cooked, will taste like a light tomato sauce. Large pieces act more like a vegetable topping, providing welcome intrusions of sweetness and acidity.

When I want tomato slices, I do not peel or seed them, but slice them very thin, no more than ⅛ inch thick.

Alternately, you can use a light coating of *marinara* sauce. I find *ragù* too heavy a taste for pizza. Those "extra-sauce" devotees would probably disagree.

AMOUNTS: Use ¾ to 1¼ cups of chopped tomatoes or sauce per 10-inch or 12-inch pizza (half the dough recipe above). You can use less when you want just a hint of tomato, but more will make the pizza soggy.

CHEESE

Mozzarella is almost synonymous with "pizza cheese," but it is only one of many possibilities. It is the most common because it melts beautifully and has a mild flavor that will not overpower the other ingredients. Other kneaded cheeses (page 25)—smoked or not—can be substituted for or mixed with mozzarella. Fontina, Gorgonzola, fresh and dried ricotta, and grated Parmesan and pecorino are all pizza-worthy.

Grate, finely chop, or crumble cheeses into small pieces so they will distribute easily and melt well.

AMOUNT: Italians use cheese quite sparingly on pizza—as little as ½ cup (4 ounces) for a 10-inch or 12-inch pizza. For that size pie, ¾ to 1¼ cups is a satisfying amount; 2 cups will not overpower. I have no guide for those of you who always order "extra cheese."

Pizza Combinations

The amount of ingredients given in each suggestion below is enough for the full quantity of pizza dough given on page 184, i.e., two 10-to-12-inch pizzas. If you want to make two or three different varieties, cut the quantities in half or quarters as needed. The recipes that follow are based on some traditional Italian combinations.

Tomato, Mozzarella, and Basil Pizza

PIZZA MARGHERITA

FOR 2 MEDIUM (10-TO-12-INCH) ROUND PIZZAS

This is not only one of the oldest tomato pizzas, it is one of the simplest and tastiest.

MAKING AHEAD
1 recipe Pizza Dough (page 184)
About 2 tablespoons cornmeal or olive oil

Prepare the pizza dough.

Preheat the oven to 500° F and set the rack, with the stone in place if you are using it, in the lower third of the oven. If you are using a stone or tiles, it is best to preheat the oven for at least 30 minutes to develop the optimum heat. The pan can go directly onto the stone or oven rack as soon as the oven is at the given temperature. Sprinkle the pizza peel with the cornmeal; the pan can be coated with either cornmeal or olive oil. Divide the dough into two equal pieces.

An experienced *pizzaiolo* stretches the dough entirely by hand, pushing, coaxing, and draping his way to the finale of tossing and spinning. My sons can toss and spin. I use this modified version. Working on a lightly floured counter, flatten one ball of dough into a disk with the heels of your hands, and then use a rolling pin to stretch the dough, rotating the circle as you do; roll firmly and swiftly, with authority, or the dough will become elastic, and no matter how much you roll, it will shrink. Using both hands, pick the circle up by the edges and let gravity pull it down; work your way around the edges until the dough is the size of the pizza you want. The circle or rectangle can be paper-thin or as thick as ¼ inch. Don't worry if your crust is not perfectly round; free-form pizzas taste just as good. When the dough is as thin as you want, transfer it to the peel or the pan, where you can continue to stretch the dough by pushing gently with the tips of your fingers.

Scatter half the tomatoes, mozzarella, and basil evenly over the dough, keeping them about 1 inch from the outside edge. Roll the edge up slightly all around to keep the topping from spilling out. Season with salt and pepper, and drizzle on enough olive oil to coat the ingredients.

If you're using the peel to transfer the dough to the oven, first tell yourself that the pizza *will* leave the wood when you want it to. Then tilt the back edge of the peel over the far end of the stone in the oven and jerk the board toward you so the pizza begins to slide off the wood. Once the crust is in contact with the stone, shuffle the peel out from under the pie so the dough slips onto the stone in a continuous movement. If you are using a pan, place it directly on the stone or the rack.

THE TOPPING

About 2½ cups peeled, juiced, and chopped fresh or canned tomatoes, or 2 cups *marinara* sauce

1½ cups finely chopped or grated mozzarella cheese

¼ cup shredded fresh basil

Salt and freshly ground black pepper

About ¼ cup extra-virgin olive oil

Bake 8 to 12 minutes. Depending on the number and density of the toppings, pizza will take anywhere from 6 to 12 minutes. It is done when the crust is firm and lightly browned on the bottom and the cheese, if using, has melted. Slide the peel under the pizza to remove it, transfer it to a cutting board, and let rest for 5 minutes before wielding your pizza wheel. Repeat with the remaining dough and topping ingredients.

VARIATION: For what is sometimes called *pizza napoletana,* make the base as above—i.e., the tomatoes or tomato sauce and the cheese—but substitute about 2 teaspoons dried oregano (or 3 tablespoons chopped fresh) for the basil, and arrange on top as many rinsed and dried anchovy fillets and/or pitted, sliced black olives as you like. Six to twelve anchovies and ¼ cup olives per pizza are about right.

VARIATION: For four 6-to-8-inch pizzas, perfect for one person, divide the dough and toppings into fourths. Shuffle the first pizza into a back corner so you have room to cook the others at the same time. Or, use all the dough and toppings at once in a 12-to-17-inch rectangular pan.

Prosciutto, Tomato, and Cheese Pizza

PIZZA AL PROSCIUTTO, POMODORO, E FORMAGGIO

FOR 2 MEDIUM (10-TO-12-INCH) ROUND PIZZAS

I sometimes make this a spicy pizza, either by using a thin layer of the *arrabiata* sauce on page 111 under the prosciutto, or by sprinkling hot-pepper flakes on top of it.

MAKING AHEAD
1 recipe Pizza Dough (page 184)
About 2 tablespoons cornmeal
    or olive oil
THE TOPPING
6 thin slices of prosciutto
1 cup finely chopped or grated
    mozzarella cheese

$^2/_3$ cup finely chopped or grated Fontina
    cheese
$^1/_3$ cup freshly grated Parmesan cheese
1 or 2 salad tomatoes, washed and thinly
    sliced
About $^1/_4$ cup extra-virgin olive oil

Preheat the oven to 500° F and set the rack, with the stone in place if you are using it, in the lower third of the oven. Sprinkle a pizza peel or pan with the cornmeal, or, if preferred, oil the pan. Stretch half the dough into the size and shape you want, and place it on the peel or in the pan.

Use half of the topping ingredients for each pizza. Put slices of the prosciutto, in one layer, on the dough. Scatter the cheeses evenly over the top, and cover with an even layer of tomato slices. Roll the edge in slightly, and drizzle on the oil. Bake 10 to 12 minutes, or until crust is firm and lightly brown and the cheese has melted. Transfer to a cutting board, and slice into pieces. Repeat with remaining dough and toppings.

VARIATIONS: **Ham or Salami Pizza.** Use boiled ham or salami in place of the prosciutto. When I use salami, I like to replace the Fontina with a more robust cheese such as provola, provolone, or an aged caciocavallo.

Potato Pizza

PIZZA DI PATATE

FOR 2 MEDIUM (10-TO-12-INCH) ROUND PIZZAS

Pizza with boiled potatoes is supposedly all the rage in Ischia, the island off the coast of Naples that was home to my grandparents. They never mentioned it; I heard about it from cookbook author and radio personality Arthur Schwartz.

MAKING AHEAD
1 recipe Pizza Dough (page 184)
GETTING READY
1 red onion, peeled and thinly sliced
3 medium waxy red or white potatoes
Salt
About 2 tablespoons cornmeal or
   olive oil

THE TOPPING
The potatoes and onions from above
Salt and freshly ground pepper
2 tablespoons chopped fresh rosemary
¼ cup extra-virgin olive oil

Soak the onion slices in cold water for 45 minutes or longer. Change the water three times during the soaking. Drain and dry the onions well. Boil the potatoes in salted water to cover just until they are tender, then drain, and rinse in cold water to cool. Peel and cut them into slices no larger than ⅛ inch thick. You should do this preparation while the dough is rising, so the onions and potatoes are ready for you.

Preheat the oven to 500° F and set the rack, with the stone in place if you are using it, in the lower third of the oven. Sprinkle a pizza peel or pan with the cornmeal, or oil the pan. Stretch half the dough into the size and shape you want, and place it on the peel or in the pan.

Divide the topping ingredients in half. Place one even layer of potatoes on top of the dough, and scatter the onions over them. Roll the edges in slightly. Season with salt, pepper, and rosemary, and drizzle with oil. Bake 7 to 9 minutes.

American-Style White Pizza

PIZZA BIANCA ALL'AMERICANA

FOR 2 MEDIUM (10-TO-12-INCH) ROUND PIZZAS

Bianca (white) refers to the fact that there are no tomatoes. In Italy, *pizza bianca* may have cheese, as this version does, or, more often, it is simply a flatbread flavored with rosemary, salt, and olive oil. In the United States, a white pizza is white with cheese.

MAKING AHEAD

1 recipe Pizza Dough (page 184)

GETTING READY

1 cup whole-milk ricotta cheese

2 tablespoons extra-virgin olive oil

1 large garlic clove, minced

½ pound mushrooms (any variety), wiped clean and thinly sliced

Salt and freshly ground black pepper

3 tablespoons finely chopped flat-leaf parsley

About 2 tablespoons cornmeal or olive oil

THE TOPPING

⅔ cup freshly grated pecorino cheese

⅓ cup finely chopped or grated mozzarella or provola cheese

The ricotta from above

The mushrooms from above

About ¼ cup extra-virgin olive oil

Put the ricotta in a sieve set over a bowl, and allow to drain for 30 minutes or more. Ricotta, especially if you have bought it fresh from an Italian grocer, often has excess liquid, which would make your pizza soggy—the straining will draw it out.

Heat the olive oil and the garlic until the garlic is golden, then put the mushrooms in the pan, season with salt, pepper, and parsley, and sauté until the mushroom juices run and are then reabsorbed, so there is no liquid left. Remove from the heat.

Preheat the oven to 500° F and set the rack, with the stone in place if you are using it, in the lower third of the oven. Sprinkle a pizza peel or pan with the cornmeal or oil the pan. Stretch half the dough into the size and shape you want and place it on the peel or in the pan.

Use half the ingredients for each pizza. Stir the pecorino and mozzarella cheeses into the ricotta, and season with salt and pepper. Spread the cheese on the dough, and scatter the mushrooms on top. Roll the edge in slightly, and drizzle on the olive oil. Bake 10 to 12 minutes.

VARIATION: **Prosciutto and Cheese Pizza.** Substitute shredded prosciutto for the mushrooms. Do not cook it before placing it on the pizza. Omit the garlic, and sprinkle the pizza with the parsley before putting on the oil.

VARIATION: Increase the mozzarella to ⅔ cup, and replace the ricotta with ⅔ cup of Fontina—it need not be strained. Use either the mushrooms or the prosciutto, or perhaps some roasted red peppers and some basil.

VARIATION: **Salted Bread Pizza with Rosemary.** A cheeseless *pizza bianca,* sometimes called "pizza of bread," *pizza di pane,* makes a very nice bread. After punching the dough down the first time, let it rise again until doubled in bulk, and then divide it in two. Stretch and roll each piece into an irregularly shaped, elongated piece about ¾ inch thick, and transfer to a pan or pizza peel. Use two knuckles to dimple the entire surface, and then brush it generously with olive oil. Bake for 8 minutes, and then brush again with oil and sprinkle with coarse salt and (optionally) some chopped rosemary. Bake 8 to 10 more minutes, until it is golden on the top and lightly browned on the bottom.

Pizza with Clams

PIZZA AI VONGOLE

FOR 2 MEDIUM (10-TO-12-INCH) ROUND PIZZAS

Use the smallest clams you can find, and steam them just until they are opened enough to shuck them. If your clams are larger than ½ inch, chop them into small pieces before using. You can substitute 1½ cups drained canned clams—two 10-ounce cans.

MAKING AHEAD

1 recipe Pizza Dough (page 184)

GETTING READY

3 medium onions, thinly sliced

¼ cup extra-virgin olive oil

About 2 tablespoons cornmeal or
    olive oil

THE TOPPING

The onions from above

1½ cups shucked clams, chopped if
    necessary (see above)

¼ cup extra-virgin olive oil

8 garlic cloves, minced

½ cup finely chopped flat-leaf parsley

¼ to ½ teaspoon hot red-pepper flakes

Heat ¼ cup of the olive oil with the onions in a large sauté pan over medium-low heat until they are very soft and golden; do not let them brown.

Preheat the oven to 500° F and set the rack, with the stone in place if you are using it, in the lower third of the oven. Sprinkle a pizza peel or pan with the cornmeal or oil the pan. Stretch half the dough into the size and shape you want, and place it on the peel or in the pan.

Spread half the onions over the dough. Toss the clams with all the remaining topping ingredients, and scatter half of them on top of the onions, being sure to take the oil with them. Bake for 6 to 8 minutes; check the pizza often to be sure the clams do not overcook and become tough.

VARIATION: **Pizza with Shrimp.** Use small, uncooked shrimp in place of the clams; check the pizza at 6 minutes.

Pizza Possibilities

In addition to the ingredients that appear in the recipes above, the following items, alone or in combination, are traditional toppings. When combining items, keep complementary flavors in mind. The amounts are about what you need for the quantity of dough on page 184. If you are having a "make-your-own" pizza party, make larger amounts and put them in individual bowls.

- 3 to 4 roasted red, green, or yellow peppers, peeled and cut into narrow strips or small squares
- 1½ pounds eggplant or zucchini, thinly sliced and roasted or grilled

- 1 to 1½ pounds sausage, removed from the casing, fried until cooked and then drained
- About 1 cup either rinsed anchovies or pitted olives, or ½ cup of each
- Small greens such as arugula and baby spinach are a nice addition to pizza; ¼ to ½ cup per 10-to-12-inch pizza is a good amount. Put them on the pie the minute it leaves the oven, so they just barely wilt.

RISOTTO

In Italy, risotto appears most often as a first course in place of pasta or soup. There are some classic exceptions when it is served as an accompaniment to meat, such as the Milanese specialty *ossobuco* and saffron risotto. Although I'm not ready to make it the rule, I don't think that the exceptions of risotto as a side dish should be so rare. It also makes a fine main course.

The Rice

To make a proper creamy risotto, you must use short-grain rice that has a very high proportion of glutinous starch. Italian Arborio rice is readily available in the United States and is the most common choice. It makes an excellent risotto, but you must be sure to remove it as soon as it is *al dente* since it can quickly overcook and become gluey. Italian-grown Vialone and Carnaroli rices are usually obtainable in specialty stores and always through the Internet. They are more forgiving than Arborio in resisting overcooking.

The Broth

The better the broth, the better the finished risotto. Its flavor—or lack thereof—will be noticed in the finished dish. You can use chicken, meat, or vegetable broth for meat, vegetable, and cheese risottos and chicken, vegetable, or fish broth for seafood dishes. Chances are you will not need all the broth called for in the recipe, but it is better to have extra in case it evaporates too quickly and you are out of broth before the rice is cooked. The broth will be added to the rice in stages and must be kept hot during the entire process of cooking so when it is ladled in it does not stop the simmering.

Risotto

SERVES 4 TO 6

So many restaurants, here and in Italy, serve so much bad risotto that it is no wonder many cooks think it is too difficult a dish to make at home. A perfect risotto is not hard to make when you pay attention to the important steps and learn what to look for. The following is a basic risotto flavored with butter and cheese. When I want the rice to include other ingredients, I cook them separately and stir them into the rice after it has cooked for about 8 minutes. This method allows better control over the initial sautéing and swelling of the rice.

THE LIQUID

About 5 cups homemade
   Chicken or Meat Broth
   (page 36)

THE START (*SOFFRITTO*)

4 tablespoons unsalted butter

1 tablespoon vegetable or
   olive oil

1 medium onion, finely
   chopped

THE RICE

1½ cups Arborio rice

½ cup dry white wine

Salt

Pour the broth into a 2-quart saucepan, bring it to a boil, and then reduce the heat so the liquid stays very hot but does not boil down. Put a small ladle in the pan so it is there when you need it.

Choose a heavy-bottomed casserole, about 12 inches wide and 6 inches deep; nonstick is fine. Melt the butter with the oil in the pan, and stir the onions into the warming fat. Cook the onion, slowly and gently, until it is completely soft and translucent, then pour in the rice. Do not rinse the rice before using; you need the starch. Raise the heat to moderate, and tickle the rice around the pan slowly until the grains turn golden and the surface starches crisp. This step is sometimes called "toasting," and when the rice is ready you can actually hear it click in the pan. Touch the grains with the side of your finger; they should feel hot. Immediately pour in all the wine and turn the heat to high, so it boils and reduces to no more than a barely visible trickle. Without hesitation, ladle in enough of the hot broth just to cover the rice. Adjust the heat so the broth simmers very gently, season with salt, and

stay close by to stir the rice often and gently to keep it from sticking, and to keep note of when more broth is needed. You do not have to stir the risotto constantly; just be close enough to watch it and stir it from time to time. Make sure that the broth is actually simmering gently and not boiling or just resting. When the rice has absorbed all the broth, add another ladleful, and continue watching and stirring from time to time.

Taste the rice after it has cooked for about 20 minutes. Like pasta, it should be *al dente,* tender with a bit of resistance at the center. If it is not, add more broth and continue. When the rice is tender and creamy, remove it from the heat and immediately use a wooden spoon to beat in the butter and Parmesan. Taste for salt, add a bit of freshly ground pepper, scoop onto warm plates, and sprinkle with more Parmesan.

THE FINISH
3 tablespoons unsalted butter, at room temperature
¼ to ½ cup freshly grated Parmesan cheese

VARIATION: You can begin risotto with all butter, all oil, or a combination as above.

VARIATION: **Saffron Risotto.** For saffron-flavored risotto, steep ½ teaspoon saffron threads in the hot broth.

VARIATION: **Radicchio-Flavored Risotto.** Radicchio is a delicious addition to risotto. It will turn the rice red, but why not? Trim away the roots from three heads (about 1 pound) of radicchio, and wash and dry the leaves. Cut them into ¼-inch-wide strips. Heat ⅓ cup of shredded prosciutto in 2 tablespoons of butter, and when it is warm, stir in the radicchio and cook it until it is completely softened, about 10 minutes. Season with salt and pepper. When the ricc has cooked with the broth for 8 minutes, stir in the radicchio, and continue to make the risotto as above.

VARIATION: **Vegetarian Risotto.** Substitute vegetable broth, page 38, for the meat broth.

VARIATION: **Mushroom Risotto.** Make 1 recipe of Sautéed Mushrooms (page 383), and stir them into the risotto after it has simmered in the broth for 8 minutes.

VARIATION: **Asparagus Risotto.** For asparagus risotto, use 5 tablespoons of butter and no oil. Keep the heat fairly low, so the butter does not color. Cook the onion as above, and when the risotto has simmered in the broth for 8 minutes, stir in 1 pound of asparagus that has been peeled, cut into ¾-inch-long pieces, blanched, cooled, and sautéed in a tablespoon of butter. Be sure to season the asparagus with salt and pepper, and do not sauté it until you are ready to add it to the rice. Use a full cup of Parmesan.

VARIATION: **Shrimp Risotto.** Purchase 2½ pounds of small shrimp in their shells. Rinse and peel them; use the shells and 5 cups of water to make a shrimp broth according to directions on page 138. Begin the risotto as in the Primary Recipe and use the shrimp broth in place of meat broth. After the rice has cooked for 15 minutes, stir in the shrimp and ¼ cup finely chopped flat-leaf parsley. You could also stir in about ⅓ pound of asparagus—blanched and cut as above—or 1 cup of fresh or thawed frozen tiny peas. Add the asparagus after 8 minutes but add the peas with the shrimp.

POLENTA

Italians serve polenta most often as a first course, in place of pasta or soup, in which case it may be dressed simply with butter and cheese, drizzled with *marinara* sauce, or topped with sautéed mushrooms. Polenta also makes a fine main dish as a bed for sautéed chicken livers or braised vegetables. I think that softly cooked polenta is the perfect accompaniment to stews and braises when some of the meat's cooking juices are trickled over the top. Polenta can also be cooled, then cut into pie-shaped pieces and fried in butter or oil, or grilled and served on the plate with an entrée.

Polenta is only cornmeal, water, and salt, but how you handle it will determine whether it is a lovely soft accompaniment or a sticky, lumpy mass. Mixing the dry cornmeal first with cold water instead of the traditional method of pouring it directly into boiling water will prevent lumps from forming. Keeping a kettle of boiling water on hand to add to the polenta as it cooks and absorbs water will ensure the proper consistency.

The Polenta Pan

The traditional pan for making polenta is a *paiolo,* a deep unlined copper pan that is larger at the top than at the bottom. Many years ago, a Florentine friend made me polenta in her tiny *cucina* using a wide, low, straight-sided frying pan. The results were perfect. I use a flat pan when I am making the amount in the recipe below and a deep nonstick soup pan for a larger amount.

If the cooked polenta has left a seemingly permanent film on the surface of your pot, fill it with tepid water and let it sit for a few hours. The film will lift right off.

The Cornmeal

You may find cornmeal in various consistencies—some are as coarse as kosher salt, others closer to regular table salt. The coarse-textured cornmeal makes a firmer polenta that is better for cutting and frying. The fine makes a better soft polenta. Quick-cooking polenta is very good and can also be cooked as below, but don't believe the box's claim that you can prepare it in 5 minutes. It needs at least 20 to remove the raw cornmeal flavor.

Working Ahead

When we were making polenta for a *Parade* magazine article some years ago, Julia Child suggested that we try making it well ahead to see how long it would last. With visions of my Italian grandmother frowning in dismay, I agreed to try. I left the finished polenta sitting over a flame tamer for a number of hours. From time to time I added more boiling water to maintain the consistency, and we were all surprised that it remained perfectly delicious.

Polenta with Butter and Cheese

SERVES 6

THE POLENTA
2 cups yellow Italian cornmeal

4 cups cold water

1 tablespoon salt

A kettle of at least 6 cups boiling water

THE FINISH
6 tablespoons unsalted butter, diced, softened

⅓ cup freshly grated Parmesan cheese

Measure the cornmeal into the cooking pan, and then gradually pour in the cold water, whisking all the time to form a smooth mixture. Add the salt and place the pan on the stove. Whisk in 3 cups of boiling water and switch to a wooden spoon. The polenta needs to cook for 40 to 45 minutes, and you should remain close by to stir it every few minutes. Taste as you near the 40-minute mark to be sure that the raw corn taste is disappearing. As the polenta cooks and bubbles it will thicken; when it becomes too thick to stir around the pot, pour in more boiling water by half cupfuls. When the polenta is ready, the wooden spoon should stand upright for a few solid seconds. When you are sure it is finished, let the pan sit over the fire undisturbed and unstirred for 30 seconds; this will create a burst of steam on the bottom that will make pouring easy. Pour the polenta out onto a wooden board or buttered platter.

Immediately dab the softened butter over the surface of the hot polenta and sprinkle on the cheese. Spoon onto plates or cut with a string and lift up with a spatula. Serve very hot.

VARIATION: *Polenta with Chicken Livers.* Make the Coltibuono-style chicken livers on page 219; do not use the anchovy-caper finish. Prepare the polenta above and top with the butter but no cheese. Pour the chicken livers on top and serve as a main course.

VARIATION: Make any of the sautéed mushroom recipes on page 383. Make the polenta as above, dot with the butter, pour on the mushrooms, and sprinkle the cheese on top.

CHAPTER 4

Meat and Poultry

The usual cookbook arrangement of meat and poultry according to types of meat—pork, veal, beef, and so on—is not very helpful if you think of cooking in terms of technique. A chicken cutlet would have more in common with a thin steak than with a cut-up chicken on the bone; veal shanks belong more with pork butt than with veal cutlets. For that reason, I have organized this chapter according to some of the most common Italian cooking techniques.

The Italian Shopper

If you have ever gone grocery-shopping with Italians, you know how finicky they can be. A few years ago, I was visiting a friend in Florence and we started out together to purchase ingredients for dinner. We didn't need much—fresh sausage, a small leg of lamb, some pasta, a bit of cheese. We walked to a nearby shop, and as Julie carefully inspected the lamb, I went over to the sausage to choose what we needed. She saw me and quickly whispered in my ear, "We'll get them across the street. They are much better there." And our afternoon shopping turned into a long adventure, crisscrossing Florence to buy the right ingredient from the best shop in the city.

I remember how people used to come from all over Rhode Island to my grandfather's meat market when he was alive. They knew how he would fastidiously choose his products, and how he and his staff would cut each steak, chop, cutlet, and roast to order. Every day they ground beef, pork, and veal and made their own sausages. There are still meat markets in his old neighborhood that purvey meat with this sense of pride.

The reality is that few of us today have a small, personal meat market, especially one with an Italian butcher. But you can choose a supermarket that employs a meat-cutter. Get to know him; you'll probably have to ring the bell a few times. Speak to the meat-department manager. Describe the cut and quality that you need. I have had supermarket meat departments both honor my requests for particular cuts and order meat for me that they did not normally carry. If you find otherwise, choose a different market.

One other option, usually a bit more expensive, is to shop on the Internet. It is a splendid source for such hard-to-find items as organically raised lamb, Italian sausages, and aged beef.

SAUTÉING

CUCINARE IN PADELLA

Some of Italy's simplest yet most memorable dishes are a result of quick pan-cooking. Cookbook author Nika Hazleton wrote that in Italy "meat was a luxury and fuel was scarce and expensive." The best solution, she said, was to cut the meat into small, thin pieces and cook them quickly in a hot pan over fairly high heat on top of the stove. What might have grown out of a shortcoming has become our gain. Veal *piccata, saltimbocca,* chicken Marsala, even the American invention veal Parmesan, owe their existence to Italian ingenuity and inventiveness in the face of meager means.

Serving Size

When a pound of meat is cut and thinned into cutlets and scaloppine, it just seems to go further, especially if it is rolled around a filling, as with the recipes below for *involtini.* This is one time when the sum of the parts equals more than the whole. My recipes yield about 4 ounces per person, a good-size serving for an average eater.

With chops and small steaks, I count on ¼ to ½ pound per person, depending on the eater, whether or not there is a bone, and the size of the rest of the meal.

The Right Pan

There is probably no better place to spend your kitchen-equipment money than on a top-quality frying pan. It can be made from any of the numerous materials designed for serious cooking, but it must be heavy-bottomed with excellent heat-conduction abilities. A thin-bottomed pan will burn the fat and the meat in a nanosecond. A pan that cannot conduct heat evenly to its entire surface will cook the meat irregularly, leaving you constantly turning and rearranging pieces to brown them evenly—and eventually overcooking them. High-quality nonstick pans work well, but beware of inexpensive ones, because they can neither withstand high heat nor capture and caramelize the meat juices, so you will have nothing to deglaze for building a sauce.

The pan should be large enough to hold at least three or four pieces of meat at one time in one layer without touching. I use an 8-to-10-inch pan when I am cooking for one or two people, and a 12-to-14-inch pan for six or more.

Flouring

A light coating of flour on meat that is to be subjected to the high heat of pan-cooking protects the fibers of delicate varieties such as chicken and veal. It also provides color and a light crust. Meat that is floured will not leave as many caramelized juices in the pan on which to build a sauce as will unfloured meat, but there will still be some. As a rule, I flour thin pieces of white meat, such as chicken and veal cutlets and scaloppine. For all others, I flour or not depending on the surface texture I want.

Aromatics and Vegetables

Aromatics and vegetables, such as garlic, shallots, onions, mushrooms, and so forth, should either be cooked and removed before the meat is browned, or added to the pan when all the cooked meat is out. Cooking them along with the meat would interfere with the surface area needed to cook the meat evenly, and you also risk burning them at the high heat needed to cook the meat. Recipes often instruct you to brown the aromatics and then push them to the side while you cook the meat. This is fine as long as you watch them carefully.

The Deglazing Liquid

Once the meat and aromatics are cooked, the fun begins. Now you are ready to build a sauce by deglazing the pan—that is, adding liquid to the hot pan to capture the meat juices that were released and concentrated during the sautéing. Common Italian deglazing liquids are water, wine, broth, fruit juices (especially lemon or orange juice), vinegar, crushed tomatoes, the soaking liquid from dried mushrooms, or any combination of these. Be cautious with salty liquids since they can become unpalatably salty when the liquid is reduced.

As the liquid reduces, its flavor will become concentrated, and no recipe can totally prepare you for the flavor the reduced liquid will have. Perhaps your oranges were a bit sweeter or your wine drier than what I used. Taste the sauce as it nears readiness, and be prepared to correct it. If the sauce reduces too much and tastes too concentrated, add a bit of warm water. Butter or cream will smooth out a too-acidic flavor; a dash of lemon or vinegar will balance too much sweetness. Sometimes all you will need is salt.

Finishes and Enrichments

When the sauce has finished reducing, it can be finished with the simple addition of chopped herbs or a fresh pat of butter. When there is an acid present—lemon juice, wine, or vinegar, for example—the butter will actually form a velvety emulsion. The butter should be at room temperature and must be unsalted.

Cream will add richness, and the reduction will go more quickly if you add it in two or three stages, reducing each addition before adding another. This way, you can adjust the amount you add. If the flavor of the reduced deglazing liquid is for some reason weaker than anticipated, all the cream called for in the recipe may be too much. A small splash of fortified wine such as Madeira or Marsala can be used to finish a sauce, but do not add table wines at the end, since they must be reduced to eliminate the raw wine flavor.

When the sauce is finished, return smaller cuts of meat to the pan and turn them around a bit so they are thoroughly coated. With larger steaks and chops, pour the sauce over them, on a platter or individual plates.

Trimming and Pounding

Meats that are going to be sautéed or fried should be of even thickness, on the thin side. It was always a bit of a drama in Italian meat markets. You order. Out comes the curved butcher's knife, and the show begins with a theatrical honing of the blade. Then, bent with concentration over the large cut of meat, the butcher slowly slices even pieces, cradling them in his palm as they are separated. Gently, he lays them apart on butcher's paper, covers them with more paper, and deftly pounds them to an even thickness before repeating the performance with another layer. You may have to do your own.

Tools

Although a heavy rolling pin or the side of a wine bottle will do the trick, a meat-pounder is a worthwhile investment. This tool is known in Italian as a *battencarne*—literally, "pound meat." I use the style that has a solid stainless-steel disk, 3½ inches in diameter, with a plastic handle rising from the center. It weighs almost 2 pounds, so it does a lot of the work for me.

To thin meat, first trim the edges of any fat or connective tissue that might be present. Then place a piece of meat under a sheet of plastic wrap. Do not actually pound down on it, but apply the weight to push the fibers out. Raise the pounder 6 to 8 inches above the meat, and strike the meat with an arclike motion, so the pounder comes down near the center but ends up off the side of the scaloppine. Repeat the motion toward you. If you can think firmly and gently at the same time, you can understand meat-pounding. Your strokes must be firm enough to stretch the meat out, but gentle enough not to tear it.

Chicken Breasts, Cutlets, and Scaloppine

When a whole chicken breast is divided along the bone into two pieces, it makes two boneless chicken breasts that are suitable for sautéing. To cook them as is, first trim the fat from around the edges. The underside of the breast has a long, thick white tendon running through it. You can remove it or not; it will shrink some during cooking, but because the breast is thick, it will not destroy the appearance of the whole piece. Pound the breasts, covered with plastic wrap, until they are as evenly thick as possible.

Italians usually divide chicken breasts into three pieces to make cutlets and scaloppine. To do this, turn the breast upside down and find the small, loosely attached tenderloin; pull it gently away. That is one piece. In this case, the thick tendon must be removed, or it will shrink during cooking and your scaloppina will not remain flat. Use the tip of a paring knife to cut around the large end of the tendon, and then hold on to it with a piece of paper towel while scraping against it with a paring knife. Pull gently as you scrape and the tendon will slip out of the meat; discard it. Place the top of the breast on the counter, skinned side up. Note the thicker side that was attached to the bone, and gently push against the opposite side to plump the boned side even more. Beginning there, use a thin knife, held parallel to the counter, to slice through the breast, dividing it into two pieces. Pound the pieces so they are about ¼ inch thick. These are cutlets.

To turn the cutlets into scaloppine, pound the three pieces so they are thinner than ¼ inch.

PORK	DESCRIPTION	USE FOR	COOKING TIME
Cutlets and Scaloppine	When scaloppine is used to indicate meat other than veal, it is modified. *Scaloppine di maiale* is pork that is cut and pounded like veal scaloppine. Pork for cutlets and scaloppine should be cut from the tenderloin. Pork tenderloins are readily available, usually cryovac, two to a package. Cut your own and freeze one if necessary. For small amounts they are sometimes sold in markets as "pork tenders."	Pan-frying with or without a breadcrumb coating. Thin scaloppine or cutlets (less than ¼ inch thick) can be stuffed and rolled.	Cook cutlets about 2 minutes per side, 2½ if they are breaded. Cook scaloppine just under 1 minute per side. Cook rolls 5 to 7 minutes.

VEAL	DESCRIPTION	USE FOR	COOKING TIME
Cutlets	Skinless, boneless, tender cuts sliced across the grain from the solid top round muscle of the leg. Cutlets are ¼ inch thick.	Pan-frying with or without a breadcrumb coating	Cook cutlets about 2 minutes per side. Add a minute or two to the total cooking time for breaded meat.
Scaloppine	The same cut as a cutlet but pounded thinner—slightly less than ¼ inch.	Pan-frying with or without a breadcrumb coating Thin scaloppine can be stuffed and rolled.	Cook scaloppine just under 1 minute per side. Cook rolls 5 to 7 minutes.
Chops	Rib or loin chops. They can be pounded as thin as ¼ inch and can be as thick as 2 inches for pan-roasting.	Sautéing, frying, with or without a breadcrumb coating Pan-broiling, broiling, pan-roasting	Sautéing and Frying: Cook ¼-inch-thick chops about 2 minutes per side; ¾-inch-thick chops about 3; 1-inch-thick chops about 4. Add 1 to 2 minutes to the cooking time for breaded meat. Pan-Roasting: Cook 2-inch-thick chops about 30 minutes.
Medallions	½-to-¾-inch-thick boneless, round pieces cut from the tenderloin and trimmed of all fat and connective tissue.	Pan-frying	Cook ¾-inch medallions about 2 minutes per side. Needs an hour or two to tenderize
Shoulder, Shanks	Choose hind shanks, which are meatier than the foreshanks. They can be cooked whole or cut into 2-to-3-inch lengths as for *ossobuco*.	Stewing, braising *Brodo* *Ragù*	

| --- | --- | --- | --- |
| Cutlets and Scaloppine | One whole boneless chicken breast yields two cutlets.

For pan-frying the cutlets should be lightly pounded to flatten them, so that no part is greatly thicker or thinner than another; they can be ⅓ to ¼ inch thick.

Instead of cooking a whole cutlet, Italians usually divide it into three pieces. The reward is not just more servings but more surface on the meat for the sauce, making the finished dish by far more flavorful. Slices of turkey breast (*petti di tacchino*) should be ⅓ to ¼ inch thick. Both chicken and turkey cutlets can be pounded to be as thin as scaloppine, that is, less than ¼ inch thick. Many markets sell poultry "cutlets" that have already been sliced and pounded, but they charge extra for their labor and the task is an easy one to do yourself. | Pan-frying with or without a breadcrumb coating

Thin scaloppine can be stuffed and rolled. | Cook boned breasts 3 to 4 minutes per side.

Cook cutlets about 2 minutes per side, scaloppine just under 1 minute per side.

Add a minute or two to the total cooking time for breaded meat. |

Veal Scaloppine with Lemon and Parsley

SCALOPPINE DI VITELLO AL LIMONE E PREZZEMOLO

SERVES 4

This simple dish was one of my grandfather's favorites. He would often arrive home from his meat market with a neatly wrapped paper package. The veal, which he had cut and pounded himself, would be carefully laid out between sheets of brown butcher's paper. Lemons and parsley were always in Nonna's kitchen, so she had his favorite on the table in no time at all.

Pay particular attention to flouring the meat; it must be done lightly, and not until it is ready to be cooked. At first, you may find it a less than rhythmic process to leave the flouring to this point, but once you have done it a few times it will become a fluid motion. I wish you could have watched my grandmother flour and fry 2 or 3 pounds of scaloppine while keeping time with Enrico Caruso on the Victrola.

THE MEAT

1 to 1¼ pounds veal scaloppine, pounded just thinner than ¼ inch thick

About ⅓ cup flour for coating

Salt and freshly ground black pepper

2 tablespoons extra-virgin olive oil

2 tablespoons unsalted butter

Dry the meat thoroughly on both sides with paper towels. Spread the flour out on a pie pan, a flat dish, or wax paper near the stovetop. Stir in the salt and pepper; the amount is up to you, but there should be enough to season the meat noticeably. I taste a bit of the flour just to be sure that I can taste salt and pepper. Heat the oil and the 2 tablespoons butter in a frying pan over medium-high heat. For sautéing, the fat should just cover the entire surface of the pan—enough to keep the meat from sticking.

While the fat is heating, begin to flour as many pieces as will fit in the pan in one layer at one time without touching. Do not be tempted to flour all the meat ahead of time, since the flour will gradually mix with the meat juices and form a paste that is always detectable. Dip the scaloppine into the flour, turn them to coat both sides, and then remove all the excess flour by patting the meat smartly between your hands. Only the thinnest veil of flour should remain.

The fat is ready when it is hot enough for the meat to sizzle audibly. If the fat is not hot enough, the meat will absorb it rather than be sealed by it. Consequently, you will run out of fat and the meat will taste greasy. Make sure by dipping one end of the floured meat into the pan and listening; if you hear it frying, the pan is ready. Slip the floured pieces of meat into the hot pan. Do not crowd the pan, or the meat juices will turn to steam and prevent the meat from browning. Cook the meat on the first side for about 40 seconds; the down side should be lightly browned, and the color will just be creeping over the edges. Flour a few more pieces of meat while the first pieces are cooking.

Turn the meat over, and fry 40 seconds or less, to brown the second side and finish the cooking. Test the meat for doneness by pressing it with your finger; it should no longer feel squishy-soft, like raw meat, but should yield with slight resistance to the pressure. You can also test the doneness by inserting the tip of a sharp paring knife into the center of a cutlet; it should penetrate and release easily.

Remove the pieces as they are cooked, and add a new piece to the pan each time you remove one. It is best not to empty the pan completely, since its temperature can quickly increase and burn the cooking fat. Keep the

cooked meat warm, either in a low oven (180° F) under a loose tent of aluminum foil, or on a plate (covered with a second plate if your kitchen is drafty) on a back burner or close to the stovetop.

When all the meat is cooked and out of the pan, discard the fat. Immediately pour in the broth or water, and let it boil aggressively until it has reduced to about 2 tablespoons; it will appear somewhat syrupy. As it is reducing, scrape the bottom of the pan continuously with a flat wooden spatula, or one of the new rubber ones fabricated to withstand very high temperatures, to pick up the meat juices that have collected and caramelized there. A spatula will cover more area at one time than other tools.

Pour in the lemon juice and heat it for 10 to 15 seconds, then toss in the 2 tablespoons of butter and the parsley, and either swirl it around by shaking the pan or use the spatula to stir it about. When the butter has melted, return the veal to the pan, with any juices that have collected on the plate. Turn the pieces in the sauce, over the heat, a few times, just to coat them, and serve.

SUBSTITUTIONS: Chicken or turkey scaloppine.

VARIATIONS: **Veal, Chicken, or Pork Marsala.** To make the dish *alla Marsala,* substitute ⅔ cup dry Marsala for the broth and lemon juice, and omit the parsley. Use with chicken, veal, or pork cutlets or the thinner scaloppine. The success of this dish will depend on the quality of the Marsala. The real McCoy, made in Sicily, will usually have a silhouette of that region on the neck of the bottle. Other brown liquids that usurp the name can be quite harsh-tasting.

VARIATION: **Veal Saltimbocca.** For *saltimbocca,* cover each scaloppina with a slice of prosciutto and one sage leaf. Thread a toothpick through the sage to secure it to the meat. Flour and brown the meat, prosciutto side down first, and deglaze the pan with ½ cup of dry white wine. (Some use Marsala.) Reduce it, swirl in a tablespoon of butter, and return the veal (without the toothpicks) briefly to the pan. The word *saltimbocca* means to "jump in the mouth," a reference to the fact that the dish is quickly made, and so appealing that one would want it to do so.

THE DEGLAZING LIQUID
½ cup homemade or low-sodium canned chicken broth or water

THE FINISH
2 tablespoons freshly squeezed lemon juice
2 tablespoons unsalted butter, at room temperature
2 tablespoons finely chopped flat-leaf parsley

Veal Chops with Rosemary

COSTATE DI VITELLO CON ROSMARINO

SERVES 2 LARGE OR 4 SMALL EATERS

Some markets only sell chops that have been precut, so the loin chops you find may be thicker than what you need for pan-frying. If this is the case, pound the meat away from the bone so that its thickness is an inch or less.

THE MEAT
4 center-cut loin chops, ¾ to 1 inch thick
About 3 tablespoons extra-virgin
    olive oil

THE AROMATICS
4 large garlic cloves, coarsely chopped
2 tablespoons fresh rosemary, not too
    finely chopped

THE DEGLAZING LIQUID
⅔ cup dry white wine

Dry the chops, and brown one side in the oil according to the Primary Recipe; ¾-inch chops take about 3 minutes per side, 1-inch chops about 4 minutes per side. Turn the chops, cook on high heat until the second side is brown, and then reduce the heat to finish the cooking. The tip of a paring knife should enter and release easily. The center will remain lightly pink. Remove the meat and keep it warm. Discard all but about 1 tablespoon of fat from the pan; if there is less, add enough to cover the bottom. The pan should be just moderately hot, so the garlic does not brown. Stir in the garlic, and keep it moving around the pan with a wooden spatula until it is just translucent. Add the rosemary, stir around the pan once or twice, and immediately pour in the wine and any juices that have collected under the meat. Scrape the pan with a wooden spatula, and boil until reduced by half. Pour over the veal, and serve.

SUBSTITUTIONS: Chicken breasts or cutlets, turkey or veal cutlets.

VARIATION: Substitute fresh sage, marjoram, or oregano for the rosemary. Use broth and lemon juice to deglaze (see page 213). Try shallots in place of the garlic.

VARIATION: For a richer sauce, finish with 2 tablespoons unsalted butter or ⅓ cup heavy cream.

Veal Medallions
in the Renaissance Manner

SERVES 4

The prolific use of spices and fruit juices in Renaissance Italian cooking inspired this recipe. A few years ago, pink peppercorns packed in water or brine were quite the rage. They were on chefs' menus and supermarket shelves across the country. As with most fads, their popularity waned, and you may not be able to find them. You can substitute brine-packed green peppercorns, which have the pungency but not the sweetness of the pink, or leave them out altogether.

The spices are mixed in with the flour, so they become part of the coating. It is a seasoning method you can use to flavor any pan-fried meat. If you opt not to flour the meat, mix the spices together and roll the meat in them.

THE MEAT

About ⅓ cup flour seasoned with salt and freshly ground black pepper for coating

¼ teaspoon ground ginger

⅛ teaspoon cinnamon

⅛ teaspoon ground mace

8 veal medallions, ½ to ¾ inch thick

2 tablespoons unsalted butter

1 tablespoon vegetable oil

THE AROMATICS

1 tablespoon pink peppercorns, water- or brine-packed, rinsed

THE DEGLAZING LIQUID

⅓ cup raspberry vinegar, sherry vinegar, or red-wine vinegar

⅔ cup freshly squeezed orange juice, from blood oranges or Valencia

THE FINISH

4 tablespoons unsalted butter, softened

Mix the spices, salt, and pepper into the flour. Dry, flour, and brown the veal in the 2 tablespoons butter and the oil according to the Primary Recipe, cooking 2 to 3 minutes per side. When all the veal is cooked and out of the pan, discard all but 2 tablespoons of fat, toss in the peppercorns, and stir around for a minute to release their flavor. Pour in the vinegar, averting your face from the acidic steam, deglaze the pan, and reduce it to 2 tablespoons, then add the orange juice and reduce it until it is syrupy. Swirl in the 4 tablespoons butter and return the medallions to the pan briefly to warm.

SUBSTITUTIONS: Pork medallions, chicken breasts, veal chops.

VARIATION: Omit the pink peppercorns (probably couldn't find them anyway), and for the aromatics use 2 finely chopped garlic cloves, the grated zest of one orange, 2 tablespoons chopped rosemary, and 1 tablespoon capers. Deglaze and finish as above with 2 tablespoons unsalted butter.

Chicken Scaloppine with Roasted Mushrooms

SCALOPPINE DI PETTI DI POLLO CON FUNGHI ARROSTI

SERVES 4

Roast the mushrooms while you are preparing the other ingredients, or use leftover vegetables you may have on hand. Sautéed zucchini, braised carrots, and roasted peppers can all enhance a simple pan-fried recipe.

MAKING AHEAD

1 recipe Roasted Mushrooms (page 391), sliced

THE MEAT

1 to 1¼ pounds chicken scaloppine, pounded just thinner than ¼ inch thick

About ⅓ cup flour seasoned with salt and freshly ground black pepper

1 tablespoon unsalted butter

2 tablespoons extra-virgin olive oil or vegetable oil

THE DEGLAZING LIQUID

½ cup dry white table wine

½ cup homemade or low-sodium canned chicken or meat broth

THE VEGETABLES

⅔ mushrooms from above (save the rest for the finish)

THE FINISH

½ cup heavy cream

⅓ mushrooms from above

1 tablespoon minced flat-leaf parsley

Dry, flour, and brown the scaloppine in the butter and oil according to the Primary Recipe, cooking about 40 seconds per side, then remove from the pan. Pour in the wine, deglaze the pan, let it evaporate, and then pour in the broth. Reduce it until it is syrupy, and toss two-thirds of the roasted mushrooms into the pan. (Reserve the rest for a garnish.)

Add the cream in two stages, reducing each addition by boiling it down (stir often, for about 2 minutes) until it thickens. Return the meat to the pan, and turn the pieces in the sauce to coat. Serve the meat garnished with the reserved mushrooms and sprinkled with the chopped parsley.

SUBSTITUTIONS: Veal or turkey cutlets or scaloppine or veal chops.

VARIATIONS: **Chicken Cutlets with Red Peppers and Tomato Sauce.** Substitute 3 roasted, peeled, and thinly sliced red peppers (see page 397) for the mushrooms. After the wine (red or white) has evaporated, stir in 1 cup of *marinara* sauce and all the peppers. Finish as above.

Veal Scaloppine with Prosciutto, Mushrooms, and Mozzarella

SCALOPPINE DI VITELLO CON PROSCIUTTO, FUNGHI, E MOZZARELLA

SERVES 6

This dish has always been a favorite company recipe of mine. As with most sauté recipes, this one is quick to prepare, but I have given you advance-preparation suggestions in the recipe so you can also make it ahead and sit down for cocktails with your guests. I have also given you proportions for six people. To serve eight to ten, increase all the ingredients by roughly one-half the amounts given.

I do not usually recommend using costly buffalo-milk mozzarella for cooking, but in this case, if you can find it, it is worth the extra expense.

THE MEAT

1½ pounds veal scaloppine, pounded
   just thinner than ¼ inch thick

About ½ pound prosciutto, thinly sliced

About ⅓ cup flour seasoned with salt
   and freshly ground black pepper for
   coating

4 tablespoons unsalted butter

1 tablespoon vegetable oil

THE VEGETABLES

1 pound mushrooms, cleaned, trimmed,
   and thinly sliced

Salt and freshly ground black pepper

THE DEGLAZING LIQUID

1 cup dry Marsala

1 cup heavy cream

THE FINISH

⅓ pound fresh mozzarella, preferably
   buffalo's-milk, very thinly sliced

3 tablespoons finely chopped flat-leaf
   parsley

Preheat the oven to 450° F. Top each piece of veal with a slice of prosciutto, trimming the ham so it just covers the top, and pound the two together lightly. Coat the scaloppine with flour, and slip them into the hot oil and butter, prosciutto side down first. The prosciutto will only tentatively cling to the meat, which is okay as long as you keep them together. Cook the veal according to the Primary Recipe, turning once. If you are preparing it ahead of time and it will cook again, sauté it no more than a total of 1 minute. Transfer the meat to a plate, and keep warm. Add the mushrooms to the pan, season with salt and pepper, and sauté until they are lightly browned and their juices run. Pour in the Marsala and any meat juices that have collected in the plate, and reduce the liquid to about 3 tablespoons, or until it is syrupy. Add the cream in two stages, reducing each addition by boiling down until it has thickened.

Pour the sauce and mushrooms into an ovenproof serving dish such as a gratin pan. The pan should be large enough so the veal is in one layer with the edges overlapping slightly. Lay the veal on the mushrooms, prosciutto side up. Arrange the mozzarella slices evenly over the top, and slide the pan into the oven for a minute or two to melt the cheese. Or set the dish aside for an hour, or refrigerate for 3 or 4 hours. Return the dish to room temperature, and put into a 450° F oven until the contents are warm and the cheese has melted, 4 to 5 minutes. Sprinkle with parsley and serve.

SUBSTITUTIONS: Chicken or turkey scaloppine.

VARIATION: Chicken Scaloppine with Leeks and Tomatoes. Top chicken scaloppine with prosciutto and cook as above. Substitute the white part of two large leeks, thinly sliced, for the mushrooms. When they are tender, stir in two plum tomatoes, peeled, seeded, juiced, and finely chopped (about 3 tablespoons pulp), and cook for a few minutes, until their juices run. Deglaze with Madeira, dry port, or dry Marsala, and finish with cream and cheese as above. I sometimes add ¼ cup of pine nuts to the leeks with the tomatoes.

Chicken Livers Coltibuono-Style

FEGATINI DI POLLO ALLA COLTIBUONO

SERVES 4

Chicken livers were by no means new to me when I brought my first cooking class to Lorenza de' Medici's school Badia a Coltibuono in Tuscany. But I had never had them made with Vin Santo, the aromatic, golden-amber specialty of that region. Lorenza used her own Coltibuono brand and prepared the typical regional hors d'oeuvres of finely minced livers spread on toasted slices of bread brushed with her own beautiful olive oil. Delicious! The recipe below leaves the livers whole for a main course (lovely with mascarpone smashed potatoes, page 357), but with the mash of a fork or the pulse or two of a food processor, they can be turned into the classic Tuscan *crostini di fegatini* (see the variation below).

Vin Santo, Holy Wine, is a dessert wine made with grapes that have been partially dried before being pressed. The result is a sherrylike wine, high in alcohol. You could substitute another sweet wine, such as a late-harvest Riesling, or a fortified one, such as Marsala or Madeira, or even a dry white wine.

GETTING READY

1 ounce dried porcini mushrooms

THE MEAT

1 pound chicken livers

THE AROMATICS

3 tablespoons extra-virgin olive oil

1/2 cup minced onion

Salt and freshly ground black pepper

The minced mushrooms from above

1 tablespoon chopped fresh sage, or 2
   tablespoons chopped flat-leaf parsley

THE DEGLAZING LIQUID

1/2 cup Vin Santo (see above)

The mushroom juices from above

THE FINISH

2 to 4 anchovy fillets, rinsed, dried, and
   minced

1 1/2 to 2 tablespoons capers, rinsed,
   dried, and chopped

2 teaspoons lemon juice

Put the mushrooms in a small bowl, and pour on enough warm water to cover them. Let them soak for at least 30 minutes. Then drain them, reserving the liquid. Rinse the mushrooms briefly under running water, feeling for any grit or sand, which should be thoroughly washed away. Dry the mushrooms well, and chop them into a very tiny mince. Pour the soaking juices through a paper coffee filter (or washed cheesecloth) that you have set in a sieve. Discard the filter, measure out 1/2 cup of juices, and keep them nearby.

Pour the livers into a strainer and rinse briefly under running water. Turn them out onto paper towels to dry, and put them on a cutting board. Trim away any green spots and bits of fat from the livers, and cut out the connective tissue that joins the lobes.

Heat the oil, and sauté the livers according to the Primary Recipe, allowing a total of about 3 minutes. The livers should remain pink in the center. Remove them to a side dish with a slotted spoon.

Reduce the heat, and stir the onion into the pan; season with salt and pepper, and cook until it is golden. Add the mushrooms and herbs, season, and cook 5 more minutes. Deglaze the pan with the wine, let it evaporate, then pour in the mushroom water and any juices that have collected on the chicken-liver plate. Reduce until syrupy, and then stir in the anchovies and capers. Heat briefly, and then return the livers with any collected juices to the pan. Season with salt, pepper, and lemon juice, stir around briefly, and serve.

VARIATION: Omit the dried mushrooms, and replace the mushroom broth with 1/2 cup of chicken broth or use slightly more wine—about 2/3 cup.

VARIATION: For a more subtle anchovy flavor, put them in the oil before the onion and mash them into it with a fork as they heat. The longer, moist cooking will make their flavor less pronounced.

VARIATION: Chicken Liver Crostini. To serve on top of *crostini,* let the cooked livers cool briefly, and then either mash them with a fork or pulse them in a food processor until minced. Do not puree them; they should maintain some texture. Cut ¼-inch-thick slices of Italian bread into pieces about 2 inches long. All the pieces will not be the same size; it is not important. Toast the bread on a baking sheet in a 400° F oven, turning once, for 2 to 4 minutes, until golden brown on each side. Immediately brush one side with extra-virgin olive oil (and rub with garlic if desired), and spread the livers on the oiled side. In Tuscany, *crostini di fegatini* are usually served on platters along with *crostini* topped with finely chopped tomatoes seasoned with oil, salt, pepper, and chopped basil, and *crostini* with garlicky Italian *olivada* (minced olive paste).

Veal Rolls with Prosciutto and Fontina

INVOLTINI DI VITELLO

SERVES 4

Involtini are thin slices of meat (or fish or vegetables) that are filled and rolled before being cooked. They are suitable for sautéing when the filling ingredients are already cooked or cured and the meat is a tender cut. Otherwise, they should be braised, so the filling has time to cook and the meat to tenderize. The meat should be as thin as scaloppine, so the heat reaches the filling, and the cheese, if you are using any, melts. The filling can be two or three large pieces of cured meat and cheese, or a minced mixture of ingredients. These little packages of flavor take slightly longer to cook than flat pieces of meat, but otherwise are treated exactly the same.

THE FILLING

¼ pound Italian Fontina or Bel Paese cheese, finely chopped

¼ pound prosciutto, finely chopped

2 tablespoons finely chopped fresh sage

2 tablespoons freshly grated Parmesan cheese

THE MEAT

1 to 1¼ pounds veal scaloppine, pounded just thinner than ¼ inch thick

Salt and freshly ground black pepper

About ⅓ cup flour seasoned with salt and freshly ground black pepper for coating

3 tablespoons unsalted butter

1 tablespoon vegetable oil

THE DEGLAZING LIQUID

½ cup Marsala wine or dry white wine

½ cup homemade or low-sodium canned meat, chicken, or vegetable broth

THE FINISH

1 tablespoon unsalted butter

Put all the filling items in a small bowl, and use your fingers or a fork to mix them together well. Lay the scaloppine on the counter or on a cutting board, and cut them into pieces approximately 5 inches by 4 inches; do not trim off any meat, just make as many similar-size pieces as possible. Season lightly with salt and pepper. Divide the filling evenly among the pieces, placing it first in the center of each and then spreading it to within ¼ inch of the edges. Beginning with the short side, roll the veal cigar-fashion, tucking the edges in slightly as you roll to secure the filling inside. Thread a toothpick lengthwise where the veal overlaps, to secure each roll closed. The toothpick should lie flat, so the *involtino* can roll around in the pan.

Dry, flour, and brown the rolls in the butter and oil according to the Primary Recipe, adding the rolls to the pan seam side down. Turn the rolls as they color, and fry until all the sides are well browned and the meat is cooked through, about 4 minutes. Insert a cake tester or toothpick into the center; if it releases easily, and the meat doesn't hold on to it, the rolls are cooked. Remove the meat from the pan, pull out the toothpicks, and keep the rolls warm in a 180° F oven or on a plate near the stovetop.

Deglaze the pan with the wine, reduce it to 2 tablespoons while scraping the pan with a wooden spatula to capture the juices, and then pour in the broth and any juices that have collected under the meat. Reduce the liquid by half, and then swirl in the butter and return the *involtini* to the pan. Turn them several times to coat and serve.

SUBSTITUTIONS: Use chicken, turkey, or pork scaloppine.

VARIATION: **Veal Rolls with Sage and Prosciutto.** Instead of making a filling of chopped ingredients, cover each piece of meat with a slice of prosciutto cut just to fit the meat. Place one or two whole sage leaves and a 2-inch-long-by-¼-inch-thick piece of cheese in the center. Roll and cook as above.

VARIATION: **Veal Rolls with Prosciutto, Cheese, and Tomatoes.** Tomatoes are a delicious addition. Make the rolls as above, and then deglaze the pan with ½ cup dry white or red wine. When it has evaporated, stir in ⅔ cup finely chopped, peeled fresh or canned tomatoes with their juices. Season with salt and pepper, and let the tomatoes simmer briskly until they have broken down and released their juices, about 8 minutes. When the juices have thickened, swirl in the butter and return the veal to the pan. Turn the rolls over a few times in the sauce, then turn off the heat and sprinkle on ¼ cup of Parmesan cheese. Cover the pan briefly, so the cheese begins to melt. Serve with a sprinkle of parsley on top.

Pork Rolls with Pancetta

INVOLTINI DI MAIALE CON PANCETTA

SERVES 4

Involtini are often covered with a slice of prosciutto before they are rolled. Here, thin slices of pancetta are used in the same way as prosciutto, but, for a change, I tried wrapping the pancetta around the outside and liked the way the rolls looked and tasted with the melting pancetta fat dissolving into the sauce. You can, of course, do it the other way and put the pancetta inside. In that case, cover each piece of pork with only one slice of pancetta, and flour the rolls before sautéing, since the meat does not have the protective fat of the pancetta on the outside.

GETTING READY

1 pint cherry or grape tomatoes,
    washed, roasted 5 minutes in a 375° F
    oven, and then cut in half

THE FILLING

1 large garlic clove, minced
¼ cup fresh breadcrumbs
½ cup grated Parmesan cheese

¼ cup minced flat-leaf parsley

Salt and freshly ground black pepper

2 tablespoons extra-virgin olive oil, plus
 3 more for cooking the meat

THE MEAT

1 to 1¼ pounds pork scaloppine

16 thin slices pancetta

THE AROMATICS

1 large onion, thinly sliced

1 tablespoon fennel seed

THE DEGLAZING LIQUID

½ cup dry white wine

THE FINISH

The tomatoes from above

Mix the filling ingredients together as in the Primary Recipe. Cut the pork into pieces approximately 5 inches by 4 inches. Lay two slices of pancetta on a cutting board or on the counter, overlapping them to make them the same size as the pork slices. Place a piece of pork on top of the pancetta, and season lightly with salt and pepper. Spread on the filling, then roll up, tucking the pancetta in at the sides to hold it to the meat. Thread a toothpick lengthwise where the meat overlaps, to secure the rolls closed.

Heat the 3 tablespoons of oil in a frying pan, and cook the pork until the pancetta is crisp and the pork is cooked through, about 4 minutes. Remove the rolls, pull out the toothpicks, and keep the meat warm. Discard all but 2 tablespoons of fat from the pan, and add the onion, salt, pepper, and fennel seed. Cook until the onion is completely softened. Pour on the wine, and boil it until it's reduced to about a tablespoon, then add the tomatoes and the pork rolls. Cook together briefly, and serve.

SUBSTITUTIONS: Veal, chicken, or turkey scaloppine.

VARIATION: **Pork Rolls with Spinach and Mozzarella.** Spinach is used often as a filling for *involtini*. Wilt 1½ pounds as directed on page 348, and then chop it very finely and squeeze it dry. Mix it with ¼ pound finely chopped mozzarella and ½ cup freshly grated Parmesan cheese. Fill and fry as above. Deglaze with wine or broth, eliminate the aromatics, and finish with the tomatoes and 2 tablespoons butter.

VARIATION: **Pork Rolls with Raisins and Marsala.** Soak 2 ounces dark raisins in ½ cup Marsala, Madeira, or dry port for about 1 hour, and then strain, reserving the liquid. Mix the raisins with ¼ cup fresh breadcrumbs, 1 tablespoon chopped fresh sage, and salt and pepper. Fill and cook as above. Omit the fennel seeds. Deglaze the pan with the raisin-soaking wine, and instead of the tomatoes, finish with 2 tablespoons butter.

Beef Rolls in Tomato Sauce

BRACIOLINE ALLA PIZZAIOLA

In southern Italy, beef *involtini* are called *braciole* or the more diminutive *bracioline*. When a recipe is cooked *alla pizzaiola*, it means that it is flavored "as a pizza," which means with tomatoes and oregano. I've called for a ready-made *marinara* to show you yet another reason to keep it on hand.

Unlike the recipes above, the beef rolls are first fried just until they are browned, not fully cooked. They finish cooking in the sauce, so the tomato flavor has time to saturate the beef and vice versa.

THE MEAT

1 to 1¼ pounds thin slices of tender beef cut from the rib, loin, or sirloin

Salt and freshly ground black pepper

About ⅓ cup flour seasoned with salt and freshly ground black pepper for coating (optional)

3 tablespoons extra-virgin olive oil

THE FILLING

2 ounces thinly sliced prosciutto

¼ pound fresh provolone or mozzarella cheese, cut into 8 pieces

2 hard-boiled eggs, each cut into 8 wedges

THE DEGLAZING LIQUID

2 cups *marinara* sauce, or 2⅔ cups chopped canned tomatoes with their juices

2 tablespoons chopped fresh oregano, or 2 teaspoons dried

THE FINISH

½ cup freshly grated Parmesan or Pecorino Romano cheese

With a sharp knife, remove the excess fat and all the connective tissue from the meat. Cut it into twelve to fourteen more-or-less even pieces, and pound them, if necessary, so they are slightly thinner than ¼ inch. The pieces should be approximately 7 inches by 5 inches. Season the side facing up lightly with salt and pepper, and lay a slice of prosciutto on top of each piece; cut the prosciutto if necessary to fit the meat. Place a piece of provolone and an egg wedge in the center and roll up. Thread a toothpick lengthwise where the meat overlaps, to secure the rolls closed.

Dry, flour if you wish, and brown the rolls in the hot oil, seam side down first. Turn the rolls as they color, and cook just until they are browned on all sides, about 1½ minutes. Remove the meat from the pan, and discard all the oil. Pour in the *marinara* sauce, season with oregano, and bring to a boil. If you are using tomatoes instead of the sauce, keep the meat in a warm oven and cook the tomatoes for about 15 minutes, until they are slightly thickened and the oil separates from the tomatoes.

Reduce the heat, and return the meat to the pan. Simmer gently, turning the rolls often for 5 to 8 minutes, until they are fully cooked. Turn off the heat, sprinkle the cheese on top, and cover the pan for a minute or two, so the cheese will begin to melt.

VARIATION: **Spicy Calabrian Pork Rolls with Cheese.** To make spicy Calabrese rolls, use scaloppine of pork tenderloin. Cover each piece with a slice of pancetta and a thin slice of hot salami. Place a slice of mozzarella or provolone in the center, and roll as above.

VARIATION: Substitute *ragù* for the *marinara*. It will produce a very rich, meaty dish.

FRYING

FRIGGO IN PADELLA

Frying is distinguished from sautéing by the amount of fat in the pan. It is the stovetop method Italians use most often for meat that has been coated with breadcrumbs or a batter. A lovely piece of meat, evenly breaded and perfectly fried to a golden color, needs nothing more. The Milanese specialty *cotoletta alla milanese,* over which people swoon in remembrance, is no more than a breaded, fried veal rib chop that was first pounded and stretched to the size of a dinner plate. It is a dramatic presentation, and a delicious dish. That's not to say that Italians don't ever do more—indeed they do—but keep in mind that a simple squeeze of lemon juice may be all you need.

The notes in the sautéing section for serving size and which pan to use (see page 204) apply also to frying.

The Amount of Cooking Fat

To fry breaded meat, there should be enough fat to reach at least a quarter of the way up the sides of the pan. Otherwise, the crumbs can come in contact with the pan and scorch. Because it is the heat of the fat and not the pan that cooks the meat, it must be hot enough to sear immediately—but not blacken—the crumbs. On the other hand, if it is too cool, the coating will absorb it and be soggy rather than crisp. Vegetable or olive oil or pure lard are the ideal choices. If you use butter, mix it with oil (or clarify it) to prevent it from burning.

Saucing Breaded Meat

Meats that are breaded and fried will not leave behind meat juices for deglazing as will uncoated meat, so any sauce needs to made separately. Sauces that contain acid, such as lemon, vinegar, wine, or tomatoes, go well with breaded meat, since the acid balances the perceived sense of sweetness and richness that breading gives.

Breaded Chicken Cutlets with Pickled Vegetables

COTOLETTE DI MAIALE CON SOTTACETI

SERVES 4

Vegetables preserved in oil and vinegar, called *sottaceti,* are a delicious complement to breaded fried cutlets. It can be your own homemade variety (see page 374), or one of the jarred Italian products on the market. Be sure to choose one that is preserved in olive oil in addition to the vinegar. Those packed in vinegar alone, usually called *giardiniera,* are too strong for this recipe.

MAKING AHEAD

1 cup *sottaceti* (page 374)

THE MEAT

2 eggs beaten with 2 teaspoons of water

About ⅓ cup flour seasoned with salt and freshly ground pepper for coating

1½ cups plain dry breadcrumbs

1 to 1¼ pounds chicken cutlets, ¼ inch thick

Extra-virgin olive oil for frying

Use either a pie plate or a bowl for the eggs, and pie plates or sheets of wax paper for the flour and crumbs. Pat a piece of chicken dry with paper toweling, and then dip both sides into the flour, slapping it well between your hands to leave only a thin coat. The flour will help the eggs adhere. Immediately drop the cutlets into the eggs. Use tongs or two forks to remove them from the egg wash and drop them into the breadcrumbs. Turn them over a few times, each time patting the crumbs so they adhere. Finally, hold them up by one end and give them a good shake to remove loose crumbs. Set them on cake racks to settle for at least 10 minutes.

The breaded meat can wait at room temperature an hour before being cooked, or be refrigerated for 2 or 3 hours. Return the meat to room temperature before cooking.

Pour enough oil into a frying pan so that it is at least ¼ inch deep. Use a moderately high heat: hot enough so the oil will sizzle when the chicken is added, but not so high as to brown it beyond a deep-golden color. Fry the cutlets in batches, so the pieces fit in the pan in one layer without touching each other. Cook about 3 minutes on a side; they should be golden brown and cooked to the center. Poke the end of a sharp paring knife or a cake tester into the center and see if it comes out easily. If the cutlet holds on to the knife, it is not cooked. Remove when cooked, drain on paper towels, and keep warm.

Empty all the fat from the pan, and wipe it out with paper towels. Return it to the stove over moderate heat and pour in the *sottaceti*. Stir them around until warm, and then pour over the chicken. Sprinkle with chopped parsley and serve.

SUBSTITUTIONS: Use pork, veal, or turkey cutlets.

VARIATION: Season the flour with ½ teaspoon ground ginger and ¼ teaspoon each cinnamon and ground mace. Omit the *sottaceti* and serve the cutlets with lemon juice and chopped parsley.

VARIATION: **Breaded Chicken Cutlets with Tomato Sauce.** Mix 2 tablespoons of grated Parmesan cheese and 3 tablespoons of chopped parsley into the breadcrumbs. Fry as above, and substitute 1 to 1½ cups of *marinara* sauce for the *sottaceti*. Heat it in the pan after the chicken is cooked as above.

THE FINISH
The *sottaceti* from above
3 tablespoons finely chopped
    flat-leaf parsley

Sweet-and-Sour
Breaded Chicken Cutlets

PETTI DI POLLO IN AGRODOLCE

Agrodolce is a sweet-and-sour sauce or marinade that Italians often used in prerefrigerator times to preserve fried meat, fish, and vegetables. Preparations similar to this one are found all over Italy under different names—*in scapece,* or *in saor,* or *in carpione,* to name a few. Here the chicken is not actually preserved, but it will taste better the longer it sits. I like to make it the day before I serve it; at the very least, leave it 3 hours. It is a good dish to serve at room temperature on a warm summer evening, or to carry along on a picnic.

GETTING READY—THE SAUCE

⅓ cup extra-virgin olive oil

1 large red onion, thinly sliced

½ teaspoon salt

½ cup red-wine vinegar

½ cup water

1 teaspoon sugar

3 tablespoons finely chopped flat-leaf parsley

3 tablespoons raisins

3 tablespoons pine nuts

THE MEAT

1 to 1¼ pounds chicken cutlets, just less than ¼ inch thick

About ⅓ cup flour seasoned with salt and freshly ground pepper for coating

2 eggs beaten with 2 teaspoons water

3½ cups plain dry breadcrumbs

Extra-virgin olive oil for frying

To make the *agrodolce* sauce, heat the oil in a 2-quart saucepan over moderate heat, and add the onion. Season with salt, cover the pan, and cook gently until the onion is very, very soft. Do not let it brown. Pour in the vinegar, water, and sugar, and simmer gently, uncovered, for 30 minutes, or until the liquid has reduced to ½ cup. Stir in the parsley, raisins, and pine nuts, and turn off the heat. Keep the sauce warm while you cook the chicken.

Bread and cook the chicken as described in the Primary Recipe. Drain on paper towels, and arrange on a nonreactive rimmed serving platter that is large enough to hold the chicken pieces slightly overlapping. Pour the warm sauce over the chicken, and let sit at room temperature, covered with plastic wrap, for at least 3 hours, or refrigerate overnight. Serve at room temperature.

SUBSTITUTIONS: Veal, turkey, or pork scaloppine.

Veal Parmesan

VITELLO ALLA PARMIGIANA

SERVES 4 TO 5

This is a fine example of the kind of Italian culinary innovation that inspired this book. In Italy, vegetables prepared *alla parmigiana* (in the style of Parma) were common fare. Veal Parmesan was unheard of. Since America offered an abundance of meat, Italians simply substituted veal or chicken for the vegetables. What a successful innovation it was! Old-style Italian-American restaurants that do not have it on the menu are rare as hens' teeth. Unfortunately, many of those restaurants took it too far and buried the veal in sauce and cheese. Properly made with a light hand, it is a delicious combination of ingredients.

THE MEAT
1 to 1¼ pounds veal cutlets, ¼ inch thick

About ⅓ cup flour seasoned with salt and freshly ground pepper for coating

Salt and freshly ground black pepper

2 eggs beaten with 2 teaspoons of water

1½ cups plain dry breadcrumbs

Extra-virgin olive oil for frying

THE FINISH
¼ pound mozzarella cheese, cut into thin round slices

1 cup warm *marinara* sauce (page 30)

⅓ cup freshly grated Parmesan cheese

Preheat the oven to 450° F. Bread and cook the veal as described in the Primary Recipe, cooking it about 1½ minutes per side. Drain on paper towels, and then put it, slightly overlapping, in a shallow ovenproof dish or platter. When all the veal is on the platter, cover each piece with some of the mozzarella and some of the sauce. Sprinkle the Parmesan over the top, and put into the oven until the cheeses melt, about 4 minutes.

SUBSTITUTIONS: Chicken or turkey cutlets.

Breaded Veal Chops Stuffed with Fontina Cheese

COSTOLETTE ALLA VALDOSTANA

SERVES 4

Italy's smallest region, Valle d'Aosta, is tucked into the northwest-ernmost tip of Italy against a splendid Alpine background. The region is justly famous for its Fontina cheese, which local cooks melt over polenta, stir into white-truffle-accented *fonduta*—the Italian counterpart to nearby Switzerland's fondue—and use to fill veal chops.

THE MEAT

4 loin veal chops, 1 inch thick

¼ pound Italian Fontina cheese, thinly sliced

About ⅓ cup flour seasoned with salt and freshly ground black pepper for coating

Salt and freshly ground black pepper

2 eggs beaten with 2 teaspoons of water

1½ cups plain dry breadcrumbs

About 4 tablespoons (½ stick) unsalted butter

About 2 tablespoons vegetable oil

Make pockets for the cheese by slitting the chops horizontally, halfway through, slicing almost to the bone. Use a quarter of the cheese for each chop, and lay the pieces flat inside the pocket, keeping them ¼ inch away from the outside edge. Pound the chops until they are only about ¾ inch thick, and to seal the edges closed.

Bread and cook the veal as described in the Primary Recipe, cooking about 5 minutes per side. Drain on paper towels and serve.

VARIATION: If you are fortunate enough to happen upon a white truffle, place a very thin slice inside the veal with the cheese.

VARIATION: Breaded Chicken Cutlets with Cheese and Truffles. For this regional specialty called *alla Castellana,* use eight chicken scaloppine. Cover four of them with thin slices of Gruyère cheese and thin slices of boiled ham or prosciutto, keeping the filling ¼ inch from the edge. Cover each with another piece of chicken, and press the edges together so they adhere. Coat with breadcrumbs, and fry as above. The classic dish usually has a few slices of white truffles tucked inside each breast. If you don't have the truffles but can find white-truffle paste in tubes, spread a little on the bottom piece of chicken before laying on the cheese.

PAN-BROILING

GRATELLATO IN PADELLA

Pan-broiling (also called pan-grilling) differs from sautéing and frying in that the meat is cooked with either a mere film of fat or none at all. The result is meat with a crust as deeply colored and flavored as one that is grilled outdoors, and the bonus of a pan rich with caramelized juices for deglazing.

Cooking meat this way creates a fair amount of smoke, and if you do not have a good kitchen-exhaust system, or if your meat is thicker than 1½ inches, you may want to sear it on top of the stove and then transfer it to a 500° F oven to finish the cooking, using the same guide to timing as on the stovetop. You can then return the pan to the top of the stove to build a sauce. Remember that the handle will be very hot. Don't cook more meat than will fit into one pan at a time. That means that this technique is best suited for dinner for one, two, or three people.

The Pan

The ideal pan is that old standard, the cast-iron skillet. A well-seasoned one (meaning one that has received a great deal of use) needs very little or no fat at all. Italian homes are rarely without a *gratella,* a cast-iron pan with surface ridges made specifically for pan-broiling. The ridges allow the fat to drip away from the meat as it cooks. Such a pan is a fine choice when you plan to serve the meat without a sauce, or with one made separately, since the ridges prevent deglazing.

Lamb Chops with Fennel Seed and Red Wine

BRACIOLINE D'AGNELLO CON SEMI DI FINOCCHIO

SERVES 2

THE MEAT

4 loin or rib lamb chops,
about 1 inch thick

Extra-virgin olive oil

Salt and freshly ground
black pepper

The meat should be at room temperature, and that means it must be out of the refrigerator 30 to 45 minutes, depending on its thickness. Dry it well; surface moisture will prevent the meat from forming a crust. Trim away all fat or all but a very thin layer of fat from the outside of the chops and coat both sides lightly with oil. Brush a thin coat of oil on a heavy cast-iron pan, large enough to hold the meat in one layer without touching. Turn the heat to a medium-high temperature, and when the pan's surface appears to be rippling, add the chops and sear one side. When small beads of juice rise to the surface and the meat will release easily from the pan, use tongs to turn it over, and season the seared side with salt and pepper. (If you are finishing the meat in the oven, transfer it at this point.) When the juices rise to the top, the meat is cooked to rare—about 4 minutes per side. For medium rare, reduce the heat, turn the meat again, and cook a few minutes more.

Remove the chops, and keep them warm; pan-broiled red meats should rest for at least 5 minutes, so the juices that have been thrown to the exterior by the high temperature will relax and settle back into the meat. If you cut the meat immediately, these juices will wind up on your cutting board.

If there is more than 1 tablespoon of fat in the pan—or if there is just 1 tablespoon but it is blackened—discard it. Reduce the heat, and stir the butter and garlic into the pan. You must be very careful when you add any dry ingredient to the pan, since it is hot and there is very little fat.

Keep the garlic moving for 20 seconds, and then pour in the wine and broth, and immediately scrape the bottom of the pan with a wooden spatula. Add the fennel seed, and reduce the liquid by at least half, or until it is syrupy. Taste to be sure the raw wine taste has disappeared.

Swirl the butter into the pan, and when the butter has melted, pour the sauce over the chops. Sprinkle with parsley and serve.

THE AROMATICS

1 tablespoon unsalted butter or extra-virgin olive oil

3 to 5 garlic cloves, coarsely chopped

2 teaspoons fennel seed

THE DEGLAZING LIQUID

⅓ cup dry red table wine

⅓ cup homemade or low-sodium canned meat or chicken broth

THE FINISH

1 tablespoon unsalted butter, softened

1 tablespoon chopped flat-leaf parsley

My Grandfather's Pan-Broiled Steaks

"STECCA" ALLA NONNO

SERVES 2 OR 3

A well-marbled, pan-grilled Delmonico has always been my favorite steak. When my grandfather knew I would be coming for dinner, he would ask if I wanted my "*stecca,*" which he then sliced from beef he had aged himself in the cold room of his meat market. I would dive into that steak for the first half, and then slow down. As much as I love it, I have never been able to eat a whole one myself. For small appetites, use a thicker steak and cut the cooked meat into thick slices after it has rested. Fan the pieces attractively on each dinner plate. The two steaks will then serve three or four smaller eaters. If you have begun the meal with a substantial first course, they will definitely feed four people.

THE MEAT
Two ¾-to-1-inch-thick steaks, Delmonico, rib eye, or sirloin
About 1 tablespoon extra-virgin olive oil
Salt and freshly ground black pepper
THE DEGLAZING LIQUID
½ cup dry red wine

½ cup homemade or low-sodium canned meat broth
THE FINISH
3 tablespoons unsalted butter
1 tablespoon minced fresh flat-leaf parsley

Trim the meat of excess fat, dry, rub with oil, and cook as in the Primary Recipe, allowing 3½ to 4 minutes per side. Remove the steaks, and let rest for 5 minutes. Pour all the fat out of the pan, and return it to high heat. Deglaze with the wine and broth, and reduce by about half. Continuing to work over high heat, drop the butter in one tablespoon at a time, and shake the pan or whisk well after each addition until it melts. Stir in the parsley, and pour the sauce over the steaks.
SUBSTITUTIONS: Other cuts of tender beef, hamburgers, lamb chops, or veal chops, ¾ to 1 inch thick.

VARIATION: **Pan-Broiled Steaks with Capers.** Capers add an entirely different dimension to the simple recipe above. Stir ¼ cup of rinsed and coarsely chopped capers into the pan with the butter and parsley.

VARIATION: **Pan-Broiled Steaks with Balsamic Vinegar.** Substitute ½ cup of balsamic vinegar for both the wine and the broth. Reduce it by half, and whisk in the butter.

VARIATION: **Pan-Broiled Steaks with Mushrooms.** Mushrooms are such a natural combination with beef that I have actually seen them packaged with it in supermarkets. To make a mushroom sauce, prepare 1 recipe of the Sautéed Mushrooms on page 383, and toss them into the pan as the broth is reducing. Omit the butter from the finish, and stir the parsley in when the mushrooms are warm.

VARIATION: **Pan-Broiled Steaks with Tomato Sauce.** For a quick version of steak *alla pizzaiola*—that is, steak seasoned in the style of the pizza man—cook the meat in the oil as above. Remove the steaks, and keep them warm. Reduce the heat, and add 3 tablespoons olive oil and 3 or 4 thinly sliced garlic cloves to the pan. When the garlic is lightly colored, pour in about 1¼ cups lightly drained and chopped canned tomatoes, salt, and 1 teaspoon dried oregano (or 1 tablespoon fresh). Cook at a lively simmer for 8 to 10 minutes, or until the sauce has thickened, and then pour over the steaks and serve. If the steaks have cooled, return them briefly to the pan to reheat.

Pan-Broiled Steaks with Arugula and Parmesan Cheese

BISTECCHE CON RUCOLA ALLA PARMIGIANA

SERVES 4

As is usually the case with "love at first bite," I remember the exact time and place I met this dish. I was in a distinguished restaurant in Montecatini Terme, in the Tuscan region of Italy, with my dear friend and frequent traveling companion, Dagmar Sullivan. We had just spent a week at a nearby villa with six of

Italy's premier cooking teachers, and I thought we had covered all the regional specialties. This was a delightful parting surprise.

The version I had that night was made with beef tenderloin filets. I have always preferred a chewier steak, so I use rib-eye or strip steaks, well trimmed of outside fat and cut in half. I usually serve the same dessert we had that evening—a small wedge of creamy sweet Gorgonzola cheese drizzled with acacia honey. I fell in love twice that night.

GETTING READY

2-ounce piece of Parmesan cheese

1 pound small leafed arugula, or larger
   leaves torn in pieces

Salt

THE MEAT

Two 1-inch-thick rib-eye or strip steaks,
   trimmed and cut in half crosswise

1 tablespoon olive oil

Salt and freshly ground black pepper

THE DEGLAZING LIQUID

⅓ cup balsamic vinegar

2 tablespoons extra-virgin olive oil

THE FINISH

The Parmesan cheese from above

Use a cheese slicer, a mandoline, or a vegetable peeler to make the thinnest possible slices of Parmesan cheese. Cover them tightly with plastic wrap to prevent them from drying out. Handle them carefully, so the pieces do not crumble.

Remove the stems from the arugula. Wash the leaves well in several changes of water if necessary to remove any sand. Dry the leaves well, and chop them coarsely if they are larger than an inch long.

Dry the meat, and cook it in the olive oil as in the Primary Recipe, about 2 minutes per side for rare, 3 for medium rare. Remove the meat to a side plate. If there is any fat in the pan, discard it, and deglaze the pan with the vinegar. Reduce it to a few tablespoons, and whisk in the olive oil. Add the arugula, and cook it only until it wilts. Remove it with tongs, and divide it among four plates. Season the steaks with salt and pepper, and place one on top of each arugula bed. Pour the pan juices over the top, and garnish with the Parmesan.

SUBSTITUTION: If you are fond of the filet, use ¾-inch-thick slices of beef tenderloin, counting on one or two per person.

VARIATION: You can substitute any tender greens for the arugula. Baby spinach is a good choice.

VARIATION: The steaks are also good with uncooked greens. Dress the greens with a small amount of olive oil, salt, and pepper, and put a small mound on each dinner plate. Place the hot, cooked steak in the center of the greens, and pour the deglazed pan juices on top.

VARIATION: **Pan-Broiled Pork Tenderloin with Prosciutto, Arugula, and Balsamic Vinegar.** To substitute pork for the beef, slice 1½ pounds of pork tenderloin into ¾-inch medallions, and cook them about 2 minutes per side. Sautéed prosciutto and garlic are really good with the pork. Before browning the meat, gently cook ⅓ pound of shredded prosciutto and 2 chopped large garlic cloves in 2 tablespoons of olive oil until the garlic is golden, about 4 minutes. Transfer the prosciutto and garlic to a plate, and sauté the pork—in batches—until brown on the outside and medium inside, 3 to 4 minutes per side; remove the meat as it is cooked. Deglaze the pan with 2 tablespoons of balsamic vinegar, reduce by half, then stir in the arugula, 1 cup of chopped, peeled fresh plum tomatoes, and the reserved prosciutto. Omit the additional olive oil and the Parmesan from the finish. Cook the tomatoes on high heat for 2 minutes to release their juices slightly, and spoon over the pork.

Pan-Grilled Steaks with Gorgonzola Butter

BISTECCHE DI MANZO CON GORGONZOLA

SERVES 2 TO 4

Flavored butters, also called compound butters, are great to keep on hand if you find yourself pan-broiling often. They are a simple and quick way to add that something extra to all pan-broiled meat (see the box below for suggested combinations). The butters freeze well, so, if you plan to use them often, triple the amounts given and freeze them in the amount that you need for 1 recipe. Bring the butter to room temperature before you use it.

GETTING READY

2 tablespoons unsalted butter, softened

2 tablespoons Italian sweet Gorgonzola
cheese, at room temperature

1 tablespoon finely chopped flat-leaf
parsley

Salt and freshly ground black pepper

THE MEAT

Two ¾-to-1-inch steaks, Delmonico, rib
eye, or sirloin

About 1 tablespoon extra-virgin olive oil

Salt and freshly ground black pepper

Put the butter and cheese in a small bowl, and use a wooden spoon to stir, mash, and beat them together until they are homogenous. Stir in the parsley, and salt and pepper to taste. Flavored butters can be made hours earlier than you need them and left at room temperature unless the day is so hot as to melt them. They can also be made many days ahead and refrigerated or frozen for a few months. Bring them back to room temperature before using.

Trim the meat of excess fat, dry, rub with oil, and cook as in the Primary Recipe. Remove the steaks to warm serving plates, and let rest 5 minutes. Spread the butter evenly over the top, and serve.

SUBSTITUTIONS: Other cuts of tender beef, hamburgers, lamb chops, or veal chops, ¾ to 1 inch thick.

Other Flavored Butters

ANCHOVY BUTTER. Mash two or three rinsed and finely chopped anchovies into 3 tablespoons unsalted butter with ½ teaspoon fresh lemon juice or lemon zest and 1 tablespoon minced parsley. Add pepper but no salt.

LEMON BUTTER. Finely mince one large garlic clove, and stir it into 3 tablespoons unsalted butter with 1 teaspoon lemon zest or juice, salt, pepper, and 1 tablespoon minced parsley.

HERB BUTTER. Butters flavored with mint or sage and lemon are especially good with pan-grilled veal chops. Use 1 tablespoon finely chopped mint or sage, ½ teaspoon lemon zest or juice, salt, and pepper with 3 tablespoons unsalted butter.

PAN-ROASTING

When my grandmother came to America in the late 1800s, she brought with her a tradition of stovetop cooking. As in much of Italy at that time, in-house ovens were a rarity in her native town. When families had a dish that required baking, such as the festive *lasagne di carnevale,* they brought it to the local baker, whose ovens were always hot and hospitable. Daily cooking took place on top of the stove. In America, Nonna gradually accepted her new oven, but she never lost the art of pan-roasting.

In pan-roasting, the meat is first sautéed to sear the outside and then cooked, covered, with a small amount of liquid, so the meat roasts in its own juices and fat. The resulting pan juices are extraordinarily concentrated and flavorful. Pan-roasting is a good choice for thick chops, small roasts, and poultry. If you are new to this technique, I think you will be pleasantly taken, as I always have been, by the deep, rich flavors it produces.

The Pan

The ideal pan for stovetop roasting is a heavy-bottomed, straight-sided, lidded pan known as a *sauteuse*. The sides should be 2½ to 3½ inches high. Use a 12-inch-diameter pan for four to six people. For larger roasts you will need a slightly deeper pan, such as an enamel-coated cast-iron casserole or a deep, wide, heavy saucepan. The snugger the meat is in the pan, the better. Avoid using a reactive material such as uncoated aluminum, since it can alter the color and flavor of the ingredients, especially when there is an acid present.

Tip on Discarding the Cooking Fat

Once you have browned the meat, you no longer need all the fat in the pan.

When the pan for browning the meat is a manageable size, tip it carefully while holding the meat in place with the lid of the pan, and pour out the fat. When the pan is too heavy or cumbersome, remove the meat from the pan and the pan from the heat. Tilt the pan, and use either a spoon or a bulb baster to remove the fat.

Veal Chops with Lemon and Sage

COSTATE DE VITELLO AL LIMONE

SERVES 4

My favorite way to cook thick veal chops!

THE START (AROMATICS)
2 tablespoons extra-virgin
   olive oil
1 tablespoon unsalted butter
6 garlic cloves, smashed and
   peeled

THE MEAT
4 large loin or rib veal chops,
   2 inches thick
Salt and freshly ground black
   pepper

THE DEGLAZING LIQUID
2/3 cup dry white wine

THE SEASONINGS
2 tablespoons chopped flat-
   leaf parsley
3 thin lemon slices
8 fresh sage leaves

Heat the oil and butter over moderate heat in a heavy, deep-sided frying pan. Stir the garlic into the warming oil, and cook until it is golden but not browned. Remove it with a slotted spoon, temporarily, while you brown the chops. Raise the heat slightly, so the fat is hot enough for the meat to sizzle gently when it is added.

Dry the chops well with paper towels, and brown them on both sides (3 to 4 minutes per side). There may not be more, but if there is, pour all but 2 tablespoons of fat from the pan; leave the meat in the pan, and season it with salt and pepper.

Turn the heat to high, and pour in half the wine, so that it flows directly to the bottom of the pan and not over the meat. Let it bubble enthusiastically until it has evaporated, and then repeat

with the remaining wine. (Adding it in stages makes the reduction go more quickly.) As the wine reduces, scrape up the meat juices from the bottom of the pan with a wooden spatula or spoon. Reach in under the chops to grab it all. When the wine has reduced to a tablespoon or two, return the garlic and put the parsley, lemon, and sage in the pan. Cover with the lid, and reduce the heat so it is just hot enough for the meat to make gentle cooking sounds. If the heat is too high, the small amount of liquid will quickly disappear, and the meat will fry instead of roast. Turn the chops once or twice as they cook, and be sure there is always a thin layer of pan juices in the bottom of the pan. If at any time the meat seems to be frying in fat instead of pan-roasting in juices, add a tablespoon or two of water to the pan. The chops will be done in about 30 minutes. When the meat is cooked through, the tip of a paring knife or a cake tester will release easily after being poked into the meat, and the juices will run yellow. Remove the cooked chops to plates, and with a rubber spatula pour and scrape the pan's contents over them.

VARIATION: When the meat is cooked and out of the pan, turn up the heat and add ¼ cup of meat broth to the pan, then reduce it by half or until it is syrupy. Swirl in 2 tablespoons of butter and 1 tablespoon of thin slivers of fresh sage; pour over the chops.

VARIATION: **Veal Chops with Mushrooms, Marsala, and Cream.** Substitute whole, small shallots for garlic, and omit the lemon and sage. Use ⅔ cup Marsala for the liquid. After the chops are cooked and out of the pan, stir ½ pound sliced mushrooms, sautéed in butter, into the pan. Stir them around on high heat until they are hot, and then pour in ¼ cup cream. Cook the cream vigorously until it has reduced by half and thickened, and then pour the mushrooms over the chops. You can substitute broth for the cream, or use nothing at all: the mushrooms themselves will provide enough of a sauce.

VARIATION: **Veal Shanks with Lemon and Sage or Rosemary.** Pan-roasting is also a lovely way to cook veal shanks. They take longer but need a minimum of attention. For two whole hind veal shanks, cook two medium-size sliced onions and four to six large garlic cloves, smashed and peeled, in 3 table-spoons each butter and vegetable oil until golden. Remove with a slotted spoon, and reserve while you brown the shanks in the same pan. Season the meat and deglaze with the wine (or dry Marsala) as in the Primary Recipe, but reduce it only by half. Use the parsley, lemon, and sage, or, instead, drop about six sprigs of rose-mary into the pan. Simmer the shanks gently for about 2 hours, turning and bast-ing often, and adding a few tablespoons more wine or a little water if the pan becomes dry. When the meat is tender, remove it and pour ½ cup of water into the pan over the heat. Boil it quickly, scraping the bottom to grab all the flavors, and pour it over the veal.

VARIATION: **Piquant Pan-Roasted Lamb Chops.** To make this Cal-abrian dish, substitute the same-size loin or rib lamb chops for the veal. For the aromatics, use 3 tablespoons of olive oil (no butter), one medium onion, and three large garlic cloves, both thinly sliced and cooked until they are limp. Set aside, and brown the lamb chops as in the Primary Recipe. Discard excess fat, and deglaze the pan with ⅔ cup dry red or white wine. Cover and cook 30 minutes, then turn the chops and for seasonings add ½ pound of thinly sliced mushrooms (porto-bello or baby bella are very nice); 2 tablespoons of rinsed, dried capers; 2 anchovies, rinsed and chopped; and ¼ teaspoon of hot red-pepper flakes. Stir them into the pan juices well, so they are coated. Cover again, and continue to cook for 30 or 40 minutes, until the lamb is cooked. May also be done with thick pork-loin chops.

Pan-Roasted Lamb

AGNELLO ARROSTO IN TEGAME

SERVES 6

In Italy, spring lamb is small enough to be cut up and fitted into a sauté pan for stovetop roasting. It is a succulent dish. Sicilians use the same-size lamb to make a classic lamb fricassee that owes its roots to classic French cooking. Unless you have an "in" with someone who raises them, you will not find lamb of such a size, but a small or a half-leg is a nice alternative.

THE MEAT

2 ounces pancetta or prosciutto

7 or 8 sprigs flat-leaf parsley

3 large garlic cloves

3-to-3½-pound leg of lamb, on the bone

4 tablespoons extra-virgin olive oil

Salt and freshly ground black pepper

THE DEGLAZING LIQUID

⅔ cup red-wine vinegar (not balsamic)

THE SEASONING

Two 6-inch sprigs fresh rosemary, or a scant tablespoon of dried

Chop the pancetta, parsley, and garlic together until they are very finely minced. Trim all the fell (the papery skin) and the outside layer of fat from the lamb. With the tip of a small, sharp paring knife, make ½-inch incisions around the top and bottom of the lamb. Stuff each pocket with some of the mixture, pushing it down below the surface. The pockets can be filled the day before the lamb is to be cooked; the flavor will be delightfully more pronounced.

Heat the oil, and brown the lamb as in the Primary Recipe. Discard the excess fat, season the meat with salt and pepper, and deglaze the pan with the vinegar. When it has reduced to 2 tablespoons, toss in the rosemary, cover the pan, and cook the meat, turning occasionally, for about 40 minutes, or until the meat is tender and an instant thermometer reads about 145° F. The meat will be medium-rare. Remove the meat to a serving platter, and pour the pan juices on top. If there is more than a tablespoon of fat, either spoon it off or separate it out into a fat separator.

VARIATION: If you have run home with the leg of lamb and are in a hurry to get dinner going, you can save some time by not stuffing the pockets but still keeping all the ingredients. Coarsely chop, rather than mince, the pancetta, parsley, and garlic. Cook them together in the oil until the garlic is golden, and then remove them with a slotted spoon before browning the meat. Once the lamb is browned, return them to the pan with the rosemary and cook as above.

Nonna's Chicken with Garlic and Rosemary

POLLO ALLA NONNA

SERVES 3 OR 4

My Nonna didn't create this dish. Both the technique and the combination of flavors are pretty traditional Italian. But I had it first at Nonna's, and that is where I learned how a few simple ingredients could make such a remarkable dish. Don't be alarmed by the large amount of garlic. By the end of the cooking, it will be so sweet that you may wish there were more. Nonna always left the rosemary whole, but for a stronger flavor you can chop the leaves or use dried.

THE START (AROMATICS)
¼ cup extra-virgin olive oil
At least 10 garlic cloves, lightly smashed
  and peeled but left whole
THE MEAT
One 3-to-4-pound chicken, cut into 10
  pieces (see box, page 248), or 3 to 4
  pounds legs and thighs

Salt and freshly ground black pepper
THE DEGLAZING LIQUID
⅔ cup dry white wine
THE SEASONING
Four 4-inch sprigs fresh rosemary, or a
  generous tablespoon of dried
THE FINISH
Fresh sprigs rosemary, if available

Heat the oil with the garlic over moderate heat until the garlic is soft and golden in color; do not let it brown or color too deeply. Remove and reserve it.

Meanwhile, rinse the chicken under running cold water and pat it dry. When the garlic is out of the pan, increase the heat, and when the oil is hot enough for the chicken to sizzle, add the pieces and brown them well on all sides. Turn the pieces often, to make sure they are well browned on all sides, for 12 to 15 minutes. Remove the breasts from the pan, since they will not need to cook as long as the rest of the bird.

Pour all but 2 tablespoons of the accumulated fat out of the pan, season the chicken with salt and pepper, and deglaze the pan with the wine. Reduce to a tablespoon or two, and return the garlic to the pan. Tuck the rosemary sprigs in between the pieces of chicken, or stir the dried herb around the pieces, and cover the pan. Cook the chicken over moderate heat for 15 minutes, then turn the pieces and return the breasts to the pan, seasoning them first with salt and pepper. Cover, and cook for 12 to 15 minutes more, until the chicken is no longer pink at the bone and the juices are yellow, not pink.

Serve the chicken with the pan juices poured over it and garnished with fresh sprigs of rosemary.

VARIATION: **Pan-Roasted Chicken with Lemon and Rosemary or Sage.** For a delightful lemony flavor, deglaze the pan with the wine, let it reduce to just a tablespoon, and then pour in ½ cup chicken broth and 3 tablespoons lemon juice. Use the rosemary, or substitute ¼ cup of fresh sage leaves.

VARIATION: Italians often pan-roast a whole chicken that is small enough to fit in the pan. Use a pan deep enough for the chicken to fit inside with a lid on top and just wide enough so you can reach in with two long wooden spoons to coax the bird to turn. Season the bird inside and out with salt and pepper, and tie the legs together. Once the garlic is golden and removed from the pan, brown the chicken, breast side down first, turning it until it is brown on all sides. Discard the fat, deglaze the pan, and finish as above. Once it is browned, a whole 3½-pound chicken will take 25 to 35 minutes to cook.

VARIATION: **Pan-Roasted Chicken with Shallots and Sage.** Lovely, large pink shallots would be a nice substitute for the garlic. Sage is commonly used in place of the rosemary. For a piquant flavor, add 3 tablespoons of lemon juice or wine vinegar with the wine and reduce as above.

Cutting a Chicken Italian-Style

With the exception perhaps of a baseball-mitt-size Tuscan *bistecca,* Italians prefer their meat in small pieces compared with common American proportions. For pan-roasting and stews, chickens are normally cut into ten pieces—two drumsticks, two thighs, two wings, and each half-breast cut in two crosswise. If you use only legs and thighs, separate them at the joint.

Creamed Chicken Italian-Style

POLLO IN CREMA ALL'ITALIANA

SERVES 3 TO 4

This is quite different from the usual creamed chicken. There is a very small amount of cream, which actually forms a pink sauce when mixed with the tomatoes.

THE START

3 tablespoons unsalted butter

1 tablespoon vegetable oil

2 medium onions, roughly chopped

2 large garlic cloves, smashed and peeled

Salt and freshly ground black pepper

THE MEAT

One 3-to-4-pound chicken, cut into 10 pieces (box, above), or 3 to 4 pounds legs and thighs or just thighs

THE DEGLAZING LIQUID

½ cup homemade or low-sodium canned chicken broth or water

THE VEGETABLES

1 pound fresh plum tomatoes, peeled, seeded, juiced, and chopped (1 cup)

⅓ cup fresh basil leaves, shredded (optional)

THE FINISH

⅓ cup heavy cream

Melt the butter and oil, and cook the onions and garlic slowly, seasoned with salt and pepper, just until softened and golden. Remove and reserve. Rinse the chicken, pat it dry, and when the onions are out of the pan, increase the heat and brown it on all sides—12 to 15 minutes. Remove the breasts, discard excess fat, deglaze the pan, cover, and cook 15 minutes. Return the breasts and the onions, add the tomatoes and basil, and season with salt and pepper. Re-cover the pan, and cook 12 to 15 minutes, or until the chicken is cooked through. Remove the chicken with tongs, turn the heat to high, and pour the cream into the pan. Stir it around, and let it reduce until slightly thickened. Pour over the chicken, and serve.

To Peel and Boil Chestnuts

For each cup of chopped chestnuts you will need approximately ½ pound of whole chestnuts in their shells. Use a small, sharp paring knife to cut a deep X in the flat side of the shells. Drop the chestnuts into a large pan of rapidly boiling water and boil for 5 minutes. Remove a few nuts at a time with a slotted spoon and, while they are still warm, peel the shells and skins off with your hands. If they don't peel off easily, return the nuts to the boiling water briefly and try again.

To cook the shelled nuts, bring enough water to cover them by 2 inches to a boil and add a teaspoon or so of salt. Put in the nuts and simmer until they are tender, about 1 hour. Drain and chop.

Pan-Roasted Stuffed Turkey Legs

TACCHINO RIPIENO ARROSTO IN TEGAME

SERVES 12 AS AN APPETIZER

I have borrowed here the flavors from my grandmother's turkey stuffing, and the idea from chef Jimmy Schmidt while he was taping the *In Julia's Kitchen with Master Chefs* series, and combined them with the pan-roasting technique to create a dish that has become a mainstay of my antipasto plate.

The turkey is as simple to cook as the above pan-roasted dishes, but there are a few ingredients and advance-preparation details that need attention.

If whole chestnuts are not available, you can use jarred ones, but be sure that they are not packed in sweet syrup. You can also substitute unsalted pistachio nuts, which you should first toast in a 350° F oven for 5 minutes.

Caul fat is the thin cobwebby lining of a pig's stomach. In the recipe below, it not only holds in the stuffing but also melts and bastes the legs as they cook. Unless you have access to an ethnic market, you may have to special-order it, or see Shopping Online, page 27. Otherwise, you can sew or tie the leg together with butcher's twine. If boning the turkey legs and thighs daunts you, you can ask your butcher to do it for you. I have found experienced supermarket butchers who are quite adept at the task.

The recipe can be cut in half, but what I do is to stuff the two legs and freeze one before it is roasted. When I want to use it, I thaw and cook it as below.

GETTING READY

1 cup chopped roasted or boiled chestnuts (page 249)

THE STUFFING

½ pound ground pork butt or sweet Italian sausage

⅓ pound prosciutto, cut into ¼-inch dice

The chestnuts from above

12 prunes, diced (½ cup)

2 apples (Golden Delicious or Cortland), peeled, cored, and cut into ¼-inch dice

Freshly grated nutmeg

2 tablespoons chopped fresh sage, or

2 teaspoons dried

Salt and freshly ground black pepper

THE MEAT

2 turkey legs, 2½ to 3 pounds each, bone-in weight, with thighs attached, boned

2 pieces of caul fat, if available

4 tablespoons extra-virgin olive oil

THE DEGLAZING LIQUID

½ cup dry white wine

¼ cup homemade chicken or turkey broth

Mix the stuffing ingredients together in a bowl. The seasoning is important, so be sure that yours is right; check it by heating a tiny bit of oil in a very small frying pan and cooking a few teaspoons of the stuffing until the pork is no longer pink. Taste and add more salt, pepper, or sage if you think it is too mild.

Lay the boned legs on the counter with the skin side down. Pound the thigh meat lightly to even out the thickness, and season it with salt and pepper. Push as much of the stuffing as possible into the drumstick cavities. Spread the rest on the thigh meat, and wrap the meat around to enclose the stuffing and reshape the leg. Wrap the caul fat securely around each leg. Alternatively, tie the legs into shape with butcher's twine.

Heat the oil in a deep, heavy pan, and when it is hot enough for the meat to sizzle, brown the turkey on all sides. Discard excess fat, and season the legs with salt and pepper. Deglaze the pan with the wine, and when it has almost evaporated, pour in the broth and reduce it to a few tablespoons. Cover the pan, and cook the turkey, turning often, for 1 to 1¼ hours. Test with a meat thermometer—the internal temperature should be 160° F. Transfer each piece, along with the pan juices, to a piece of aluminum foil large enough to enclose it eventually. Cool to room temperature, and remove the twine if you have used it. Wrap each leg tightly in foil, and refrigerate for at least 3 hours or up to 3 days. Cut into thin slices to serve.

VARIATION: The turkey legs are perfectly delicious hot. If you would like more sauce on them, stir about 1½ cups of chicken broth or turkey broth, made from the bones that were removed, into the pan after the turkey is out. Reduce by half, and pour over the turkey slices.

STEWING/BRAISING

SPEZZATINO/IN UMIDO

Long before I can even smell the aroma, the words "braise" and "stew" make me hungry. They are techniques that promise moist, tender meat and a rich marriage of flavors. The initial steps—cooking and removing aromatics, browning the meat, and deglazing the pan—are exactly the same as those of pan-roasting. Then, unlike a pan-roast, a measurable amount of liquid is added to the pan. Italian stews are often called *spezzatini* because the meat is cut into small pieces, not because they have a large amount of liquid, as typical American stews do. They are meant to be eaten with a fork, not a spoon.

The Pan

When a 3½-to-4-inch-deep pan with a lid is large enough to hold all the ingredients in two layers, I use that. Otherwise I use a 6-inch-deep casserole.

For large pieces of meat, I like to begin with two pans—one for browning the meat, and the other for cooking the aromatics and finishing the entire dish. That's because a pan that is deep enough to hold all the ingredients for the actual braising is usually too deep to brown the meat conveniently. Choose a heavy frying pan for browning the meat, and a good heavy casserole or pot with a tight-fitting lid for cooking. A thin-bottomed pan will cause you endless problems by "grabbing" on the bottom and producing scorched bits of food that will ruin the dish.

To use one pan, cook the vegetables and the meat at different times. It doesn't matter which you do first. Remove the aromatics or meat with a slotted spoon before cooking the other items, and make sure there is enough fat to cover the bottom of the pan. Add more if necessary. Cooking vegetables and meat separately gives you more control over the browning. Recipe instructions often tell you to push the meat or vegetables aside while you brown the other ingredients. Why have to worry whether one is browning too much while the other is just getting started?

The Braising Liquid

The choices of liquids and the caveat about overly salted ones are the same as the deglazing liquids for sautéing on page 203, only use more of the liquid.

Braising Large Pieces of Meat

Large, less tender pieces of meat will cook a long time, so the pan should be very tightly covered, with foil and the lid, to force the steam created by the meat's juices and the simmering liquid to stay in the pan. The pressure of this steam is what converts tough connective tissue into tender meat. As the tenderizing is happening, the flavor of the braising liquid and the meat juices form one harmonious taste.

Take a sheet of heavy-duty aluminum foil, and use the flat of your hand to push it right down flush on top of the meat in the pan. Holding it in place with one hand, use the other to push the rest of the foil up and over the sides of the pan. Squeeze it tightly over the sides, and then cover the pan with its lid.

Chicken Hunters'-Style

POLLO ALLA CACCIATORA

SERVES 3 TO 4

"Hunters'-style" usually means that there are mushrooms present, and in the Tuscan version of this dish there are. The classic Neapolitan dish is traditionally just a chicken-and-tomato stew. I prefer this Italian-American version with red and green peppers but no mushrooms.

I ordered chicken cacciatore so often when my family went out to dinner that my brothers made clucking noises at me the minute the waiter approached the table. My good friend Kay Cameron's Italian stepfather, Nano, must have felt the same way. He was a whiz in the kitchen, and when he took on the preparation of his first American Thanksgiving dinner, an invited guest sent him a large, splendid turkey to roast. When they were well into the abundant meal, the confused guest was still looking for his bird, and finally asked Nano if he had not had time to cook it. With equal confusion, Nano pointed to the stew on the table and asked, "You don't like it cooked cacciatore?"

A note on the chicken. I prefer to use only the dark meat of chicken—legs, thighs, and wings—for stews and braises because it stays moist and can cook long enough to contribute its flavor to the rest of the dish. I save the breasts for sautéing. There may be times, however, when you want to include them. If you do, follow the directions for browning and removing them. This way they will not overcook and dry out, but they also will not absorb all the flavor of the longer-cooking pieces.

THE MEAT

3½ to 4 pounds chicken legs
and thighs or one 3-to-4-
pound chicken, cut into
10 pieces (page 248)

3 tablespoons extra-virgin
olive oil

THE AROMATICS

2 large onions, roughly
chopped

Salt

½ hot red pepper or ¼ teaspoon red-pepper flakes

THE DEGLAZING LIQUID

½ cup dry white wine

THE VEGETABLES

2 pounds fresh plum toma-
toes, peeled, seeded,
juiced, and chopped or
2 cups drained canned
tomatoes, chopped

1 medium green and
2 medium red peppers,
peeled if desired, seeds
and ribs removed and cut
into pieces about ½ inch
wide and 3 inches long

Rinse the chicken under cold running water and pat the pieces until very dry with paper towels. In order for meat to sear properly it must be dry or the water will create a steam that will prevent it from browning. Heat the oil in a straight-sided frying pan large enough to hold all the ingredients in one slightly overlapping layer. When the oil is hot enough to make the chicken sizzle, put the chicken pieces into the pan in a single layer to brown. If the pan is too small for all the chicken, either use two pans or brown the chicken in stages. Work over a medium heat and allow 15 minutes for the pieces to be properly browned on all sides.

When the chicken is browned, remove it from the pan and discard all but 2 tablespoons of fat. Reduce the heat so the onion (or any other aromatics you might choose) will not scorch. Put the onion in the pan, season with salt and hot pepper, and cook until golden. Return the chicken to the pan. If you have used chicken breasts, keep them aside; the white meat of the breasts will dry out if cooked as long as dark meat. Season with salt and pour in wine. Turn the heat to high so the wine boils while you scrape the bottom of the pan to deglaze it. Push under the chicken with a wooden spatula to capture all the pan juices.

When the wine has reduced to a few tablespoons, pour in the tomatoes, bring to a boil, season, cover the pan, reduce the heat, and simmer for 15 minutes. Return the breasts to the pan, stir in the peppers, cover, and continue to cook for 15 minutes more or until the chicken is cooked and the peppers are tender. Prick the chicken to see that the juices run yellow, not pink.

VARIATION: **Chicken-and-Tomato Stew.** For a chicken-and-tomato stew without the peppers, use the onions or substitute 4 garlic cloves, smashed and peeled. Deglaze the pan with the ½ cup chicken broth, reduce it to a few tablespoons, and then use 3 cups chopped canned tomatoes, with their juices for the cooking liquid. Stir 2 tablespoons chopped fresh rosemary, or 2 teaspoons dried, into the tomatoes, and cook as above.

VARIATION: **Chicken-and-Mushroom Stew.** For a Tuscan chicken-and-mushroom stew without tomatoes, before browning the chicken cook three chopped garlic cloves in the oil without the hot pepper. Substitute 1 pound cleaned and sliced mushrooms for the peppers, and sauté them, seasoned with salt, pepper, and 3 tablespoons chopped parsley or rosemary, until their juices run and are reabsorbed. Remove them from the pan while you brown the chicken. Use 1½ cups broth or water, and return the mushrooms to the pan when you return the chicken breasts.

VARIATION: **Chicken-and-Olive Stew.** One of my favorite combinations is chicken with olives. When lemon is also present, it positively sings of the hills of southern Italy. Brown and remove the chicken as above. Put two thinly sliced large onions and three minced large garlic cloves in the pan, and when the onions are soft, return all but the chicken breasts. Deglaze the pan with ½ cup lemon juice, and season the chicken with 1 tablespoon fresh or 1 teaspoon dried oregano. Return the chicken breasts to the pan, and fold in ⅔ cup pitted and quartered green olives. I often finish this dish by stirring in four to six rinsed and minced anchovy fillets and 3 tablespoons chopped parsley for the last 5 minutes. If you like the look of whole lemons, deglaze the pan with water or broth and cook one thinly sliced medium lemon with the chicken.

VARIATION: **Nonna's Veal and Peppers.** Instead of the chicken, use 2 pounds of boneless stewing veal, such as shoulder, trimmed of excess fat and cut into 1-inch cubes. Brown and remove the meat as above; it will not take as long as the chicken to brown. Cook the onions, return the meat, and deglaze the pan with red or white wine. Pour in the tomatoes, cook for 30 minutes, then stir in 3 medium to large red peppers (do not use green peppers), cut into 1-inch strips. Simmer until the veal is tender, about 30 minutes.

VARIATION: **Veal Stew with Peas.** Prepare the veal as in the above variation, and substitute 3 pounds, unshelled weight, of fresh peas for the peppers. Add the peas during the last 15 minutes of cooking.

Sweet-and-Sour Lamb Stew

SPEZZATINO D'AGNELLO IN AGRODOLCE

SERVES 6

This lovely lamb stew is a specialty of Apulia, the heel of the Italian boot. It is an example of the best of Arab and Greek influences on the food of that region. As with all stews, this one will improve with age and can easily be doubled, so it makes a great party dish. I always serve it with soft polenta (page 200).

THE MEAT
3 to 5 tablespoons extra-virgin olive oil
4 pounds boneless shoulder lamb,
    trimmed of excess fat and cut into
    1½- to-2-inch cubes
Salt and freshly ground black pepper
THE AROMATIC
2 medium-size yellow onions, thinly
    sliced

THE DEGLAZING LIQUID
½ cup red-wine vinegar
THE BRAISING LIQUID
⅓ cup tomato paste
1 tablespoon sugar
About 1½ cups homemade meat broth
THE FINISH
⅓ cup pine nuts
⅓ cup raisins

Heat the oil, then dry, brown, and remove the meat as in the Primary Recipe. Discard all but 2 tablespoons of fat, and sauté the onions. Return the meat to the pan, avert your face, and pour in the vinegar. Scrape the bottom of the pan with a wooden spatula to capture the caramelized meat juices, and reduce the liquid by half. Whisk the tomato paste and the sugar into ¾ cup of the broth, and pour it into the pan. Bring the liquid to a boil, and then reduce the heat to low, so the meat just barely simmers. Cover the pan, and simmer for 1 hour, turning the meat from time to time. Check the pan regularly to make sure the liquid is not boiling. If, during cooking, the liquid evaporates, add more broth, ¼ cup at a time.

At the end of the hour, stir the pine nuts and raisins into the pot, cover again, and cook another ½ to 1 hour, until the meat releases easily when poked with a cake tester or fork tine. If during cooking the juices have reduced below the 1-inch level, add a little more warm broth or water to the pan. If, on the other hand, they are very thin, remove the meat with a slotted spoon and boil them until they are thick enough just to coat the meat. Serve the stew with the pan juices poured on top.

VARIATION: **Lamb and Tomato Stew.** Substitute red onions for the yellow, and cook three large coarsely chopped garlic cloves and 3 tablespoons minced parsley with them. Deglaze the pan with 1 cup dry red wine, and use 2 cups chopped fresh or canned tomatoes with their juices for the braising liquid. Cook as above, without the raisins or pine nuts.

VARIATION: **Lamb and Potato Stew.** The northern-Italian region of Alto Adige serves a lovely braise of lamb on the bone and potatoes. Cook the same aromatic as above; use about 4½ pounds of lamb shoulder with the bones attached, trimmed of excess fat, and deglaze the pan with red wine. For the braising liquid, use the broth, 2 tablespoons of tomato paste, and no sugar. Use one bay leaf and 3 tablespoons of chopped fresh marjoram, or a teaspoon dried. After the first hour of cooking, instead of the raisins and pine nuts, add to the pan three large boiling potatoes, peeled and cut into large pieces.

Pork and Turnip Stew

SPEZZATINO DI MAIALE CON RAPE

SERVES 5 OR 6

As passionate as I am about Italian food, I am no match for Dagmar Sullivan when it comes to hunting down that obscure, out-of-the-way, hidden restaurant, located in a town that is a mere speck on the map but lauded by those in the know for one particular dish served only at a certain time of the year. I remember well our journey through Friuli: four very hungry people, three of us ready to stop at any promising establishment, and Dagmar insisting that gastronomic paradise had to be just around the next bend and wasn't it a nice ride. Walter Sullivan commented that it was too dreary and gray outside to know! We were starving; she was stalwart; and finally there it was. Not much to look at, but, oh, the pork and platter of steaming hot polenta were well worth the trip!

GETTING READY

10 ounces small white boiling onions

THE AROMATICS

3 tablespoons vegetable oil

1 large yellow onion, coarsely chopped

3 large garlic cloves, coarsely chopped

Salt and freshly ground black pepper

THE VEGETABLES

The boiling onions from above

2 medium or 1 large white turnip,
    peeled and cut into 1-inch cubes
    (about 3 cups)

THE MEAT

3½ pounds stewing pork (shoulder or
    butt), cut into pieces about 1½ inches
    large, preferably with bones attached
    and trimmed of excess fat

Flour for coating

1 teaspoon ground cloves

1½ teaspoons ground allspice

THE DEGLAZING LIQUID

½ cup dry white wine

THE BRAISING LIQUID

1 to 1¼ cups homemade or low-sodium
    canned chicken broth

Blanch and peel the boiling onions (page 348). Heat the oil with the yellow onion and garlic, seasoned with salt and pepper, and cook until the vegetables are slightly soft and somewhat golden in color. Remove them with a slotted spoon. Fry the boiling onions and the turnips in the same pan until they are lightly browned, and reserve them separately from the aromatics. Dry and flour the meat; shake it in a sieve to remove excess flour. Brown the meat in the reserved oil as in the Primary Recipe. Season with salt, pepper, cloves, and allspice, and return the sliced onion and garlic to the pan. Deglaze with the wine, reduce to a few tablespoons, and pour in 1 cup broth. Bring it to a boil, reduce the heat, cover the pan, and simmer gently, adding more broth if necessary to maintain liquid in the pan. After 40 minutes, add the onions and turnips, and continue to simmer for 40 more minutes, or until the meat and vegetables are cooked.

Chicken in Red Wine

POLLO IN VINO ROSSO

SERVES 3 OR 4

Note that the vegetables, the boiling onions, and the mushrooms are added to the pan at different times, according to how long they need to cook. I mention this because you may be ready to make this dish and find that you have leeks and carrots instead of onions and mushrooms and are not sure when to put them in the pan. Determine their cooking times—pages 343–49 give you a guide—and add them so they are cooked but not overcooked when the meat is ready.

Choose a light-bodied red wine, such as a young Chianti, to make this dish, and enjoy a glass along with it.

GETTING READY

16 small white boiling onions

THE MEAT

2 tablespoons unsalted butter

1 tablespoon vegetable oil

One 3-to-4-pound chicken, cut into 10 pieces (page 248), or 3½ to 4 pounds chicken legs and thighs

Salt and freshly ground black pepper

THE VEGETABLES

¼ pound thinly sliced pancetta, cut into pieces about 1 inch long by ¼ inch wide

½ pound mushrooms, thickly sliced

1 small carrot, thinly sliced

3 garlic cloves, thinly sliced

The boiling onions from above

THE DEGLAZING AND BRAISING LIQUIDS

1½ cups dry red wine

½ cup homemade chicken broth

THE AROMATICS

3 tablespoons chopped fresh marjoram

1 bay leaf

Blanch and peel the onions (page 349). Heat the butter and oil, and dry and sear the chicken as in the Primary Recipe, about 15 minutes. Remove the chicken from the pan, discard excess fat, and put the pancetta in the pan. When it has released its fat and become slightly crisp, put the mushrooms into the pan, and sauté until they are lightly browned. Remove the mushrooms and pancetta to a side dish. Discard all but 2 tablespoons of fat, and cook the carrot and garlic in the same pan until the garlic is golden. Toss in the boiling onions, and sauté until they are lightly browned. Return all the chicken pieces except the breasts to the pan and season. Use ½ cup of the wine to deglaze the pan, reduce it to a few tablespoons, and pour in the rest of the wine and the chicken broth. Bring to a boil, reduce the heat, add marjoram and bay, and simmer, covered, 15 minutes, then return the pancetta, mushrooms, and breasts, season, cover, and cook 15 minutes more or until chicken is cooked.

VARIATION: **Chicken with Marsala, Pancetta, and Mushrooms.** Cook the chicken, pancetta, and mushrooms as above. Omit the carrot, garlic, and boiling onions. Deglaze the pan with ½ cup Marsala and cook the chicken, covered, for 15 minutes. Return the mushrooms and pancetta, and cook for 15 minutes more or until chicken is done. Remove the chicken and mushrooms from the pan and swirl 2 tablespoons butter and 2 tablespoons chopped parsley into the pan juices. Pour over the chicken and serve.

Braised Lamb Shanks
with White Beans

SERVES 6

The shank of the animal is one of the tastiest cuts, and particularly well suited for braising, since the long cooking renders it fork-tender. When lamb shanks are combined with beans, they are in my opinion the ultimate comfort food.

MAKING AHEAD

3 cups cooked white beans, cannellini or
   Great Northern (page 40)

THE AROMATICS

2 tablespoons extra-virgin olive oil, plus
   3 more for browning the meat

1 large carrot, peeled, coarsely chopped

2 large onions, coarsely chopped

6 large garlic cloves, coarsely chopped

THE MEAT

3 lamb shanks, about 3 pounds, trimmed
   of excess fat

Salt and freshly ground black pepper

1 tablespoon paprika

THE DEGLAZING LIQUID

1 cup dry red wine

THE BRAISING LIQUID
AND FLAVORS

About 3 cups chopped canned tomatoes,
   seeded but with juices (see page 21)

Grated zest of 1 lemon

3 sprigs fresh thyme

2 sprigs fresh rosemary

$\frac{1}{3}$ cup chopped fresh flat-leaf parsley,
   plus more for finishing

Preheat the oven to 325° F. I like to cook long-braised food in the oven so that there is even heat around the entire pan. If, for some reason, you cannot use your oven—perhaps pies or cakes are occupying it—you can braise on top of the stove, but watch the temperature carefully so that the liquid only simmers and does not boil, which would toughen the meat. You should also turn the meat in stovetop braising more often than in the oven.

    Choose a heavy casserole for the aromatics, and heat the 2 tablespoons olive oil in it. Stir in the carrot, onions, and garlic, and cook over low heat until the onions are softened but not browned.

Meanwhile, heat the 3 tablespoons oil in a heavy frying pan. Dry the lamb well with paper towels and, working in batches, brown the pieces on all sides. As the pieces are browned, transfer them to the casserole, on top of the aromatics. When all the lamb is in the pan, season it with salt, pepper, and paprika.

Discard the fat from the frying pan, turn the heat to high, and pour in the wine. Bring it to a boil, and deglaze the pan by scraping the bottom with a flat wooden spatula. When the wine is reduced by about half, transfer it to the casserole with the meat. Stir in enough of the tomatoes to reach a third of the way up the side of the meat. The exact amount needed will depend on the size of your pan, how full it is, and how long the meat is going to cook. As a guide, for braises that cook an hour or less, the liquid should be about 1 inch deep in the pan. For those that cook longer, as this one does, it should reach about one-third the way up the contents of the pan. Too little liquid will evaporate quickly and leave the meat frying; too much will dilute the flavor. If you have too little liquid, add some broth, or water, or more tomato juices, or even the liquid in which the beans were cooked. Bring the liquid to a boil, stir in the zest, thyme, and rosemary, and then turn off the heat while you cover the pan with the aluminum foil, as described on page 252. Place the lid firmly on top, and put the casserole in the oven. Turn the meat every 30 minutes or so, and be sure to replace the foil tightly. After 2 hours, gently fold in the beans and parsley, replace the foil and lid, and cook for 30 minutes, or until the meat is tender enough to fall from the bones. If during cooking the juices have reduced below the 1-inch level, add a little warm water or broth to the pan. To test for doneness, pierce the meat with a skewer or a fork with long tines; the tines should slip in and out with no resistance. If the meat holds on to the skewer or fork, cook it longer.

The fat content of meat can be so unpredictable. You may have trimmed it well and still find an unappealing amount floating on top. If so, tip the pan and spoon it off. Or, if the meat is to be served the following day, refrigerate it; the fat will congeal in the cold and be easier to see.

When a braised dish has finished cooking, the pan juices should be rich and dense. If you find that they are thin, remove the meat, and place the casserole over high heat. Boil the juices until they have reduced and thickened. Break large pieces of lamb from the bones and serve with beans, juices, and a sprinkle of chopped parsley.

VARIATION: **Braised Lamb Shanks with Madeira and Mushrooms.** Cook the aromatics in 2 tablespoons butter. Brown the shanks in oil, and add them to the casserole. Omit the paprika, and deglaze the pan with ½ cup of Madeira wine. Pour the deglazed juices and another cup of Madeira into the casserole. Add enough meat broth to reach a third the way up the side of the meat. Use a bay leaf and two sprigs of thyme for the herbs, and replace the beans with ½ pound of small mushrooms, wiped clean.

VARIATION: In spring you may find smaller lamb shanks, in which case you can serve 1 per person. They will take slightly less time to cook.

Milan-Style Braised Veal Shanks

OSSOBUCO ALLA MILANESE

SERVES 6

This classic Italian braised recipe is deservedly one of the best known and loved. Traditionally it is served with saffron-flavored risotto (page 255) and the combination makes a splendid meal. I also serve the shanks with mashed potatoes.

The Milanese will argue about the inclusion of tomatoes in this dish. I think most would say they don't belong in it. I like the rich dimension they add, but if you prefer to leave them out, do so. As for the veal, ask for hind shanks, because they are meatier.

THE AROMATICS (*SOFFRITTO*)

6 tablespoons unsalted butter

2 medium yellow onions, peeled and
    finely chopped

4 large garlic cloves, finely chopped

1 medium carrot, peeled and finely
    chopped

1 large celery stalk, finely chopped

Salt and freshly ground black pepper

THE MEAT

6 pieces of meaty veal shank, 2 inches
    thick

¼ cup vegetable or olive oil

About ½ cup flour mixed with salt and
    pepper for coating

THE DEGLAZING LIQUID

1 cup dry white wine

THE BRAISING LIQUID AND
FLAVORS

About 1½ cups drained and seeded
    canned Italian plum tomatoes, finely
    chopped, or 1½ cups fresh plum
    tomatoes, peeled, seeded, and
    chopped (pages 20–22)

About 1¼ cups homemade or low-
    sodium canned meat broth

2 dime-size pieces of lemon rind

2 tablespoons chopped fresh flat-leaf
    parsley

THE FINISH (*GREMOLADA*)

1 medium garlic clove, minced

2 tablespoons chopped flat-leaf parsley

Grated rind of 1 lemon

Preheat the oven to 325° F. Melt the butter in a casserole, and cook the aromatics slowly until softened.

Meanwhile, tie a piece of butcher's twine around the middle of each piece of veal to hold the meat on the bone while it cooks. Heat the oil in a frying pan over high heat. Working with a few pieces at a time, dry, flour, and brown the veal in the hot oil on all sides until they are a deep-brown color. As pieces brown, remove them to the top of vegetables. Discard the fat from the pan, and deglaze the pan with the wine. Reduce by half, and pour over the veal.

Pour in the tomatoes and enough broth to bring the level of the liquid a third of the way up the sides of the meat. Bring to a boil, reduce the heat, and stir in the lemon peel and the 2 tablespoons parsley. Cover and braise as in the Primary Recipe, allowing 1½ to 2 hours; a skewer should pierce the meat and release easily without the meat's grabbing on to it.

While the shanks are cooking, mix together the seasonings for the finish. Transfer the shanks to a serving platter, remove the strings, and pour the pan sauce on top. Sprinkle with the *gremolada* and serve.

VARIATION: **Southern Italian–Style Ossobuco with Cavatelli.** I enjoy this southern Italian preparation of veal shanks with *cavatelli* pasta every bit as much as the dish above. For the aromatics, cook ¼ pound chopped pancetta, two sliced medium onions, and four large garlic cloves, sliced, seasoned with salt and pepper, in 3 tablespoons olive oil until the onions and garlic are golden; remove. Flour and brown the meat as above. Deglaze with the wine, and use the tomatoes and meat broth for the braising liquid, but for the braising flavors, instead of the lemon peel and parsley, use one small whole lemon, thinly sliced, 2 tablespoons fresh rosemary (or 1 teaspoon dried), and 1 tablespoon each chopped fresh marjoram and thyme (or 1 teaspoon each dried). Braise as above, and when the meat is just about tender, stir 12 ounces fresh, frozen, or dried *cavatelli* into the pan. Cook, uncovered, for 20 minutes, or until the pasta is tender. Do not use the *gremolada*.

Tuscan Braised Beef

STRACOTTO DI MANZO ALLA COLTIBUONO

SERVES 6 TO 8

Stracotto means "long cooked," and when it is a Tuscan *stracotto* it means in Chianti wine. There are many styles—and price ranges—of Chianti. Choose what your budget allows, but I would save that special Chianti Riserva to drink with the meal.

THE AROMATICS (*SOFFRITTO*)

2 tablespoons extra-virgin olive oil

3 ounces pancetta, thinly sliced and cut
   into ¼-inch-wide strips

1 large yellow onion, finely chopped

4 large garlic cloves, finely chopped

1 large celery stalk, finely chopped

1 medium carrot, peeled and finely
   chopped

Salt and freshly ground black pepper

THE MEAT

3 tablespoons extra-virgin olive oil

4-to-4½-pound piece of stewing beef
   (chuck, shoulder, or rump)

Salt and freshly ground black pepper

THE DEGLAZING
AND BRAISING LIQUID

2 cups dry red wine, preferably Chianti

1 cup peeled, chopped fresh or canned
   tomatoes, seeded but with their
   juices (pages 20–22)

1 tablespoon tomato paste

About 1 cup homemade or low-sodium
   canned meat broth

Preheat the oven to 325° F. Slowly cook all the aromatics together in a heavy casserole until the pancetta has rendered its fat and the onions are golden.

Meanwhile, heat the oil in a heavy frying pan and brown the beef. Transfer to the casserole, and season with salt and pepper. Discard the fat, and deglaze the pan with ½ cup of the red wine, reducing it to a few tablespoons. Pour the liquid over the meat, and pour in the rest of the wine and the tomatoes. Blend the tomato paste into the liquid, and pour in enough broth to come a third of the way up the meat. Bring to a boil, then cover and braise as in the Primary Recipe, allowing 3 to 4 hours, until the meat is tender. Serve with mascarpone smashed potatoes (page 357).

VARIATION: **Chianti-Braised Lamb Shanks.** Substitute lamb shanks for the beef. The lamb will need only 2 to 2½ hours to cook.

Working Ahead

All stews and braises not only *can* but *will* taste even better if they are served a day or two after being made. Cool the meat, and then refrigerate it in the pan in which it cooked if it will fit in your refrigerator. If the meat has released excess fat, the cold will congeal it and make it easy to spoon off. Reheat the braise gently on top of the stove.

CHAPTER 5

Seafood

Italians have a pretty simple approach to seafood. If it's good, it needs very little done to it; if it's not, don't buy it. The "very little" is summed up in the Italian saying, *Il pesce prima nuota nell'acqua, poi deve nuotare nell'olio, e poi nel vino*—"Fish first swims in water, then must swim in oil and then in wine." In other words, all you need is a perfect piece of fish, some fine-tasting olive oil, and a little wine or other acid, and you'll have a delicious Italian fish dish.

The "perfect fish" is easier for most Italians than it is for many of us. Most of the fish sold in the colorful, boisterous markets of Italy are whole, plump, glossy fellows that spill out of ice-filled baskets onto the walkways next to pails of still-wiggling small creatures. Even the unpracticed eye—and nose—can tell that these are perfect creatures. Unless you live near a reliable, active fish market, your selection will be more limited. I have lived near the ocean all my life, and even for me, excellent fish is not always easy to find. Whenever I intend to have fish for dinner, I go to the fishmonger looking for the best fish available—not necessarily one called for in a particular recipe. I always plan a non-seafood backup, so if none of the fish is perfect I can cook something else.

Buying

Claiming that fish is "fresh" really says nothing. How was it caught? How was it handled once it was caught? How soon was it eviscerated? Was it iced down as soon as possible? These are the conditions that determine seafood quality, and good fishmongers should be concerned about them, but, incredibly, many markets pay little attention. So it is up to you to be a discerning consumer.

Seek out the best fish market, or a supermarket with a top-notch fish department. If you frequent restaurants where the fish is always delicious, ask them their opinion of local fish markets. Although chefs buy wholesale, I have found that they also know where the retail fish is good. When you are checking out the market, let your nose lead you. A strong, unpleasant "fishy" odor is a signal to vacate the premises immediately. The smell indicates old or poorly stored fish and an unclean area. Fish and shellfish should be sitting on ice in a cold case, and not piled so high that the top pieces are too far from the ice to be properly chilled.

The eyes of whole fish should be clear, not cloudy, the gills should be bright red, and the tail moist with no signs of shriveling. Fillets and steaks should look moist, glistening, and translucent. Whether the fish is whole or in pieces, its flesh should be taut, leaving no indentation when pressed with your finger. Ask to use one of the salesman's rubber gloves and test it. And while you are poking, check for bruises, which would indicate that the fish was mishandled.

Clams and mussels should be in closed shells, or, if slightly opened, they should close tightly when tapped against each other. Scallops are usually sold out of their shells, whether sea scallops or the smaller bay scallops. Always try to buy "dry" scallops, meaning that they are stored in their own juices, as opposed to "wet" ones, which are stored in a saline bath, because the salt solution will seep out during cooking and prevent browning.

We have many varieties of shrimp available to us, and they can be used interchangeably. I like to buy shrimp in their shells and peel them myself. I am particularly happy to find them with the heads still attached, but that does not happen often. With the exception of some local varieties, all shrimp arrive frozen at the market, where they are then defrosted. Freezing does not destroy the quality, so, if I have the choice, I prefer to buy them that way than to wonder how long ago the market defrosted them. Thaw them in the refrigerator or at room temperature in a plastic bag set in a bowl of very cold water.

When you have found the market that meets your expectations, try to get to know the owner or manager. If he or she knows you care, he will tell you what fish is particularly splendid, when the snapper arrived, where the trout was farmed or, perhaps, caught.

Storing

Fish should stay cold until you are ready to prepare it. When you have found your perfect fish, ask the salesman to put the wrapped fish in a plastic bag with another plastic bag of crushed iced. In warm weather, I keep a small insulated thermal bag in the car, and slip the fish in for the ride home. At home, if it is to be stored more than 30 minutes, lay a plastic bag of ice in the bottom of a shallow dish or bowl, place the fish in its wrapper on top, and cover it with another bag of ice.

Substituting Species

The fish that is recommended in a particular recipe may well be unavailable to you, or it may be in the market but you have a similar, local variety that is ever so much better than the fish suggested. Choose what looks best, selecting your fish by characteristics, such as size and "firm-fleshed or delicate," "lean or oily," rather than the specific kind called for in the recipe. The substitutions suggested after the recipes describe what to look for.

Readying the Catch

Whole Fish

Most fish you purchase has already been scaled, but it is prudent to check for any pieces left behind. Run your hands carefully over the skin, and scrape off any scales you find with the blunt side of a table knife or a fish scaler. Check carefully behind the head. If the fins and gills are still attached, cut them off with kitchen scissors. Wash the fish under cold running water, paying particular attention to the inside, where all signs of blood and bits of viscera must be washed away. Pat the fish dry inside and out.

Steaks and Fillets

If the skin is still on, check it for scales as above. Rinse the pieces briefly under cold running water, and pat dry. Run your fingers carefully over the flesh to feel for small bones that may have eluded the fishmonger. Remove any you find with your fingers, tweezers, or small pliers.

Clams

Clams are harvested from sandy beaches, and careful washing is necessary to remove excess sand. Cover the clams with cold water in the kitchen sink, and use a stiff brush to scrub the outside. As you wash, be aware of any that are open and won't close when thumped against another clam; they are most likely dead and should be discarded. Lift the washed clams out of the water, rinse the sink, and then repeat with fresh cold water. Do this at least three times, until you are sure there is no sand left in the sink. Clams may be washed and stored in the refrigerator covered with a damp towel to keep them moist for 2 or 3 days.

Mussels

Discard any mussels that are open and refuse to close when they are tapped against a hard surface. Mussels should not be washed until an hour or two before being cooked. Store unwashed mussels, covered with a damp paper towel, in the refrigerator for a day or two. Run the mussels under running water—don't soak them—and use a stiff brush to scrub the outside. Wild mussels will need a bit of scraping with a knife to remove the barnacles; farm-raised mussels are usually barnacle-free. Use the sharp side of the blade of a small paring knife to pinch and pull off the beards—the tufts of hair on the side of mussels. While washing the mussels, check them carefully for any with empty shells or, worse yet, any that are full of mud. Do this by firmly pushing the top and bottom shells in opposite directions with thumb and index finger. Empty shells or "mudders" will break open.

Shrimp

To peel a shrimp, twist off the head if it is attached. Grab the feet on the underside of the body, and twist them around to remove the main part of the body shell. You can leave the tail shell attached, or pinch it while pulling the body to release the tiny tail of meat. Rinse shrimp well under cold running water. If you wish to remove the vein, cut a shallow trench in the back and pick it out with the tip of a small knife. I only do so with very large shrimp when the dark vein is so obvious that it is visually unappealing. The vein has no unpleasant taste or texture—its removal is for purely aesthetic reasons.

Scallops

A scallop has a small off-white strip on its side; this is what attached the animal to its shell. The bands should be removed from sea scallops, because they will toughen during cooking; it is not necessary to do this with the smaller bay scallops. Do not wash scallops; they will absorb the water and release it during cooking. If you want small pieces but can only find the large scallops, slice them horizontally into two or three pieces, or quarter them vertically.

Squid

Most squid you buy will have been frozen; this does not injure its quality. Most likely the squid has been cleaned, but if you are faced with a whole, slithery creature, do not fret; it is an easy process. I find it quite fun, actually, because the fish comes apart so easily. Grab hold of the tentacles and pull gently; they will slip out of the body with the head. Use a sharp knife to cut off the head just below the eyes. Discard the head, and squeeze the cut end of the tentacles to remove the tiny, bony beak. Feel inside the body for the hard quill-like bone, pull it out, and throw it away. Working under cold running water, peel off the gray skin and rinse the inside of the body well. Pull off the flaps on the side of the body; do not discard them, they also can be cooked.

Serving Size

An average serving of fish steaks or fillets per person is 6 to 8 ounces, depending on the appetite of the diner and how simply or elaborately the fish is prepared. An average eater, for example, may easily consume an 8-ounce fillet of simply grilled fish but be sated by a smaller amount that has been sauced or braised with vegetables. When purchasing a whole fish, estimate 10 to 16 ounces of fish per person to compensate for the inedible parts, such as head, tail, and bones.

Timing

Even with the carefree Italian notion of fish snatched from the water, slipped into oil, and dressed with wine, there is that matter of timing that needs your attention. Overcooked fish is disappointingly dry and tasteless, and, unfortunately, there is not much leeway between almost done and overdone. No need for such disasters; there are ways to make educated guesses as to how long the fish should cook, and definite methods for knowing when it is done.

For finfish, whole or in pieces, lay the fish flat on the counter the way it will rest in the cooking pan. Place a ruler perpendicular to it at its thickest point. The measure at this point is a relative guide to the approximate amount of cooking time you should allow. For every inch of thickness, the fish will take somewhere from 8 to 12 minutes of cooking. The variance will depend on the overall size of the fish; small 1-inch-thick steaks, for example, should take a total of 8 minutes to cook, whereas a very large 1-inch-thick fillet may need 12 minutes or more. This means of calculating is merely a guide; begin to test the fish after it has cooked a few minutes, before your total calculated cooking time.

Knowing When the Fish Is Cooked

There are several indications that the fish is cooked. The tines of a fork or tip of a narrow knife should pierce the fish easily, and the flesh should show a willingness to separate into large pieces. The color will have changed; raw fish is translucent, cooked fish is opaque with just the barest amount of translucency left near the bone or the center.

There is also the temperature test, particularly helpful for fish that is wrapped in parchment or foil. Push a metal skewer into the thickest part of the fish, and hold there for 30 seconds, then remove and touch it to the back of your hand or your lip; it should feel warm. Or use an instant-read thermometer at the thickest part of the fish; a temperature of 140° F indicates that your fish is cooked or very near so. Remember, fish will continue to cook a bit after it is removed from the heat, so it is better to stop the cooking a little before rather than after it is fully cooked.

Shellfish and shrimp cook very quickly and can go from succulent to tough in a heartbeat. Clams and mussels are done when their shells open; scallops, when they turn opaque, 2 to 8 minutes depending on their size; shrimp, when they turn pink and feel firm and their tails just begin to curl, 2 to 10 minutes, depending on their size and how they are cooked.

OVEN-ROASTING/BAKING

Roasting is one of the quickest and easiest ways to cook fish—as simple as placing it in an oiled pan, brushing it with oil, and slipping it into a hot oven. Technically, roasting (*arrostimento*) is done on a spit over an open fire, and baking happens in the oven (*al forno*), but the terms are often used interchangeably. Both are dry-heat methods, meaning that there should be no, or just the smallest amount of, liquid in the pan.

Breadcrumb Coating, Topping, and Stuffing

You can dress up your simple roasted fish by using breadcrumbs as a coating, a topping, or a stuffing.

COATING: A thin breadcrumb coating gives the fish a nice color and a crispy texture. Use fine dry breadcrumbs (page 17), and if you are not planning on eating the skin, remove it before coating the fish. If the fish has been marinated, pick it up with the oil clinging to it and roll it in the crumbs. Otherwise, brush the fish with oil or melted butter, and then coat it. Roll the heads and tails of whole fish as well as the bodies for an even appearance. Lay the coated fish on a lightly oiled baking sheet and drizzle or spray oil over the top. If you are cooking more than one fish, keep the pieces separated by a couple of inches, so the sides will brown.

TOPPING: Breadcrumb toppings are used for fillets and steaks and are put only on one side. They offer a pleasantly crisp contrast to the texture of the fish. Measure about ¼ to ½ cup fresh or dried breadcrumbs (page 17) per pound of fish, enough to cover each piece lightly, and season them with salt and pepper. If there are herbs elsewhere in the recipe, add some of the same ones to the crumbs. Otherwise, use an herb of your choice; parsley, oregano, and mint are Italian favorites with fish. You can also add grated lemon rind, and/or finely minced garlic. Contrary to what you may have heard, Italians do sometimes add grated cheese such as pecorino or Parmesan to the crumbs. Another nice Italian touch—but not if you are using grated cheese—is to moisten the crumbs with white-wine vinegar or lemon juice, using just enough barely to coat them, not to make them wet.

In order to crisp and brown in the oven, the crumb topping must be coated with oil or melted butter, and there are a few ways to do this. You can scatter the crumbs on the fish and then drizzle oil or melted butter over them with a spoon, or use one of those atomizer bottles available in kitchen stores, into which you pour your own good olive oil and then mist the tops of the crumbs. Another option is first to toss the crumbs in a bowl or sauté pan with olive oil or melted butter, using about 2 teaspoons of fat per ½ cup of crumbs.

STUFFING: Any whole fish can be filled with a breadcrumb stuffing before cooking, thereby providing the starch component to a meal. The backbone should be removed before stuffing, a task you can easily accomplish with small fish (see sardines, page 284), but for larger fish you may want to ask the fishmonger to do it for you.

For every pound of fish, use about ½ cup of fresh or dried breadcrumbs and 2 tablespoons of oil or melted butter—enough so the mixture will loosely clump together when pinched. A stuffing with fresh crumbs will be dense and spongy; one with dried crumbs will be crispy and textured. If you are using fresh bread-crumbs, soak them first to cover in cold milk for about 10 minutes and then squeeze them to remove the liquid. Flavor the breadcrumbs with salt and pepper and any or all of the following: chopped herbs, minced garlic, grated lemon rind, or a bit of vinegar or lemon juice. To add other ingredients, such as onions, celery, zucchini, bacon, pancetta, mushrooms, spinach, etc., chop them finely, and sauté them first in the fat measured for the crumbs until they are softened, and then toss in the crumbs and seasonings. For large fish, sew, tie, or skewer the opening closed to hold the stuffing in place.

Roasted Whole Fish

PESCE ARROSTO

SERVES 4 TO 6

The first time I ate dinner in a seafood restaurant on the Bay of Naples, with its halo of lights and shadowy outline of Vesuvius, I understood why so many Neapolitan songs are soulful odes to the bay and its fishermen. When the waiter presented the herb-scented and wood-oven-roasted whole fish at our table, tuneful strains of "O Marinara" ran through my head. Roasting a whole fish is easier than singing the song.

This recipe calls for red snapper; it is a round fish that is commonly sold whole and readily available in many areas of the country. I don't know what species you may find in the market or, for that matter, catch, but as long as it will fit in the oven, it is a good candidate for this method. At the end of the recipe, I have given directions for dealing with a flatfish as well as the round snapper in case you meet up with a whole turbot, *orata,* or small halibut.

THE FISH

About 4 pounds whole red
    snapper, scaled and gutted

Salt and freshly ground black
    pepper

Extra-virgin olive oil

6 to 8 large sprigs thyme,
    tarragon, or rosemary

1 lemon, thinly sliced

Preheat the oven to 400° F. I like to roast fish at temperatures between 400° F and 450° F. The larger the fish, the lower the temperature should be, so the center cooks through without the outside's becoming charred or overcooked.

Rinse the fish inside and out under running water and check for scales (see directions for cleaning whole fish on page 271). You may have to cut off some of the tail to fit the fish into your pan. It would be a shame to remove the head, which seals in the juices, but if it must go, then cut it away and use it to make a fish broth. Sprinkle the fish inside and out with salt and pepper, rub the cavity with olive oil, and tuck in some of the herb sprigs and a few lemon slices. Put the remaining herbs and lemon slices in the bottom of a shallow, generously oiled roasting pan, baking dish, or rimmed baking sheet, and place the fish on top. When the fish will fit, I like to use an oval dish that is attractive enough for the table. Make sure that there are at least 2 inches between the fish and the sides of the pan; and, in the case of smaller fish, between the pieces. A tight fit would prevent the heat from reaching as much surface as possible and could cause the fish to steam rather than roast.

Brush the top of the fish with oil, and when you are positive that the oven is up to temperature, slip the pan in the oven. Roast the fish without turning, but baste it with more oil a couple of times as it cooks, to keep the skin moist. The fish will take approximately 40 minutes to cook, but begin to test it after 30 minutes of roasting. Pierce the fish at its thickest part with a skewer or the tip of a sharp knife; it should slip in and out easily and feel warm on your lip or hand after being in the fish for 30 seconds. (See page 274 for testing for cooked fish.)

At the table serve portions of the fish on warm plates drizzled with a tablespoon or so of your very best extra-virgin olive oil and a squeeze of lemon, or serve with one of the fish sauces on page 301.

SUBSTITUTION: Use the above method for any whole fish that will fit in your oven.

VARIATION: **Whole Roasted Fish Marinated in Lemon and Herbs.** You can marinate the fish before roasting it. In a shallow glass baking dish or a platter large enough to hold the fish, whisk together ¼ cup olive oil and the juice of one lemon. If you like, add three or four minced garlic cloves to the dish. Season the fish inside and out with salt and pepper, put the herbs and lemon slices inside as above, put the fish in the marinade, turn over to coat both sides, and spoon some inside. Scatter the rest of the lemon slices and herbs into the dish, cover with plastic wrap, and marinate 2 hours in the refrigerator. Bake the lemons, herbs, and fish as above.

Serving and Carving Whole Fish

When you have roasted or grilled a whole fish, the drama should continue at the table, so present it whole on a warm platter or in its baking dish. Use a sharp knife to make shallow cuts below the head and above the tail. If you do not want to serve the skin, lift a corner of it near one of the cuts and gently pull it off.

Flatfish

Flatfish have two top fillets, which you should separate before removing them from the bone. Make an incision down the center of the top of the fish from the head to the tail, between the fillets, cutting only as deep as the bone. Working at the cut, slip a thin spatula or fish server under one fillet, parallel to and above the bone, and lift it off. Repeat with the other side. Carefully pull out the bone rack, taking care not to leave any bones in the bottom flesh. Cut between the bottom fillets, and either lift them off the skin or slice through it to include.

Round Fish

For round fish, make an incision the length of the backbone, lift off the whole top fillet, remove the bone, and then pick up the bottom fillet. If the fish is very large, you may want to divide the top and bottom fillets into serving-size pieces before lifting them from the fish.

Whole Roasted Trout
with Pickled Onions

TROTA AL FORNO CON SOTTACETI

SERVES 4

Acids such as lemon juice, vinegar, and wine enhance the flavor of seafood, and that is why one of them is so often part of a fish recipe. But you don't have to stop at the liquids; acidic foods have the same effect. *Sottaceti* are vegetables that have been pickled in vinegar, so roasting them with fish provides not only the acid but also a lovely garnish.

MAKING AHEAD
1 recipe pickled red onions (variation, page 377)
THE FISH
4 freshwater trout, 8 to 12 ounces each, scaled and gutted

Salt and freshly ground black pepper
1 small lemon, thinly sliced
12 small bay leaves
Extra-virgin olive oil
THE AROMATIC
The onions from above

Preheat oven to 425° F. Season the insides of the trout with salt and pepper, and tuck in a few lemon slices and two bay leaves. Scatter half the onions and remaining bay leaves in the bottom of a lightly oiled baking dish, and lay the fish on top. Brush or spray the fish with oil, and arrange the rest of the onions and bay leaves over the fish. Roast for 10 to 12 minutes, basting occasionally and turning once.

SUBSTITUTION: Extensive fish-farming has made trout of one species or another readily available nationwide. Not all of it is handled properly. I would definitely give the flesh a good poke to be sure it springs back and is not watery and squishy. Of course, wild trout have a gutsier flavor. The above recipe can also be made with one or two large trout if you find or catch them, or other freshwater fish or ocean fish. The recipe is best suited to a full-flavored, slightly oily fish.

VARIATION: Substitute other *sottaceti* for onions. If you use a store-bought product, it is best to rinse it first in boiling water, since they are often overly acidic.

VARIATION: **Whole Roasted Fish with Green Olives.** Clean the fish, and season with salt and pepper. Instead of the *sottaceti,* tuck two or three sprigs each of rosemary and thyme inside the fish, and pour ¼ cup of extra-virgin olive oil and 2 tablespoons of wine vinegar inside and over the fish. When it is about 5 minutes from being fully cooked, stir ¾ cup of pitted and sliced green olives into the pan. Serve each fish with some olives and pan juices spooned over it.

Roasted Hake in the Style of the Marches

NASELLI ALLA MARCHIGIANA

SERVES 4

If you picture Italy as a boot, the Marche region, The Marches, lies near the top of the calf, on the Adriatic Sea, below Emilia-Romagna and just above Abruzzo. Students of music appreciate it as the birthplace of Rossini; gourmands salute the food. The long stretch of coastline, and numerous rivers that run to the sea, provide one of the largest and most varied selections of seafood in Italy. The *marchigiani* provide some of the tastiest ways to cook it.

GETTING READY—MARINATING THE FISH

4 pounds whole hake or Atlantic whiting, 2 or 3 fish, cleaned

Salt and freshly ground black pepper

2 small onions, thinly sliced

3 garlic cloves, thinly sliced

About ⅓ cup extra-virgin olive oil

THE FISH

2 cups fine dried breadcrumbs (page 17)

The fish from above

THE SAUCE

6 tablespoons unsalted butter

1 anchovy, deboned if necessary, rinsed and dried

¼ cup white-wine vinegar or lemon juice

1 tablespoon chopped flat-leaf parsley

Sprinkle the fish inside and out with salt and pepper. Put the fish, the onions, and the garlic in a glass baking dish or other shallow dish large enough so the fish can rest in one layer. Pour the oil over the ingredients, and give them a few good turns to distribute the flavors. Marinate the fish at least 1 hour; there is no acid in the marinade, so the fish can sit in it for several hours in the refrigerator.

Preheat the oven to 425° F. Scatter the breadcrumbs on a large plate or piece of wax paper or foil. Lift the fish out of the marinade, letting most of it drip off, and then roll them in the breadcrumbs. Arrange the fish in a lightly oiled baking dish, and drizzle a little of the oil from the marinade on top; do not brush it on, or you will dislodge the crumbs. Roast for 8 to 12 minutes, depending on the size of the fish; turn once—carefully since the fish is delicate. Use a spoon to drizzle on more of the marinade if the crumbs appear dry.

While the fish roasts, melt the butter in a small saucepan; do not let it get so hot as to take on any color. Still over low heat, mash the anchovy into the butter with a wooden spoon. When the anchovy has disintegrated into the butter, pour in the vinegar or lemon juice, add the parsley, and keep warm until the fish is cooked. Serve the fish napped with the warm sauce.

SUBSTITUTION: Use other mild-flavored, lean, delicate white fish; use four 1-pound fish or two 2-pounders. Or use one large fish with the same characteristics. You could also use large fillets of cod, scrod, or pollack.

VARIATION: **Roasted Breaded Sardines or Anchovies.** Very small fish such as sardines and anchovies are lovely roasted this way, and served with or without the sauce, as an antipasto. Behead and bone (see page 284) about three dozen small fish, and add 2 tablespoons of vinegar to the above marinade. After no more than 1 hour, remove them from the marinade and roll in the breadcrumbs. Drizzle or spray with oil, and bake at 450° F until the fish are browned and cooked, 5 minutes or less. I like to drizzle a little fresh vinegar on top as they come out of the oven. Serves four to six as an antipasto.

Marinating

Marinating fish before cooking is optional, but I like to do it, especially with lean fish that is going to be roasted or cooked by other dry, high-heat methods such as broiling or grilling. A marinade not only protects the fish's moisture but also enhances the flavor. Italian marinades are usually very simple—some oil, acid, a few aromatics. The acid—wine, vinegar, lemon juice—both perks up the fish's flavor and encourages the marinade flavors to permeate the flesh. However, extended contact with acid can alter the texture of the flesh of delicate raw fish. When there is an acid present, marinate large fish and fillets no more than 2 hours, and small fish a maximum of 1 hour. Approximately 5 tablespoons of marinade are sufficient for 2 pounds of fish. Always use glass or other nonreactive pans or dishes that are large enough to hold the fish in one layer, and marinate in the refrigerator, turning the fish over a few times as it sits.

Remember, marinating is an option, and if you are pressed for time you can simply brush the fish well with oil before cooking.

Roasted Stuffed Sardines

SARDELLE RIPIENE ALL'ADRIATICO

SERVES 4, OR 8 AS A FIRST COURSE

Oh, how my father and grandfather loved fresh sardines and smelts! And, how I hated them! I tried them once when I was about 6 and immediately swore off them for life—for my whole life! I don't know what possessed me to break my vow years later, when I was in Ravenna, on the Adriatic coast of Italy, but it was indeed an epiphany. A small plate of these is a worthy antipasto for any seafood meal.

The sardines are beheaded and boned not just because they are being stuffed, but also because it is easier to serve and eat small fish without having to deal with those parts.

THE STUFFING

About 1½ cups dried or fresh breadcrumbs (page 17)

¼ cup chopped fresh mint or parsley, or
2 teaspoons dried oregano

2 or 3 large garlic cloves, minced

Salt

½ teaspoon crushed hot red-pepper
flakes

About 6 tablespoons extra-virgin
olive oil

THE FISH

About 2½ pounds fresh
sardines

Salt and freshly ground pepper

Lemon juice or red- or white-wine
vinegar

About 2 tablespoons extra-virgin
olive oil

THE FINISH

2 tablespoons lemon juice or vinegar

Preheat the oven to 450° F. Mix together the breadcrumbs, parsley, garlic, a pinch of salt, hot pepper, and oil.

Wash the sardines, and snap off the heads by pulling downward toward the stomach; leave the tails attached. Run your finger along the stomach to open the fish up, and pull out the innards and the backbone, being careful not to tear the fillets apart. Wash the sardines well, and pat them dry. Season inside and out with salt and pepper and lemon juice or vinegar.

Spread the stuffing inside the fish cavities, and then close the top fillet down so that it covers the stuffing. Put them in one layer in a baking dish, nestled close to each other, drizzle on the olive oil, and roast for 8 to 10 minutes, until a skewer easily pierces the fish. Remove from the oven, sprinkle with the lemon juice or vinegar while they are still in the pan, and serve hot or at room temperature.

VARIATION: This is a good recipe for any small oily whole fish that has its bones removed—smelts, mackerel, trout, and fresh anchovies. I leave the heads on mackerel and trout.

VARIATION: Vary the flavors of the breadcrumbs—oregano or rosemary or 2 teaspoons crushed fennel seed in place of the mint; add the grated rind of a lemon to any of the combinations.

VARIATION: **Sicilian Stuffed and Roasted Sardines.** Sicilians stuff sardines with the breadcrumbs, and snuggle them close together in a baking dish with their tails pointing up, so they resemble little birds—after which the dish is named, *sarde a beccafice* (a type of warbler). To the breadcrumbs above, add ½ cup raisins, ½ cup pine nuts, and 2 tablespoons rinsed and dried capers. Spread and smear the inside of each sardine with just enough to cover the flesh. Beginning at the neck end, roll each sardine tightly to the tail. Put the fish in an oiled baking dish, their tails poking up and close together to keep the rolls intact. Sprinkle any remaining breadcrumbs on top, drizzle or spray with about 3 tablespoons olive oil, and roast, without turning, at 400° F. Depending on the size, the rolls will take 10 to 15 minutes to cook.

VARIATION: **Venetian Stuffed Sardines.** In the Veneto, they flavor the breadcrumbs with grated Parmesan cheese. Replace 3 tablespoons of the crumbs with grated Parmesan. Some Venetian chefs use half breadcrumbs and half cheese. Flavor the crumbs with garlic, and parsley or rosemary. Fill and roast as in the Primary Recipe.

VARIATION: **Roasted Prosciutto-Wrapped Mackerel or Trout.** Use four small mackerel or trout, center bones removed but heads left on. Substitute chopped fresh sage for the mint. Wrap one thin slice of prosciutto around each body, and roast as above, 8 to 10 minutes.

VARIATION: **Baked Stuffed Shrimp.** In many Neapolitan-American homes, Baked Stuffed Shrimp was a standard part of the Christmas Eve seven-fish dinner. Since I avoided the eel (what child wouldn't?), I had two helpings of shrimp to complete my requisite seven. Use parsley and three or four large cloves of garlic, and substitute melted butter for the oil in the above stuffing recipe. Peel, but leave the tails on, 2 pounds of jumbo shrimp. Butterfly the shrimp by cutting from the tail to the head along the inside curve, cutting almost all the way through. Open the bodies out flat with the inside facing up. Season with salt, pepper, and lemon juice, and press some of the filling inside each body. Lay the shrimp, filled sides up, in a generously buttered baking dish, and use a spoon to drizzle 2 to 3 tablespoons of melted butter over the tops. Bake at 450° F for 8 to 12 minutes, until the shrimp are pink and the tails are just beginning to curl up. I'm not sure when Ritz crackers became part of Italian-American cuisine, but I know many cooks who substitute the ground-up crackers for half or all of the breadcrumbs.

Fish Roasted in Pork Fat

PESCE ARROSTO IN PORCHETTA

Porchetta is a small roasted pig flavored with wild fennel, garlic, and rosemary, so to cook fish *in porchetta* is to flavor and roast it somewhat like the pig. The recipe is a specialty of the landlocked region of Umbria, where they use large lake carp, known locally as *regina* (queen). It is a regal way to cook any whole fish.

You may be lucky enough to live in an area where wild fennel is showing up in markets or backyards. The dried crushed buds, called fennel pollen, are available by mail order. Although different in flavor and aroma, fennel seed makes a fine substitute.

¼ pound fatback or fatty prosciutto

2 garlic cloves, peeled and coarsely chopped (optional)

1 medium carrot, peeled

1 small onion

1 celery stalk

1 tablespoon fresh rosemary

1 tablespoon fennel pollen or crushed fennel, or 2 tablespoons whole fennel seed

¼ teaspoon hot red-pepper flakes

1 whole carp, about 4 pounds, or 2 smaller ones

Puree the fat, garlic, carrot, onion, and celery in a food processor. Pulse in the rosemary, fennel, and hot pepper. Rub the puree inside and over the entire surface of the fish. Refrigerate it for 2 hours or overnight, so the fat can solidify.

Preheat the oven to 400° F for the large fish, 450° F for smaller fish. If you have a sauté pan large enough to hold the fish, put it on top of the stove over high heat. (Do not oil the pan, since the fish has a coating of fat.) When it is almost smoking, lay the fish with the coating attached into the pan, and sauté for 2 minutes, or until the skin has crisped. Turn the fish over, and transfer the pan to the oven. (See below regarding sautéing and then roasting fish.) Or lay the fish in a shallow baking dish or roasting pan, and roast according to the Primary Recipe, turning the fish once and basting it from time to time, for 25 to 30 minutes for the larger fish, 12 to 15 for smaller fish.

VARIATION: Use other lean freshwater fish, such as two to four perch, or a largemouth bass. The recipe is equally good with ocean fish such as sea bass or red snapper.

VARIATION: **Stuffed Fish Roasted in Pork Fat.** Before baking, stuff the fish with about 2 cups of breadcrumbs tossed with 3 tablespoons of the puree and 2 tablespoons of vinegar.

The Sauté-Then-Roast Method

Sautéing fish before roasting is a restaurant technique that has good home application. The quick stovetop blast gives the fish good surface color and a crispier skin, if it is attached. Remember to reduce the oven time given in a recipe by the number of minutes the fish was cooked on top of the stove.

Choose an ovenproof sauté pan large enough to brown and then roast the fish in one layer without crowding. Put the sauté pan on the stovetop, coat with a light film of oil, and heat until it is hot enough for the fish to sizzle when it is added. For a nicely browned outside, dredge the fish lightly in flour. Sear the fish on one side for 2 minutes, or until it will release easily, then turn over, scatter the seasonings called for in the recipe around the fish, and transfer the pan to the oven, preheated to the temperature called for in the recipe, to finish cooking.

Fillets and Steaks

With the increase of ethnic populations, especially Asian, in the United States, the appearance of whole fish even at supermarket fish counters is becoming more common, but most of the fish you find will already be cut into fillets or steaks. They can be cooked in many of the same ways that Italians use for whole fish, and they also lend themselves to numerous simple variations, such as crisp breadcrumb toppings, colorful beds of sautéed or roasted vegetables, and quick pan sauces.

Roasted Turbot Fillets with a Thousand Herbs

ROMBO ARROSTO CON MILLE ERBE

SERVES 4

Italians do love to exaggerate, although if you counted each little piece of minced herb there may well be a thousand. The abundance of herbs not only flavors the fish but also absorbs its juices to create a flavorful crust. Vary them according to what you like—chervil, marjoram, savory, mint, and tarragon are all possibilities—but do use some parsley and chives in the mixture.

Although it is making cameo appearances here and there, chances are that true European turbot—a noble fish—will not be in your market. If it is, grab it; otherwise, this incredibly simple method is delicious for any of the flatfish suggested below. Watch thin fillets closely, because they cook quite quickly, in less than 5 minutes, and, if possible, cook them on a nonstick baking pan so they release easily.

Season both sides of the fillets with salt and pepper. Whisk or stir the olive oil and vinegar or lemon juice together in a glass dish or bowl. Put the fish in the marinade, turn over a few times, and marinate in the refrigerator, turning over occasionally for 20 minutes or up to 1 hour.

Preheat oven to 425° F, and spread the herbs out on a sheet of wax paper. Pick up the fish fillets with some of marinade still clinging to them and roll them in the herbs so the pieces are completely covered. Set them down in one layer on a lightly oiled rimmed baking sheet or in an oven-to-table baking dish. Pour the wine into the pan, and roast the fillets, without turning, until they are cooked, 3 to 6 minutes, depending on the thickness. The tines of a fork will pierce the fish easily, and the fish will be opaque. Serve with lemon wedges and, if you like, a fresh drizzle of olive oil. If there are pan juices, pour them over the fish.

SUBSTITUTION: The fillets of the delicately flavored turbot are ideal for oven-roasting because of their firm texture. Other flatfish to consider are gray sole, Dover sole (wouldn't it be lovely!), and plaice (fluke). You can sometimes find small halibut fillets, but halibut steaks, cod, haddock, and striped-bass fillets are other suitable choices; increase the roasting time accordingly to account for the thicker fish (page 274).

VARIATION: **Roasted Fish Steaks.** To roast firm-textured, ¾-to-1-inch-thick fish steaks such as halibut, cod, or swordfish, either marinate as above, or eliminate the marinade and brush both sides of the fish with olive oil. Brush the baking dish with olive oil, and scatter 3 tablespoons of fennel seed, or another herb of your choice, over the bottom. Put the fish on top, and drizzle 3 tablespoons of white wine around it. Roast, turning once, and basting with more oil, for a total of 8 to 10 minutes.

VARIATION: **Roasted Breaded Scallops or Shrimp.** For scallops or peeled shrimp, marinate as above, using lemon juice, and then toss the fish in about 1 cup of dried breadcrumbs mixed with 3 tablespoons of chopped parsley. Drizzle with oil and roast at 450° F; they will cook in 3 to 5 minutes.

THE FISH
About 2 pounds skinless turbot fillets, rinsed and dried
Salt and freshly ground black pepper
3 tablespoons extra-virgin olive oil
2 tablespoons white-wine vinegar, lemon juice, or white wine
2 cups minced fresh herbs, a combination of parsley, chives, and savory
3 tablespoons dry white wine

FOR SERVING
Lemon wedges

VARIATION: **Roasted Fish Fillets or Steaks with Butter and Sage Leaves.** Instead of oiling the baking dish, butter it, and scatter a good handful of sage leaves on the bottom. Put the fish in the dish, scatter more sage leaves on top, pour in the wine, and drizzle the fish with melted butter.

VARIATION: **Roasted Fish Fillets with Crumb Topping.** Use 2 pounds of striped-bass fillets, or other thick white fish fillets, cut into four equal pieces. Melt 6 tablespoons of unsalted butter in a small frying pan. Toss 1½ cups of dried breadcrumbs with salt and pepper and 1 tablespoon of chopped fresh oregano or 1 teaspoon dried. Season the fish with salt, pepper, and a bit of lemon juice, then roll in the melted butter; there will be some butter left. Dip the top of the fillets in the breadcrumbs, pressing so they adhere, and place, unbreaded side down, in a baking pan. Scatter as many more breadcrumbs on top as will hold, and spoon the rest of the melted butter on top. Roast as above without turning, 12–15 minutes, or until a fork pierces them easily.

VARIATION: **Roasted Salmon Antipasto.** Salmon fillets, cut into very thin slices and roasted, are ready in a flash, making an easy and delicious antipasto. Make one recipe of Lemon-Herb Sauce with Hard-Boiled Eggs (page 302). Cut, or have your fishmonger cut, 2 pounds of skinless salmon fillets into twelve slices, each ¼ inch thick. Lightly oil the bottom of a large ovenproof platter, and arrange the salmon on the platter, overlapping the slices slightly. Brush them with olive oil, and season with salt and pepper. They can be refrigerated, covered with plastic wrap for up to 3 hours. Roast in a 400° F oven for about 4 minutes, and serve warm with the sauce. Serves six as a first course; three or four for lunch with Italian potato salad and some dressed greens.

> The Italian expression for all talk and no action—or, as cowboys used to say, "All hat and no horse"—is *Tutto fume, niente arrosto* (All smoke, no roast).

Roasted Monkfish
with Roasted Red Pepper Sauce

CODA DI ROSPO ARROSTA CON SALSA DI
PEPERONI ARROSTI

SERVES 4

If you grew up in an Italian household, you know that a little *marinara* sauce was always on hand. When Nonna baked fish, she would often scoop a few ladlefuls into the roasting pan when the fish was finished. The fish had the seared characteristics of dry-heat cooking but also a sauce flavored with the roasting juices. There is no need to stop at *marinara*, however; other lean vegetable sauces, such as this one made with roasted red peppers, are very good with fish.

GETTING READY—
MAKING THE SAUCE

3 medium to large red bell peppers

2 tablespoons extra-virgin olive oil

2 tablespoons balsamic vinegar, red-wine vinegar, or lemon juice

1 teaspoon sweet paprika

Salt

THE FISH

2 pounds monkfish fillets (tail), rinsed and dried

Salt and freshly ground black pepper

1/3 cup extra-virgin olive oil

1 tablespoon wine vinegar or lemon juice

THE FINISH

The pepper sauce from above

Roast and peel the peppers according to directions on page 397. Cut the peppers into large chunks and put them in a blender or food processor with the olive oil, vinegar or lemon juice, paprika, and salt. Run until the sauce is liquid and smooth.

Preheat oven to 450° F. Monkfish is sold still in need of some additional trimming. Use a paring knife to remove the thin gray membrane covering the fish, and cut away and discard any dark meat. Season the fish all over with salt and pepper, and then roll it in the olive oil and vinegar and let sit 20 minutes to 2 hours. Alternatively, just brush the fillets with olive oil before roasting.

Roast the fish as in the Primary Recipe, turning a few times to brown all sides, 20 to 25 minutes, depending on the thickness. Remove the fish and keep it warm. Put the roasting pan on the stovetop over medium heat, and pour in the pureed peppers. Use a flat wooden spatula to incorporate the pepper puree into the pan juices. Reduce to a sauce consistency, and keep warm while you slice the fillets into ⅓-to-½-inch-thick medallions. Spoon the warm sauce over the fish, and serve.

NOTE: If your piece of monkfish is decidedly thinner at one end, tuck that end under the rest of the fish, and tie the tail at 1-inch intervals with kitchen twine.

SUBSTITUTION: Substitute other large, lean, firm-textured fillets, such as striped bass or halibut.

VARIATION: For a tangy addition to the sauce, add to and puree with the peppers ⅓ cup oil-packed sun-dried tomatoes, drained, and ¼ teaspoon hot red-pepper flakes.

VARIATION: **Roasted Monkfish with Tomato Sauce.** Substitute 3 cups of *marinara* sauce for the pepper sauce.

VARIATION: **Roasted Fish Fillets with Lemony Asparagus Sauce.** A lemony asparagus puree is especially good with mild white fish fillets. Remove the tips from 1 pound of asparagus, and boil the tips and stalks separately until they are tender (see page 343). Puree the stalks in a blender with the juice of one large lemon, salt, and pepper. Simmer the puree in a small saucepan until it has reduced by about a third. Season well with salt and pepper. Roast the fish as in the Primary Recipe, and pour the asparagus puree into the roasting juices and reduce. Serve the fish napped with the sauce and garnished with the tips warmed in a little butter.

VARIATION: **Roasted Monkfish with Creamy Red Pepper Sauce.** For a rich, creamy pepper sauce, do not marinate the fish, but brush it with melted butter, and roast as above. Make the pepper sauce by sautéing two small chopped onions in 4 tablespoons of butter with salt and pepper until they are translucent and tender. Add two peeled and chopped plum tomatoes and two roasted, peeled, and roughly chopped red peppers to the pan; cook 10 minutes, then pour in ½ cup of fish broth and simmer and reduce by half, about 5 minutes. Puree the vegetables, and put them in a saucepan over medium heat. Pour in ¼ cup cream, reduce slightly, and whisk in 4 tablespoons of butter. Season with lemon juice, pour over the roasted fish, and enjoy!

Fish on a Bed of Roasted Peppers, Tomatoes, and Prosciutto

PESCE ARROSTO CON PEPERONI, POMODORI,
E PROSCIUTTO

SERVES 4

A bed of vegetables not only flavors the fish but also provides you with a tasty accompaniment. The vegetables can first be roasted, as in this recipe, or sautéed as in Roasted Salmon Fillets with Fennel (page 294). Vegetable bases can be cooked ahead and held for several hours until you are ready to cook the fish.

THE VEGETABLE BASE

2 medium onions, cut into eighths

2 medium red or yellow peppers,
  cleaned and cut into ½-inch-wide
  strips

1 cup cherry or grape tomatoes, rinsed
  but uncut

2 ounces prosciutto, thinly sliced,
  shredded

4 to 6 sprigs fresh rosemary or thyme

Salt and freshly ground black pepper

¼ cup extra-virgin olive oil

THE FISH

2 pounds striped-bass fillet, in 2 pieces,
  rinsed and dried

Salt and freshly ground black pepper

Extra-virgin olive oil

Flour for dredging

Preheat the oven to 425° F. Put the onions, peppers, tomatoes, prosciutto, and rosemary in a roasting pan that is large enough to hold them in one layer and in which the fish will fit. Season the vegetables with salt and pepper, and pour the ¼ cup oil over them; toss to coat completely. Roast for about 20 minutes, turning often, until the onions and peppers are just tender.

Meanwhile, season and coat both sides of the fish with salt and pepper. Pour an ⅛-inch layer of olive oil into a sauté pan, and set over moderately high heat. Dredge the fish on both sides in flour, shake off the excess, and when the oil is hot enough for the fish to sizzle, put it in the pan and brown, 2 to 3 minutes a side, or until it is nicely colored and releases easily from the pan. Use a slotted spatula to transfer the fish to the pan with vegetables. If the sautéing oil is not blackened, drizzle it over the fish; otherwise, baste with fresh oil. Roast, without turning, until the fish is cooked through, about 20 minutes depending on its thickness. Serve the fish with the vegetables spooned on top.

SUBSTITUTION: Use large, firm-textured fish fillets, or tuna or swordfish steaks.

VARIATION: Marinate the fish before roasting in 3 tablespoons of olive oil, 1 tablespoon of white-wine vinegar, and 3 sprigs of rosemary for up to 2 hours. Place the fish on top of the vegetables, without sautéing first, and roast as above.

Roasted Salmon Fillets with Fennel

SALMONE CON FINOCCHIO

SERVES 4

In this case, the vegetable, fennel, is cooked on top of the stove, and the fish is marinated and not fried.

GETTING READY

2 medium bulbs fennel

THE FISH

4 salmon fillets, about 6 ounces each

Salt and freshly ground black pepper

3 tablespoons extra-virgin olive oil

1 tablespoon lemon juice

½ the chopped fronds from above

THE VEGETABLE BASE

¼ cup extra-virgin olive oil

4 medium garlic cloves, thinly sliced

The fennel from above

Salt and freshly ground black pepper

The remaining chopped fennel fronds

½ cup water

Cut the fennel heads where the stalks meet the bulbs. Pull the feathery fronds from the stalks, and finely chop enough to make about ⅓ cup. Remove the core, and slice the fennel bulbs into ¼-inch-thick crosswise slices. Rinse in a bowl of cold water, drain, and pat dry.

Season the fish on both sides with salt and pepper. Stir together, in a glass dish large enough to hold the fish, the olive oil, lemon juice, and chopped fronds. Turn the fish in the marinade, cover, and refrigerate for up to 1 hour.

While the fish is marinating, heat the ¼ cup of olive oil in a 12-inch sauté pan with the garlic, and when it is golden put the fennel in the pan and sauté, turning over several times to coat with the oil, for 2 minutes. Reduce the heat, and season with salt, pepper, and the remaining chopped fronds. Pour in the water, cover the pan, and simmer until the fennel is just tender, about 10 minutes. Check to make sure the pan is not dry, and add more water if it is.

Preheat the oven to 425° F. If the pan with the fennel is large enough to hold the fish, put the fillets on top of the vegetables; otherwise, transfer the fennel to a roasting pan. Arrange the fish on top, and roast for 15 to 20 minutes, or until a fork easily pierces the fish. Serve the fish with the fennel on top.

SUBSTITUTION: Use thick white fillets of lean or oily fish.

VARIATION: **Roasted Shrimp with Fresh Fennel.** The fennel makes a delicious base for shrimp. Marinate 2 pounds of peeled large shrimp as above, and cook the fennel with ¼ cup of dry white wine and ¼ cup of water. Place the shrimp on top of the fennel, and roast at 450° F for 6 to 8 minutes, or until the shrimp are pink and the tails are just beginning to curl.

IN A PACKAGE

IN CARTOCCIO

Cooking fish *in cartoccio*—literally, "in a bag"—is a centuries-old technique employed by Italians as well as many other cultures. Although the action happens in the oven, it is not so much a method of baking as of steaming. The tightly closed wrapping seals in the exuding fish—and optional vegetable—juices. The result is a succulent combination of flavors. You will not have the searing that occurs with baking or roasting, but you will have delicious taste and a bit of drama for the table.

The traditional case for wrapping the fish is parchment paper, but aluminum foil is often suggested as a substitute. I think it is because for a long time parchment paper was difficult to locate in the United States. Today, average supermarkets usually stock it. If you can't find it, use foil, and wrap with the shiny side in.

Fish in a Package with Olives, Fennel Pollen, and Lemon

PESCE IN CARTOCCIO CON OLIVE, FIORE DI FINOCCHIO, E LIMONE

SERVES 4

The aromatics that are included in the package should be either precooked or ingredients that need no cooking. There is not enough oven time for raw vegetables to cook unless they are cut into infinitesimally small pieces and you use just a few spoonfuls per package.

When you are estimating the time the fish will cook, keep in mind that fish cooked in a package will take longer to cook, as much as 5 minutes longer, than it would by other means.

THE FISH

Extra-virgin olive oil

2 pounds sea-bass fillets, about 6 ounces each, with skin attached, washed and dried

Salt and freshly ground black pepper

THE VEGETABLE BASE

½ cup pitted and sliced green olives

1 large lemon, thinly sliced

4 sprigs fennel pollen, or 4 teaspoons fennel seed

Preheat the oven to 450° F. Cut parchment paper or foil into four pieces about 12 by 16 inches. The ingredients must all fit on half of the paper, and the other half has to wrap around the fish generously with several inches to spare at the sides in order to seal the packages. Fold the paper pieces in half lengthwise to determine the center, and then unfold.

Brush the bottom with olive oil. Season the fish on both sides with salt and pepper, and lay a fillet on one half of the paper, about 1½ inches from the fold and the sides. Scatter an equal amount of olives, lemons, and fennel over the fish. Fold the top of the paper over the fish, and then cut the open side into a half-moon shape. Roll the edges of the paper together to form a tight seal; do not roll the paper tight against the ingredients, since some puffing room is needed. Place the packages on a baking sheet and bake 10 to 15 minutes; insert a skewer through the package and into the fish. (Do this carefully, since steam can rush out and catch your hand.) The skewer should pierce the flesh with just the barest amount of resistance at the center. It is best to remove the fish before it is fully cooked, since the packages will rest 2 to 3 minutes before being cut open, and the fish will continue to cook.

After the brief rest, place a wrapped fish in front of each diner and use scissors to cut the packages open *con brio*.

SUBSTITUTIONS: Any whole fish or thick steak or fillet can be cooked in a package. Because of the olives, I would choose a lean fish for the recipe above; red snapper, cod fillets, and halibut steaks are all good candidates. For a 2-to-2½-pound whole fish, use a larger piece of paper and cook for 20 to 30 minutes, depending on the fish. When you test the whole fish with the skewer, touch the skewer to your lip to see if it feels warm, or use an instant-read thermometer and remove the fish when it is at 140° F.

VARIATION: **Fish Cooked in a Package with Tomatoes and Herbs.** For an oily fish such as whole pompano or butterfish, chop six peeled and seeded plum tomatoes and mix together with ½ cup of chopped basil, one large minced garlic clove, salt and pepper, 2 tablespoons of olive oil, and 2 teaspoons of wine vinegar. Spoon it over the fish, wrap, and bake as above.

VARIATION: **Fish Cooked in a Package with Lemon and Herbs.** Make a fresh-herb flavoring of ¼ cup each of parsley and basil. Add a tablespoon each of rosemary, thyme, and marjoram. Season with salt, pepper, one small minced garlic clove, 2 tablespoons of lemon juice, and 3 tablespoons of extra-virgin olive oil. Divide it among the packages, and bake as above.

GRILLING/BROILING

Just as popular with Italians as roasting seafood is grilling it, whether it is over an outdoor fire, under a broiler, or on a *graticola*—a special cast-iron grill pan that fits atop the stove and is ubiquitous in Italian kitchens. Essentially, grilling and broiling differ from each other in that foods are grilled *over* the heat source and broiled *under* it. Think of the two techniques as upside-down versions of each other. They are both dry-heat methods and are usually interchangeable. The broiler will not impart the same grilled flavor as a wood fire does, but it will produce the same crispy outside and juicy inside. It is good to remember that you have the option, if the fish is marinating and a sudden downpour interferes with your outdoor intentions, or if you simply don't have a grill or, for that matter, a backyard.

Grilled or Broiled Fish

PESCE AI FERRI

EACH POUND OF WHOLE FISH
SERVES 1 OR 2 PEOPLE

Nothing says Italian summer quite like a freshly hooked whole fish roasting outdoors on the grill. I say "summer" because I am not quite as stalwart as a friend of mine who will stand up to his knees in snow, attending to his catch with thickly mittened hands. Grilling is the only cooking method he finds worthy of a whole fish.

There have been volumes written about grilling techniques that discuss the pros and cons of wood, charcoal, gas, etc. I am beginning with the conjecture that you have a grill and use it in a way that satisfies you.

Season the fish inside and out with salt, pepper, and olive oil. Use only a thin coat of oil on the outside, to prevent flare-ups. Squeeze the lemon juice inside, or slice the lemon and put the pieces in the cavity. Tuck the herbs inside.

TO GRILL: Prepare the grill according to your preference, but in time for it to be up to temperature before putting on the fish. Just as in roasting, the larger the fish, the lower the temperature, so adjust your fire accordingly. Whole fish can be tricky to turn on the grill, especially if you have a large brute, and very small ones can slip through the cracks, so I like to put any fish for grilling in a hinged basket specifically designed for this purpose; some are even fish-shaped. Brush the basket with oil so the fish won't stick, or, in the absence of a basket, brush the grill itself, and put the fish on to grill, turning it once halfway through its cooking. Baste

THE FISH

1 whole large fish, up to 3 pounds, or a number of smaller ones that will fit on your grill

Salt and freshly ground black pepper

Enough extra-virgin olive oil to coat the fish inside and out

1 large lemon

A generous handful of fresh herbs, chopped or in sprigs

FOR SERVING
Extra-virgin olive oil
Lemon juice

it often with oil as it cooks. A large 2½-to-3-pound fish will take from 15 to 30 minutes; small 1-pounders, 8 to 15 minutes depending on their thickness. Brush the top with oil when you turn the fish, being careful not to drip it into the fire. If the fish is not in a basket, use two wide spatulas for a large fish, tongs for the smaller ones.

TO BROIL: Cover the bottom of a broiling pan with aluminum foil, shiny side down (the foil is used to save on cleanup and is optional). Put a rack in the pan and brush it with oil. Position the oven rack so the fish will be about 6 inches from the source of heat; small fish can be 4 inches away, and fillets and steaks as close as 2 inches. Arrange the fish in one layer on the rack, separating the pieces by an inch or so. Set the pan squarely under the broiling unit and cook, basting often. You can do this with herb sprigs dipped in olive oil *al mio amico* (see sea bass, page 302); turn the fish once, halfway through the cooking.

Serve with olive oil and lemon juice, or one of the suggested sauces below.

SUBSTITUTION: Any fish that will fit on the grill or under the broiler. You can also grill or broil thick steaks or fillets over 1 inch thick. Marinate fillets and steaks in oil, lemon juice, and herbs for at least 20 minutes before grilling or broiling.

VARIATION: Grilled or Broiled Fish with Green Sauce. We usually think of serving fish hot, but room-temperature fish makes a lovely summer meal. This variation from coastal Ancona, in the Marche region, calls for *orata,* a fish similar to sea bream. It is available in large cities in the United States, but the recipe is equally good with a whole salmon or large salmon fillets, or thick tuna or swordfish steaks. Marinate the fish in 2 cups white wine, ¼ cup olive oil, two chopped scallions, four thyme sprigs, and a crushed bay leaf; leave for 2 hours. Grill as above, let cool at room temperature, and serve with the *salsa verde* or Lemon-Herb Sauce with Hard-Boiled Eggs below. The fish is also good served hot with either of the sauces, or with lemon juice and olive oil.

Little Sauces for Fish

SALSINE PER PESCE
Fish is perfectly delicious served with nothing more than a bit of lemon and perhaps a drizzle of olive oil. When you want to cook the fish simply but dress up its flavor, consider one of the following sauces. They can all be made several days ahead, stored in the refrigerator, and brought to room temperature before being spooned over the cooked fish. Whatever amount of sauce isn't used will keep a week in the refrigerator.

SAUTÉED HERB SAUCE: ½ cup extra-virgin olive oil, two minced garlic cloves, ½ cup chopped parsley, ½ cup chopped basil, 2 tablespoons chopped mint. Soften garlic in the oil over medium-low heat, then add the herbs, salt and pepper, and a teaspoon of fresh lemon juice. I like to put in some grated lemon peel as well. Cook gently 3 to 5 minutes. This sauce can also be used to marinate fish before cooking.

PICKLED RED PEPPER SAUCE: Use this for full-flavored fish. I particularly like it with grilled tuna, which I serve hot, as well as cold in a salad (see the cold variation for *salmoriglio* on page 305). Gently cook ⅓ cup sliced scallions (or onions), 1 to 2 tablespoons rinsed capers, ½ cup finely chopped pickled red peppers, ½ cup minced flat-leaf parsley, and 2 tablespoons chopped fresh oregano in ½ cup extra-virgin olive oil. Do not fry the ingredients, but cook at a low temperature just to blend their flavors. Stir in ¼ cup lemon juice or wine vinegar. Or make a pickled-onion sauce by substituting ½ cup of pickled red onions (page 377) for the peppers, and keep everything else the same.

LEMON-CAPER SAUCE: Especially good with grilled or broiled tuna, swordfish, trout, and salmon. Gently sauté 1 medium yellow onion, finely chopped, in ½ cup extra-virgin olive oil until it is softened; do not let it brown. Stir in ¼ cup rinsed and chopped capers, and cook 30 seconds or so and then add ¼ to ½ teaspoon hot red-pepper flakes and ¼ cup fresh lemon juice. Reduce the juice by about a third, and stir in 3 tablespoons chopped parsley.

Raisins are a nice addition. Plump 2 or 3 tablespoons of golden or dark raisins in water for about 5 minutes, then drain, and sauté with the onions after they have begun to soften.

For a quicker Lemon-Caper Sauce, stir together 3 tablespoons chopped fresh parsley, 2 tablespoons snipped fresh basil, salt and pepper, and 2 tablespoons lemon juice. Gradually beat in ½ cup extra-virgin olive oil, then stir in 3 tablespoons rinsed and dried capers.

GREEN SAUCE (SALSA VERDE): This classic Italian tangy green sauce finds its way on top of hot and cold seafood, vegetables, boiled meat, grilled chicken, and even hard-boiled eggs. It is one of my favorite sauces. Soak for at least 15 minutes one ½-inch-thick slice of day-old but not stale Italian bread in 3 tablespoons red-wine vinegar, or enough to soak the entire slice. Meanwhile, put 2 cups of leaves from flat-leaf parsley in the blender or food processor with one or two smashed and peeled garlic cloves, and salt and pepper to taste. Optionally, you can also add any or all of the following: 3 tablespoons of drained capers, three rinsed anchovy fillets, 3 tablespoons of minced red onion soaked for 45 minutes in three changes of cold water. Squeeze the bread to remove the vinegar, and add it to the blender. Run the machine, and gradually drizzle 1 cup of extra-virgin olive oil through the top as the ingredients puree. The texture will be slightly coarse because of the bread. For a smoother sauce—one I prefer for fish served cold—omit the bread and add a tablespoon of vinegar or lemon juice to the blender with the other ingredients. Taste carefully for seasoning.

LEMON-HERB SAUCE WITH HARD-BOILED EGGS: I mix the ingredients by hand, because I like the texture. If you use a food processor, pulse it so some texture remains. Press four hard-boiled egg yolks through a sieve into a bowl. Use a wooden spoon to mix in four or five rinsed and finely minced anchovy fillets (or 2 teaspoons anchovy paste), 3 tablespoons chopped fresh parsley, 2 tablespoons chopped basil, 2 tablespoons lemon juice, and (optionally) 2 tablespoons rinsed and drained capers. Still using the spoon, beat in ¾ cup extra-virgin olive oil and salt and pepper.

Sea Bass with Fennel Seed

SPIGOLA CON SEMI DI FINOCCHIO

SERVES 4 TO 5

I have a Neapolitan friend who is delightfully spontaneous and animated in all he does. (Some may say that this is the definition of Neapolitan.) He has a small hibachi-type grill on his second-story patio—an area that he considers a miniature urban farm but which looks more like a dense jungle. Herbs and vegetables, many of questionable genus, sprout from pots, cans, and containers of all shapes and sizes. On one occasion, as he was grilling fish, he beheaded a pot of wild fennel, dramatically threw a handful into the fire, and dipped the rest into oil to baste the fish. The flavor, though subtle, was delicious. You will probably not find fresh wild fennel, but you can mail-order dried pieces for the fire and fennel pollen or fennel seed for flavoring.

GETTING READY
1 tablespoon fennel pollen or whole
　fennel seed

THE FISH
4 sea bass, about 1 pound each, cleaned
　but with heads and tails left on
Salt and freshly ground black pepper
Enough extra-virgin olive oil to coat the
　fish inside and out

2 tablespoons lemon juice
The fennel seed or fennel pollen from
　above
4 large garlic cloves, smashed and
　peeled

FOR SERVING
Lemon wedges

If you are using the whole fennel seeds, put them in a small plastic bag and pound them with the bottom of a heavy pan or a rolling pin to crush slightly.

Season both sides of the fish with salt and pepper. Rub the fish inside and out with the oil and lemon juice. Tuck some of the fennel and a garlic clove inside each fish.

Grill or broil the fish as in the Primary Recipe, turning once, for about 6 minutes a side. Serve the fish with lemon wedges.

SUBSTITUTION: The same suggestions as in the Primary Recipe, page 300.

VARIATION: **Grilled Fresh Fennel.** If you are grilling the fish, wedges of grilled fresh fennel are a lovely accompaniment. Count on two medium or four small heads of fennel for four people. Trim the bulbs (page 294), quarter large bulbs, and cut the smaller ones in half. Marinate the pieces in olive oil while the fish is marinating, and grill for 20 to 30 minutes, or until tender; turn to cook both sides.

Grilled Bruschetta/Oven Crostini

As long as the grill is going, take the opportunity to make Italian toast the way it tastes best—over the fire. *Bruscare* is Italian for cooking over an open fire, so when *crostini* are cooked that way as opposed to in the oven, they are called *bruschetta*.

BRUSCHETTA: Cut firm-textured Italian bread into slices, on an angle if you want lovely long pieces, about ½ inch thick. Cut two per person. Put the slices directly on the grill rack, and toast, turning once, for 5 to 7 minutes, or until the pieces are lightly brown on both sides. Immediately brush or drizzle one side with your best extra-virgin olive oil.

CROSTINI: If the grill is not going, put the sliced bread directly on an oven rack when the temperature is at 400° F, and toast, turning once, until lightly browned on both sides, a total of 4 to 5 minutes. Finish the baked *crostini* as below.

GARLIC BRUSCHETTA/CROSTINI: Before brushing on the oil, rub one side with the cut side of a halved garlic clove (no need to peel it).

LEMONY GARLIC BRUSCHETTA/CROSTINI: Mix 2 teaspoons of lemon juice into ¼ cup of extra-virgin olive oil, and brush this on each *bruschetta* after rubbing it with garlic. Sprinkle fresh parsley and a bit of salt on top.

HOT PEPPER BRUSCHETTA/CROSTINI: Brush the toasted bread with piquant oil, *olio santo* (page 6).

TOMATO BRUSCHETTA/CROSTINI: Chop 1 pound of beautifully ripe salad tomatoes in half. Squeeze gently to remove the seeds and a little juice, but do not squeeze dry. Chop the pulp into a small dice, and put it in a bowl. Gently stir in ¼ cup of coarsely chopped basil, 1 teaspoon of minced garlic, 2 tablespoons of extra-virgin olive oil, and salt and freshly ground black pepper. Spoon a good tablespoon on top of each hot *bruschetta*.

Swordfish Salmoriglio

PESCE SPADA AL SALMORIGLIO

SERVES 4 OR 5

Cooking fish *al salmoriglio* is a specialty of the southern Italian regions of Sicily and Calabria. The name is derived from the Italian word *sale* (salt) and refers to the fact that at one time the dressing was actually flavored with seawater. Traditionally, the fish is cut into rather thin pieces, as below, but you can cook thicker fish steaks if you prefer. Thin slices of fish are perfect for a hurry-up meal, because they cook so quickly.

GETTING READY—MAKING THE *SALMORIGLIO* SAUCE

2 tablespoons lemon juice

1 teaspoon salt

¼ cup extra-virgin olive oil

A generous amount of freshly ground black pepper

1 tablespoon chopped fresh oregano

THE FISH

2 pounds swordfish steaks, ½ inch thick

Salt and freshly ground black pepper

3 tablespoons extra-virgin olive oil

2 tablespoons white-wine vinegar

Pour the lemon juice into a small bowl, and add the salt. Gradually whisk in the olive oil, and season with pepper. Keep the *salmoriglio* at room temperature, and just before using, whisk in the fresh oregano.

Season the fish steaks on both sides with salt and pepper, and coat them with oil and vinegar. Marinate 20 to 30 minutes. Grill or broil close to the heat source, turning once, for 2 to 3 minutes a side. Put the fish on a platter, poke the tops lightly with the tines of a fork, and pour the *salmoriglio* over them.

VARIATION: Swordfish is the usual choice for *salmoriglio,* but the sauce is equally good with tuna or halibut steaks.

VARIATION: **Grilled Swordfish or Tuna Salad.** Firm fish cooked and sauced this way is delicious served cold for an antipasto or lunch. Whenever I have some left over, I cut it into large chunks and refrigerate it overnight. The next day, I let it sit at room temperature for about 15 minutes and then put it on a bed of leafy lettuce dressed with a little oil and lemon and garnish it with small cherry tomatoes, black olives, and lemon wedges. Boiled and cooled vegetables, such as thin green beans that are dressed with oil and lemon, are just right with the fish salad.

VARIATION: **Grilled Salmon Fillets with Sautéed Herb Sauce.** Thin slices of salmon fillet broil very nicely and quickly. Use 2 pounds of ½-inch-thick slices of salmon, cut on an angle from the fillet. Marinate in a combination of 3 tablespoons olive oil, 2 tablespoons lemon juice, and 3 tablespoons chopped parsley. Grill or broil as above, and serve with the Sautéed Herb Sauce on page 301, or unsauced on top of a leafy salad tossed with olive oil and lemon juice with broiled or grilled *bruschetta* on the side (page 304).

Grilled Tuna Brochettes

SPIEDINI DI TONNO MARINATO

SERVES 4

We would be hard-pressed to get so much drama for so little work as we do from an array of fish and vegetables that are skewered and grilled, *allo spiedino.* Your presentation will be even more dramatic if you have a set of ornate skewers. For the fish, choose only firm-textured varieties and cut it into large cubes, or you will watch in dismay as the fish disintegrates into the fire.

GETTING READY

8 to 10 wooden skewers, 8 to 10 inches long

THE MARINADE

6 tablespoons extra-virgin olive oil

3 tablespoons lemon juice

The zest of 1 lemon

2 large garlic cloves, minced

3 tablespoons chopped fresh oregano

THE VEGETABLES

2 medium zucchini

1 medium eggplant

24 cherry tomatoes

THE FISH

2 pounds tuna, cut into 3-inch squares

Salt and freshly ground black pepper

FOR SERVING

Wedges of lemon

Submerge the skewers in cold water and let sit for at least 30 minutes. This will prevent them from charring. If you are using metal skewers, there is no need to soak them.

In a large rectangular glass baking dish, mix together the olive oil, lemon juice, zest, garlic, and oregano. Wash the zucchini, trim the ends, and cut it lengthwise in half. Cut each half crosswise into 8 pieces. Wash and trim the eggplant, and cut it in half lengthwise. Use a spoon to scrape out the seeds, and then cut the pieces in half again, lengthwise, and cut those into 8 pieces crosswise. Rinse the tomatoes.

Season the fish with salt and pepper. Thread the fish and vegetables on the prepared skewers, alternating them, and roll the skewers in the marinade. Marinate for at least an hour but no more than 2, turning the skewers often.

Grill or broil as in the Primary Recipe, gripping the *spiedini* firmly with tongs to turn, so the ingredients actually turn and do not spin around on the skewers. Serve with lemon wedges and couscous (see box, page 308) flavored with chopped parsley, olive oil, and a bit of lemon juice.

VARIATION: Use another firm-fleshed meaty fish, such as swordfish.

VARIATION: Grilled Tuna or Swordfish Skewered with Sage and Pancetta. Use tuna or swordfish cut as above. Omit the vegetables. Thread the fish onto the skewers, sliding a fresh sage leaf and a piece of pancetta about ¼ inch thick and as long as the fish between each two pieces of fish. Marinate and grill as above. If you have fresh bay leaves, use those in place of the sage, or cover dried bay leaves with boiling water and soak for 10 minutes, or until softened; drain and pat dry.

Couscous

You may not think of couscous as Italian, but Sicilians would quickly set you straight. Known in the regional dialect as *cuscusu,* it is especially popular in Sicily, where it is commonly served with fish. The region has some rather intricate recipes for this coarse semolina grain, most using the long-cooking variety, but I like to use the quick-cooking type and prepare it simply.

Nantucket chef Ron Suhanosky shared this way of making it with me, and it is by far the best for the instant grain. He learned it from a Moroccan chef; North Africa is the most likely source of this grain in Italy, so he knew his couscous.

I buy couscous at health-food stores, because they sell so much of it that their supply is always fresh.

SERVES 4

1 cup quick-cooking couscous
2 tablespoons extra-virgin olive oil
Salt and freshly ground black pepper
1½ cups boiling water or broth

Put the couscous in a 1-quart mixing bowl. Drizzle the oil over the grains, and rub them between the palms of your hands to coat each grain with the oil. Season with salt and pepper, and pour in the boiling water. Cover the bowl tightly with plastic wrap. Let sit for 5 minutes, and then transfer the couscous to a flat dish or baking sheet and toss with two forks. Serve at room temperature or cold. Ron likes to sauté it the next day for a snack.

VARIATION: The above is perfectly plain couscous, but it needn't be. The boiling water or broth can be flavored with a tablespoon of tomato paste, or a teaspoon of saffron. Chopped herbs—mint and parsley are particularly good with seafood—and spices can be added to the grain with the salt and pepper. Once the couscous has absorbed the water, toss in finely chopped cooked vegetables or raw cucumbers, radishes, tomatoes, more fresh herbs, and a bit of lemon juice or vinegar.

SAUTÉING

Sautéing, cooking on top of the stove in a frying pan, is one of the fastest and most gratifying ways to cook fish. If you have ever reeled in a few perch or trout out of the water and cooked them in a skillet over a hot fire, you know what I mean.

Coating the Fish

Flour is the simplest and most common coating for fish that is to be sautéed, although contemporary Italian chefs are taking advantage of their Italian pantries and using cornmeal, semolina, and rice flour for coating—all quite crisply delicious. I always coat delicate fillets. It is optional for very firm fish, but it does provide a slightly crisp and golden protective coating. Ground spices, alone or mixed with flour, are also an option.

The Deglazing Liquid

Once the fish is sautéed, the pan will hold the makings of a delicious, simple sauce that can be captured with a deglazing liquid. It can be water, fish broth, wine, vinegar, tomatoes, lemon juice, lime juice, orange juice, or a combination. See page 314 for a Quick Fish Broth using clam juice, and page 138 for a quick shrimp broth.

Sautéed Tuna Steaks with Prosciutto and Tomatoes

TONNO IN PADELLA CON PROSCIUTTO E POMODORI

SERVES 4

Tuna steaks will be juiciest if they are removed from the heat while they are still slightly translucent at the center. Some people prefer them just barely seared on the outside and still quite raw inside. Adjust the timing of the tuna according to your taste. The timing below is for medium rare.

THE FISH

2 pounds tuna steaks, ¾ inch thick, washed and dried

Salt and freshly ground black pepper

About 3 tablespoons extra-virgin olive oil

¼ pound prosciutto, thinly sliced, cut, or shredded into thin julienne strips

½ cup flour

Fish for sautéing is easiest to handle when it is between ¼ and ¾ inch thick. Season both sides with salt and pepper. I like the seasonings to sit on the fish, so I season it directly rather than adding the salt and pepper to the flour, as I do with meat. Heat the oil with the prosciutto in a heavy sauté pan over medium heat. Cook the prosciutto for 3 or 4 minutes, until some of its fat is released into the pan, and then remove it with a slotted spoon and reserve. Make sure that there is enough fat in the pan to cover the bottom; if not, add more oil.

Flour as many pieces of fish as will fit in the pan at one time, patting off the excess. When the fat is hot enough for the fish to

sizzle—test by dipping a corner of a piece into the pan and listening to be sure it makes a sound—slip the fish into the pan, a few slices at a time if necessary so as not to crowd the pan. Cook for 4 minutes, and then turn over—a wide, slotted fish spatula will keep delicate fish intact and leave the oil behind in the pan for cooking the other side. Cook on the second side for 3 to 4 minutes. The tines of a fork or the tip of a paring knife should pierce the flesh easily with just the slightest resistance at the center. Transfer to a heated plate and keep warm; you can tent the fish with foil and keep near the stovetop, or put the fish on a warm plate in the oven set at its lowest temperature. Cook the remaining pieces of fish.

When all the fish is out of the pan, increase the heat to high, and pour in the wine or water. Boil and reduce to 2 tablespoons, then pour in the tomatoes. Season with salt and pepper, and cook over high heat until the tomatoes are almost completely dry, about 5 minutes. Toss in the arugula and vinegar, season with salt and pepper, and cook just until the arugula wilts, about 3 minutes. Make a small bed of the vegetables on four dinner plates, top with the fish, and garnish with the prosciutto.

SUBSTITUTION: Use other firm-fleshed steaks or fillets, such as cod, swordfish, halibut, or monkfish medallions.

VARIATION: **Sautéed Fish Steaks with Spinach, Pine Nuts, and Raisins.** Substitute chopped pancetta for the prosciutto, and after it has cooked in the oil for 4 or 5 minutes and is just beginning to crisp, stir in ¼ cup of pine nuts and ¼ cup of raisins. When the pine nuts are just golden, use a slotted spoon to remove the contents of the pan. Flour and cook the fish as in the Primary Recipe, and use ½ cup of fish broth and 2 tablespoons of lemon juice (no tomatoes) to deglaze the pan. Reduce to 2 tablespoons, and toss in ½ pound of baby-spinach leaves. Season with salt and pepper, and toss in half the pancetta mixture. Divide the spinach among four plates, top with the fish, and garnish with the remainder of the topping.

THE DEGLAZING LIQUID
¼ cup dry white wine or
   water
1 cup peeled, seeded, and
   chopped fresh or canned
   tomatoes (about 1 pound)
THE FINISH
½ pound arugula, washed,
   stems removed
2 tablespoons balsamic
   vinegar

VARIATION: **Sautéed Fillet of Sole with Asparagus and Prosciutto.** The same recipe can be used for fillet of sole with asparagus and prosciutto. Trim, peel, and boil 1 pound of thin asparagus for 1 minute, or until just barely tender; cool, and cut into 1-inch pieces. Replace the olive oil in the Primary Recipe with 3 tablespoons of unsalted butter and 1 tablespoon of vegetable oil, and after the prosciutto has cooked for 3 minutes, toss the asparagus and ¼ cup of pine nuts into the pan and cook just until the pine nuts begin to color; remove with a slotted spoon. Coat with flour and sauté 2 pounds of fillet of sole for 1 to 1½ minutes per side. Remove and keep warm. Discard the fat, and deglaze the pan with ½ cup of dry white wine or water and 1 tablespoon of lemon juice. Reduce by half, return the asparagus, prosciutto, and pine nuts to the pan, and swirl in 2 tablespoons of butter. Pour the sauce over the fish.

Sautéed Monkfish Medallions with Pancetta and Cream

MEDAGLIONE DI CODA DI ROSPO CON
PANCETTA E PANNA

SERVES 4

Maureen Pothier was the chef-owner of the former Blue Point Oyster Bar and Grill in Providence, Rhode Island. I know few people who know as much about seafood as Maureen. This rather elegant recipe, always one of my favorites, is based on one of hers.

THE DEGLAZING LIQUID

⅔ cup white wine

⅔ cup homemade or low-sodium canned fish or chicken broth

1 large shallot, minced

1 teaspoon chopped fresh thyme

Grated zest of ½ lemon

3 or 4 parsley stems

THE FISH

2 pounds monkfish fillets (tail)

Salt and freshly ground black pepper

2 tablespoons extra-virgin olive oil

⅓ pound pancetta, finely chopped

About ½ cup flour

THE FINISH

2 tablespoons chopped fresh lemon verbena (optional)

⅔ cup heavy cream

Put all the ingredients for the deglazing liquid in a small saucepan, and simmer until it has reduced to about ½ cup. Strain and reserve.

Meanwhile, use a paring knife to remove the thin gray membrane that covers the fish. Cut away and discard any dark meat, and remove any bone fragments from the fish, then slice it into ¼-inch-thick round medallions. Season the fish on both sides with salt and pepper. Heat the olive oil and pancetta in a sauté pan, and when the pork has released its fat and crisped slightly, remove it with a slotted spoon and reserve.

Flour and sauté the fish, as in the Primary Recipe, for 1½ minutes per side, removing it when it is just shy of being fully cooked, and keep warm. Discard all the fat from the pan, and pour in the deglazing liquid, the pancetta, and lemon verbena. Bring to a simmer, and whisk in the cream in two stages, reducing it until the sauce is thickened. Slip the fish back into the pan along with any juices that have collected on the plate. Shake the pan gently as the fish heats and finishes cooking.

VARIATION: You can substitute small whole skinless fillets, such as sea bass, for the monkfish medallions. Or use halibut fillets or steaks cut into serving-size pieces.

Quick Fish Broth

MAKES ABOUT 1 1/2 CUPS

1 cup clam juice

2 cups water

2/3 cup dry white wine

1 large shallot, finely chopped

2 teaspoons chopped fresh thyme, or 1/2 teaspoon dried

1 small bay leaf

4 parsley stems

Put all the ingredients in a saucepan, and reduce to slightly less than half. Strain.

Spicy Bay Scallops with Capers and Lemon

CANESTRELLI PICCANTI CON CAPPERI E LIMONE

SERVES 4 OR 5

All coastal regions have seafood cycles that are celebrated by the inhabitants. Here in Nantucket, September marks the beginning of scallop season. It is not unusual to see scallop-harvesting paraphernalia hanging by the back door of most island homes. I'm not sure that the same situation exists in Venice, but it must, because the tiny, succulent scallops the Venetians use for this recipe are well worth the wading.

THE FISH

1¼ pounds bay scallops, or sea scallops
    cut into 3 slices

Salt and freshly ground black pepper

2 tablespoons extra-virgin olive oil

THE AROMATIC

⅓ cup pickled green *peperoncini,* cut
    into thin rings

THE DEGLAZING LIQUID

¼ cup lemon juice

THE FINISH

Deep-fried capers (page 318) (optional)
    or grated lemon zest, and 1 table-
    spoon chopped parsley

Season the scallops with salt and pepper. Heat the oil in a sauté pan, and when it is hot enough for the scallops to sizzle, slip them into the pan and cook, tossing often, for 1 minute. Stir the *peperoncini* into the pan, and cook for another minute or so, until the scallops are cooked. They will be just springy to the touch and no longer translucent inside. Remove the scallops with a slotted spoon, discard all but a tablespoon of fat if there is more, and deglaze the pan with the lemon juice as in the Primary Recipe. Garnish with the deep-fried capers or lemon zest and parsley.

VARIATION: Use the same recipe for peeled shrimp, or firm-fleshed fillets cut into narrow pieces.

VARIATION: **Sautéed Scallops with Wine and Parsley.** Instead of the *peperoncini,* toss one or two minced garlic cloves and 2 tablespoons chopped parsley into the pan, and deglaze with ¼ cup white wine or fish broth. Finish with a tablespoon of unsalted butter.

VARIATION: **Sautéed Cod Fillets with Peperoncini, Anchovies, and Capers.** This piquant dish is a specialty of the province of Istria, in the region of Venezia Giulia. Substitute 1¼ pound cod fillets for the scallops. Coat them with flour, sauté, and remove them when they are just shy of being cooked. Pour 2 tablespoons fresh oil into the pan, and add the *peperoncini* as above as well as ½ small minced onion, 2 finely minced garlic cloves, 2 tablespoons finely chopped parsley, two rinsed anchovies, and 2 tablespoons rinsed capers. Mash the anchovies into the pan so they dissolve. When the onion is just golden, deglaze the pan with ⅔ cup fish or chicken broth and 2 tablespoons lemon juice, and reduce by half. Return the fish to the pan until it is cooked.

VARIATION: **Shrimp Scampi.** Forget that this Italian-American favorite translates to "Shrimp, shrimp"; we know what it means—garlicky shrimp with lots of olive oil. For the fish use 1½ pounds of peeled large shrimp. Season them with salt and pepper and sauté them as above in ⅓ cup of extra-virgin olive oil. After one minute, toss 3 to 5 minced garlic cloves (it's up to you) into the pan. When the shrimp turn pink, carefully pour in ¼ cup dry white wine. Boil the wine until it has reduced to a few tablespoons, and then season the shrimp with ¼ cup chopped flat-leaf parsley and a tablespoon of fresh lemon juice.

Sautéed Shrimp with Fennel "Dust"

SCAMPI IN FINOCCHIO

SERVES 4

If you frequent trendy restaurants, then you are most likely in tune with the innovative descriptive terms that are constantly creeping into chef-speak. "Dust" refers to an ingredient that has been pulverized to a powder. Many "dusts" are what we used to know as ground spices, such as ground fennel, and are common on most supermarket shelves and a staple of Italian groceries. I have now taken to calling such things "dust" because I like the modern sound.

This recipe begins with making a quick shrimp broth that is used for deglazing. If you have bought shrimp without the shells or want to prepare a faster meal, deglaze with water instead.

GETTING READY
1½ pounds large shrimp, with their
 shells
1¾ cups water
Just a pinch of salt
THE FISH
The peeled shrimp from above
Salt and freshly ground black pepper
About ¼ cup ground fennel

About 2 tablespoons extra-virgin
 olive oil
THE DEGLAZING LIQUID
The ½ cup shrimp broth from above, or
 ⅔ cup water
1 to 2 tablespoons lemon juice
THE FINISH
2 tablespoons extra-virgin olive oil, or
 1 each of oil and unsalted butter

Rinse the shrimp well under cold running water. Peel them, and put the shells in a small saucepan. Pour in the water, season with the salt, and bring to a boil. Cover the pan, and simmer for 15 minutes, then strain, pushing firmly on the shells to extract as much flavor as possible. You should have about 1⅓ cups of delicately flavored broth. Measure out ½ cup for this recipe, and freeze the rest for use in another seafood dish.

Pat the shrimp dry, and season on both sides with salt and pepper. Spread the fennel out on a dish, and coat one side of the shrimp with it. I find that coating both sides gives too strong a flavor, but you might like it. Heat the 2 tablespoons oil in a sauté pan until hot enough for shrimp to sizzle. Put the pieces in the pan, fennel side down, and cook about 1 minute. Turn, and cook another minute, or until cooked through. Remove from the pan, deglaze with broth or water, and reduce the liquid by half. Stir in the lemon juice, cook a few seconds, and finish with the oil. Pour over the shrimp.

SUBSTITUTION: **Sautéed Fish Fillets with Fennel "Dust."** Small fillets of white fish can be substituted for the shrimp.

VARIATION: Fennel pollen (see page 286) can be used in place of the ground fennel.

FRYING

Frying is stovetop pan-cooking, similar to sautéing but using more fat. When Italians fry fish, they usually coat it first, either with breadcrumbs (*alla milanese*), or with beaten eggs, or with a light batter called *la pastella*. The coating helps to keep delicate fillets in one piece, seals in their moisture, and imparts a delicious crisp contrast to the soft fish flesh.

Coatings for Fried Fish

BREADCRUMBS

Dip the fish in flour, pat the excess off, then dip it in eggs beaten with a small amount of water, and finally in fine dried breadcrumbs. The breadcrumbs can be flavored with chopped herbs or grated cheese. A breadcrumb coating becomes quite crisp when fried.

BEATEN EGGS

Dip the fish in flour, then in eggs beaten with a small amount of water or milk. This is a delicate, light coating that gives a lovely golden color to fish.

BATTER

La pastella can be a simple batter of water or milk and flour, or it may contain eggs as well. Sometimes the fish is soaked in milk and then dipped in flour to produce a kind of semi-batter. Fish that is cooked this way has a golden, lightly crusty coating that clings airily to the fish. The batter-fried squid on page 323 is a sample of a simple *pastella*.

Finishes for Fried Fish

A good, healthy squeeze of lemon juice and a sprinkle of parsley are always a fitting finish for fried fish. If you want to build a sauce in the pan that cooked the fish, check the fat first. Since it has been at high temperature to cook the fish, it may be burned and unsuitable for building a sauce. Furthermore, there is the possibility that small amounts of the coating, especially breadcrumbs, will have slipped into the pan, and can ruin your sauce. If the fat is burned, either make the sauce (they are very quick to do) in a separate pan, or remove the oil from the pan that cooked the fish and wipe it out before adding sauce ingredients. The recipes suggest sauces, but keep in mind some of the tart sauces on page 301. The Lemon-Caper Sauce, Salsa Verde, and Sautéed Herb Sauce found there are some examples of piquant sauces that are good with fried fish.

Deep-Fried Capers

These crisp capers are a good, quick garnish, especially for fried, breaded fish.

½ cup capers, rinsed and patted dry
½ cup extra-virgin olive oil

Heat the oil in a small frying pan until it is very hot. Drop the capers into the oil. They should crackle. Fry 45 seconds, until golden and crisp, and then drain on paper towels.

Breaded Fillets of Sole with Sage Butter

FILETTI DI SOGLIOLA FRITTI CON SALSA DI SALVIA

SERVES 4

The northern Italian region of Piedmont serves a lovely trout sautéed in butter with sage leaves. It is a simple but memorable dish. On a day when I was unable to find fresh trout but the sole was remarkable and the garden overflowing with sage, I made this dish instead. In the recipe below, the fish is breaded, but you could make a more delicate dish by omitting the breadcrumbs and frying the sage with the fish. (See the *piemontese* variation below). If you don't have access to fresh sage—it is easy to grow, even in cold climates—do not use dried. Substitute another fresh herb, such as oregano, basil, chervil, or flat-leaf parsley.

Put the flour in a pie pan and mix in the salt and pepper. Break the eggs into a wide bowl, add 1 teaspoon of water, and beat until liquefied. Pour the breadcrumbs into another pie pan or onto a large sheet of wax paper. Season the fish on both sides with salt and pepper and piece by piece, dredge it on both sides in the flour, and then pat the excess away so only a thin veil remains. Immediately drop the fillets into the beaten eggs, and then, using tongs to keep your fingers clean, transfer the fish from the eggs to the breadcrumbs. Turn them over, and pat the crumbs well, so they adhere to the fish. Set the fillets on a wire rack in the refrigerator to settle for at least 10 minutes. The rest will help the crumbs adhere to the fish and prevent

THE COATING
About ⅓ cup flour
Salt and freshly ground black pepper
2 large eggs
About 1⅔ cups fine dried breadcrumbs (page 17)
THE FISH
2 pounds skinless sole fillets, rinsed and dried

THE SAUCE

6 tablespoons unsalted butter

About 16 small sage leaves, or
     larger ones torn in pieces

2 teaspoons lemon juice

FOR FRYING

4 tablespoons (¼ cup)
     unsalted butter

3 tablespoons extra-virgin
     olive oil

them from falling into the pan while the fish fries. They can rest for about 3 hours, but bring to room temperature before cooking.

Make the sauce before you begin to cook the fish—when you are frying, your attention should be on the fish, and once it is cooked it should be eaten as soon as possible, while the coating is at its crispiest. Melt the butter in a small saucepan, season with salt, pepper, sage, and lemon juice. Keep it warm while you cook the fish.

Put the butter and olive oil in a high-sided frying pan; there may be some spattering, and the high sides will contain the fat. The fat should be at about ½ inch deep in the pan; if it's not, add more butter and oil. The fat can be deeper, since, properly fried, the fish does not absorb it. Heat the fat until it is so hot that it bubbles gently around the fish when it is added—not quite smoking. If the fat is not hot enough to start the fish frying immediately, then the coating will absorb some of it, so it will be soggy and you'll be disappointed. Dip one corner of the fish into the pan to test the heat; you should hear it sizzle and see small bubbles around the edges. Cook only as many pieces at one time as will fit comfortably in the pan with "swimming" room around them. When the down side is nicely golden, turn the fish, and reduce the heat slightly to finish cooking; the total cooking time should be 2 to 4 minutes, depending on the thickness. A fork should pierce through the flesh easily. Remove the fish to paper towels to drain and keep warm while you are cooking the rest of the fish.

Serve with the warm sage sauce drizzled on top and lemon wedges on the side.

FOR SERVING

Lemon wedges

SUBSTITUTION: Use any small fish fillets, such as flounder, tilapia, orange roughy, or trout.

VARIATION: **Breaded and Fried Trout Fillets with Sage Butter.** For the *piemontese* variation, use small trout fillets, with or without the skin. Coat the fillets in flour as above, but do not use the egg or breadcrumbs. Heat 5 tablespoons of butter and 1 tablespoon of vegetable oil in a sauté pan, and when the fat is hot, drop in the sage leaves and cook for a minute; leave them in the pan, and sauté the fish with them, turning once, as above. When the fish is cooked, remove it from the pan, grabbing the sage with it. If the butter is not burned, you can add 2 or 3 tablespoons of lemon juice to it and pour it over the fish; otherwise, melt 4 tablespoons of butter separately and season with lemon juice, salt, and pepper. Pour over the fish, and serve.

VARIATION: **Breaded and Fried Fish Fillets with Sweet-and-Sour Sauce.** *In carpione, in saor,* and *in scapece* are various regional terms for food that is fried as above and then marinated in a delicious combination of sweet and sour flavors. It is a dish that I make often for summer buffets; it can be made ahead and served at room temperature. Make the sweet-and-sour sauce, *agrodolce,* for chicken cutlets on page 230. Bread the fish as above, and then fry it in all olive oil with no butter. Remove the fish to a large platter, and pour the *agrodolce* sauce over it. Marinate at least 3 hours or overnight before serving at room temperature. If you would like a more delicate finish, omit the egg and breadcrumbs and dip the fish only in flour before frying in olive oil. I like it both ways.

VARIATION: **Breaded and Fried Fish Fillets with Marinated Vegetables.** If your pantry holds the vegetable relish *sottaceti* (page 374), you can quickly make a splendidly tangy dish. Fry the fish as above, wipe out the pan, and stir about 1½ cups of the marinated vegetables into it. Stir around just until they are hot, and spoon some over each piece of fish. You can substitute other vegetables preserved in oil and vinegar, either your own or jarred ones imported from Italy.

Sicilian Fried Fillets with Orange Sauce

FILETTI FRITTI ALL'ARANCIA SICILIANA

SERVES 4

The common Sicilian orange is the blood orange, with its startling red flesh and juice. Less acidic than our juice oranges, it makes a lovely sauce if your sense of color is not disturbed by the unusual color contrast with the fish. Here the fish is coated with flour and eggs, but you could just as well coat it with breadcrumbs, or simply with flour.

THE SAUCE

2 small blood oranges or juice oranges

¼ cup dry white wine

3 tablespoons white-wine vinegar, or the juice of 1 small lemon

Salt and freshly ground black pepper

3 tablespoons unsalted butter

2 tablespoons chopped flat-leaf parsley

THE FISH

About 2 pounds sole or flounder fillets, rinsed and dried

Salt and freshly ground black pepper

THE COATING

½ cup flour

2 eggs beaten with 2 teaspoons water or milk

FOR FRYING

About ¾ cup vegetable oil

To make the sauce, grate the orange peel, being careful to avoid the bitter white pith. Blanch the grated rind for 1 minute in a small amount of boiling water, and then drain and dry it. (You can omit the peel if you are pressed for time.) Put the peel in a saucepan with the juice of the two oranges (about 1 cup) and the wine. Boil and reduce by half, then stir in the vinegar or lemon juice, salt, and pepper. Keep the sauce warm, and just before using, raise the heat and whisk in the butter and parsley.

Season the fish on both sides with salt and pepper. Dip in the flour, shake off the excess, then dip in the eggs. Fry in hot oil, 1 to 1½ minutes per side, and drain as in the Primary Recipe. Serve with the orange sauce.

SUBSTITUTION: Use other lean, delicate-flavored, thin fillets.

VARIATION: **Breaded and Fried Fish Fillets with Lemon-Caper Sauce.** Fry the fish as above, and serve with the Lemon-Caper Sauce on page 301.

Batter-Fried Squid with Peperoncini

CALAMARI FRITTI IN PASTELLA CON PEPERONCINI

SERVES 4 TO 6 AS A FIRST COURSE

You would be hard-pressed to find an Italian-American restaurant that does not offer fried calamari as an appetizer. Italian seafood antipasti are quite often piquant and to my taste, always a delicious introduction to dinner.

Traditionally, the milk and flour for a *pastella* are beaten together before the fish is added. Ron Suhanosky, chef at Nantucket's Sfoglia, uses this more modern technique of soaking the fish in milk and then dipping it in the flour. It makes a lighter coating that I prefer to the batter. The secret to tender squid is to cook it either a very brief time or a very long time— 2 minutes or 45; anything in between will produce fish too rubbery to be eaten. When frying, cook for the brief time.

GETTING READY
About 1½ pounds squid
3 tablespoons whole flat-leaf parsley
  leaves
½ lemon, cut into very thin slices
Enough milk to cover the squid
THE SAUCE
1 large garlic clove, thinly sliced
¼ cup extra-virgin olive oil

⅓ cup thinly sliced pickled green
  peperoncini
2 teaspoons lemon juice
THE FISH
Vegetable oil for frying
The squid from above
About 2 cups flour seasoned with salt
  and freshly ground black pepper

Clean the squid according to directions on page 273. Cut the squid bodies into ½-inch-wide rings, and the tentacles in two pieces. Put the pieces in a bowl, and scatter on the parsley and lemon slices. Pour on enough milk to cover the squid. Ron likes to let the fish soak in the milk for 2 hours or up to 24 hours, but I let them sit only long enough to make the sauce.

Make the sauce first. Gently cook the garlic in the olive oil in a small sauté pan until translucent. Stir in the *peperoncini* and lemon juice, and keep warm.

Meanwhile, pour enough oil into a heavy, deep saucepan (or deep-fryer) to reach a depth of 3 inches, and set the pan over moderately high heat. The oil temperature must be hot enough for the squid to fry quickly, about 375° F. Use a slotted spoon to remove the squid, parsley, and lemons from the milk, and toss them into the flour. Working with a few pieces at a time so as not to crowd or cool the oil, shake the squid, parsley, and lemons briefly in a strainer to remove excess flour, and drop them into the hot oil. Fry for about 2 minutes, until the coating is golden and the squid is cooked. Drain on paper towels, and keep warm.

When all the squid is cooked, put it on a warm serving plate and pour the sauce over it.

SUBSTITUTIONS: Octopus and cuttlefish can be substituted for the squid.

VARIATION: **Batter-Fried Sole with Green Sauce.** I borrow this from the French preparation known as *goujonettes*. Cut fillet of sole into small pieces, about 3 inches long and ½ inch thick, coat and fry them as above. I like the sole with *salsa verde* (page 302) as well as the piquant sauce here.

BRAISING

When fish is simmered partially covered by a liquid, which serves as a sauce for the finished dish, it is being braised. Braising usually indicates long cooking, and that is the case with sturdy creatures, such as squid, cuttlefish, and octopus. In the case of finfish, which will not cook very long, braising refers to the fact that the fish is not "drowned" in liquid, as in poaching, but is merely humid, *umido*. Recipes for braised finfish represent pure Italian home cooking and usually assume that you have caught a whole fish down the road.

The Aromatic Base

Onions, garlic, shallots, leeks, fennel, peppers, marjoram, sage, thyme, olives—the list is endless. Choose the base ingredients according to the flavor of the fish: delicate flavors for delicate fish, and robust tastes for fish with character. Because they will not cook very long once the fish is added, the aromatics for finfish recipes should be precooked long enough so they are tender and almost cooked by the time the fish goes into the pan. The chart on pages 343–49 in the vegetable chapter gives a guide to the time needed.

The Braising Liquid

There should be an acid in the braising liquid. Remember the last step in the Italian fish adage: the fish must swim in wine. Wine is one form of acid; others are lemon juice, vinegar, orange juice, tomatoes. Acid alone would be overwhelmingly puckering, so other liquids, such as fish broth, light chicken broth, or water, should be combined with it.

Braised Trout in the Style of Piedmont

TROTA IN UMIDO PIEMONTESE

SERVES 4

This is a favorite *piemontese* method of preparing the trout that fill their swift mountain streams. It is quite delicious with any of the substitutions listed below, or with most fish you yourself might snag. I say "most" because braising is best suited to whole fish, with their heads and tails, or to medium-size firm-fleshed fillets with their skin attached, or to large firm-fleshed, skinned fillets or steaks.

GETTING READY

¼ cup raisins, preferably golden

THE AROMATICS

3 tablespoons extra-virgin olive oil

1 medium onion, sliced

2 medium garlic cloves, thinly sliced

1 celery stalk, finely chopped

2 sprigs rosemary, or 6 to 8 fresh sage leaves

Salt and freshly ground black pepper

Soak the raisins in warm water to cover for 15 minutes, then drain. Squeeze them gently to remove the excess water.

Choose a large, straight-sided sauté pan or casserole that is 2 to 3 inches deep and large enough to hold the fish in one layer; or use two pans. Do not use aluminum or other reactive material to braise the fish, since there is acid in the braising liquid. I prefer enamel-coated cast iron.

Warm the oil in the sauté pan; it should just coat the entire bottom of the pan. Stir the aromatics into the warming oil, and cook gently so they soften slowly, about 10 minutes.

Meanwhile, look over the fish flesh carefully. Trout always seems to have pinbones left behind; remove them with needle-nose pliers or tweezers. Season the fish inside and out with salt and pepper. When the aromatics are cooked, stir in the lemon rind and raisins and cook for 30 seconds, stirring the ingredients together.

Lay the fish on top, then pour in the vinegar and enough broth to come a third of the way up the sides of the fish; add water if necessary. Bring the liquid to a quick boil, then reduce the heat, and cover the pan first with a sheet of parchment or wax paper, so it touches the top of the fish, and then the pan's lid. Simmer gently for 10 to 15 minutes, until the tip of a small knife easily pierces the fish and the flesh is no longer translucent. Turn the fish once as it cooks.

Carefully transfer the fish to a serving platter, and remove the skin if you wish; trout skin can get rubbery when it braises. The braising juices should be thick enough to coat the fish; if they are not, boil them down over high heat, and then spoon them over the fish.

SUBSTITUTION: The recipe is best with lean or oily whole fish, such as small perch, whiting, or butterfish, or with medium to large fillets with skin attached, or with thick firm-fleshed steaks.

VARIATION: **Oven-Braised Fish.** Fish can be braised in a 375° F oven as well as on the top of the stove. If your sauté pan is ovenproof, lay the fish on top of the cooked aromatics as above, cover with parchment or wax paper, top with the lid, and transfer to the preheated oven. Or cook the aromatics, spread them out in a baking dish just large enough to hold the fish, and put the fish on top. The fish will take slightly longer in the oven.

THE FISH

2 pounds (2 medium or 4 small) whole boneless trout, with heads and tails, rinsed and dried

Salt and freshly ground black pepper

THE BRAISING LIQUID AND INGREDIENTS

Grated rind of 1 small lemon

The drained raisins from above

3 tablespoons red- or white-wine vinegar

About 1¼ cups fish or light chicken broth

Braised Striped Bass with Tomatoes

PESCE ARROSTO CON POMODORI

SERVES 4

One of the great boons of living so near the ocean is having many friends who love to fish. In my area of the world, a summer's early-morning call from Scooter, Pierre, or Ken usually means that he has caught more striped bass than he can eat, and we are ever so grateful for his luck. Recipes for cooking fish steaks and fillets in tomatoes exist all over Italy. This was Nonna's way. Unlike the whole fish in the Primary Recipe, the fish here is browned lightly before braising, to give it color. If your liquid ingredients are thin, such as broth and wine, flour the fish before sautéing; it will help thicken the pan juices.

THE FISH

About 2 pounds striped-bass fillets or halibut steaks, in 4 pieces, rinsed and dried

Salt and freshly ground black pepper

Extra-virgin olive oil

THE AROMATICS

3 tablespoons extra-virgin olive oil

3 large cloves garlic, thinly sliced

1 medium yellow onion, thinly sliced

Salt

Pinch hot red-pepper flakes

⅓ cup chopped flat-leaf parsley, or 1 teaspoon dried oregano

THE BRAISING LIQUID

3 tablespoons dry white or red wine

1½ cups fresh or canned peeled and coarsely chopped tomatoes, with juices

Season both sides of the fish with salt and pepper. Pour enough oil into a sauté pan to cover the bottom by ⅛ inch, and place it over moderate heat. When the oil is hot, put the fish in the pan, in batches if necessary, and brown lightly on each side, about 1 minute per side. Remove it with a slotted spatula, and set aside.

Add enough oil to the pan to make about 3 tablespoons, and put in the garlic, onion, salt, and red pepper. Cook slowly until completely softened but not browned, and then stir in the parsley and cook for 30 seconds. Put the fish on top of the aromatics, pour in the wine and tomatoes, bring to a quick boil, then reduce the heat, cover, and braise, turning once as in the Primary Recipe, allowing 15 to 20 minutes, or until a fork easily pierces the fish and the flesh is no longer translucent. If the pan juices are too thin to be a sauce, remove the fish, and boil the tomatoes down until they thicken.

SUBSTITUTION: Use any thick, firm fish steak or fillet, such as halibut, cod, or monkfish.

VARIATION: **Striped Bass Braised in Tomato Sauce.** If you have 2 cups of *marinara* sauce on hand, you can omit the aromatics, brown the fish as above, and then pour in the sauce and the wine, season with a little hot pepper and the parsley or oregano, and braise as above.

VARIATION: **Striped Bass Braised with Onions, Tomatoes, and Cream.** This variation of the tomato-sauce braise produces a richer dish. Do not brown the fish first. Increase the onions in the aromatics to two large, thinly sliced ones. Cook them, without the garlic and hot pepper, in 3 tablespoons of butter and 1 tablespoon of vegetable oil until completely softened; use parsley or chervil to season. Tuck in the fish, and use ¾ cup of chopped fresh tomatoes—peeled, seeded, and juiced—and 3 tablespoons of dry white wine. Braise as above, and when the fish is cooked, remove it from the pan, leaving the onions and tomatoes behind. Turn the heat to high, and pour in ½ cup of heavy cream. Reduce it until it is thickened enough to coat the onions and tomatoes. Spoon the vegetables over the fish.

VARIATION: **Tuna or Swordfish Steaks Braised with Peppers.** Peppers make a flavorful bed, especially for thick—at least 1¼-inch—swordfish and tuna steaks. Season, brown, and remove the fish as in the Primary Recipe. Cook one sliced medium onion and three chopped garlic cloves in 3 tablespoons of olive oil until they are golden. Stir in two large sweet peppers (a red and a yellow one would be nice) that have been cleaned and cut into ¼-inch strips. Cover the pan, and cook slowly until they are very tender, about 15 minutes. Season with ¼ cup each parsley and basil leaves. Use three large, fresh tomatoes, peeled and chopped, with their juices, and 3 tablespoons of wine or balsamic vinegar for the braising ingredients. Cover and braise as above, watching the pan carefully; if it gets dry, add small amounts of warm water.

VARIATION: **Shrimp Fra Diavolo.** The "brother Devil" of this popular Italian-American dish refers to the heat provided by a generous amount of hot pepper flakes. Cook the aromatics above, using the oregano and about ½ teaspoon of red pepper flakes—more or less depending on how hot a dish you want. Pour the braising liquids into the pan and simmer for 15 minutes before adding 1½ to 2 pounds of peeled large shrimp. Simmer for about 4 minutes or until the shrimp are cooked through. Some Italian-Americans serve this over thin spaghetti.

Braised Squid with Peas

CALAMARI IN UMIDO CON PISELLI

SERVES 4

The steps for braising squid are the same as those in the Primary Recipe, except that there is a greater volume of braising liquid, and the squid goes into the pan after the aromatics. Squid is a strong fish and can be stirred around the pan to sauté without worry of its breaking into pieces, as would finfish. Either butter or oil can be used to begin the dish; the butter will give a richer flavor.

THE AROMATICS

4 tablespoons extra-virgin olive oil or
  unsalted butter

4 medium garlic cloves, minced

1 small onion, minced

3 tablespoons each chopped fresh flat-
  leaf parsley and basil

THE FISH

2 pounds squid, untrimmed weight

Salt and freshly ground black pepper

THE BRAISING LIQUID

½ cup dry white wine

2 cups peeled, seeded tomatoes, finely
  chopped or passed through a food
  mill, with their juices

THE VEGETABLE

2 cups fresh peas (shelled measure), or 2
  cups frozen tender tiny peas

Cook the aromatics as in the Primary Recipe. Meanwhile, clean the squid according to directions on page 273, wash and dry well, and then cut the bodies into ½-inch-wide rings. Cut large tentacles in three pieces, small ones in half. Season with salt and pepper.

When the aromatics are tender, put the squid in the pan and sauté for 2 or 3 minutes, until it becomes opaque. Pour in the wine, reduce by half, and add enough tomatoes just to barely reach the top of the squid. Bring to a quick simmer, reduce the heat, season with salt and pepper, and cover the pan. Braise for 40 minutes, then add fresh peas to the pan (frozen peas should be added nearer the end) and cook another 10 or 15 minutes, until squid is tender and peas are cooked.

SUBSTITUTION: Cuttlefish, if you can find it, can be cleaned and cooked the same way. Remove the ink sac if the fishmonger has not done so.

VARIATION: **Neapolitan Braised Squid with Raisins and Pine Nuts.** For Neapolitan-style braised squid, use olive oil, two minced onions, two minced garlic cloves, 1 teaspoon of fresh oregano or ¼ teaspoon dried, and a half or whole minced small hot red pepper (or ¼ to ½ teaspoon of dried red-pepper flakes) for the aromatics. Use a tablespoon of red-wine vinegar in place of the wine (do not reduce), and use the tomatoes as above. Omit the peas, and add 2 tablespoons each of raisins (softened in water for 15 minutes and squeezed dry) and pine nuts to the pan after 40 minutes of cooking. Stir a generous amount of chopped parsley into the finished dish.

Stuffed Squid in Malvasia Wine

CALAMARI RIPIENI AI MALVASIA

SERVES 5 TO 6

I first had this dish at a tiny seafood restaurant (I can't recall the name) on the volcanic island of Lipari, off the coast of Sicily. It was a simple place—the dining room was a deck that sat out over the water. That and the kitchen were all there was, unless you count the tiny armada of fishing boats tied just outside. The night I was there, a great hullabaloo occurred in those boats and in the kitchen, when one of the fishermen displayed his day's booty— a giant, surely 2½-foot-long, blue lobster. It was a female, and the mass of roe that clung to her was like nothing I had ever seen. She was returned to the water to birth her young, and we ate this stuffed and braised squid. It was delicious, but I have always wondered what that blue lobster would have tasted like.

The cook braised the fish in local Malvasia di Lipari, a golden, highly aromatic and flavorful sweet wine, which gives the dish a special, delicious finesse. If you cannot find it, see Gasbarro's on page 29, or ask your wine store for a similar white wine.

MAKING AHEAD

1 recipe braised sweet-and-sour red
   onions (page 377, variation)

THE STUFFING

1¾ pounds squid (about 15 bodies with
   tentacles), cleaned (page 273)

2 tablespoons extra-virgin olive oil

3 garlic cloves, minced

3 tablespoons pine nuts

5 tablespoons finely chopped flat-leaf
   parsley

Salt and freshly ground black pepper

½ cup fresh dry breadcrumbs (page 17)

⅔ cup grated pecorino cheese

THE FISH

2 tablespoons extra-virgin olive oil

The readied squid from above

THE VEGETABLES

The red onions from above

THE LIQUID

½ cup Malvasia wine

Set the squid bodies aside, and chop the tentacles and body flaps into small pieces. Heat the olive oil with the garlic in a sauté pan until the garlic is golden, add the pine nuts and chopped squid, and sauté over low heat, stirring, for 2 minutes. Season with the parsley, salt, and pepper, turn off the heat, and stir in the breadcrumbs and cheese.

Divide the filling evenly among the squid bodies, stuffing it inside and leaving about ½ inch of space at the top for the stuffing to expand. Secure the tops closed with a toothpick.

Heat 2 tablespoons of olive oil in a sauté pan large enough to hold the squid bodies in one layer. When the oil is hot enough for the squid to sizzle, pat the bodies dry and slip them into the pan. Turn the bodies as they brown, and when they are lightly colored on all sides, stir in the onions and pour in the wine. Bring to a quick boil, then reduce the heat, cover the pan, and simmer the fish gently for 45 minutes, or until the squid is tender. Discard the toothpicks, and cut each squid into 1-inch-thick slices. Serve warm with the onions spooned on top.

POACHING

Like braising, poaching is cooking fish in liquid, but in this case the fish is totally submerged. The Italian word *affogato* also means to be drowned, so it is easy to get the picture.

Poaching is not boiling. That is a crucial point to keep in mind. I remember a time when a young chef invited me to view his kitchen and the dinner he was preparing for an event at which I was a guest. The first course was to be poached scallops, and I watched sadly as the lovely little creatures were being cruelly shriveled to inedible nuggets by boiling milk. Boiling will toughen firm-fleshed fish and break flaky ones apart. The poaching temperature should not go above 205° F; there will be just the gentlest of rippling on the surface—a tremor, not an eruption.

The Poaching Liquid

Italians poach fish primarily in aromatic, salted, and acidulated water (*court bouillon* in French), in olive oil, or in light tomato sauces. The soups in Chapter 2 with whole pieces of fish and tomato broth are examples of poaching fish in tomato sauce.

Water is acidulated by adding wine, lemon juice, or vinegar or a combination of two or all three. For a general poaching liquid, I use a proportion of 1 cup of dry white wine or ¼ cup of vinegar or lemon juice for each quart of water; or 1 cup of wine *and* 2 tablespoons of vinegar or lemon juice. You can use equal portions of wine and water for a high-acid poaching liquid that will produce a firmer fish but will also leave the flavor of the wine—not a shortcoming when that is what you want. In some parts of Italy, they use red wine in place of the white for whole dark-fleshed fish such as trout. The common aromatics are onions, carrot, celery, and such herbs and seasonings as thyme, bay leaf, parsley, salt, and pepper. Other seasonings, such as fennel seed, rosemary, and oregano, can be used, but their taste will flavor the fish; again, acceptable when that is what you are looking for. Once used, the liquid can be strained and refrigerated for 3 days, or frozen for months, and used in fish soups or to poach fish again. Always boil it to begin the second time around, to kill any bacteria.

Poached Cod with Green Sauce

MERLUZZO AFFOGATO CON SALSA VERDE

SERVES 4

Fish that is poached this way can be served hot, cold, or at room temperature. Either way, unless you are strongly into minimalism, the fish should have a sauce, even a simple one. My favorite is Green Sauce (*salsa verde*), which I serve with cod whether it is hot or cold.

MAKING AHEAD

One recipe for Green Sauce
(page 302)

THE POACHING LIQUID

2 medium onions, peeled and
thinly sliced

2 medium carrots, peeled and
cut into large pieces

1 medium celery stalk with
tops, cut into large pieces

2 cups dry white wine

2 quarts water

2 tablespoons white-wine
vinegar

1 bay leaf

8 to 10 parsley stems

5 whole black peppercorns,
or 1 teaspoon ground

1½ teaspoons salt

Put all the poaching-liquid ingredients in a large, deep pan, wide enough to hold the fish in one layer. You need enough liquid to cover the fish totally; if you need more, increase the ingredients proportionately. Bring the liquid to a boil, and simmer for 20 minutes.

With the liquid still visibly bubbling, gently slip the fish into the pan; immediately adjust the heat so the liquid is just trembling. The initial high heat is necessary to firm and seal the outside flesh, but from this point on it should never boil.

To serve the fish hot, cover the pan and poach until fully cooked—8 to 12 minutes, depending on its size. A fork or knife tip should pierce the fish easily. Remove the fish with large slotted spatulas, and put on a serving platter. Cut the fish into pieces, and serve with the sauce.

To serve the fish cold, put it in the boiling liquid, simmer for 3 minutes, then cover the pan and turn off the heat. Let the fish cool in the liquid before removing it and chilling in the refrigerator 2 hours or overnight. Cut into pieces, and serve with *salsa verde*.

SUBSTITUTION: Use other firm-fleshed fillets or steaks. Check steaks and small fillets after about 5 minutes of poaching. If you are poaching a whole fish with the skin on, cool the poaching liquid to room temperature after it has simmered 20 minutes, add the fish to the cooled liquid, then bring to a simmer and poach. This will prevent the skin from bursting.

VARIATION: **Poached Halibut with Fennel Seeds.** Substitute a large piece of halibut for the cod. Add to the poaching liquid 1 tablespoon of fennel seed. Make the Lemon-Caper Sauce with cooked onions on page 301, but substitute 1 tablespoon of fennel seed for the capers.

VARIATION: **Poached Tuna Steak Salad with Pickled Red Pepper Sauce.** Make the Pickled Red Pepper Sauce on page 301. Poach 2 pounds of skinless tuna steaks, 1½ to 2 inches thick, as in the instructions above for fish served cold. Cut the cooled fish into ¼-inch-thick slices and serve napped with the sauce, or cut it into 1-inch chunks, toss with the sauce, and serve atop a bed of leafy greens.

VARIATION: **Poached Halibut or Salmon with Fennel Seed—Orange Sauce.** Make the Sicilian orange sauce on page 322, adding 2 teaspoons of fennel seed to the pan with the orange juice. Add 1 tablespoon of fennel seed to the poaching

THE FISH
2 pounds skinless and boneless codfish fillets (1 or 2 large fillets)

liquid, and poach 2 pounds of halibut fillets or salmon fillets as in the instructions above for serving poached fish hot. The fillets will cook in 6 to 9 minutes, depending on their size. Remove them immediately with a slotted spatula, and serve with the warm orange-fennel sauce.

VARIATION: **Poached Shrimp with Green Sauce.** Poached shrimp served in *salsa verde* is not only delicious but pretty to look at. Serve it cold or at room temperature as an antipasto or light lunch with wilted greens or fennel braised in olive oil. Make a poaching liquid with 2 quarts of water and ¼ cup of lemon juice and the aromatics in the Primary Recipe. Simmer it for 20 minutes, and then let it cool. Shrimp should not be added to a hot poaching liquid or they will toughen. Put 2 pounds of medium shrimp in their shells into the cooled liquid, bring to a boil, and simmer 3 minutes, or until the shrimp turn pink and their tails begin to curl. Remove, and rinse in cold water so they are comfortable to peel. Alternatively you can put the shrimp in the cooled poaching liquid, bring to a boil, immediately turn off the heat, and let the shrimp cool in the broth—then peel.

> If we lavished as much love on the cooking of fish as
> we do on the catching, we would do very well indeed.
> —COOKBOOK AUTHOR JEAN ANDERSON

Trout Poached in Oil
with Capers

TROTA AFFOGATA CON CAPPERI

SERVES 6 TO 8 AS AN ANTIPASTO OR 4 AS A MAIN COURSE

Chances are, if you see lovely pieces of cooked fish bathing in olive oil on an antipasto table in Italy, they were cooked this way. Serve the fish at room temperature for a first course or lunch, with plenty of good bread to dip in the oil.

THE FISH

4 rainbow trout, with skin, but with
    heads, tails, and backbones removed

Salt and freshly ground black pepper

THE POACHING OIL

Extra-virgin olive oil

1 small lemon, thinly sliced

20 small whole sage leaves

⅓ to ½ cup capers, rinsed

¼ teaspoon hot red-pepper flakes

FOR SERVING

¼ cup chopped flat-leaf parsley

Cut each fish into two fillets, and rinse and pat dry. Check for pinbones, and remove with needle-nose pliers or tweezers. Season with salt and pepper. Choose a sauté pan large enough to hold all the fish in one layer, or use two pans. Pour in enough oil to come ½ inch up the sides of the pan. Put the fillets in the oil, skin side down, and scatter on all the other poaching ingredients. Turn the heat on low, so the oil becomes very warm, barely shimmering but not hot enough to fry the fish; definitely do not let it boil. Poach for 5 to 8 minutes, or until the fish just turns white and is easily pierced with a fork. Turn off the heat, and let the fish cool in the oil. Serve each piece with some of the oil, lemons, and capers spooned on top. Garnish with chopped fresh parsley.

SUBSTITUTION: Use any small to medium lean or oily fish fillet, with or without the skin.

VARIATION: To serve the fish hot for dinner, use 2 pounds of skinless lean fish fillets such as halibut, scrod, or cod, no more than 1 inch thick. Poach them in the oil as above until they are fully cooked, allowing about 20 to 25 minutes. Remove the fish from the oil as soon as they are fully cooked, and serve warm with a little of the oil, lemons, and capers as above. I sometimes substitute golden raisins for the capers.

CHAPTER 6

Vegetables, Frittatas, Salads

I have always been fascinated by the Italian reverence for vegetables. The profusion of produce is remarkable; the riot of colors at the outdoor markets is breathtaking. In restaurants, enraptured diners make entire meals of plate-size porcini mushrooms, twirl bowlfuls of long buttery strands of monk's beard, and savor mounds of tiny garlicky artichokes. Waiters spin off long lists of vegetable antipasti, main courses, and *contorni* (side dishes). Vegetables are serious business.

Such veneration for vegetables would hardly be warranted were the vegetables not deserving. Many Italians prefer to grow their own whenever possible, and when it is not, they choose with great care from a trusted greengrocer. My grandparents in America grew what they could on a tiny patch of city land, and for all else they relied on the pushcart. Nonna was not an easy sell. She purposely approached the cart with a suspicious look. Her practiced hands would pinch garlic, squeeze tomatoes, slide over the skin of eggplant and zucchini, and raise peppers to her nose for a determining sniff. She was extremely particular, and, to this young girl holding on to her skirt, sometimes embarrassingly skeptical.

If you live in a climate with long and numerous growing seasons, as do most Italians, by all means follow the cycles and choose what the nearest farmer has just harvested. Elsewhere you must learn to be selective. The chart on pages 343–49 and notes throughout this chapter give you details on choosing produce.

With all this care going into the selection of vegetables, Italians don't want to muck them up. Consequently, the majority of recipes for vegetables are fairly simple and straightforward. There are delicious, elaborate exceptions, especially in the form of vegetable appetizers, main courses, and what the Italians call *intermezzi* (in-between courses). You'll find good ideas there for fine vegetarian meals.

Serving Size

With the exception of leafy vegetables (see page 342), a pound to a pound and a quarter of vegetables will serve 3 to 4 people, depending on what else is served and the diner's appetite. Some vegetables undergo a great deal of trimming before they are cooked, so you will need to buy as much as 2 pounds to wind up with the right amount. I give you the weight as a guide, but what I do is pick up a fistful of loose vegetables for every diner, mentally discarding stems and pods, or visually dividing heads into pieces. Remember, a little more or less in a recipe is not its ruination.

Italian Vegetable Names

VERDURE: The general term used for all vegetables. It comes from the root *vert-,* meaning "green."

CONTORNO (CONTORNI): Literally meaning "contour," it indicates vegetables that accompany a main course. The implication is that they round out the meal.

LEGUME (LEGUMI): Vegetables that grow in pods, such as peas, beans, lentils.

Boiling/Steaming

BOLLIRE/AL VAPORE

Let the vegetables do the work! If you have chosen the pick of the crop, they will have superb flavor and texture. Boiling and steaming are two methods that will maintain their personalities with little effort on your part. Once they are cooked, you need do no more than add a dab of butter or a drizzle of olive oil and a bit of lemon juice. The flavored butters on page 240 are delicious with vegetables. Toss with the hot vegetables until the butter melts.

Another common way to finish boiled vegetables is to sauté them. (See the section on sautéing beginning on page 378.) In this instance, the vegetables are boiled only until they are partially cooked. "Parboiling" or "blanching," as the method is called, is used to begin the cooking for a vegetable that will then be sautéed, roasted, or braised, thereby reducing the time of the secondary cooking. Vegetables are also blanched to facilitate peeling, as with small onions, or, in the case of bitter or sharp vegetables such as broccoli rabe, to tame the sharpness.

Buying, Trimming, Boiling, and Steaming Vegetables

General Rules

The directions for preparing and boiling or steaming each vegetable are in the chart on pages 343–49. Some general rules to keep in mind:

- The water for boiling vegetables should be salted, so that the vegetable's natural salt, which holds in its flavor, will remain in the vegetable and not seep out into the water.
- The water for steamed vegetables should not come into contact with the steamer. Sprinkle salt on the vegetables.
- Recipes will indicate whether or not you should peel the vegetable. If it says to peel, I really mean it, since the vegetable's dark outer layers are tougher than the centers or tips, and by the time the skin has become tender the rest will be mush. A vegetable peeler or a small paring knife will accomplish the task.
- Vegetables that grow aboveground, such as green beans, asparagus, or peas, should not be covered as they cook, since they will lose their color. Underground growers, like carrots and beets, can be covered.

I have given you directions for boiling and steaming whenever that is a technique I use for that vegetable. When blanching or parboiling is the only method I use, that is the only timing given. If a vegetable is not listed, that means I never cook it by this method; you will find it elsewhere in the chapter. Begin timing once the water returns to a boil.

Cooking Leafy Greens

Not all greens will render the same amount when they are cooked. Therefore, you will have to adjust the volume of raw greens according to the variety and how many people you are feeding.

FOR 4 PEOPLE

Use about 1½ pounds	Use about 2 pounds	Use about 2½ pounds
Collard greens	Swiss chard	Spinach
Kale	Beet greens	Mizuna
	Escarole	Arugula
		Mesclun

Holding Boiled Vegetables

Boiled and steamed vegetables can be dressed and eaten at once, or cooled and held for use later, when they can be reheated in a pan with butter or oil and seasonings or finished by roasting or sautéing. Once vegetables are boiled to the point you want, drain at once, either by emptying the pan into a colander in the sink or by scooping the vegetables out of the water with a strainer or slotted spoon. Immediately plunge the drained vegetables into a bowl of ice water; swish them around just until they have cooled, and then drain and dry them well. Don't leave them sitting in the cold water or they will become waterlogged. Keep the cooled vegetables wrapped loosely in a kitchen towel until you are ready to use them. Do not wrap green vegetables tightly or place them in a tightly closed plastic bag, because they will lose their color. The vegetables will hold for several hours prior to finishing.

VEGETABLE	LOOK FOR	PREPARATION AND COOKING	TIMING
Asparagus	The stalks should be ramrod-straight and bright green. Their ends should be moist and the tips should be green and firmly closed.	Holding the top of the stalk in one hand and the bottom in the other, gently bend the asparagus until it snaps. Discard the broken stalk end, which will be too tough to use. Unless the remaining stalks are pencil-thin, peel them up to the tips. **BOILING:** Bring enough water to boil in a large frying pan just to cover the vegetable when it is laid flat in the pan in no more than two layers. Salt the water, slip in the asparagus, and boil gently. **STEAMING:** Cut so the spears lie flat in the steamer, and season with salt.	**BOILED:** 3 to 10 minutes, depending on thickness **STEAMED:** 5 to 15 minutes, depending on thickness The stalks are completely cooked when the tip of a paring knife easily pierces the thickest part. Hold an asparagus upright by the stem end; it should bend slightly.

VEGETABLE	LOOK FOR	PREPARATION AND COOKING	TIMING
Beets	The beets should be firm and unblemished. Their greens should look fresh and crisp.	Leave the root end attached, and cut the tops so 1 inch remains attached to the beet. This will prevent the color of the beets from seeping out into the water. Wash well in cold water, but do not peel. BOILING: Drop beets into a large pot of boiling salted water.	BOILED: Small beets—15 minutes Medium beets—20 to 25 minutes Large beets—35 to 40 minutes Beets are cooked when a cake tester or skewer can pierce them easily. Drain, and peel when they are cool.
Broccoli	Broccoli heads should be bright green and the stalks firm; ignore those with yellow spots and flabby stalks.	Cut into spears, or divide into stalks and flowerets. Cut or break the tops from the stalks, and divide them into bite-size pieces. Peel the stalks (discard a slice from the root end), and cut them into pieces about the size of the flowerets. BOILING: Bring a large pan of water to a rapid boil, add salt, and pour in the stalks; boil 3 to 4 minutes, then add the flowerets; or boil each separately until done. STEAMING: Put the stalks in the bottom of the basket, steam about 8 minutes, then cover with the flowerets. Season each layer with salt.	BOILED: Stems—6 to 10 minutes Flowerets—3 to 8 minutes, depending on size STEAMED: Stems—15 to 20 minutes Flowerets—10 to 15 minutes Broccoli is cooked when it is tender with just the slightest hint of crispness. There should be no hint of a grassy taste.

VEGETABLE	LOOK FOR	PREPARATION AND COOKING	TIMING
Broccoli Rabe	Broccoli rabe should be bright green, with no yellowing buds. Choose bunches that have a good number of small bud clusters attached.	The stems of rabe are tough and stringy and should be peeled. Use a paring knife to destring the stems in the same way you would with celery. Cut into pieces as desired. Blanch to remove excess bitterness by dropping into large amount of boiling salted water.	Blanch 2 minutes to remove bitterness
Carrots	Carrots should be firm and deeply colored; flabby ones are woody and tasteless. Avoid those that are split.	Peel the carrots, and trim off both ends. Cut into whatever shape is called for. BOILING: Boil the carrots whole and then cut into desired size, or cut first and then boil. STEAMING: Cut carrots into desired shape, and lay evenly in a steamer; season with salt.	BOILING: Matchsticks and slices up to $\frac{1}{2}$ inch thick—4 to 6 minutes Quartered large carrots— 7 to 10 minutes Whole—10 to 12 minutes, depending on thickness STEAMING: 15 to 35 minutes, depending on size The tip of a knife should easily pierce the pieces, with a slight resistance at the center.

VEGETABLE	LOOK FOR	PREPARATION AND COOKING	TIMING
Cauliflower	Cauliflower heads should be firm and white and have no withering brown spots. The cradle of green should be bright green.	Although cauliflower can be broken into tops and stalks like the broccoli above, I prefer to cook it whole and cut the cooked cauliflower into pieces. Cut into the bottom of the head to remove the core, and then plunge a narrow paring knife into the core, about 2 inches into the stalk, in the shape of a cross. This will hasten the cooking. BOILING: Submerge the head, top side down, in a large pan of boiling salted water. A small squeeze of lemon juice will keep the cauliflower white. STEAMING: Put in a steamer, head side down, and season with salt.	BOILED: 10 to 15 minutes STEAMED: 30 to 45 minutes The tip of a knife should pierce the stem easily, with a slight bit of resistance at the center.
Fresh Fava Beans	Look for bright-green pods, the smaller the better, but most that arrive at the supermarket are the fat, mature ones. Select those that have a number of beans inside.	Split the shell to release the beans. The skin needs to be removed. If it does not slip off easily, blanch in boiling water for 1 minute, drain, and drop into ice water. Use your thumbnail to peel off the skin. Or cook the beans fully in the boiling water and then peel.	BOILED: 5 to 10 minutes, depending on size They should be tender but hold their shape and have a bit of crunch at the center.

VEGETABLE	LOOK FOR	PREPARATION AND COOKING	TIMING
Fennel	Fennel should have a shiny, firm, crisp appearance even though there may be some brown spots on the outer layers. The feathery tops should be perky.	Trim off the feathery tops, discard bruised outer leaves, and cut bulbs in half or in quarters, depending on how large they are. Remove the small knob and the hard inner core from the root end. Soak the fennel in cold water for 20 minutes to wash and crisp before cooking. Drop into large amount of boiling, salted water.	BOILED: 8 to 15 minutes Pierce with a skewer to test if it is tender with a bit of resistance at the center.
Green Beans	Whenever possible, buy young, thin bright-green beans. They are a treat. Larger ones are fine if they have no brown spotting or decaying ends.	Thanks to modern agricultural technology, the strings are gone, and young, thin beans need no trimming. With thicker and older beans, I cut away the ends. BOILING: Drop the washed beans into a large pan of rapidly boiling salted water. STEAMING: Distribute them evenly in a steamer, season with salt; turn over from time to time as they cook.	BOILED: Thin—5 to 7 minutes Thick—8 to 12 minutes STEAMED: Thin—8 to 10 minutes Thick—12 to 20 minutes Test by biting into one. It should be tender with just the slightest hint of crunch. Undercooked beans will taste "grassy."

VEGETABLE	LOOK FOR	PREPARATION AND COOKING	TIMING
Leafy Greens (see page 342 for individual names)	Greens should have a bright, crisp look and feel. Avoid leaves that are wilted or wet.	To "wilt" greens—a process somewhere between boiling and steaming—trim off any tough stems or remove leaves from center core. Fill the sink with lukewarm water, submerge the greens, swish them around, and then lift them out. Rinse the sink, and repeat 2 or 3 more times. Don't skimp on the washing; even a residual grain of sand can spoil a dish. Shake the washed greens vigorously, and put them in a large saucepan with only the water clinging to them. Season with salt, cover the pan, and cook just until they have wilted.	Greens are ready to be eaten when they have completely wilted, all water has evaporated, and they are tender. To continue cooking in another manner, remove the greens when they are just wilted and squeeze them completely dry in a kitchen towel.
Small Boiling Onions	Look them over carefully, for signs of rotting beneath their papery coats. Squeeze them; they should be firm.	Blanch in order to facilitate peeling. With the tip of a small paring knife, make two cross-cuts in the root ends. Drop into boiling salted water. Remove and plunge into cold water, then drain and pat dry. Slip off the skins.	Boil 1 minute

VEGETABLE	LOOK FOR	PREPARATION AND COOKING	TIMING
Potatoes	Potatoes should be firm, unblemished, and unsprouting.	Waxy potatoes (Red Bliss, new potatoes, Yukon Gold) can be boiled in their well-washed skins and then peeled or not, depending on the recipe; russets and all-purpose can be peeled and then boiled. Potatoes should be started in cold water, since dropping them into rapidly boiling water can cause them to break apart. Put them in a saucepan large enough for them to move about, and cover them by 1 inch with cold water. Add salt and bring to a boil. If they are to be mashed, remove a cup or so of the boiling water before draining; keep it nearby to loosen the potatoes if they become too stiff.	Whole unpeeled potatoes or peeled potatoes cut into large chunks—12 to 40 minutes, depending on size. Pierce the potatoes with a sharp paring knife or a cake tester. They should be tender through to the center.

Boiled Asparagus with Butter and Parmesan Cheese

ASPARAGI CON BURRO E PARMIGIANO

SERVES 4 OR 5

A Parmesan finish makes any simple vegetable seem elegant. Vary the amount of cheese according to your taste, but make sure to use enough to season all the vegetables. Refer to the chart on page 343 for a more detailed look at trimming and boiling asparagus.

THE VEGETABLE

2 pounds asparagus
  (untrimmed weight)

Salt

Trim off the ends of the asparagus, and if the stalks are thick, peel them. Bring water to a boil in a large sauté pan, and add salt and the asparagus. Boil, uncovered, until the asparagus are completely tender, anywhere from 3 minutes for pencil-thin ones to 10 minutes for great thick trunks.

When the asparagus are cooked, hold a pan lid over the top and drain the water out, or pour the asparagus into a strainer and then return them immediately to the pan. Put the pan back on the flame and toss about for 30 seconds, or until any excess water has evaporated.

Season with pepper, drop in the butter, and shake the pan until the butter melts. Sprinkle on the Parmesan, turn off the heat, cover the pan, and peek in after a moment or two. When the cheese has melted, serve.

VARIATION: **Boiled Peas or Sugar Snaps with Parmesan Cheese.** Substitute boiled peas or sugar snap peas (*mange-tout,* or in Italian *taccolè*) for the asparagus. When the peas are cooked, drain and return them to the pan as above. Pour ¼ cup of heavy cream into the pan and raise the heat; reduce it until it is thick enough just to coat the peas (or, in place of cream, use 3 tablespoons of butter as above), and then sprinkle on ½ cup of grated Parmesan cheese, cover, and let it melt. In Piedmont, they add a few tablespoons of veal broth with the cream to peas, and finish the dish with thin shavings of a white truffle. If you have both on hand, I can think of few ways better to use them.

THE FINISH
Freshly ground black pepper
3 tablespoons unsalted
    butter, softened
½ to 1 cup freshly grated
    Parmesan cheese

Vegetables, Frittatas, Salads   351

Herbed Green Beans

FAGIOLINI CON ERBE AROMATICHE

SERVES 4 TO 5

I find herbs extremely satisfying to grow, because, in spite of my lack of any great know-how, they always seem to thrive. An admirable selection not only graces my small garden, but in the summer also finds a home in patio pots. This recipe combines parsley and mint, but I am not choosy—I pick enough from any two or three plants that seem to need a bit of pruning to make up about ⅓ cup.

THE VEGETABLE

2 pounds green beans, washed and
    trimmed

THE FINISH

3 tablespoons extra-virgin olive oil or
    unsalted butter

2 garlic cloves, minced

2 tablespoons minced fresh mint

2 tablespoons minced fresh flat-leaf
    parsley

2 teaspoons grated lemon rind

Salt and freshly ground black pepper

1 teaspoon white-wine vinegar or lemon
    juice (optional)

Drop the beans into a large pot of rapidly boiling water and boil, uncovered, until they are tender, 6 to 8 minutes. Drain, and immediately return to the pan over the heat to evaporate any excess water.

Pour in the oil or butter with the garlic and remaining seasonings, and toss for a minute or so to blend the flavors.

VARIATION: **Herbed Carrots.** Substitute carrots for the beans, or combine green beans and carrots, cutting the carrots into matchstick sizes to match the beans. Boil the vegetables separately (use the same water), so you can control the cooking times.

Red Potatoes with Basil and Olive Oil

PATATE ROSSE CON BASILICO E OLIO

SERVES 4 OR 5

These simple potatoes are a perfect accompaniment to any braised or roasted fish or meat dish. Vary the herb to complement the meal: parsley, oregano, rosemary.

THE VEGETABLE

2 pounds small red new potatoes, of equal size, about 1¼ inches in diameter

Salt

THE FINISH

3 to 4 tablespoons extra-virgin olive oil

Salt and freshly ground black pepper

¼ cup finely shredded fresh basil

Wash the potatoes in cold water. Use a vegetable peeler or a paring knife to remove a strip of peel about ¼ inch wide around the center of each potato. This will give the oil a place to seep in. Put the potatoes in a deep pot, and cover with cold water by 1 inch. Add salt, and bring the water to a boil. Cook until the potatoes are tender, about 20 minutes after the water boils. Drain, and return to the pot over the heat to remove excess liquid.

Pour in the oil, and season with salt, pepper, and basil. Toss well until the vegetables have absorbed the oil and the basil has wilted; add more oil if the potatoes seem dry.

VARIATION: Red Potatoes with Butter and Basil. Substitute butter for the oil.

Warm Potato Salad

INSALATA CALDA DI PATATE

SERVES 4 TO 6

Italian-style potato salads are simpler than their mayonnaise-laden American counterparts. Serve this as part of an antipasto plate or an accompaniment to any simple meat or fish dish. The potatoes below are cut into a large dice, but you can just as well slice them. The recipe for pickled onions is in the box on page 377, but you could use store-bought ones, even the cocktail size.

THE VEGETABLE
2 pounds large all-purpose potatoes,
   peeled and washed
2 teaspoons salt

THE FINISH
2 tablespoons white-wine vinegar
1 tablespoon capers (optional)

⅓ cup chopped pickled white onions
   (page 377)
2 tablespoons finely chopped flat-leaf
   parsley
Salt and freshly ground black pepper
⅓ cup extra-virgin olive oil

Put the potatoes in a large saucepan, and pour in enough cold water to cover them by 1 inch. Add the salt, bring to a boil, and cook until the potatoes are just about tender, 20 to 25 minutes after the water returns to the boil.

While the potatoes are cooking, stir the vinegar, capers, onions, parsley, salt, and pepper together in a bowl large enough to hold the potatoes with some tossing room. Drain the cooked potatoes, and cut them into ½-inch squares, adding them to the bowl with the dressing as you cut. Gently turn the warm potatoes over and around in the dressing, so all the pieces have a chance to absorb the flavors; do this gently so as not to break them—a large rubber spatula is the ideal tool. Taste for seasoning, drizzle on the oil, and toss together again. Serve warm or at room temperature.

VARIATION: In place of the pickled sauce above, dress the warm potatoes with any of the sauces in the box for vegetable sauces opposite. Serve at room temperature as an antipasto, or as a salad for a cold buffet.

Some Lively Sauces for Boiled/Steamed Vegetables

Oh, how appealing it is to enter an Italian restaurant and pass by an antipasto table resplendent with color and texture! Most of the splendor is contributed by an assortment of vegetables boiled, dressed, and served at room temperature. As well as antipasti, marinated vegetables make an appetizing lunch, with cured meats, a piece of cold chicken on the bone, canned tuna, or hard-boiled eggs.

Or you can dress the warm vegetables with a few tablespoons of the same and serve as a side dish. Cook each vegetable according to the chart on pages 343–49 and drain. Cut large vegetables into bite-size pieces, and if you are mixing two or three together, cut them into similar sizes. While the vegetables are still warm, either dress them simply with olive oil, salt, and a bit of lemon juice or vinegar, or toss them with one of the dressings below. For antipasti plan on steeping them at room temperature at least 2 hours. They can be refrigerated, covered with plastic wrap, overnight, but return them to room temperature before serving. Note that acids (vinegar or lemon juice) will discolor green vegetables after an hour or so; if the color disturbs you, leave the acid out of the marinade, and add it just before serving.

The dressings themselves can be made in quantities and kept in the refrigerator for a few weeks. Bring enough to room temperature to coat the vegetables, and keep the rest refrigerated for another time.

Piquant Sauce

Put ½ cup minced flat-leaf parsley, ½ cup extra-virgin olive oil, ⅓ cup sliced scallions, 2 tablespoons capers (rinsed), half a small *peperoncino* finely chopped, and 2 tablespoons lemon juice into a small saucepan, and heat gently for about 7 minutes. The cooking is only to blend the flavors, so do not allow the ingredients to fry.

USE FOR: Broccoli, green beans, cauliflower, carrots, asparagus. Or use a combination of cauliflower and broccoli, or of carrots and green beans; cut the carrots to the size of the beans.

Parsley-Anchovy Sauce

Stir together about ½ cup finely chopped flat-leaf parsley, three rinsed and mashed anchovies (or 1 teaspoon anchovy paste), 3 tablespoons minced red onion soaked in cold water for 1 hour, 2 tablespoons capers, 1 tablespoon minced garlic, and ¼ cup lemon juice. Season with salt and pepper, and beat in ¾ cup olive oil.

USE FOR: Cauliflower, carrots, broccoli, sliced potatoes, fennel. For a mixed antipasto salad, use about ¼ pound each carrots, asparagus, green beans, and zucchini. Boil the vegetables whole and separately until each is cooked. Then cut them all into pieces about 1½ inches long and similar in shape, or even in a smaller dice. Toss them together with the anchovy sauce.

Basil Sauce

Put about 2 cups destemmed basil leaves, two or three chopped garlic cloves, 2 teaspoons lemon juice, salt and pepper, and 3 tablespoons pine nuts in the food processor or blender, and pulse until the ingredients are minced. On the lowest speed, or by hand, blend in 6 to 8 tablespoons extra-virgin olive oil until the mixture is blended. It should be loose. (Were you to omit the lemon and stir in ½ cup grated Parmesan, a few tablespoons grated Pecorino Romano, and 3 or 4 tablespoons softened unsalted butter, you would have a traditional pesto sauce.)

USE FOR: I particularly like to pour this over sliced boiled potatoes, green beans, and hard-boiled eggs.

VARIATION: A pesto sauce made with parsley is also delicious. Substitute the leaves of flat-leaf parsley for the basil, and use ⅔ cup walnuts in place of the pine nuts.

Smashed and Mashed Boiled Potatoes

"Smashed" is a contemporary term for potatoes that are boiled with their skins on and then pummeled with an old-fashioned potato masher just until they are broken into a textured mass. It is my favorite way to prepare them, because it is fast and easy and I love the contrasts of textures that the skin and uneven potato pieces give to the dish. For mashed potatoes (sometimes called "whipped"), peel them either before or after boiling and then mash them. For a more refined finish, squeeze them through a potato ricer and then use a wooden spoon to beat in hot milk or potato water, butter, and seasonings.

Smashed and mashed potatoes are always best served as soon as they are finished. If they have to wait, set them over a flame tamer, drizzle the top with 2–3 tablespoons of warm milk, and keep them covered and warm. Mash in the milk before serving.

Smashed Potatoes
with Mascarpone Cheese

PATATINE CON MASCARPONE

SERVES 4 TO 6

I am particularly fond of the Yukon Gold variety for this dish, but other waxy potatoes such as Red Bliss, Yellow Finn, and New Whites make excellent smashed potatoes. Use potatoes that are 1½ to 2 inches in diameter.

THE VEGETABLES

2 pounds small boiling potatoes, with their skins

1 large bunch scallions, white parts and about ½ inch of green only

1½ teaspoons salt per quart water

THE FINISH

8 ounces mascarpone cheese, at room temperature

3 tablespoons minced flat-leaf parsley

Freshly ground black pepper

Put the potatoes and scallions together in a large saucepan—the potatoes need some elbow room—and pour in enough cold water to cover them by 1 inch. Add the salt so the water tastes lightly salty, bring to a boil, and cook until the potatoes are tender through to the center when pierced with a cake tester, 15 to 20 minutes after the water comes to the boil.

Drain the potatoes, reserving 1 cup of the cooking water, and smash them with a hand masher, adding the mascarpone, parsley, and pepper as you pound. If the potatoes are too stiff, mash in some of the cooking water to loosen them.

VARIATION: Any soft cheese that melts easily can be substituted for the mascarpone. Try a soft herbed goat cheese or Gorgonzola.

VARIATION: **Garlicky Smashed Potatoes and Greens.** Smashed potatoes cooked with greens and finished with olive oil are so good! Use 1 pound of chard, beet greens, or escarole, washed, trimmed, and torn into pieces that will fit into the palm of your hand. Substitute three or four large cloves of peeled garlic for the scallions, and boil the potatoes as above, adding the greens to the water after the potatoes have cooked for 8 minutes. Drain as above, reserving the water in case you need it, and smash the potatoes and greens with 3 tablespoons extra-virgin olive oil, or to taste, and salt and pepper. Any of the greens on page 342 can be used; since there are also potatoes, use half the amount listed for four servings.

Parmesan Mashed Potatoes Cooked in Milk

PATATINE AL LATTE CON BURRO E PARMIGIANO

SERVES 4 TO 6

The milk gives a subtle dairy finish to the potatoes. You can make the same recipe boiling them in water instead.

THE VEGETABLES

2 pounds baking or all-purpose potatoes, peeled and quartered
Enough milk to cover potatoes by about
  1 inch
2 teaspoons salt

THE FINISH

6 tablespoons unsalted butter, softened
1 cup freshly grated Parmesan cheese,
  or to taste
Salt and freshly ground black pepper

Put the potatoes in a large pot, and cover them with cold milk. Add the 2 teaspoons of salt, and boil the potatoes until they are tender when pierced, 15 to 20
minutes. Drain, reserving a cup of the cooking milk. Mash in the butter, ½ cup of
the reserved hot milk, the Parmesan cheese, salt, and pepper. Whip with a spoon
for a fluffier texture. Add more of the reserved milk if necessary.

VARIATION: Herbed Mashed Potatoes. To add a hint of herbs, tie the
stems of 3 or 4 sprigs of fresh rosemary or thyme together, boil them with the
potatoes, and remove after the potatoes are drained. Or, for a more pronounced
flavor, blend 1 tablespoon of chopped fresh herbs with the softened butter, and
mash them together into the hot potatoes.

BRAISING

IN UMIDO

Braising vegetables means cooking them in a small amount of liquid, in a pan that
is snugly covered so that the flavor of the vegetable is captured in the pan along
with all the flavors of whatever else is added. The flavors are very concentrated,
because there is not enough liquid to water them down. The Italian term says it
well—*in umido*—humid as opposed to drenched.

Note that, because there is so little liquid and because the pan is covered,
bright-green vegetables will not keep their color. If this is unappealing to you (it is
not to me), choose another cooking method.

The Braising Fat

Before liquid is added to the vegetables, they should be tossed in a small amount of
fat, which helps the vegetables to absorb the flavors in the braising. It can be butter, olive oil, vegetable oil, pork fat, or a combination of any of these. You need

just enough to coat the bottom of the pan but can use more if you like. I toss the vegetables in the warm fat over moderate heat for a few minutes and then add the liquid. If you want the vegetables to color, toss them over a slightly higher heat until they are lightly browned.

The Braising Liquid

Vegetables can be braised in a wide variety of liquids. Water, broth, citrus juices, vinegar, and tomatoes are just some of the possibilities. Vegetables with high moisture content will release their own juices, so they may need only a very small amount of liquid—even none at all. If the vegetables are tender and there is excess liquid in the pan, remove the cover and boil the juices down.

Covering the Pan

The lid that covers the pan should be snug, so that the liquid does not evaporate before the vegetables are cooked. If your pan allows great gusts of moist steam to escape, cover the vegetables first with a sheet of wax paper that touches the vegetables and drapes over the sides before placing the lid on top.

> Tomatoes and oregano make it Italian; wine and tarragon make it French. Sour cream makes it Russian; lemon and cinnamon make it Greek. Soy sauce makes it Chinese; garlic makes it good.
> —ALICE MAY BROCK

Carrots Braised in Marsala Wine

CAROTE AL MARSALA

SERVES 4 OR 5

For this simple dish to taste extraordinary, you need the best-quality Italian dry Marsala. Others would give a harsh taste or none at all to the dish. I know from experience. If you can't find one, use another braising liquid, such as chicken, meat, or vegetable broth.

Choose a straight-sided sauté pan that has a tight-fitting lid and is just large enough to hold the vegetables in one or two layers. A pan that is too large will allow the liquid to evaporate too quickly; if it is too small, the vegetables will be piled too high to braise evenly.

THE START
4 tablespoons unsalted butter

THE VEGETABLE

1¼ pounds carrots, peeled
   and cut into large matchsticks or ¼-inch-thick slices

Salt and freshly ground black
   pepper

Small grating of fresh nutmeg

½ teaspoon sugar

THE BRAISING LIQUID

½ cup dry Marsala

Melt the butter over moderate heat, so that it melts without taking on any color. Stir the carrots into the pan, and season with salt and pepper, nutmeg, and sugar. Turn the carrots over several times with a heatproof rubber spatula or wooden spatula or spoon to coat them well with the butter and seasonings. Cook gently—do not fry—stirring often, for about 2 minutes, to release the vegetable's flavor, and then pour in the Marsala. Bring to a quick boil, and then adjust the heat so the carrots just barely simmer. Cover the pan tightly and braise, shaking it well from time to time, for 12 to 15 minutes, or until the carrots are tender. Check the pan occasionally, and if the liquid has evaporated before the carrots are cooked, add small amounts of hot water. When the carrots are tender, there should be only enough liquid left just to coat them. If there is more, turn the heat to high and boil it off.

VARIATION: **Carrots Braised in Lemon and Parsley.** Before adding the carrots to the butter, cook one finely chopped small onion until it is tender. Substitute water or broth for the Marsala, and add a teaspoon of lemon juice. When the carrots are tender, stir in 3 tablespoons of finely chopped flat-leaf parsley, and toss a minute before serving.

VARIATION: **Braised Carrots with Parmesan Cheese.** Braise the carrots with broth or water, and when they are cooked, turn off the heat and sprinkle on ⅓ cup or more grated Parmesan cheese.

Braised Brussels Sprouts with Pancetta

CAVOLI DI BRUSSELLE IN UMIDO

SERVES 4

Cutting the Brussels sprouts in half or quarters reduces the cooking time and exposes the insides, which more readily absorb flavors. Use salt sparingly—the pancetta is already salty.

THE START
2 tablespoons butter or olive oil
¼ pound pancetta, in ¼-inch dice
  (optional)
4 to 6 large shallots, peeled and
  quartered
Salt and freshly ground black pepper

THE VEGETABLE
1¼ pounds Brussels sprouts, ends and
  bruised leaves trimmed away,
  quartered
THE COOKING LIQUID
½ cup good-quality white-wine vinegar

Heat the butter and pancetta in a 12-inch sauté pan over medium-low heat until the pork has rendered its fat and become slightly crisped, 8 to 10 minutes. If necessary, add more butter or oil to make 3 tablespoons of fat; if there is more, discard the excess. Reduce the heat so that the pan is not so hot as to brown the shallots, and drop them into the fat. Season with salt and pepper, and cook gently until the shallots are golden. Toss in the Brussels sprouts, turning them over with a spatula to coat on all sides, season, and sauté gently for about 2 minutes. Pour in the vinegar, and braise as in the Primary Recipe, allowing about 15 minutes.

VARIATION: **Braised Savoy Cabbage with Pancetta.** Brussels sprouts are of course members of the cabbage family, and other cabbages will lend themselves to the same flavors that work for these small cousins. Substitute four cloves of sliced garlic for the shallots, add one large red or yellow onion, thinly sliced, and cook these with the pancetta, and butter or oil. In place of the sprouts, use a large head of Savoy cabbage, trimmed and cut into wedges.

VARIATION: Use 3 to 4 tablespoons of butter, no pancetta, and the juice of one small lemon in place of the vinegar.

VARIATION: **Braised Brussels Sprouts with Parmesan Cheese.** For Brussels sprouts *alla parmigiana*, omit the pancetta and use 3 tablespoons of butter. Substitute ⅓ cup of chicken or vegetable broth for the vinegar, and cook as above. When the sprouts are cooked, raise the heat if necessary to evaporate any liquid, then turn off the heat, and sprinkle with ½ cup of grated Parmesan cheese. Put the cover on just long enough for the cheese to melt.

VARIATION: **Braised Fennel with Parmesan Cheese.** In place of the Brussels sprouts in the variation *alla parmigiana* directly above, use 2 pounds of fennel (three or four heads), cut into quarters or thick slices. The fennel takes a long time to braise, at least 40 minutes, but you can reduce the time by parboiling it for 5 minutes before braising, or by cutting it into very thin slices.

Oven-Braising

Vegetables can be braised in the oven as well as on top of the stove. It is a good method for those that take a long time to cook, since the oven provides more evenly surrounding heat. Preheat the oven to 350° F. Use part of the fat called for in the recipe to coat a baking dish. Put the vegetables in the pan, and scatter pieces of butter or drizzle oil on each layer; season each layer with salt and pepper and whatever other seasonings are called for. Pour the braising liquid into the dish, cover tightly with foil, and bake until the vegetables are tender and the liquid has evaporated. To add a Parmesan finish, boost the oven up to 400° F when the vegetables are tender, and sprinkle on the grated cheese. Bake uncovered for about 10 minutes, or until the vegetables are golden.

Braised Peas with Pancetta

PISELLINI CON PANCETTA IN UMIDO

SERVES 4 TO 6

This is a good method for cooking peas that are a little older and less sweet than those lovely, tiny treasures that begin the season.

THE START
1 tablespoon extra-virgin olive oil
¼ cup finely chopped pancetta or
  prosciutto
½ cup minced onion
THE VEGETABLE
3 pounds peas (unshelled weight),
  shelled

Salt and freshly ground black pepper
¼ cup finely chopped Italian flat-leaf
  parsley
THE BRAISING LIQUID
½ cup homemade or low-sodium canned
  meat broth or water

Heat olive oil, pancetta, and onion in a 12-inch sauté pan over low heat until the onion is softened. Stir in the peas, salt, pepper, and parsley, and cook about 2 minutes. Pour in the broth, and braise as in the Primary Recipe, allowing 15 to 20 minutes, depending on the peas' size and age.

VARIATION: To use frozen peas, thaw two 10-ounce boxes and proceed as above, using only ¼ cup broth. The peas will be cooked through in 5 to 6 minutes.

VARIATION: Braised Peas and Lettuce. Omit the pancetta, and substitute 3 tablespoons of butter for the oil. Gently cook 1 cup of finely shredded lettuce in the fat until it wilts. Replace the parsley with fresh mint.

VARIATION: Braised Fava Beans. Substitute 3 pounds (unshelled weight) of fresh fava beans for the peas. Peel according to the chart on page 346 before braising in butter with no pancetta. Small young favas will need 8 to 10 minutes to cook, large ones as long as 20. In Sicily, they cook the favas with small quartered artichokes and tiny young peas. Trim and braise the artichoke hearts for about 15 minutes, or until they are just tender; add the favas, and when they are close to being done, stir in the peas for 5 minutes, or until they are cooked.

Braised Sweet-and-Sour Peppers with Almonds

PEPERONI IN UMIDO

SERVES 4 OR 5

Bell peppers of any color can be cooked this way. The red and yellow ones are sweeter than the green, and I always make them part of the recipe. You can also use long green Italian frying peppers, which are, again, sweeter than the green bell ones.

Peppers are always a bit more elegant—and some say digestible—when peeled before cooking, but it is not a speedy task. To peel raw peppers, use a vegetable peeler, and run it lightly from the top to the bottom of the pepper with a light sawing motion.

THE START

3 tablespoons extra-virgin olive oil

1 large garlic clove, smashed and peeled

⅓ cup slivered almonds

½ cup dark raisins soaked in warm water
   to cover 20 minutes and drained

THE VEGETABLE

5 large bell peppers, stems, seeds, and
   ribs discarded, in ½-inch-wide slices

Salt

THE BRAISING LIQUID

1 tablespoon sugar dissolved in 3 tablespoons red-wine vinegar

Heat the oil and garlic until the garlic is lightly brown; discard the garlic, and stir the almonds into the pan. Cook, stirring often, for 2 minutes without letting the almonds brown. Stir in the raisins and cook 1 minute more. Add the peppers to the pan, season with salt, and sauté about 2 minutes. Pour on the liquid, cover the pan, and braise as in the Primary Recipe, allowing 10 to 15 minutes.

VARIATION: **Braised Peppers, Onions, and Tomatoes (Peperonata).** *Peperonata* is a braised dish of peppers, onions, and tomatoes. It is a delicious side dish for roasted meats as well as a handy condiment to have on hand. I add it to scrambled eggs and *frittate* for brunch or lunch. Omit the almonds and raisins from the recipe above, and instead cook thin slices from three medium yellow or red onions in the oil with the garlic. When the onions are soft and golden, sauté the peppers. Omit the vinegar and sugar, and for the braising liquid use 1 cup of peeled, chopped tomatoes with their juices.

Braised Leeks and Onions

PORRI E CIPOLLE IN UMIDO

SERVES 4

These braised leeks and onions are more like a relish than a vegetable side dish. Serve them with a simple roasted chicken or a piece of poached fish. I often use this combination in other recipes that contain fish, such as the leek-and-shrimp lasagna on page 179. The large amount of lemon makes the finished dish quite tangy. You can cut down on it (unless you are making this for the shrimp lasagna), or substitute water or broth.

GETTING READY
4 large leeks (about 2 inches in
    diameter)
THE START
4 tablespoons unsalted butter

THE VEGETABLES
The leeks from above
2 large onions, cut in half and then into
    thin half-rounds
Salt
THE BRAISING LIQUID
Zest and juice of 1 large lemon

Slice away the green tops and root ends from the leeks. Make a long slice through the white bulb, from the top almost to the root, and then hold the top under cold running water, gently spreading the leaves back, to wash away any traces of sand. Finish the cut to the end, and then slice the leeks into half-rounds about ⅛ inch thick.

Melt the butter in a sauté pan, and stir in the leeks and onions, season with salt, and cook very slowly, over medium-low heat, stirring frequently, until the vegetables are slightly golden in color, about 6 minutes. Don't allow the onions to brown. Add the zest and juice of the lemon, cover the pan, and braise as in the Primary Recipe, allowing 10 to 15 minutes. The leeks and onions should be completely tender. Serve warm or at room temperature.

VARIATION: Use ¼ cup chicken or vegetable broth in place of the lemon juice and zest. Add 2 to 3 tablespoons chopped fresh parsley or marjoram.

VARIATION: **Braised Fennel.** Substitute two large fennel bulbs (about 2 pounds) for the leeks, and 4 tablespoons of olive oil for the butter. Trim the heads, and cut the bulbs into thin slices, about ⅛ inch thick. Omit the onions, sauté the fennel in the oil as above, and then pour in ½ cup dry white wine, ⅓ cup water, three fresh thyme sprigs or ½ teaspoon dried, salt, and pepper. Braise as above, and if desired stir in some of the chopped fennel tops when the fennel is almost cooked.

VARIATION: **Creamy Braised Leeks and Tomatoes.** Braise the leeks in ¼ cup chopped, peeled tomatoes with their juices, and when the leeks are tender, pour in ½ cup heavy cream. Reduce the cream by half, and serve warm.

Artichoke Hearts

Although canned or frozen artichoke hearts are acceptable in some recipes, they are just not as tender or flavorful as the real McCoy. Trimming artichokes is not a task for the impatient, but the rewards are delicious.

Choose artichokes that feel heavy and have tightly closed leaves. If the leaves have some brown at the edges and a touch of white blistering, it is a sign that the vegetable has been "winter-kissed"—that is, touched by frost—which improves its flavor.

Cut a lemon in half, and squeeze one half into a bowl of cold water large enough to hold all the trimmed artichokes. Drop the squeezed half into the water. Use the other half of the lemon to rub all cut and trimmed surfaces as you work, to avoid discoloration. Working with one artichoke at a time, bend back and pull off the outer green leaves until only the pale-yellowish-green leaves remain. Use a large stainless-steel knife to cut off the top third of the vegetable and discard the tips. With a small stainless-steel paring knife, peel the dark green away from the stem and around the bottom. Quarter, cutting through the stem and all the way to the top. Cut out the choke (the fuzzy and purple parts), and drop the remaining heart into the lemon water. Trim the other artichokes.

Eating an artichoke is like getting to know someone really well.

—WILL HASTINGS

Braised Whole Artichokes

CARCIOFI IN UMIDO

I once read an article that asked a number of chefs and celebrities which foods they always liked to have in their refrigerators. No one gave what would have been my answer—roasted red peppers and braised whole artichokes. I think artichokes are the perfect snack food—a leaf here, a leaf there—they always taste good. They are, of course, just as delicious hot.

GETTING READY
1½ lemons
4 large globe artichokes
THE START
3 tablespoons extra-virgin olive oil
4 large garlic cloves, smashed and
    peeled (optional)

THE VEGETABLE
The trimmed artichokes from above,
    drained and patted dry
Salt
THE BRAISING LIQUID
¼ cup water or homemade or low-
    sodium canned chicken or vegetable
    broth
Juice of ½ lemon

Cut the lemons in half and squeeze half of one into a bowl of cold water large enough to hold all the trimmed artichokes. Drop the squeezed half into the water. Use another half-lemon to rub all cut and trimmed surfaces as you work, to avoid discoloration. Save half a lemon for braising. Working with one artichoke at a time, use a stainless-steel knife to cut off the stem so the artichoke will sit flat. Peel the dark-green outer layer off the stem, and drop the trimmed piece into the lemon water.

Use stainless-steel scissors to cut the tips off the leaves, if you wish. They are sometimes too sharp for young children. Remember to rub the cut parts with the lemon.

If you wish to remove the prickly choke before cooking, turn the trimmed artichoke upside down, and squish it on the counter to open the leaves out a bit. Right side up, press the center of the leaves out until you can see the purple tips and fuzzy choke. Pull the purple leaves out, discard, and then use a spoon (a grapefruit spoon is perfect) to scrape out the fuzzy choke. Otherwise leave it in and remove it when you have eaten your way down to it. Drop the trimmed artichoke into the lemon water, and trim the others.

Choose a wide, deep nonreactive pot that will hold the artichokes in one layer standing up—be it ever so snugly. Heat the oil and garlic in the pot until the garlic is golden. Remove and reserve the garlic. Put the artichokes and stems in the pan, and sauté on all sides. You may have to work with two at a time. When they are all browned, stand them upright, tuck the stems in and around where you find room, season with salt, and pour in the liquid and the garlic. Bring to a quick boil, cover with wax paper, and braise according to the Primary Recipe, allowing 25 to 40 minutes, depending on their size. The leaves should release easily when pulled.

I like to reduce the braising liquid until it is pleasantly lemony and use it as a dip for the leaves.

VARIATION: **Spicy Braised Artichokes.** For a spicy addition, cook 1 small hot red pepper, minced, or ½ teaspoon red-pepper flakes with the garlic.

VARIATION: **Braised Artichokes with Garlic and Mint.** The artichokes can be stuffed with herbs and chopped garlic before they are sautéed. In this case, do remove the choke before braising. Mix ¼ cup of finely chopped fresh mint, four or five minced garlic cloves, and the zest from one lemon with a tablespoon of olive oil and some salt and pepper. Push the mixture firmly down into the leaves. Or use parsley in place of the mint.

Some Artichoke History

With its thorny tips, prickly choke, and fibrous, only partially edible leaves, the artichoke was called "one of the earth's monstrosities" by the Roman naturalist Pliny. Yet he and untold millions since have loved the globed vegetable. First cultivated in Sicily, where Arab Saracens named it *al quarshut,* the artichoke came to America with the Spaniards. In the 1890s Italian farmers in California marketed artichokes so successfully to enthusiastic New Yorkers that soon the racketeers muscled in and Mayor Fiorello La Guardia had to ban their sale. However, the ban lasted only a week, because the mayor loved his artichokes too much to give them up.

Caramelized Onions

CIPOLLE IN CARAMELLATA

SERVES 4

Onions have a great deal of natural moisture, and may indeed exude enough to braise in their own juices. If, however, the bottom of the pan begins to get brown, pour in 2 to 3 tablespoons of the water or wine. This will deglaze the pan and actually hasten the caramelizing process. If necessary, repeat this several times during the cooking. As the onions soften and release their sugars, they will slowly turn a rich caramel color.

THE VEGETABLE
2 very large onions
4 tablespoons butter (½ stick)
Salt

THE LIQUID
½ to 1 cup water or white wine, as needed

Cut the onions in half from tip to root, then cut the halves into thin half-moon slices. Melt the butter in a 12-inch frying pan over moderate heat, and scatter the onions in the pan. Season with salt, cover, and braise as in the Primary Recipe until the onions are completely wilted and caramelized. Check the pan from time to time, and add a bit of water or wine if the pan is dry.

Potatoes in Tomato Sauce

PATATE ALLA PIZZAIOLA

SERVES 4

Alla pizzaiola means "in the pizza-maker's style," indicating that the food shares the flavors of pizza—that is, tomatoes, garlic, olive oil, and oregano. This typical Neapolitan treatment is used for fish and meat as well as for vegetables.

THE VEGETABLE

2 pounds medium-size russet potatoes, peeled

About 1½ teaspoons salt

THE START

3 tablespoons unsalted butter

1 tablespoon vegetable oil

1 small onion, thinly sliced

Salt and freshly ground black pepper

THE LIQUID

3 tablespoons chopped fresh oregano, or 1 tablespoon dried

2 cups lightly drained, chopped canned plum tomatoes

Put the potatoes in a large pot, and cover by 1 inch with cold water. Add the salt and bring to a boil. Parboil the potatoes until the outside is tender but they still show some resistance at the center, 10 to 12 minutes.

Meanwhile, heat the butter, oil, and onions, seasoned with salt and pepper, in a 12-inch sauté pan until the onion is golden. Drain the potatoes, and while they are still warm, cut them into ¼-inch-thick slices. Transfer them immediately to the sauté pan, season with salt, pepper, and oregano, and toss for a few minutes. Pour in the tomatoes, season with salt and pepper, and braise according to the Primary Recipe 15 to 35 minutes, until the potatoes are tender but hold their shape. I can't explain the discrepancy in time; I have had some potatoes cook quickly, and then sometimes they seem to take forever. The good news is that they reheat beautifully—even the next day.

VARIATION: **Braised Winter Squash with Tomatoes.** Substitute parboiled slices of winter squash, such as butternut, for the potatoes. It is a delicious combination. I'm not sure whether or not she invented it (Italians don't eat a lot of squash), but my aunt Irma made it that way often and was justly acclaimed for it.

Smothered Broccoli Rabe

BROCCOLI DI RAPA AFFOGATO

SERVES 4

Before we considered fat the enemy, my family made this recipe with enough olive oil so it made a puddle on the plate. That was the point, because there was always plenty of bread on the table to sop it up. Use as much or as little as you like; if you have chosen to serve it my way, put it on its own plate so the oil does not run away.

GETTING READY

1½ pounds broccoli rabe

THE START

4 to 6 tablespoons extra-virgin olive oil

3 large garlic cloves, thinly sliced

1 or 2 small hot red peppers, finely chopped, or 1 teaspoon hot red-pepper flakes

THE VEGETABLE

The broccoli rabe from above

Salt

THE LIQUID

3 or more tablespoons water

Wash, peel, and parboil the broccoli rabe according to the chart on page 345, then cut it into 3-inch-long pieces.

Heat the oil, garlic, and hot pepper in a 12-inch sauté pan, over gentle heat, until the garlic is golden. Put the rabe in the pan, salt lightly, and stir over heat for 2 minutes. Pour in a tablespoon of water, and braise according to the Primary Recipe, adding more water as needed, allowing about 15 minutes. The rabe will have lost its green color but should be very tender.

VARIATION: **Broccoli Rabe with White Beans.** Broccoli rabe and white beans served over Italian toast have sustained more than a few Neapolitan families. Stir 3 cups of cooked white beans into the pan when the rabe is just about cooked, heat, and serve over thick slices of Italian bread that have been toasted and drizzled with olive oil.

Braised Marinated Vegetables

SOTTACETI

Throughout history, Italians have been master gardeners. No matter how small or rugged the patch of land, whether it is on the steep rocky hills of the Amalfi coast or a front yard in Cambridge, Massachusetts, they garden. What these prolific gardeners do not eat or give away, they preserve. Braising them in vinegar, *sottaceto*, is one way to store overflowing produce; *agrodolce* (sweet and sour) is another. Although used mainly as a garnish or on an antipasto platter, these vegetable preserves are a delicious ingredient to have on hand for stirring into a pan after frying meats or fish to make a quick finish.

Any reasonable combination of vegetables will work for this recipe. You will need a total of about 12 cups in addition to the garlic and onions.

GETTING READY

1 small eggplant, trimmed, washed, and cut into ½-inch cubes (about 2 cups)

Salt

THE START

¾ cup extra-virgin olive oil

4 large garlic cloves, minced (about 2 tablespoons)

2 medium onions, thinly sliced (about 4 cups loosely packed)

1 small hot red pepper, minced, or ½ teaspoon hot red-pepper flakes

THE VEGETABLES

The eggplant from above

3 large bell peppers, any color, in strips ¼ inch wide by 2 inches long (about 6 cups)

2 small zucchini, about 1 pound, halved lengthwise, then sliced into thin half-moon shapes (about 3 cups)

½ pound mushrooms, wiped clean, trimmed, and thinly sliced

¾ cup assorted black and green olives, pitted and quartered

THE LIQUID

1 cup red-wine vinegar

Scatter the eggplant pieces in a colander, lightly salting the layers. Place a plate on top of the eggplant, and a weight, such as a large can of tomatoes, on top of the plate. Let drain for 45 minutes, then rinse and pat dry.

Pour the olive oil into a 4-to-6-quart saucepan with a heavy bottom, and set over medium-low heat. The heat during the entire cooking process must remain low enough to prevent any of the vegetables from burning. While the oil is warming, stir in the garlic, onions, and hot pepper. Season lightly with salt, and cook slowly until the onions begin to soften. Stir in the eggplant and peppers, season lightly with salt, and continue to cook for 5 minutes, until the eggplant is slightly brown. Add the zucchini and mushrooms, season lightly with salt, and continue cooking another 5 minutes. Stir in the olives, and pour in the vinegar. Cover, and braise as in the Primary Recipe, allowing 15 to 25 minutes. All the vegetables should be very soft and wilted.

Storage: These vegetables will keep in the refrigerator covered for several weeks.

VARIATION: **Caponata.** *Caponata* is a traditional Sicilian form of braised marinated vegetables made primarily from eggplant. Use 2 pounds eggplant, cut and salted as above. Omit the hot pepper from the start, and cook 2 cups diced celery with the onions and the garlic. Add 2 medium red bell peppers, and cook until they are just beginning to soften, about 5 minutes. Remove the vegetables with a slotted spoon to make room for the eggplant. Add another few tablespoons of oil to the pan, since eggplant is so absorbent, then raise the heat and brown the eggplant; work in batches if necessary. Return the reserved vegetables to the pan, and pour in 3 cups chopped canned tomatoes, 2 tablespoons tomato paste, 2 tablespoons drained capers, ¼ cup pitted and sliced green olives, ¼ cup red-wine vinegar, 1 tablespoon sugar, and salt and pepper, and cook as above until the sauce has thickened. Stir ¼ cup chopped fresh parsley into the finished dish, and reserve as above. Optionally, you can garnish the finished *caponata* with sliced almonds.

Sweet-and-Sour Onions

CIPOLLINE IN AGRODOLCE

SERVES 4

Agrodolce translates to "sour/sweet" and refers here to vegetables that are cooked in a sweet (*dolce*) and sour (*agro*) combination of sugar and vinegar. More a condiment than a side dish, sweet-and-sour onions will keep a week or so in the refrigerator and are a common addition to antipasto tables, where they are served at room temperature. Try the equally delicious but speedier-to-make variation using sliced red onions.

GETTING READY

2 pounds small white boiling onions

THE START

3 tablespoons extra-virgin olive oil

2 ounces fatty prosciutto, finely chopped

THE VEGETABLE

The onions from above

⅓ cup dark raisins

1 bay leaf

Salt and freshly ground black pepper

THE LIQUID

1 tablespoon tomato paste

1 tablespoon sugar

1¼ cups water

½ cup red-wine vinegar

Parboil and peel the onions according to the chart on page 348.

Heat the olive oil with the prosciutto over a moderate flame until the fat begins to run, about 3 minutes. Do not let the prosciutto crisp. Put the onions in the pan and sauté, turning often, until lightly golden, about 8 minutes. Stir in the raisins, bay leaf, and salt and pepper. Whisk the tomato paste and sugar into the water and vinegar until the sugar and paste have dissolved, and then pour the liquid into the pan, cover, and braise according to the Primary Recipe, allowing about 1½ hours to cook. The onions should be very tender and the liquid a glaze. Remove the bay leaf before serving at room temperature.

VARIATION: Sweet-and-Sour Red Onions. Substitute 1 pound (about 2 large) red onions for the boiling onions. Do not parboil, simply peel and thinly slice. Omit the prosciutto, and cook the onion slices in ¼ cup olive oil for about 8 minutes. Use ½ cup water, ½ cup white-wine vinegar, 1 teaspoon sugar, and no tomato paste for the liquid. For seasonings, use 8 whole cloves and ¼ cup raisins. Braise 25 minutes, or until onions are completely softened. Remove cloves before serving.

Uncooked Preserved Vegetables

SOTTACETI CRUDI

Pickling vegetables without cooking them is another way Italians fill their pantries with the garden's overflow. These vegetables need at least 2 weeks to cure, so plan ahead. You can double or triple the recipe; the peppers especially make lovely house gifts, because they add such color to your arrival.

FOR 2 POUNDS

THE VEGETABLES

2 pounds of small white onions, about 1 inch in diameter, peeled

THE PICKLING BRINE

1 teaspoon salt

2 cups white-wine vinegar

3 to 5 sprigs fresh thyme

2 to 3 sprigs fresh oregano or marjoram

Cut three slashes ⅓ inch deep in both ends of the onions. Drop into a perfectly clean 1½-quart glass jar, or 3 or 4 smaller ones. Sprinkle on the salt and pour in the vinegar. Add enough cold water to come to the top of the jar. Put in the herbs, tucking some along the side of the jar for show, and cover the jar. Store at room temperature for at least 2 weeks and up to 6 months before using.

To serve as part of an antipasto, remove the onions from the brine, rinse quickly, dry, and dress with fresh herbs, minced garlic, and olive oil. If desired, drape with a few anchovies and/or garnish with brine-cured olives.

VARIATION: A combination of red and yellow peppers makes an impressive splash of color, to say nothing of a delicious condiment. Prepare four onions as above, and drop them into the jar. Wash, quarter, and remove the seeds and stems from about 1¾ pounds of sweet peppers, half red and half yellow. Put into the jar, cover with the brine, and store as above.

SAUTÉING

Sautéing is a fast stovetop method of cooking in a small amount of fat—just enough to keep the vegetables from sticking to the pan. The fat becomes part of the finished dish. Soft vegetables, such as mushrooms, can begin and end their cooking in the sauté pan. Harder vegetables are usually partially boiled or steamed before sautéing in order to hasten their cooking time.

Broccoli with Garlic, Oil, and Lemon

AGLIO, OLIO, E LIMONE

SERVES 4 OR 5

The amount of olive oil is up to you. Perhaps it's left over from my Italian-American youth, but I like the larger amount for finishing shredded escarole, broccoli rabe, and regular broccoli that is chopped into small pieces. The excess oil that seeps out just cries out to be mopped up with bread. If you use the larger amount, serve the vegetable on a side dish—as Italians usually do—so the oil doesn't run into the rest of your meal.

Divide the broccoli into stems and flowerets, and boil or steam according to the chart on page 344, cooking the stems about 5 minutes, or until they can be easily pierced, and the flowerets 3 minutes. Cool immediately, and chop into pieces about ½ inch small.

Pour the oil into a sauté pan large enough to hold the broccoli in one slightly overlapping layer, so you can keep the vegetables moving about to brown on all sides. If they are too crowded, they will steam instead of sauté. Place the oiled pan over medium-low heat, and slip the garlic and red pepper into the warming oil. Season the garlic with a pinch of salt, and cook gently until the garlic is just golden; be very careful not to let the garlic brown.

GETTING READY

1 large head broccoli

THE START

4 to 6 tablespoons extra-virgin olive oil

3 to 6 medium garlic cloves, peeled and thinly sliced

½ small hot red pepper, or ¼ to ½ teaspoon hot red-pepper flakes

Salt

Vegetables, Frittatas, Salads   379

THE VEGETABLE

The broccoli from above

Salt and freshly ground black
  pepper

1 tablespoon minced parsley

Raise the heat a bit, and when the pan is hot enough for the broccoli to sizzle quietly, drop it into the pan, season with salt and pepper and parsley, and either shake or toss it around until it is fully cooked, 5 to 7 minutes. It is important to keep sautéing vegetables moving ("sauté" actually means "to jump"), either by tossing the pan or by using a spatula to toss them around—otherwise, they will not sear or cook evenly.

When the broccoli is as tender as you like, serve hot or at room temperature.

VARIATION: Stir ⅓ cup pitted and sliced black olives into the oil after the garlic is golden. Heat for a minute before tossing in the broccoli.

VARIATION: **Sautéed Carrots with Lemon and Parsley.** Substitute about 1¼ pounds carrots, peeled and cut into large matchsticks or ¼-inch-thick slices, for the broccoli. Boil or steam them until they are tender on the outside but still offer resistance at the center, about 3 minutes. Use 4 tablespoons of olive oil or 2 tablespoons each of butter and olive oil, and finish the carrots with a tablespoon of lemon juice and 3 tablespoons of parsley.

VARIATION: **Sautéed Spinach and Romaine Lettuce.** Use 4 tablespoons of olive oil, and substitute ¼ cup pine nuts and ⅓ cup of golden or dark raisins (soaked and drained) for the garlic and hot pepper. When the pine nuts are lightly colored, toss in one medium head of romaine lettuce, trimmed and finely shredded, and 2 pounds of washed and shredded spinach. If your pan does not hold all the greens at once, wait for the first batch to wilt and make room for more. Or wilt the spinach first, according to directions in the table on page 348, and squeeze it dry very well. Season with salt, pepper, and nutmeg, and when the greens are cooked, sprinkle on ¼ cup of freshly grated pecorino cheese.

Cauliflower Southern Italian–Style

CAVOLFIORE ALLA MEZZOGIORNO

SERVES 4 OR 5

This is a less than shy way to flavor cauliflower and calls for a very simply prepared entrée. *Mezzogiorno* means "noon" but also means the south of Italy, because its days are as sunny as though the high-noon sun shone from morning to night.

GETTING READY

1 large head cauliflower

3 tablespoons dark raisins

THE START

4 to 6 tablespoons extra-virgin olive oil

1 small onion, finely chopped

3 medium garlic cloves, finely chopped

½ small hot red pepper, or ¼ to ½ teaspoon red-pepper flakes (optional)

Salt

2 anchovy fillets, rinsed and finely
chopped (optional)

THE VEGETABLE

The cauliflower from above

THE FINISH

¼ to ½ cup slivered, pitted black olives

The raisins from above

3 tablespoons pine nuts

Trim away the green leaves of the cauliflower, drop it upside down into boiling salted water, and cook until almost tender but still offering some resistance, 8 or 9 minutes. Drain, cool, and cut the head into 1-inch pieces. Soak the raisins in water to cover for 15 minutes, then drain and squeeze dry.

Heat the oil, and add the onion, garlic, and red pepper (if using) to the warming oil. Season very lightly with salt, and cook gently until the onion is soft. Keep the heat low enough to prevent the garlic and onions from browning. If using, stir the anchovies into the pan and push them into the oil with a wooden spoon, so they dissolve, then stir in the olives, raisins, and pine nuts.

Turn up the heat and toss in the cauliflower. Continue to toss until the cauliflower is tender, about 6 minutes.

VARIATION: Substitute broccoli or green beans for the cauliflower.

VARIATION: **Sautéed Piquant Vegetables with Pasta.** As well as for flavoring vegetables, Italians use this piquant combination to dress small pasta, such as *cavatelli* or *orecchiette*. To use on pasta, increase the oil to ½ cup, and boil the pasta in the water used to cook the vegetable—cauliflower, broccoli, and broccoli rabe are especially good. Sauté the vegetable as above, and toss the cooked pasta into the pan. Finish with pecorino cheese. Or, if you have prepared this as a vegetable and have some left over, reheat it in more olive oil and toss it with pasta for another meal.

Asparagus in Balsamic Butter

ASPARAGI AL BALSAMICO

SERVES 4 OR 5

When an acid, such as vinegar or lemon juice, is heated and agitated in the pan with butter, the resulting sauce will become somewhat creamy. This is an unstable emulsion that will not last long, so work quickly. The vinegar will color the vegetables, but that is secondary to the remarkable flavor.

GETTING READY

2 pounds asparagus

THE VEGETABLE

4 to 6 tablespoons unsalted butter, softened

The asparagus from above

Salt and freshly ground black pepper

3 tablespoons balsamic vinegar

Trim, peel if necessary, and boil the asparagus until they are just tender but still offer resistance—2 to 4 minutes, depending on how thick they are. Drain and cool.

Melt 2 tablespoons of the butter in a frying pan. Cut the remaining butter into tablespoon-size pieces. Toss the asparagus into the pan, and sauté until they are just about fully cooked and lightly browned on all sides, 3 to 5 minutes. Season with salt and pepper, and pour on the vinegar. Boil until it is reduced to a tablespoon and then begin to toss 2 to 4 tablespoons of the remaining butter, a tablespoon at a time, into the pan, waiting for each to melt before adding the next. Use as much or little as you like. Constantly and vigorously shake the pan as the butter is added. When it has all melted, serve the asparagus immediately.

VARIATION: **Sautéed Carrots with Balsamic Vinegar.** Substitute carrots, cut into thick sticks, for the asparagus.

VARIATION: **Sautéed Carrots with Orange Juice and Balsamic Vinegar.** Instead of all balsamic vinegar, use 2 tablespoons of blood-orange or Valencia-orange juice and 1 tablespoon of balsamic vinegar.

VARIATION: Olive oil can be used in place of the butter. Drizzle it into the pan as you shake.

Sautéed Mushrooms

TRIFOLATI

SERVES 4

Mushrooms are a soft vegetable and do not need to be boiled before sautéing. *Trifola* is a dialect word for "truffle," so to cook vegetables *trifolati* is to cook them in the manner of truffles—that is, thinly sliced and sautéed in olive oil and parsley. Other seasonings often include capers, white wine, anchovies, or lemon juice. Use any variety of mushrooms.

THE VEGETABLE
1½ pounds mushrooms
3 tablespoons unsalted butter
1 tablespoon extra-virgin olive oil or
    vegetable oil
2 large garlic cloves, chopped

Salt and freshly ground black pepper
Small squeeze of lemon juice
THE FINISH
¼ cup chopped flat-leaf
    parsley

Trim away the ends of the mushroom stems, and use a damp towel to wipe the mushrooms clean. If they are impossibly dirty, dip them quickly into cold water and pat dry. Cut them into thin slices.

Heat the butter and oil in a sauté pan, and cook the garlic until it is just golden, then toss the mushrooms into the pan, season with salt, pepper, and lemon juice, and sauté as in the Primary Recipe. The mushrooms will release and then reabsorb their liquid before they are finished. When they are cooked, stir in parsley and cook for a minute more.

VARIATION: **Sautéed Mushrooms with Marsala or Madeira and Cream.** Omit the parsley above, and when the mushroom liquid has evaporated, pour ¼ cup of dry white wine, Madeira, or Marsala into the pan and boil until it evaporates. Finish by adding a tablespoon or two of heavy cream and reducing slightly.

VARIATION: **Sautéed Diced Zucchini.** Substitute zucchini, trimmed and cut into ½-inch dice, for the mushrooms.

VARIATION: **Sautéed Diced Eggplant.** Whereas the mushrooms above are said to be cooked like truffles, Neapolitans cook eggplant like mushrooms. Go figure! Cut one medium eggplant, without peeling, into a small dice. Put it in a colander with a little salt on each layer and a weight on top, and leave to drain for an hour. Rinse and dry well, and cook as above, using a bit more oil to start, since the eggplant absorbs some, which it will release as it cooks.

VARIATION: A nice treatment for Jerusalem artichokes (sun chokes). Scrub under running water 2 pounds of Jerusalem artichokes, and cut away any blemishes. Their knobs make them close to impossible to peel, so I don't try. Slice them as thin as possible and if you are not cooking them right away, store them in water with a bit of vinegar to keep them from discoloring. Cook two cloves of sliced garlic in ⅓ cup olive oil until golden, add the chokes, season with salt and pepper, and sauté until tender, about 10 minutes. Toss with 2 tablespoons of chopped flat-leaf parsley, and serve.

FRYING

Frying vegetables entails cooking them on the stovetop over high heat in a measurable amount of fat. The fat does not become part of the dish; the vegetables are removed from it and drained before serving. Vegetables that are to be fried are sometimes coated first with flour or eggs or breadcrumbs or a combination.

Pan-Fried Potatoes

PATATINE FRITTE IN TEGAME

SERVES 4 OR 5

Undeniably one of the most delicious ways to cook potatoes! If you have children, you had better double the recipe.

THE VEGETABLE
1½ pounds all-purpose potatoes
Vegetable oil
Salt

Peel the potatoes, and cut them into a ½-inch dice. Rinse them in cold water to remove the excess starch. You will actually see the water run white and then become clear. Pat the potatoes very well to dry them completely, since surface moisture will spatter in the fat.

Pour enough oil into a 12-inch frying pan to reach ½ inch up the sides. Turn the heat under the pan to high, so the oil is hot enough to make the potatoes sizzle. To fry any vegetables properly, the initial heat must be high enough to seal the surface, so they do not absorb the fat. The oil is merely a source of heat; it is actually the steam created in the vegetables by the heat that cooks them.

Carefully slip the potatoes into the pan. Keeping the heat on high, use a large slotted spatula to turn the potatoes over and over until all the sides are golden in color and feel crusty. Then reduce the heat to medium and continue to cook until the potatoes are tender inside, 20 to 25 minutes. Toss them about from time to time, and make sure that they are actually cooking and not just sitting in warm oil—listen for the sound. When the potatoes are cooked, remove with a slotted spoon to paper towels to drain. Salt just before serving, and encourage the kids to try them without ketchup!

VARIATION: To season with garlic or rosemary, put the herbs in the oil before adding the potatoes, and when they are deeply colored (not blackened), remove and discard them.

Fried Plum Tomatoes

POMODORI FRITTI

SERVES 4 OR 5

It was after seeing the movie *Fried Green Tomatoes* that I chauvinistically thought, "Hey, fried ripe Italian plum tomatoes have to be as good." Moist vegetables, such as tomatoes, zucchini, and eggplant, are usually coated before frying, to hasten a crust and to prevent the hot oil from spattering the juices. Here the tomatoes are dipped in flour before frying, but they can also be dipped in cornmeal.

THE VEGETABLE
8 to 10 large, ripe plum tomatoes
Extra-virgin olive oil

Flour for coating
Salt

Wash the tomatoes, and cut out the cores. Cut each tomato from stem to bottom into three slices. The slices should be about ¼ inch thick. If your tomatoes are large, you may get 4 slices. Heat the oil as in the Primary Recipe, and when it is hot enough for the tomatoes to sizzle, dip the slices in the flour and coat lightly on each side. Slip them into the oil—do not crowd the pan—and cook 30 to 40 seconds on each side until they are a golden color. Drain on paper towels, and salt just before serving.

VARIATION: Drizzle a bit of vinegar on the fried tomatoes.

VARIATION: Before cooking the tomatoes, fry whole basil leaves in the oil until crisp, and use them as a garnish.

ROASTING

Vegetables that are roasted are cooked as they would be over a fire—that is, in a very high heat with as much of the surface exposed to the heat as possible. It is one of the simplest and most delicious ways to prepare vegetables. The intense dry heat concentrates the vegetables' flavor as in no other way I know. The higher temperature will brown the vegetables and small ones, such as green beans and asparagus, will shrivel producing a homey, country look rather than an elegant appearance. When my sons were young, "wrinkled vegetables" were a frequent request, in spite of their withered appearance.

Liquid Additions

Since this is a dry-heat method, any liquid should be added only after the vegetables are cooked, either by drizzling a small amount on top or by deglazing the roasting pan with a larger amount, which should then be reduced. If, however, during roasting you notice that the bottom of the pan is beginning to char, add a small amount of water. You may lose the vegetable crust, but you will save the vegetable. This should not happen if your pan is the right size (see Primary Recipe below).

Roasted Green Beans

FAGIOLINI ARROSTITI

SERVES 4

I included this recipe in an article I wrote for *Food & Wine* magazine. When the editors published an issue with their favorite recipes from the past 10 years, this was included. I think that was a fine tribute to simple Italian food.

Preheat oven to 450° F. Make certain that it is up to temperature before putting the vegetables in the oven. Use a shallow roasting pan—metal is best—just large enough so that the vegetables are in one layer. If they are piled up, the heat cannot circulate around them and the vegetables will partly steam. If the pan is too large, it will overheat and can burn the vegetables.

Put the beans, garlic, and thyme in the pan. I leave garlic cloves whole and herbs in sprigs for roasting, since the high heat can burn small pieces. Season with salt and freshly ground pepper, and pour on the olive oil. If you wish to reduce the oil, do so, but always use enough to coat all the vegetables, so they do not dry out. Toss the ingredients together till they are evenly coated with the oil, and then spread them out in one layer.

Put the pan in the oven and bake 12 to 15 minutes, tossing the beans occasionally, until they are cooked. They will be slightly brown.

Remove from the oven, and stir the anchovies, lemon peel, and lemon juice into the pan with the beans. Toss well, and serve warm or at room temperature.

THE VEGETABLE

1 pound green beans, trimmed and washed

3 garlic cloves, smashed and peeled

3 sprigs fresh thyme

Salt and freshly ground black pepper

¼ cup extra-virgin olive oil

THE FINISH

3 anchovies, mashed

Grated zest of 1 lemon

2 to 3 teaspoons lemon juice

VARIATION: **Roasted Green Beans, Carrots, or Asparagus with Balsamic Vinegar.** Omit the above finish ingredients and dress the beans with a dash of balsamic vinegar. Or remove the roasted beans from the pan, place the pan on a stovetop burner, and pour in ⅓ cup balsamic vinegar. Boil and scrape the pan until the vinegar reduces to a few tablespoons, and pour over the beans. Use this variation for carrots or asparagus as well.

VARIATION: **Mixed Roasted Vegetables with Balsamic Vinegar.** For a splendid mixed-vegetable roast, cut four medium carrots, one large red onion, two zucchini, one red and one yellow pepper, and one small head of broccoli into similar pieces just larger than bite-size. Toss them in the roasting pan with salt, pepper, 1 tablespoon fresh or 1 teaspoon dried oregano or 2 tablespoons fresh basil, three garlic cloves, and ½ cup of olive oil. Roast and deglaze the pan with balsamic vinegar as above.

Roasted Butternut Squash

ZUCCA ARROSTATA

SERVES 4 TO 6

If your only experience with winter squash is the boiled and mashed Thanksgiving variety, I think you will be amazed at how roasting concentrates and enhances the flavor. The cooking method is exactly the same as in the Primary Recipe, but the finish is handled differently. I use this method of finishing with vegetables that release juices and sugars into the roasting pan.

THE VEGETABLES

1½ pounds butternut squash, peeled and cut into ¾-inch cubes

2 small yellow onions, peeled and cut into 1-inch chunks

2 tablespoons extra-virgin olive oil

Salt and freshly ground black pepper

3 sprigs fresh thyme

Grated nutmeg or allspice

THE FINISH

⅔ cup dry Marsala

3 tablespoons minced flat-leaf parsley

Preheat oven to 450° F. Roast the squash, onions, and seasonings as in the Primary Recipe, allowing 20 to 25 minutes, or until the vegetables are tender and lightly golden in color. Remove the vegetables to a serving bowl, and place the roasting pan on top of a burner. Pour in the Marsala, and deglaze the pan juices by scraping the bottom of the pan with a wooden spoon or spatula. Allow the liquid to boil and reduce to almost a glaze. Use a rubber spatula to scrape it all out of the pan and onto the vegetables to coat them. Don't waste a drop! Sprinkle with parsley, and serve.

VARIATION: Any winter squash can be cooked this way, or substitute small whole carrots.

VARIATION: Substitute orange juice mixed with about a tablespoon of red-wine vinegar for the Marsala; or use Madeira.

Roasted Mushrooms

FUNGHI ARROSTITI

SERVES 4

Roasted mushrooms are a fine accompaniment to grilled or roasted meats. I also like to scatter slices on top of sautéed chicken or veal as a garnish. Use this method for any variety of mushrooms—porcini, cremini, cultivated, or baby bellas.

THE VEGETABLE
10 ounces to 1 pound fresh mushrooms
3 garlic cloves, smashed and peeled
½ teaspoon salt

Freshly ground black pepper
3 to 4 tablespoons extra-virgin olive oil
THE FINISH
1 tablespoon chopped flat-leaf parsley

Preheat the oven to 450° F. Clean the mushrooms, and either quarter them or cut them into thick slices; very small mushrooms can be left whole. Toss with the garlic, salt, pepper, and oil, and roast as in the Primary Recipe, allowing 10 to 15 minutes, until they are lightly brown and cooked through. Whole mushrooms, depending on the variety, will need 20 to 30 minutes. Toss the parsley in the pan with the hot mushrooms and serve.

VARIATION: **Roasted Mushrooms with Marsala.** Finish the roasted mushrooms with Marsala or Madeira, as in the preceding recipe for Roasted Butternut Squash.

Roasted Potatoes with Garlic and Rosemary

PATATE CON ROSMARINO AL FORNO

SERVES 4

Rosemary with potatoes is quite common in Italy, and deservedly so, since it is a satisfying combination. You can use any herb that you like.

THE VEGETABLE

2 pounds russet potatoes, peeled and cut into pieces about 2 inches large

2 tablespoons fresh rosemary, chopped, or 2 teaspoons dried

5 large whole garlic cloves, smashed and peeled

Salt and freshly ground black pepper

½ cup extra-virgin olive oil

Preheat oven to 450° F. Toss all the ingredients together in a large metal roasting pan, and roast the potatoes according to the Primary Recipe, allowing 45–55 minutes, until the potatoes are lightly brown on the outside and tender within.

VARIATION: **Roasted Potatoes and Onions.** Add two medium onions, peeled and cut into eighths, to the pan.

VARIATION: **Roasted Whole Potatoes.** Use 2 pounds of Red Bliss or Yukon Gold potatoes and do not peel them. Cut them in half or quarters if they are too large.

VARIATION: **Roasted Potatoes with Prosciutto.** Toss 1 ounce of shredded prosciutto and 1 medium red onion, coarsely chopped, into the potatoes in any of the above recipes.

Roasted Gratineed Tomatoes

POMODORI GRATINATI

SERVES 3 TO 6

Roasted tomatoes are a colorful, flavorful accompaniment to meat and fish dishes. They seem to say that you fussed over the meal, whereas in truth they are a snap to prepare. The tomatoes are roasted at a slightly lower temperature than other vegetables to prevent their skins from bursting.

MAKING AHEAD
1 cup dried breadcrumbs (page 17)
THE VEGETABLE
6 medium round tomatoes
Salt and freshly ground black pepper
The breadcrumbs from above
¼ cup freshly grated Parmesan cheese

3 tablespoons finely chopped flat-leaf parsley
1 large garlic clove, minced
3 tablespoons extra-virgin olive oil

Preheat oven to 400° F. Cut the tomatoes in half, and slice a thin piece from each round end so the tomatoes sit flat. Squeeze out the seeds and most of the juice, and set tomatoes in a lightly oiled baking pan. Season the insides with salt and pepper. Mix together the breadcrumbs, cheese, parsley, garlic, and salt and pepper. Scatter the topping evenly over the tomatoes, and drizzle with the olive oil. Brush some oil on the outside of the tomatoes. Bake 20 minutes, or until the topping is brown and the tomatoes are soft.

VARIATION: Add a tablespoon of rinsed capers and a tablespoon of chopped fresh oregano (or a teaspoon dried) to the recipe.

VARIATION: **Cheese-Stuffed Roasted Tomatoes.** In place of the above filling, mix together about ½ pound of grated mozzarella or provolone cheese and ¼ cup of snipped basil. Use this to fill the tomatoes, and bake as above.

Roasted Artichokes

CARCIOFI ARROSTI

SERVES 4 TO 6

In Italy, spring is heralded by the market arrival of small, choke-less artichokes. Platters brimming with this vegetable from the thistle plant are often the focal point of picnic tables. Since we don't get the chokeless variety in our markets, use the following preparation to do away with the pesky center choke.

THE VEGETABLE
2 lemons, cut in half
6 globe artichokes
4 large garlic cloves, minced

1 large bunch Italian flat-leaf parsley, minced
⅓ cup extra-virgin olive oil
Salt and freshly ground black pepper

Preheat the oven to 450° F. Fill a large bowl with cold water, and squeeze in the juice from two of the lemon halves. Drop the squeezed lemons into the water. Using a stainless-steel knife, trim the ends of the stems from the artichokes, but leave the stems themselves attached. Cut the dark green away from the outside of the stem, leaving only the pale center. As you work, use the remaining lemon halves to rub all cut and trimmed surfaces, to avoid discoloration. Remove the tough small leaves from around the base, and then cut the artichoke in quarters. Remove the choke, the prickly center, with a small sharp knife. Drop the trimmed artichokes into the bowl of lemon water.

Mix together the minced garlic and the parsley. Moisten with a few table-spoons of the olive oil, and season with salt and pepper. Remove the artichokes from the water, pat dry, and push the parsley mixture between the leaves. Put the artichokes in one layer in a large roasting pan. Drizzle with the remaining olive oil, season with salt and pepper, and roast according to the Primary Recipe 16–20 minutes, until a fork easily pierces the heart (the spot between the stems and the leaves) and the leaves come off easily when pulled. Mound the artichokes on a platter, and serve warm or at room temperature. Pull the leaves off one by one, and eat the tender part at the base.

Roasted and Mashed Butternut Squash

PASSATO DI ZUCCA ARROSTATA

SERVES 4

When I want mashed squash, I prefer roasting to boiling, because the flavor is so much more intense. Squash-filled ravioli served with butter and Parmesan cheese is one of Italy's most memorable dishes. If you make your own ravioli, you can use this recipe for a filling. It is what I use for the lasagna filling on page 177.

THE VEGETABLE

1 medium-size butternut squash (about
   1 1/2 pounds)

Salt and freshly ground black pepper, to
   taste

Olive oil for the pan

1/4 teaspoon grated nutmeg

3/4 teaspoon chopped fresh thyme,
   or 1/4 teaspoon dried

Preheat the oven to 400° F. Wash and cut the squash in half lengthwise. Scoop out the seeds and strings, and season with salt and pepper. Lay the halves, cut side down, in an oiled baking pan. Roast for about 1 hour, or until the squash is very soft. Check the oven from time to time to be sure that the residual sugar from the squash is not caramelizing too much in the pan; if it looks even close to blackening, pour 2 to 3 tablespoons of warm water into the pan. Repeat as necessary. When the squash is cooked and out of the oven, scrape the pulp into a bowl and discard the skin. Season the squash with nutmeg, thyme, salt, and pepper, and mash the pulp with a fork.

VARIATION: Use this method for any winter squash. If you like, mash in a few tablespoons of olive oil or some butter, and Parmesan cheese.

Roasted Peppers

PEPERONI ARROSTITI

As most Italians did, my grandmother charred peppers over the stovetop's gas flame, usually leaning them against the side of a pan that was simmering something on top of the stove—there was always a pan simmering something on Nonna's stove. Charring peppers over a gas flame or under the broiler is the way I do it when I want to peel peppers but don't want them fully softened (see box, page 397). That way they can be cooked again, such as with the stuffed-and-baked recipe on page 399, without falling apart. When I want peppers tender enough to eat as is, I roast them at a high temperature. Roasted peppers are a popular and delicious Italian antipasto, served as is or dressed with olive oil and perhaps a bit of parsley or oregano and a splash of vinegar.

THE VEGETABLE

6 red bell peppers

Few tablespoons extra-virgin olive oil

1 teaspoon red-wine vinegar (optional)

Salt and freshly ground black pepper

About 3 tablespoons chopped flat-leaf parsley

Preheat the oven to 500° F. Rub the peppers with the olive oil, and place them directly on the oven rack. Roast, turning often, until the peppers are soft and the skins are shriveled and black, 15 to 20 minutes. Use tongs to turn the peppers, and be careful not to break them or the juices will spill out. Remove the peppers, and enclose them in a paper bag or put them in a bowl and cover them with plastic wrap, for at least 10 minutes. The wait allows the peppers both to cool enough to be handled, and to continue steaming so the skins will come off more easily. Slip off the skins, cut in half lengthwise, and remove the stems, ribs, and seeds. Cut the peeled peppers into 1½-to-2-inch-long slices, and put in a shallow dish. Drizzle with oil, vinegar if you like, salt, pepper, and parsley. Serve at room temperature. They will keep a week in the refrigerator.

VARIATION: **Roasted Peppers with Garlic and Ricotta Cheese.** While the peppers are warm, sprinkle 2 teaspoons of minced garlic over them, as well as the oil and parsley, and grate 4 ounces of dried ricotta cheese on top.

VARIATION: **Roasted Peppers with Anchovies and Black Olives.** Tuck 6 to 10 rinsed and dried anchovy fillets among the peppers, and garnish with black olives. Season evenly but lightly with extra-virgin olive oil, vinegar, and chopped parsley. Serve as an antipasto.

To Roast and Peel Peppers

To char peppers for peeling without cooking them completely, do not oil them first. Place them on an oven rack so the peppers are about 2 inches from the broiler. Watch the peppers carefully and turn them with tongs as soon as the skin turns black and blisters. Transfer them to a bag as above and then peel. Cut the peppers in half and remove the stems, ribs, and seeds.

Roasted Peeled Peppers

SPEZZATINO DI PEPERONI ARROSTI

SERVES 6

The flavor of these peppers, which are peeled first and then roasted, is different from the peppers in the preceding recipe, which are roasted whole. It is richer. Use these peppers as a side dish, or spread them on top of toasted and oiled Italian bread for a simple appetizer *bruschetta*. I'm sure if you have a plate of them waiting in the refrigerator a number of delicious ideas will come to mind.

THE VEGETABLE

6 large red bell peppers

¼ cup extra-virgin olive oil

Salt

THE FINISH

1 tablespoon balsamic or red-wine
   vinegar

Preheat the oven to 400° F. Run a vegetable peeler lightly down the sides of the peppers to remove the thin layer of skin. Cut the peppers in quarters, and remove the seeds and ribs. Cut the flesh into slices ½ inch wide, and spread them out in a large roasting pan. They should be no more than 1½ layers deep. Pour on the oil, season with salt and roast for about 30 minutes, until they are tender and slightly charred on some edges.

Remove the peppers from the oven, and while they are still warm, dress with the vinegar. Taste for seasoning, and serve warm or at room temperature.

VARIATION: The same as those for roasted whole peppers (preceding recipe).

BAKED VEGETABLE DISHES

Given Italy's passion for vegetables, it is not surprising that they are often stuffed, layered, sauced, or molded into meals in themselves. They become elegant antipasti, main courses, and, in a very elaborate Italian meal, a course between the antipasto and the main course known as *intermezzo*. They are known by such melodious names as *sformato, timballo,* and *tortino.*

This section includes recipes in which the vegetables are stuffed or layered with other ingredients. Most times the vegetables are boiled, steamed, or roasted before eventually finding their way into a baking dish with sauces, cheese, and/or other vegetables. There is no Primary Recipe since each dish is handled differently. What is worth considering, however, is how you might substitute vegetables in casserole-like dishes that contain meat.

Gratineed Pepper Antipasto

ANTIPASTO DI PEPERONI GRATINATI

SERVES 6 AS AN APPETIZER OR 4 AS A MAIN COURSE

Traditionally served as an antipasto, these flavorful stuffed peppers with a tossed salad also make a very tasty lunch. The peppers can be stuffed and held for several hours before baking.

GETTING READY

2 tablespoons dark raisins

6 medium (about 3 pounds) bell peppers, mixture of red and yellow

ASSEMBLING THE PEPPERS

1 cup dried or fresh breadcrumbs (page 16)

2 tablespoons capers, chopped

The raisins from above

¼ cup pitted and chopped brine-cured green olives

2 medium garlic cloves, minced

2 anchovies, rinsed and minced

3 tablespoons pine nuts

3 tablespoons chopped flat-leaf parsley

3 tablespoons basil, or 2 teaspoons dried oregano

½ teaspoon salt

Generous grinding of black pepper

About ⅓ cup extra-virgin olive oil

Cover the raisins with warm water, soak for 15 to 20 minutes to soften, then drain and squeeze dry. Char the peppers either directly over a gas flame or under a broiler, on the oven rack, until the skins are blackened on all sides but the peppers retain their shape as much as possible. Put the peppers in a closed paper bag or in a bowl covered with plastic wrap, and let sit for 10 minutes, then peel. Carefully pull off the stems and cut the peppers in half lengthwise; scrape out and discard the seeds. Arrange the peppers, in one layer, cut side up in a lightly oiled baking dish.

Preheat the oven to 350° F. Toss the breadcrumbs into a mixing bowl, and add all the remaining ingredients except the olive oil. Mix well, and then drizzle in enough olive oil to coat the ingredients. Depending on your breadcrumbs, you may need a bit more or a bit less than ⅓ cup. Spoon the filling in even amounts into the peppers, drizzle the crumbs with a little more oil, and bake for 30 minutes, until the peppers are tender and the filling is lightly browned. Serve warm or at room temperature.

VARIATION: **Baked Stuffed Zucchini.** Substitute six small zucchini or yellow squash for the peppers. Trim the ends, and blanch them whole in boiling salted water for about 5 minutes; they should be tender when pierced but still hold their shape. Cut the squash in half lengthwise, and use a spoon to scoop out and discard the seeds. Scoop out enough flesh so the shells are about ¼ inch thick. Chop the flesh, and add it to the stuffing. Fill the shells with the above stuffing and bake as above.

VARIATION: Sprinkle about 1 cup of grated Pecorino Romano cheese on top of the peppers (or the squash) before drizzling with oil, and bake as above.

VARIATION: **Meat-Stuffed Zucchini.** To make a more substantial dish, sauté one small minced red or yellow onion, two minced garlic cloves, and ½ pound of ground lamb or beef in 2 tablespoons of olive oil until the meat is no longer pink. Drain off the excess fat, and toss the meat with the breadcrumbs—use fresh breadcrumbs. Stir in 1 beaten egg. Omit the anchovies and capers, but use the olives, raisins, pine nuts, and some herbs—mint is fitting with the lamb. Sprinkle with grated cheese before baking as above.

Baked Endive
with Pancetta and Cheese

INDIVIA CON PANCETTA E FORMAGGIO

SERVES 6

This dish always makes me think of Sunday lunch or supper, especially since it can be assembled on Saturday and baked when needed. A simple leafy salad or, in summer, sliced tomatoes are all that is needed to go with it.

MAKING AHEAD
2 cups White Sauce (page 35)
GETTING READY
Salt and freshly ground white or black
  pepper
Juice of 1 lemon
4 large or 8 small Belgian endives (about
  1½ pounds)

ASSEMBLING THE DISH
16 very thin slices pancetta
The endive from above
2 tablespoons butter
The white sauce from above
¾ cup grated Gruyère cheese
⅓ cup fresh breadcrumbs (page 16)
⅓ cup freshly grated Parmesan cheese

Bring about 3 quarts of water to a boil, add salt, and pour in the lemon juice. Drop the endives into the water, and boil small ones 10 minutes, large 15 minutes. Plunge them into cold water, and squeeze gently from root end to tip to remove all excess water. Trim a thin piece from the root end, and cut large bulbs in half lengthwise. Meanwhile, put the white sauce in a small saucepan to heat.

Enrobe each endive in two slices of pancetta. Use the butter to coat the bottom and sides of a baking dish large enough to hold endives snugly in one layer (or use individual dishes). Season the warmed white sauce with salt and pepper if necessary, and stir in the Gruyère until it melts. Pour a third of the sauce into the baking dish, arrange the endives on top in one layer, and cover with remaining sauce. Sprinkle on the breadcrumbs and Parmesan, and bake 30 minutes, until the endives are tender and the tops are lightly browned.

VARIATION: Use thin slices of prosciutto in place of the pancetta.

VARIATION: **Ham-and-Cheese-Stuffed Zucchini.** Use six medium zucchini in place of the endives, and ¼ pound of chopped boiled ham in place of the pancetta. Trim and parboil the zucchini for 5 minutes, then cut in half and use a spoon to remove the seeds and make a deep trench in the center of each piece. The sides should be at least ¼ inch thick. Stir the ham into the white sauce, and use all of it to fill the zucchini. Arrange them in a buttered baking dish, sprinkle on the cheese and breadcrumbs, and bake as above.

VARIATION: **Baked Cauliflower and Cheese.** Substitute one head of parboiled cauliflower for the endive and ¼ pound of shredded prosciutto for the pancetta. Cut the head into 1-inch pieces, and mix with the white sauce that has been enriched with the Gruyère. Spread it in the dish. Cover with breadcrumbs and Parmesan, and bake until tender.

Baked Asparagus with Fried Eggs

ASPARAGI ARROSTI CON UOVA

SERVES 2 OR 4

Many regions of northern and central Italy claim this recipe as a specialty of their area. Some towns have even named it for themselves. The truth is most likely that many cooks thought of it on their own, simply because eggs and asparagus are a delicious combination. Think of the popularity of asparagus with egg-based hollandaise sauce. Serve this dish for a light lunch or supper.

Since the asparagus spears are cooked twice, it is best to choose asparagus with thick stalks so they do not overcook.

GETTING READY

2 pounds thick-stalked asparagus,
    untrimmed weight

Salt

ASSEMBLING THE DISH

4 tablespoons unsalted butter, diced

The asparagus from above

Salt and pepper

1 cup freshly grated Parmesan cheese

FOR THE EGGS

2 tablespoons butter from above

4 eggs

Trim off the ends of the asparagus and peel the stalks. Bring water to a boil in a large sauté pan; add salt and the asparagus. Drain the stalks when they are tender on the outside but still slightly firm at the center, about 3 minutes after the water returns to the boil. Cool and dry them.

Preheat the oven to 450° F. Use ½ tablespoon of the butter to coat the bottom of a baking dish large enough to hold the cooked asparagus in two or two and a half layers. Lay the asparagus in the pan with all the tips pointing in one direction; if they are very short, you can lay them tip to end in one layer. Sprinkle each layer with salt, a dot of butter (use 1½ tablespoons), and a sprinkle of Parmesan. Make the top layer Parmesan and butter. Bake until the asparagus are tender and the top is lightly brown, about 12 minutes.

When the asparagus are nearly cooked, melt the 2 tablespoons of butter in a sauté pan, and fry the eggs gently, without turning, until they are set. Season with salt and pepper as they cook. Divide the asparagus between two or four plates, and cover each serving with one or two eggs. If there is melted butter in the bottom of the baking dish, it's awfully nice spooned over the eggs.

Baked Mashed Potatoes

PATATE GATTÒ

SERVES 6

I often double this Neapolitan specialty and make and use it as an accompaniment to simple meat or chicken dishes for a buffet. The dish can be assembled the day before, refrigerated overnight, and baked when you are ready. The perfect party dish! Neapolitans often add a savory filling (see suggested variations) and make it a main course.

GETTING READY

2 pounds all-purpose potatoes, peeled and quartered

Salt

5 tablespoons unsalted butter, softened

2 eggs, lightly beaten

½ cup grated Parmesan cheese

Freshly ground black pepper

ASSEMBLING THE DISH

4 tablespoons unsalted butter, softened

About 2 cups dried breadcrumbs (page 16)

The potatoes from above

¼ cup whole basil or flat-leaf parsley leaves

½ pound grated Italian Fontina cheese or smoked provola

Put the potatoes in a deep pot, and cover with cold water by 1 inch. Add salt and bring to a boil. Boil until cooked throughout, about 20 minutes. Pierce with a cake tester or skewer; the potatoes should be tender through to the center. Drain, return to the pot, and shake over the heat briefly to dry; remove from the heat. If you have a potato ricer, this is a good place to use it; otherwise, use a potato masher to mash them until there are no lumps left. Beat in the butter, eggs, Parmesan, salt, and pepper.

Preheat the oven to 375° F. Use 1 tablespoon of the butter to smear the bottom and sides of a 2-quart shallow baking dish or a springform pan. Coat the bottom and sides with breadcrumbs, saving some for the top. Put three-quarters of the potatoes into the pan, and spread them over the bottom and up the sides. Cover with all the basil, and scatter the Fontina over the herb. Carefully spread on the remaining potatoes so as not to dislodge the filling; I drop on spoonfuls and then pat them into place. Sprinkle the remaining breadcrumbs evenly over the top, and dot with the remaining 3 tablespoons of butter, cut into small pieces. Bake 40 minutes, or until the top is nicely browned. Serve the potatoes directly from the baking dish, or be dramatic and unmold them!

VARIATION: **Mashed Potatoes Baked with Tomato Sauce.** Make one recipe for Quick Ragù (page 116). Use enough sauce to cover the bottom layer of potatoes, and save the remaining to serve hot over the top. Substitute mozzarella for the Fontina, omit the basil, and sprinkle ½ cup of Parmesan over the mozzarella.

VARIATION: **Mashed Potatoes Baked with Hard-Boiled Eggs.** Add four hard-boiled eggs, peeled and sliced into ¼-inch rounds, with the Fontina and, if you like, ¼ pound of shredded prosciutto.

VARIATION: **Mashed Potatoes Baked with Vegetables.** With a vegetable filling, the *gattò* can be a main course, a first course, or a very generous vegetable side dish. Possible vegetable fillings to use in place of the Fontina:

- The Sautéed Mushrooms on page 383 or any of the variations of it. If you choose the one with eggplant, use olive oil to coat the dish and drizzle on top, and serve the *gattò* with warm marinara sauce.
- The Braised Leeks and Onions on page 366, but use ¼ cup of meat or chicken broth in place of the lemon juice and zest for braising.
- The Braised Peas with Pancetta (page 364), exactly as it is written.

Zucchini "Parmisagna"

ZUCCHINI "PARMISAGNA"

SERVES 4 TO 6 AS A MAIN COURSE

My son Brad came up with this name when we turned zucchini
Parmesan into zucchini lasagne. There are no lasagna noodles;
instead, long thin slices of zucchini are layered as one would use
the noodles. The resulting dish, which looks and tastes much like
lasagna, makes a very satisfying vegetarian main course or, cut
into small servings, a first course. And, just like lasagna, the dish
can be assembled ahead of time and baked when you need it. For
a double recipe, use a 9-by-12-inch pan.

MAKING AHEAD

3 cups *marinara* sauce (page 30)

GETTING READY

3½ pounds zucchini of equal length,
 washed, ends trimmed

About ¼ cup extra-virgin olive oil

Salt and freshly ground black pepper

The *marinara* sauce from above

3 tablespoons chopped fresh basil,
 plus ½ cup whole basil leaves for
 assembling

ASSEMBLING THE DISH

The tomato sauce from above

The zucchini from above

½ cup freshly grated Parmesan cheese

½ cup grated Italian Fontina cheese

½ cup grated fresh mozzarella

The whole basil leaves from above

Preheat oven to 400° F. Cut the zucchini into ¼-inch-thick slices lengthwise, and
lay them on a lightly oiled baking sheet. Do not crowd the pan, or the slices will
steam and not brown. Brush the tops with some of the oil, sprinkle with salt and
pepper, and roast, turning once, for 5 minutes per side, or until tender and slightly
browned. Remove the zucchini from the oven.

Meanwhile, heat 1 tablespoon of the olive oil in a medium-size frying pan, and
add the tomato sauce and the chopped basil. Simmer until the sauce is reduced to
2½ cups and has thickened.

Spread a light coating of the sauce in the bottom of an 8-by-8-inch baking pan. Cover the sauce with a single layer of slightly overlapping zucchini slices. Save the prettiest slices for the top layer. Top the bottom layer with more tomato sauce, one-third of the Parmesan, and a sprinkling of half the other two cheeses and half the whole basil leaves. Tear very large leaves in half. For the second layer, repeat all the above steps, saving one-third of the Parmesan for the top. Add the final layer of zucchini, arranging them carefully, and sprinkle them with the reserved Parmesan. Drizzle lightly with remaining olive oil, and bake 25 minutes, or until bubbly and brown. Let rest 10 minutes before cutting into squares.

VARIATION: **Eggplant "Parmisagna."** Use baked slices of eggplant in place of the zucchini. Before roasting the eggplant, put the slices in a colander, salt and weight them, and drain for 45 minutes. Rinse, pat dry, and then bake as above.

Eggplant Parmesan

PARMIGIANA DI MELANZANE

SERVES 4

People often ask me what my favorite recipe is in my first book, *We Called It Macaroni*. Julia Child would call this an unanswerable "media question" in the category of that "favorite meal," "favorite restaurant," and so forth. I agree that all the possibilities cannot be reduced to one sole survivor. I do have, however, one that is definitely in the running. My grandmother's eggplant Parmesan is the best rendition of this ever-popular dish. I repeat it here in case you don't have a copy of *Macaroni* (tsk, tsk), and because this recipe and the variations that follow demonstrate the different ways to coat vegetables for frying.

MAKING AHEAD
1½ cups *marinara* sauce (page 30)
GETTING READY
1 medium eggplant (about 1¼ pounds)
Salt
FOR FRYING
4 large eggs

Salt and freshly ground black pepper
Extra-virgin olive oil for frying
The eggplant from above
FOR ASSEMBLING THE DISH
The *marinara* sauce from above
2 tablespoons freshly grated Parmesan
   cheese

Peel the eggplant, and cut it into paper-thin slices. Place the slices in a colander, salting each layer, and put a plate and a weight on top. Let sit at least an hour to draw out the water. Rinse and dry well, squeezing gently to remove all excess liquid.

Beat the eggs in a pie pan with some salt and pepper, and then pour enough oil into a sauté pan to reach at least ½ inch up the sides. Dip the eggplant in the eggs, hold them up so the excess egg drains off, and then fry as in the Primary Recipe, turning once, until they are golden on each side, less than 20 seconds a side. Drain on paper towels or brown paper bag, and repeat with remaining slices.

Preheat the oven to 400° F. Oil a baking dish lightly, and layer the eggplant with a light coating of *marinara* sauce. Sprinkle the cheese on the top layer, and bake for 10 minutes. Once assembled, the eggplant can wait a few hours before baking.

VARIATION: To coat the eggplant or other vegetables with breadcrumbs for frying, dip them first in the eggs, and then turn them in a separate dish of dried breadcrumbs. When vegetables are coated with breadcrumbs, let them sit on wire racks for at least 10 minutes, so the crumbs have time to adhere. This will keep the crumbs from falling into the oil.

FRITTATAS

When Neapolitans suggest making a *frittata,* they don't refer to it as a "delicious *frittata*" or a "good *frittata*" but as "*una bella frittata.*" They serve these lovely, golden flat omelets warm for a light lunch or supper; or at room temperature, cut into wedges, for an antipasto; or tucked inside Italian bread or focaccia for sandwiches. They may be seasoned simply with a few herbs and a bit of cheese, or chock-full of the foods you love best. They are indeed beautiful.

Depending on how lavish a filling you use, you will need six to eight eggs for four people, three to four for two people. For a *frittata* of medium thickness, use a 10-to-12-inch frying pan for the larger number of eggs and a 6-to-8-inch for the lesser amount. The size of the pan will determine the thickness of the finished dish, so if you want a great, fat *frittata* use the smaller pan for the larger number of eggs. It will take a bit longer to cook. A sturdy nonstick frying pan is a help but not essential.

Filling ingredients that need cooking should be completely cooked and cooled before they are added to the eggs. Obviously, this is a superb way to use leftovers such as boiled, braised, or roasted vegetables; pasta with or without sauce; rice, shellfish, and small pieces of sausage and meatballs.

The technique of making a *frittata* differs from that of a French omelet in that the eggs are not folded over a filling. An omelet is meant to be eaten while still runny—*a la baveuse,* as the French say. A *frittata* is firm, with the eggs completely set.

I know few Italians who do not remember *frittate* as being a standard part of their family's home cooking. And I don't know two who make them the same way. This is my way.

Asparagus Frittata

FRITTATA DI ASPARAGI

SERVES 4 FOR A LIGHT MEAL OR 6 AS AN ANTIPASTO

The *frittata* is equally delicious hot or at room temperature. The recipe may be doubled, but cook it in two separate batches or the eggs will get away from you! I have begun the recipe with directions for cooking the asparagus—I like them roasted—but you can substitute any cooked vegetable that you have on hand, or any raw one you want to cook.

Preheat the oven to 400° F. Put the asparagus in a single layer in a large roasting pan. Add the garlic to the pan. Season the asparagus with salt and pepper, and coat with the 2 tablespoons of olive oil. Roast for 5 to 6 minutes, or until asparagus are tender and slightly colored. Watch carefully, and turn once or twice during cooking. Cut the cooked asparagus into 1-inch-long pieces, and let cool until tepid.

Using a fork, beat the eggs with the salt and pepper just until the whites and yolks are blended; do not beat them so long that they foam. Add the cheese, parsley, and asparagus.

Heat the 3 tablespoons of olive oil in a 10-inch frying pan. When the oil is hot enough so that a drip of water will sizzle in the pan, pour in the eggs, and immediately reduce the heat to medium. As soon as the eggs are in the pan, begin to swirl them with the flat side of the fork, continually breaking the bottom to allow the uncooked egg to run through. At the same time, shake the pan well to keep the eggs from sticking on the bottom. When the eggs begin to form large

GETTING READY

½ pound asparagus, peeled

2 cloves garlic, smashed and peeled

Salt and freshly ground black pepper

2 tablespoons extra-virgin olive oil

THE FRITTATA

6 large eggs

Salt and freshly ground black pepper

¼ pound scamorza or mozzarella cheese, grated

2 tablespoons flat-leaf parsley

The asparagus from above

3 tablespoons extra-virgin olive oil

curds on top, pat them into a flat, round shape with the fork and leave them until they are softly set but still moist on the top. Check the bottom color by picking up a corner and looking; you want it to be lightly brown. When it is, place a serving-size plate or flat cookie sheet over the pan, and reverse the *frittata* onto it. Slide the *frittata* back into the pan to brown the second side— a minute at most. Slide onto serving plate or cutting board.

VARIATION: Potato-Tomato Frittata. In place of the asparagus, use ½ pound of either Roasted Potatoes with Garlic and Rosemary (page 392) or Pan-Fried Potatoes (page 385). Add them to the six eggs along with 1 cup of chopped tomatoes. Use the cheese as above, and ⅓ cup snipped basil in place of the parsley.

VARIATION: Frittata Verde (frittata with herbs and greens). Instead of the asparagus, stir 1 cup of chopped mixed fresh herbs and greens into the eggs. Use a combination of about five different ones, choosing perhaps from parsley, basil, mint, baby spinach leaves, arugula, sage, chervil, sorrel, lovage, celery leaves, and marjoram. Chop the greens into small pieces, and mix them together. In place of the cheese above, use 3 tablespoons freshly grated Parmesan or pecorino, and when the *frittata* is cooked, sprinkle 2 tablespoons of red-wine vinegar over the top.

Spaghetti Frittata

FRITTATA DI SPAGHETTI

SERVES 4

Maybe it's only because they are an instant transport to my childhood, but *frittate di pasta* are *bellissima frittate!* Make them with spaghetti with *marinara,* ziti with *ragù,* noodles with Alfredo—it matters not. They are delicious.

MAKING AHEAD
About 4 cups leftover spaghetti with
 sauce, at room temperature
THE FRITTATA
6 large eggs
Salt and freshly ground black pepper
½ cup freshly grated Parmesan cheese

The spaghetti from above
3 tablespoons extra-virgin olive oil
FOR THE FINISH
½ cup hot *marinara* sauce (optional)
Freshly grated Parmesan cheese

Beat the eggs with the salt and pepper as in the Primary Recipe. Stir in the cheese and the spaghetti. Heat the oil in a 10-to-12-inch frying pan, and when it is hot, pour in the eggs. Stir with a fork until softly set, then reverse and cook the second side as directed in the Primary Recipe. Serve with additional tomato sauce and more Parmesan if desired.

SALADS

INSALATE

Salads can show up at one of three places during an Italian meal: they may begin the meal as an antipasto, or accompany the entrée as a vegetable (*contorno*), or arrive at the end of dinner, just before the fruit, cheese, or, if there is one, dessert. Although some salads may be versatile enough to be served at any one of the three courses, most are intended for a specific purpose and place.

An antipasto salad is there to stimulate the appetite and can be quite substantial—in ingredients, not size. It may contain cheese and seafood as well as raw or cooked vegetables. The box on page 356 has a number of suggestions for boiled and then marinated vegetables to begin a meal. Many antipasto salads are satisfying as main dishes for lunch or ideal additions to a cold buffet. I am always happy to sit down to a noon meal of a loaf of bread, a jug of wine, and tuna fish with tomatoes and boiled white beans; or *insalata caprese,* with ripe tomatoes, fresh mozzarella, basil, and olive oil; or thin slices of fennel and mushrooms with shaved Parmesan.

Salads served with the meal are considered a vegetable and must balance or contour (*contornare*) the main course. They may be tossed greens or cooked and marinated vegetables, but they should not include strongly flavored or substantial ingredients that will vie with the entrée for attention. The salad at the end of the meal is meant to refresh the palate and aid in digestion. Nonna called it "the stomach's toothbrush."

When you make a mixed salad, keep in mind the character of the lettuce and other ingredients: are they bitter or sweet, crunchy or soft, salty or acidic? Select contrasting tastes and textures, so the mix is appealing and interesting.

Salad Greens

Italian salads are usually classified as *insalata verde* (green salad) or *insalata mista* (mixed salad). A green salad is made with lettuce of one or several varieties. Mixed salads have the addition of other seasonal produce. Typical Italian greens are loose-leaf heads such as our Boston and Bibb lettuces and the firmer romaine lettuce. Bitter greens are a favorite addition to salads, and I know many an Italian-American grandfather who could be seen picking wild dandelions in the backyard for dinner. Other sharp salad greens include chicory, arugula, watercress, and escarole. If an Italian were to guide you in buying lettuce at the market, he would instruct you to choose *insalata in stagione,* the greens in season.

Italian Salad Dressing

In all my years of living at home, salad dressing was always on the table—in two bottles, one holding olive oil, the other vinegar. That was all we knew of as "Italian dressing." When we wanted garlic, we rubbed the bowl with it; herbs we tossed into the greens. Dining out, I felt as finicky as Sally of *When Harry Met Sally,* because I would order the salad without any dressing and ask the waiter to bring oil and vinegar on the side. And if he brought the salad before the meal, in the typical American fashion, I left it there until after I finished my main course and then dressed and ate it. Even adjusting to lemon juice instead of vinegar was monumental.

Italians dress a salad by pouring just enough oil, vinegar or lemon juice, and salt and pepper directly onto the ingredients and tossing. That is the way I usually prepare my salad, but not the only way. I do not think the integrity of the flavors suffers at all if you put the dressing ingredients in a jar and shake them, or whisk them together in the bottom of the salad bowl before tossing in the greens. What will make the dressing taste un-Italian is adding a heap of ingredients that don't belong there. That's not to say that your salad dressing won't be good, it just won't resemble any you ate in Italy.

Arugula Salad

INSALATA DI RUCOLA

SERVES 5 OR 6

A very simple salad in which the sweetness of the Parmesan balances the sharp taste of the arugula, and the crunch of pine nuts offers a contrast of texture. The inspiration for this salad came from Patricia Wells' book *Trattoria*. She was inspired by a tightly layered salad she had eaten in Florence. All this inspiration must be proof of the perfect marriage of ingredients.

GETTING READY

¼ cup pine nuts

THE SALAD

2 to 3 bunches arugula (about 10
　　ounces)

The pine nuts from above

1-ounce piece of Parmigiano Reggiano

THE DRESSING

3 to 4 tablespoons extra-virgin olive oil

1 tablespoon fresh lemon juice

Salt

Freshly ground black pepper

Preheat the oven to 350° F. Spread the pine nuts in a single layer on a baking sheet, and toast for 5 minutes, or until golden. Remove and cool.

Remove the tough stems from the arugula. Wash and dry the leaves well. A salad spinner is one of the greatest kitchen treasures. With so little effort on your part, it removes the excess water from the leaves, which would wilt your lettuce, water down your dressing, and leave your salad lifeless. Roll the arugula in a kitchen towel to dry it completely. Tear very large pieces in half; small bite-size leaves can remain whole. Drop the arugula into a salad bowl, and if not ready to serve, cover it with a sheet of damp paper towel and refrigerate. If your bowl doesn't fit in the refrigerator, then wrap the leaves in a damp towel and refrigerate.

Toss the pine nuts with the arugula. Use a vegetable peeler to shave long, thin slivers of cheese directly on top of the salad. Drizzle on the oil and lemon juice, and season with salt and pepper. Toss together carefully, so as not to break the cheese more than necessary. Serve immediately.

SERVING: As well as a good finish to dinner, this salad is a nice accompaniment to simple broiled or grilled meats.

VARIATION: **Tender Greens Salad.** Instead of all arugula, use a combination of tender baby greens sold in markets as "mesclun." These mixes usually contain some bitter greens such as arugula but if not, buy a little and toss it in. The sharpness is a good contrast to the cheese.

Mixed Salad

INSALATA MISTA

6 TO 8 SERVINGS

When I was about 12 years old, I decided with a group of my friends that we should have traveling dinners. I don't remember if they were the rage at the time or if I had read about them somewhere, but we were thrilled with the concept and began our JUG (just-us-girls) "eat-arounds." For our first roving meal, my father helped me construct the most dazzling mixed salad that any one of the girls had ever seen. From that meeting on, mine was the salad home, and if not the most popular, then surely a close second to Claire O'Keefe, who together with her mother set out a make-your-own-ice-cream-sundae smorgasbord.

Italian mixed salads are not always as copious as ours was. See the variations below for less abundant mixes. My father and I arranged our salad as described here, but it is more common to toss all the ingredients together in the bowl.

GETTING READY

1 red onion, peeled and thinly sliced

THE SALAD

Salt

1 large garlic clove, unpeeled, cut in half

1 large or 2 small heads Boston or Bibb
    lettuce, trimmed, washed, and dried

1 small head romaine lettuce, trimmed,
    washed, and dried

1 medium cucumber, scrubbed but
    unpeeled unless waxed

1 bunch radishes, washed, thinly sliced

The red onion from above

1 yellow or red pepper, washed, stem
    and seeds removed, cut into thin rings

1 cup black olives, pitted

2 medium ripe red tomatoes

THE DRESSING

About 6 tablespoons extra-virgin
    olive oil

About 2 tablespoons red-wine vinegar

Salt and freshly ground black pepper

Drop the onion slices into a bowl of cold water, and soak for 45 minutes to an hour. Change the water three times during its soak. Drain and pat dry.

Sprinkle the inside of a salad bowl—preferably wood—with about a teaspoon of salt. Take one of the garlic halves and, using the cut side, rub the salt around the bowl, pressing hard so the garlic juice is released into the bowl. Repeat with the other half. Discard the garlic.

Take the largest leaves of the Boston lettuce and stand them around the bowl so their spines are down and the leafy tops frame the bowl's rim. Break the remaining Boston lettuce and all the romaine into bite-size pieces, toss them together, and make a bed on the bottom of the bowl.

Working nearest the large leaves of lettuce, make a ring of cucumber, slightly overlapping the slices. Lay any extra slices on top of the torn lettuce. Next, arrange a ring of radishes just on top of but not hiding the cucumbers. Put extras in the middle with the cucumbers. Arrange a row of onions, and then of peppers. Scatter the olives attractively around the salad. I don't add the tomatoes until I am ready to present the salad. Cover salad with a damp paper towel, and refrigerate until serving time.

Make a nest of tomatoes in the center of the salad. Put the oil, vinegar, salt, and pepper in a glass jar with a tight-fitting lid, and shake them together. When everyone has had a chance to admire the salad, drizzle the dressing over all and toss well.

SERVING: As a vegetable side dish, or to finish a meal.

VARIATION: Soak the red onion as described above. Use one small head each of Boston lettuce and romaine. Toss them together with 1 cup fresh mint or basil leaves and the onion, and dress with 6 tablespoons olive oil and 3 to 4 tablespoons lemon juice, salt, and pepper.

VARIATION: Use vegetables that are fresh and in season. Slivers of carrots, cherry tomatoes in place of the salad tomatoes, thin slices of fennel can all be part of the mix.

Radicchio and Pancetta Salad

INSALATA ALLA VICENTINA

SERVES 6

Roy Bailey, my fiancé, taught me a great way to handle offers of foods that I may think I don't like. If I am about to cook something new to our menu, I usually ask him, "Do you like such-and-such?" If he does not, his reply is always, "Well, I don't, but maybe I've just never had it prepared right." I should have been so diplomatic a few years back, while visiting Vicenza, in the region of the Italian Veneto. When grappa was offered after our meal, I stated without hesitation that I did not care for its harsh taste. We were then presented with a tall bottle that held a long, graceful, red-leafed radicchio suspended in the liquid. I took a sip. Somehow this treasure of Treviso, this "king of salads," had tamed the fire of that distilled spirit. It was prepared right.

Radicchio is member of the chicory family of lettuces. The long variety in the bottle was Treviso radicchio, prized for its red leaf and agreeable sharpness, and available here in specialty-food stores at very dear prices. More common are the small cabbage-shaped heads with white bottoms. Either one can be used in this salad.

THE SALAD

3 heads radicchio, about 12 ounces

THE DRESSING

2 tablespoons extra-virgin olive oil

¼ pound pancetta, finely chopped

3 tablespoons red-wine vinegar

Salt and freshly ground black pepper

Separate the radicchio leaves from the head, and wash them well in several changes of cold water. Dry the leaves well, and tear them into large pieces. Put them in a salad bowl, cover with a damp paper towel, but do not refrigerate.

Heat the olive oil and pancetta in an 8-to-10-inch sauté pan over moderate heat. Cook slowly, so the meat crisps without the fat's burning, about 10 minutes. When the pancetta is as crisp as well-done bacon, season lightly with salt and pepper. Raise the heat, and pour in the vinegar—carefully, in case it snaps. Let it evaporate completely, and then pour the pancetta and fat from the pan over the radicchio, and serve immediately.

SERVING: As an antipasto or a vegetable side dish.

VARIATION: **Endive and Pancetta Salad.** Substitute Belgian endive for the radicchio.

VARIATION: **Wilted Spinach Salad.** Remember wilted-spinach salad? A nice twist on the Treviso salad is spinach with the dressing above made with balsamic vinegar. Pour the hot dressing over about 1 pound of baby spinach leaves tossed with ½ cup of thinly sliced green onions (scallions). Use some of the green parts of the onions as well as the white bulbs.

Fennel, Mushroom, and Parmesan Salad

INSALATA DI FINOCCHIO, FUNGHI,
E PARMIGIANO REGGIANO

SERVES 4

Although this salad is popular throughout much of northern Italy, I associate it with Venice and a restaurant that hugged one of its quieter canals. The mushrooms were large, meaty wild ones, but I have made it quite successfully with the cultivated kind.

GETTING READY	The fennel from above
1 small head fennel	2-to-3-ounce piece of Parmesan cheese
THE SALAD	THE DRESSING
½ pound firm white mushrooms, wiped clean	⅓ cup extra-virgin olive oil
	1½ tablespoons lemon juice
1 lemon, cut in half	Salt and freshly ground black pepper

Slice off the stalks of the fennel bulb, and discard any bruised or discolored outer leaves from the bulb. Cut out the core, and then slice the bulb in half lengthwise. Cut the bulb into the thinnest possible slices, and drop them into a bowl of very cold water; let soak for 20 minutes before draining and drying.

Trim away the dried ends of the mushrooms, but leave the stems attached. Cut the mushrooms into very thin slices, about ⅛ inch thick. Squeeze a little lemon juice over them to keep them from discoloring.

Choose the most attractive fennel slices, and make a ring around the outside edges of four salad plates. Fill the center of the plates with the remaining pieces, and then cover them with a neat arrangement of mushrooms. Use a vegetable peeler to shave the cheese into very thin pieces, and divide them evenly in the centers of the salads.

Drizzle the olive oil and lemon juice evenly over the salads and season each with salt and pepper, or shake the dressing in a jar and drizzle it on top of each salad.

SERVING: Serve as an antipasto, or make one large salad and include it as part of a cold buffet. If you eliminate the mushrooms and increase the amount of fennel, the salad is quite refreshing at the end of a meal.

Beet and Walnut Salad

INSALATA DI BARBABIETOLA E NOCE

SERVES 4 TO 6

Put the beets on the lettuce just when you are ready to serve the salad or they will bleed into the lettuce.

GETTING READY
6 medium beets, red, yellow, or 2 of
    each
THE SALAD
1 small head Boston or Bibb lettuce
The beets from above
¾ cup walnuts
3 tablespoons chopped chives or
    scallions

THE DRESSING
⅓ cup extra-virgin olive oil
1½ tablespoons lemon juice or red-wine
    vinegar
Salt and freshly ground black pepper

Cut off all but 1 inch of the tops of the beets; leave the root ends on so the beets will not lose their color. Wash well, but do not peel. Drop the beets into a large pot of boiling, salted water, and cook until tender when pierced with a cake tester or skewer, 15 to 20 minutes. Drain, and let cool. Scrape off the peel, and dice the beets into pieces of about ½ inch.

Separate the leaves of the lettuce, leaving them whole. Wash well, dry, and wrap in a towel until serving time. Chop the walnuts so they are about the same size as the beet pieces. Toss the beets and walnuts together in a bowl with the chives or scallions. Pour on the oil, add lemon juice or vinegar, and season with salt and pepper. Toss together well, and chill for at least an hour. Serve on top of lettuce leaves.

SERVING: Serve as an antipasto or a vegetable.

VARIATION: Beet, Celery, and Walnut Salad. Cut four tender inside stalks of celery the same size as the beets. Marinate with the beets.

VARIATION: Beet Salad with Hard-Boiled Eggs. For an antipasto, garnish the salad with finely chopped hard-boiled egg and 3 tablespoons of minced parsley.

VARIATION: Shake the dressing ingredients together with a generous tablespoon of Dijon-style mustard. The tang of the mustard is lovely with the beets.

VARIATION: Garnish the salad or the variations with slivers of pecorino cheese—about 2 ounces.

CHAPTER 7

Desserts

When I was growing up, we didn't expect sweet desserts at the end of a meal, although they were available for special occasions and mid-morning or afternoon snacks. At daily meals, there was always a plate of fresh fruit and a bowl of nuts in their shells on the table. When fresh peaches were in season, my grandfather would cut them up and drop them into a little wine for us. A nutcracker was permanently tucked into the nut bowl, but my uncle Frank had long ago shown us how to squeeze two nuts together to crack their shells, so we eschewed the gadget for the more impressive, seemingly worldly method. Nonna sometimes put little boxes of the Italian nougat candy, *torrone,* in the bowl with the nuts, and we were as pleased by the pretty boxes as we were by the sweet inside. Altogether, it was a most satisfying end to dinner.

This does not mean that there is a dearth of Italian sweets. Indeed, they could fill volumes. Italian bakeries are as predominant in Italian neighborhoods as shops with dangling salami and provolone. Fancy-pastry cases overflow with the cream-filled *zeppole,* crunchy biscotti, sugared *wandi,* and flaky sfogliatelle that Italians usually buy rather than bake at home. Whenever we visited "the aunts" (a Sunday and holiday ritual) or dropped in to see a *paesan,* we followed the Italian custom of stopping at the Italian bakery for a selection of traditional pastries to bring along with us. Many of the choices were filled with such a strong rum-flavored cream that I can still call up the powerful scent that emanated from the box.

On a work-free, casual day, I may well be inspired to roll, beat, pipe, and fry up one of those traditional bakery items. But for the busy days when I know someone may ask, "What's for dessert?" I'm ready with a homey and simple-to-make Italian sweet, *dolce casalingo.* The desserts that follow are some of my favorites.

PUDDINGS

It fascinates me how inventive Italian home cooks can deftly turn kitchen staples into delicious desserts. Cooked rice, pasta, semolina, polenta, as well as soft ricotta cheese—all provide the makings of homespun puddings. Unlike typical creamy American puddings, these Italian creations are more like dense, moist cakes. You may find such puddings referred to by the name *migliaccio*, from the Italian for "millet," from which both sweet and savory puddings were made.

The basic elements of puddings are simply starch, eggs, milk, and a sweetener, but they can be combined and treated differently to create simple or elaborate results. For a lighter-textured pudding, keep the number of eggs constant, but separate some of the whites and beat them as described on page 425. Fold them into the completely cooled pudding base. For a crusty exterior, butter and sugar the dish; for a tender pudding all around, bake it in a water bath.

[In the early twentieth century in Rome, when one had a party it was an unspoken but common practice to rent a number of showy desserts from a bakery.]

They were beautiful tortes, covered with fancy sugar icing and figurines of butter cream. A small rental fee was charged . . . but the host only paid in toto for those that had actually been cut. At the end of the party, the caterer came to fetch them, and, undoubtedly, to rent them out again the next day. To [Aunt Giulia's] credit . . . she never watched them as some of her friends did with terror in their hearts, lest a guest should demand a slice . . . thereby ruining completely the chance of returning it.

—NIKA STANDEN HAZELTON,
Reminiscence and Ravioli

Ricotta Pudding

BUDINO DI RICOTTA

SERVES 6 TO 8

Budino di ricotta is a specialty of Rome, and if the name had not been on the menu, I could not have guessed what was in that first bite I took so long ago. My taste buds were saying "fallen citrus soufflé," but there was the word "ricotta" right in front of me. The dessert is meant to be served at room temperature or cold, but if you eat it warm with Orange-Flavored Crema (page 451) poured over the top, you will think soufflé. For this pudding the ricotta provides the milk and the flour is added for the starch.

Depending on the source of your ricotta, it may contain an excess of residual water. If you notice a milky white moisture surrounding the cheese, then scoop the ricotta into a sieve and let it sit for about 15 minutes, shaking it from time to time, so the excess water drips off. If it does not appear wet, just proceed with the recipe.

Preheat the oven to 325° F. Generously butter the bottom and sides of a 2-quart baking dish.

GETTING READY

1 pound ricotta cheese

THE PUDDING BASE

The drained ricotta from
    above

5 eggs

⅔ cup sugar

2 tablespoons flour

Pinch salt

It can be round or square or oval, but the sides should be at least 2 inches deep. My favorite is a white ceramic oval dish that is about 8 inches across and 12 inches long. Sprinkle sugar into the dish, and tip the dish around so the sugar covers the butter, then turn it upside down and tap the bottom to remove excess sugar.

Push the ricotta through a sieve into a large bowl. This will lighten and smooth it. Separate four of the eggs, and set the four whites aside. Beat the one whole egg and the four yolks together in a small bowl or cup until they are well blended. Use a wooden spoon or a sturdy whisk to beat the eggs into the cheese. When they are completely mixed in, beat in the sugar, flour, and salt. Stir in the cinnamon, lemon and orange zests, liqueur or extract, and the candied peel if you have it.

In a separate and perfectly clean bowl, beat the egg whites with a pinch of salt until they form peaks but are not dry. Stir a quarter of the beaten whites into the cheese base to lighten it, and then fold in the remaining whites.

So as not to deflate the whites, hold the mixing bowl close to the baking dish, and pour and scrape in the batter. Put the dish in the middle of the oven, and bake for 30 to 40 minutes, until a cake tester inserted an inch from one of the sides comes out clean.

Remove from the oven, and sift confectioners' sugar over the top. Serve at room temperature or cold.

THE FLAVORS
1 teaspoon cinnamon

Grated zest of ½ small lemon

Grated zest of 1 orange

2 tablespoons orange liqueur, or 1 tablespoon orange extract

3 tablespoons finely chopped candied orange peel (optional)

THE FINISH
Confectioners' sugar

VARIATION: Raisins are often added to a ricotta pudding. Soak about ¼ cup of raisins in water or rum to cover for 15 minutes, and then drain. Stir them into the pudding base with the zests.

VARIATION: Lemon-Ricotta Pudding with Blueberry Sauce. Instead of the orange zest and orange liqueur, use the zest of one whole lemon and 1 tablespoon vanilla. Serve the pudding with the cooked blueberry sauce on page 453.

VARIATION: Chefs often unmold this pudding to make a more sophisticated presentation. It is a nice touch if you are called upon to bring a dessert to a gathering of appreciative eaters. Grease and flour a 2-quart springform pan, Bundt pan, or fancy pudding mold. If the pan is deep, count on approximately 45 minutes baking time. Let the cooked pudding rest in the pan for 20 minutes, then unmold (on a paper lace doily), and sprinkle generously with confectioners' sugar.

Beating Egg Whites

Can there be a kitchen miracle more impressive than the conversion of a few viscous tablespoons of albumen into a giant bank of puffy white clouds? The phenomenon of beaten whites relies on a few simple principles that will determine the size of your clouds. The whites should be at room temperature. If you are starting with cold eggs, warm them, in their shells, in a bowl of hot water for 10 to 15 minutes.

The whites and the bowl must be free of any fat that will interfere with their mounting. Wash and dry the bowl and the beaters well before beginning. Egg yolks have fat in them, so if even a small drop gets into the whites it can prevent them from achieving their full potential. Because there are few more disheartening culinary disasters than separating a dozen eggs only to have the last yolk break and dribble into the whites, use three bowls to separate the eggs. Break one egg, and, using your hands or an egg separator, divide the two parts and put the white into one bowl and the yolk in another. If the white is perfectly clean, transfer it to the third bowl. Break another egg, and if that white is untainted, transfer it to the bowl with the good white. If you break a yolk and contaminate the white, save it for scrambled eggs.

Perfectly clean, warm whites will mount better and remain more stable when an acid is present. An unlined copper bowl provides natural acid, but hand-beating is not for everyone. To beat with an electric mixer, moisten a paper towel with some vinegar and rub the inside of the bowl and the beaters with it. Do not rinse with water after rubbing. You can also add a pinch of salt or cream of tartar to the whites, which helps stabilize the pouf.

Lastly, the "peaked but not dry" part. Overbeaten egg whites cannot be incorporated into a base. As you fold, they break up into small and smaller white globs but never blend in. Until you can definitely tell by eye when they are ready, place an egg in its shell on top of the whites when they have developed peaks. The egg should sink down ¼ inch. They are ready at that point. If you have inadvertently overbeaten the egg whites, add one raw egg white to the mixture and beat again until the whites have softened to the perfect point.

Semolina Pudding

BUDINO DI SEMOLINA

SERVES 6 TO 8

This is a firm but light pudding with an elusive and addicting flavor. I am able now to find semolina in my supermarket, in the flour section. If it is not in yours, try specialty-food stores or Italian markets, or use the American cereal farina, which is in fact semolina.

FOR THE PUDDING

3 cups milk

Pinch salt

½ cup semolina

⅔ cup sugar

5 tablespoons unsalted butter, softened, plus more for buttering the baking dish

Grated zest of 1 small lemon

1 tablespoon pure vanilla extract

6 large eggs

FOR THE FINISH

2 to 3 tablespoons confectioners' sugar

FOR SERVING (OPTIONAL)

1 recipe Almond Crema made with 1 tablespoon flour or cornstarch (page 451)

1 recipe Dried Tart-Cherry Sauce (page 454)

Pour the milk and the salt into a deep (about 3-quart) saucepan—nonstick if available—and place the pan over medium heat. Once the milk shows signs of tiny bubbles around the edge, watch it carefully so you can see the first bubble that is a sign of boiling. Immediately begin to add the semolina in a slow, steady stream, whisking rapidly to prevent it from lumping. When all the semolina has been added, switch to a wooden spoon, and reduce the heat slightly. If the heat is too high, the pudding will spit bits of semolina all over you and the stove; at the right temperature, it will make small, gentle poufs. Stir continuously, being sure to reach down to the bottom and around the sides. After 6 to 7 minutes, the semolina should have thickened enough so that when you stir it pulls from the sides and bottom of the pan. Remove from the heat, and immediately use the wooden spoon to beat in the sugar and butter. When the butter has melted, stir in the lemon zest and vanilla, and then transfer the pudding to a large bowl to cool for 30 minutes, stirring it from time to time.

Preheat the oven to 350° F and set a rack in the center of the oven. Butter an 8-cup round or oval baking dish that is 2½ to 3 inches deep. Sprinkle sugar on top of the butter so the dish is completely coated, and then tap out the excess sugar.

Separate four of the eggs, and set the whites aside in a bowl for beating. Use a fork or a whisk to beat the two whole eggs with the four yolks, and then stir them into the semolina. Beat the egg whites until they are peaked but not dry, and stir one-third of them into the semolina to lighten it. Fold in the remaining whites, and pour the batter into the prepared pan.

Put the pudding in the oven and bake for 35 to 40 minutes; the center of the pudding should be lightly brown and swelled but still jiggly. A cake tester or small knife plunged an inch from the side of the pan should come out clean. Remove the pudding to a wire rack, immediately sift the confectioners' sugar on top, and cool completely. The center will sink slightly. When it is cool, cover the pudding with plastic wrap, and refrigerate for 3 hours or overnight. Serve drizzled with *crema* and cherry sauces if desired.

VARIATION: **Semolina Rum Pudding with Raisins.** Soak about ¼ cup raisins in 4 tablespoons of rum. Stir the raisins, with the soaking rum, into the pudding with the vanilla and lemon rind. Serve the pudding with a rum-flavored *crema,* if you wish.

VARIATION: **Thin Spaghetti Pudding.** Noodle pudding is a specialty that my grandmother brought from her native Ischia. Substitute ¼ pound of capellini or angel hair pasta for the semolina. Break it into pieces about three inches long and boil it in milk until it is tender. Do not separate the eggs but beat them together. When the pasta is tender, beat in the butter and sugar, then gradually beat in the eggs. Bake as above and serve dusted with confectioners' sugar and without the sauces. Nonna often added about ⅓ cup of chopped candied orange peel or citron to the pudding before baking.

VARIATION: **Sweet Cornmeal Pudding.** This old Neapolitan recipe uses cornmeal in place of the semolina. It calls for the fine cornmeal known as Bergamo, which may be difficult to find outside of specialty Italian food stores. Make the pudding as above, substituting the same amount of cornmeal for the semolina. Flavor it with the lemon peel and vanilla, and add ¼ cup each of raisins and pine nuts to the base. Candied fruit is also frequently added.

BREAD PUDDINGS

BUDINI DI PANE

I have never known an Italian cook to throw away a piece of bread. Quite a feat when you consider how large some of those Italian loaves are. If that stale bread is not made into crumbs, crostini, or stuffing, it may well wind up as a dessert.

The Bread

The frugal home cook often uses whatever leftover bread is on hand. It may be the remains of a Christmas *panetone* or the heels of yesterday's *ciabatta*, but it will soon be pudding. Although any type of bread can be used, the results will be different with different types. Dense bread will produce a dense pudding; light, airy loaves with many holes will let you taste more of the custard. The bread should be slightly stale so that it does not become a soggy mess before it is baked; if it is not, toast or sauté it to creat a crust.

The Custard

The bread is bound with an egg custard. The recipes below call for four large eggs and two egg yolks. The extra two yolks make a richer custard. You can eliminate them and still have a perfectly delicious dessert. You can also beat the two extra whites and fold them into the cooled base to make a fluffy bread pudding.

Neapolitan Bread Pudding

BUDINO DI PANE ALLA NAPOLI

SERVES 6 TO 8

If my family is any yardstick, then yours will gobble up this pudding any time it appears. I like it for breakfast; after all, it does contain most of the major food groups. If you used whole-wheat bread, you would be pretty much all set.

Italian bread puddings contain the same basic elements as all bread puddings—stale bread and egg custard. The Italians, however, often handle the bread differently: they beat it into a mass after it has soaked in milk or in custard. The region of Lombardy, known for its puddings, calls a beaten bread pudding *miascia*. With any of the bread puddings or their variations, you can either leave the bread in chunks as below, or beat it as described in the Chocolate Bread Pudding recipe on page 432. The beaten bread puddings will have a smoother, more puddinglike texture.

Put the raisins in a small bowl, and cover with rum or warm water. Let soak in rum for at least 45 minutes, or in water for 15 minutes, then drain. If you like, you can use the drained-off rum with the vanilla to flavor the custard below. Butter a 2-quart, shallow baking dish, and find a roasting pan large enough to hold the baking dish without its touching the sides.

GETTING READY
½ cup raisins
4 tablespoons rum (optional)

THE PUDDING BASE

5 to 7 slices of slightly stale Italian or other firm-textured bread (about 12 ounces)

5 tablespoons unsalted butter

⅓ cup pine nuts

The raisins from above

2 tablespoons sugar

2 teaspoons cinnamon

FOR THE CUSTARD

3 cups whole milk

4 large eggs

2 egg yolks

½ cup sugar

1 tablespoon pure vanilla extract

Small grating of fresh nutmeg

If the crusts are hard, trim them off the bread. Break the bread into small (about ½-inch) pieces. You should have 4 cups of lightly packed pieces. Melt the butter in a large frying pan, and toss in the bread and the pine nuts. Turn to coat all over, and continue to toss over medium heat until the bread and pine nuts begin to color slightly. Stir in the raisins, and sprinkle on the 2 tablespoons sugar and the cinnamon. Stir and cook until the sugar has melted and the bread is completely coated. Spread the bread out evenly in the pudding dish.

Heat the milk until small bubbles appear around the edges (scalding). Whisk the eggs and egg yolks together just until they are mixed. Whisk in the ½ cup sugar just until it is incorporated; do not overbeat. When the milk is hot, gradually whisk it into the eggs and sugar; go slowly at first, so the eggs warm and do not scramble from the heat of the milk. Stir in the vanilla and nutmeg, and pour through a strainer over the bread. Push top pieces down to submerge. Let the bread sit to absorb the custard for 45 minutes.

Preheat the oven to 325° F.

Bring a large saucepan of water to a boil to use for a water bath. Put the roasting pan in the oven, set the custard dish in the center of the roasting pan, and pour enough boiling water into the larger pan to come halfway up the sides of the pudding dish.

Bake the pudding 45 minutes to an hour. To test if it is done, plunge a small knife an inch from the side of the pan; it should come out clean. Plunge it into the center and it should have a few bits of custard clinging to it. Remove the pudding from the water bath, and serve warm or cold with the rum-flavored *crema* if desired.

VARIATION: **Panetone Bread Pudding.** The Italian "big bread," *panetone* (or another egg bread, such as challah or brioche), makes a delicious bread pudding. Even though *panetone* has raisins in it, I still add the amount called for above. Prepare the pudding exactly as in the recipe above, substituting the same amount of *panetone* for the regular bread.

VARIATION: **Puffy Bread Pudding.** Beaten egg whites will make a lighter, puffy pudding. When the custard and bread are completely cooled, beat the two extra egg whites and fold them into the pudding. Bake as above.

VARIATION: **Apple-and-Pear Bread Pudding.** For an apple-and-pear pudding, stir about 1 cup each of chopped apples and pears into the bread after it is soaked—and beaten, if you choose to do it. You can also add ¼ cup chopped walnut halves if you like. Bake as above, and while the pudding is still hot, brush it with some melted marmalade.

FOR SERVING
1 recipe rum-flavored *crema* made with 1 tablespoon flour or cornstarch (variation, page 451), optional

Un buon uomo e buono comme un pane.
A good man is as good as bread.
—ITALIAN SAYING

Chocolate Bread Pudding

SERVES 6 TO 8

The method here is basically the same as in the Primary Recipe, but there are a few optional changes. I do not use a water bath for baking, because I want to develop a bit of crust on the edges. I butter and sugar the baking dish to create the crust, and so as not to disturb it before baking time, I mix the pudding in a bowl and transfer it to the baking dish when it has rested. I usually beat the bread for chocolate pudding, because I like the finer texture, but it is also good with the bread left in ½-inch pieces.

FOR THE BREAD

5 to 7 slices of slightly stale Italian or other firm-textured bread (about 12 ounces)

5 tablespoons unsalted butter, plus more to grease pan

2 tablespoons sugar

3 tablespoons unsweetened cocoa

FOR THE CUSTARD

3 cups whole milk

4 ounces bittersweet chocolate, chopped

4 large eggs

2 egg yolks

½ cup sugar, plus 3 tablespoons to coat dish

1 tablespoon pure vanilla extract

FOR SERVING

¼ cup confectioners' sugar

Lightly sweetened and whipped cream (optional)

Trim away any hard crusts, and break the bread into small (about ½-inch) pieces. You should have 4 cups of lightly packed pieces. Melt the butter in a large frying pan, and toss in the bread. Turn to coat all over, and continue to toss over medium heat until the bread begins to color slightly. Sprinkle on the 2 tablespoons sugar and the cocoa. Stir and cook until the sugar has melted and the bread is completely coated. Transfer the bread to a large bowl.

Heat the milk until small bubbles appear around the edges. Drop the chocolate into the milk, turn off the heat, and let the chocolate melt. While the chocolate is melting, whisk the eggs and egg yolks together just until they are mixed, then whisk in the ½ cup sugar just until it is incorporated. Whisk the milk to distribute the chocolate; if it has not completely melted, return it to the heat, then gradually whisk it into the eggs and sugar. Stir in the vanilla, and pour the custard through a strainer over the bread. Let the bread sit to absorb the custard for 45 minutes.

Preheat the oven to 325° F. Butter the bottom and sides of a 2-quart shallow baking dish, sprinkle sugar over all the surfaces, and then tip out the excess sugar. Beat the bread with a fork or a whisk until the crumb is very small, and pour it into the dish. Bake for 45 minutes to an hour, until a knife tests clean an inch from the sides. Remove the pudding from the oven, and sift the confectioners' sugar over the top. Serve at room temperature or cold with the whipped cream if desired.

VARIATION: **Chocolate Pandoro Bread Pudding.** *Pandoro* is chocolate-studded Italian egg bread, and I usually buy it just to make this pudding. Use 12 to 14 ounces of the bread in place of the white bread above.

"COOKED CREAMS"

PANNA COTTE

These smooth, silky puddings are amazingly no more than stabilized, sweetened, and flavored cream. *Panna cotte* are traditionally molded in individual ramekins and then turned out onto dessert plates. Because they contain so little gelatin, the unmolded creams wriggle and shimmy on the plate much like that old standard, junket. The flavor and texture, however, are much more exciting. Unmolding is not difficult, and the little creams are charming. But if you want to avoid the last-minute action and still have a nice presentation, make the creams and scoop them into pretty stemmed glasses.

Gelatin

A package of gelatin contains approximately 2¼ teaspoons and is enough to soft-set 3 cups of cream or a combination of milk and cream. If you want a firmer *panna cotta,* decrease the liquid to 2½ cups but do not use less—the pudding will be rubbery.

In order for the gelatin to gel and not remain grainy, it must first be softened for five minutes in 3 to 4 tablespoons of a cold liquid and then heated until it is completely dissolved. Do not skimp on these important steps. Once the pudding is refrigerated, allow about three hours for it to set.

"Cooked Cream"

PANNA COTTA

SERVES 6

Raspberries and cream. Such a lush combination! But it is only one of the numerous possibilities. Use any fresh berries in place of the raspberries. Or top the pudding with the Chocolate-Espresso Sauce on page 455 or with one of the berry sauces on pages 452 and 453.

GETTING READY

3 tablespoons water

1 package unflavored gelatin

FOR THE CREAM

2 cups heavy cream

1 cup whole milk

½ cup sugar

1 whole vanilla bean, split lengthwise, or 1½ teaspoons pure vanilla extract

The melted gelatin from above

Pour the water into a small glass measuring cup or heatproof bowl and sprinkle the gelatin on top. Let sit, without stirring, for 5 minutes, or until the gelatin has softened. Put the cup with the softened gelatin in about ½ inch of simmering water in a small frying pan. Simmer, stirring a few times, until the gelatin is melted. Turn off the heat. Line up on a tray that will fit in your refrigerator six small ramekins or custard cups, each with a capacity of at least ½ cup.

Stir the cream, milk, and sugar together in a 2-quart saucepan. Drop in the vanilla bean; if you are using the vanilla extract, wait until the cream has boiled before adding it (see below). Place the pan over medium-high heat, bring the cream to a boil, and then remove the pan from the flame. Remove the vanilla bean. Use a small spatula to scrape the gelatin from the bowl into the hot cream, and then stir it around well so it is evenly distributed. If you are using vanilla extract, stir it in now. Ladle the cream in equal proportions into the ramekins. Transfer the creams to the refrigerator, and when they are no longer hot to the touch, stretch pieces of plastic wrap taut over the tops of the cups. Refrigerate for 3 hours, or until set. The creams will keep up to 3 days. About 30 minutes before serving, toss the raspberries with the sugar.

To unmold, dip the bottoms of the ramekins one by one in a shallow bowl of hot water for about 3 seconds, then run a sharp knife around the edge. Place a dessert plate on top of the cup, and then reverse it so the cream drops into the center of the plate. Wiggle a little if necessary to make the cream slip out. Spoon the raspberries over and around the *panna cotta,* and garnish with a sprig of mint if you like.

VARIATION: To serve the *panna cotta* without unmolding, ladle the hot cream into small stemmed glasses and chill as above. When ready to serve, divide the berries evenly over the tops of each, and garnish with the mint.

VARIATION: Steeping the vanilla bean in the milk before mixing the ingredients together will render a more intense vanilla flavor. Cut the vanilla bean in half and scrape the seeds into the cup of milk in a small saucepan. Put in the pods, and heat the milk until bubbles just begin to form around the edges of the pan. Turn off the heat, cover the pan, and let steep for 45 minutes. Strain the milk, and use as above.

VARIATION: **Buttermilk Panna Cotta.** For a pleasantly tangy taste, substitute one cup of buttermilk for the whole milk, or, for a richer dessert, substitute half-and-half.

FOR SERVING

About 3 cups fresh raspberries

1 tablespoon sugar, preferably superfine

6 sprigs mint (optional)

Lemon "Cooked Cream" with Berries

SERVES 6

A "cooked cream" is a delicate dessert, and any flavoring should be subtle. For this delicate lemon flavor, the rind is steeped in the milk and then removed before the milk is added to the other ingredients. Of course, if delicacy is not your style, you could also add a teaspoon of lemon extract to the hot cream. The recipe below calls for the *panna cotta* to be served in glasses on top of cooked berries. If you prefer to unmold the desserts, pour the cream into the ramekins as in the preceding recipe, and pour the sauce over the top of each unmolded dessert.

GETTING READY

1 large lemon

1 cup whole milk

1 recipe cooked blueberry sauce
  (page 453)

3 tablespoons water

1 package unflavored gelatin

FOR THE CREAM

2 cups heavy cream

The lemon-flavored milk from above

½ cup sugar

The melted gelatin from above

Wash the lemon in warm water, and then use a vegetable peeler to remove long strips of peel; take only the yellow skin and not the white pith beneath it. Put the peel and the milk in a small saucepan, and set it over medium heat. When bubbles appear around the edges, turn off the heat, cover the pan, and let steep for 45 minutes to an hour. Strain the milk, and discard the lemon.

Spoon a generous tablespoon of the berries into the bottom of six stemmed glasses each with a capacity of at least ⅔ cup. Reserve the remaining berries for garnish. Put the glasses in the refrigerator to chill. Chilling the fruit will make it less likely to float once the cream is added.

Soften and melt the gelatin in the water as in the Primary Recipe.

Stir the cream, milk, and sugar together in a 2-quart saucepan and bring to a boil. Scrape in the gelatin, and then transfer the cream to a large measuring cup or a bowl and refrigerate for about 1 hour, or until the cream is cool but has not begun to set up. (You can speed this up by setting the bowl in an ice bath and stirring it for about 15 minutes.) The cream is cooled so its heat will not dislodge the juices when it is poured over the berries. Carefully ladle equal amounts of the cool cream into the glasses, over the berries. If some of the berry juices bleed into the cream, it is fine. Chill, covered with plastic wrap, for at least 3 hours or up to 3 days, as in the Primary Recipe. Serve from the glasses with another small dollop of berries in the center.

VARIATION: **Coffee Panna Cotta.** For a coffee-flavored *panna cotta,* instead of the lemon peel, stir 2 to 3 teaspoons of instant espresso coffee into the scalded milk. Stir it well, to be sure it has dissolved, and heat again if it has not. The coffee milk is ready to use as soon as the coffee is dissolved. Mold coffee *panna cotta* in individual ramekins, chill, and unmold according to the Primary Recipe. Serve with Chocolate-Espresso Sauce (page 455) drizzled on top instead of the layer of berries.

"DELIGHTS"

DELIZIE

A *delizia* is a composed dessert that is built with sponge cake, pound cake, or ladyfingers. The cake is brushed with a flavorful liquid, such as strong coffee or a combination of liqueurs, and then layered with a filling that can be pastry cream, fruit, mascarpone, sweetened ricotta, whipped cream, or a combination of any of those. *Delizie* can be haphazardly assembled or elaborately constructed and decorated. Chefs often make these simple home desserts in individual small molds, so they appear to be elegant, intricate desserts when they are in truth child's play. *Tiramisù, zuppa inglese,* and the Sicilian *cassata* are some of the best-known examples of these composed desserts.

Whole Egg Sponge Cake

MADDALENA

MAKES ONE 9- OR 10-INCH ROUND OR SQUARE CAKE

Italians bake this cake primarily to use in composed desserts. The relatively dry texture makes it perfect for soaking up syrups and liqueurs. Whether swathed with blankets of pastry cream or drenched with pools of *zabaglione,* this tender, butterless cake will absorb the flavors, like the sponge it is, and make the parts whole. I like to keep pieces of sponge cake, even irregularly sized trimmings, in the freezer. Wrapped well they will keep for two or three months and are a great boon when I want to make a fancy dessert fast.

There is no leavening ingredient in this cake; the swelling of the egg proteins is what makes it rise. It used to be that the only way to inflate the eggs enough to make the cake rise was to beat them over heat. Kitchen technology has given us high-speed electric mixers, which beat the eggs rapidly enough to create the heat necessary to increase their volume. If you do not have a heavy-duty, freestanding mixer, then follow the directions below for the heat method.

GETTING READY
4 large eggs in their shells
Confectioners' sugar
THE CAKE
Butter and flour for the cake pan
The 4 warm eggs
²/₃ cup sugar

¼ teaspoon salt
The grated rind of one lemon (optional)
1 tablespoon pure vanilla extract
1 cup sifted cake flour

Put the eggs, in their shells, in a bowl of very warm water for 6 to 8 minutes, until they feel warm. Pour very hot or boiling water into the mixing bowl and over the whisk, let sit a few minutes, and then dry them well. Warming the eggs and the bowl before beginning to beat will encourage the eggs to swell to their maximum amount. Spread a kitchen towel over a cake rack and dust it generously with confectioners' sugar.

Set the oven rack in the bottom third of the oven, and preheat the oven to 325° F. Generously butter the bottom and sides of the cake pan, and lightly dust the bottom only with flour. Turn the pan upside down, and tap out the excess flour. The butter on the sides of the pan, without the flour, will grab the cake and help it rise.

In the bowl of a heavy-duty electric mixer fitted with the whisk attachment, beat the eggs on high speed until they begin to foam and swell. To work over heat instead, break the eggs into a metal bowl, set it on a flame tamer or in a skillet of barely simmering water over low heat, and use a handheld electric mixer. When the eggs are foamy and about double in volume, gradually beat in the sugar and the salt, and continue beating until the batter is pale and about tripled in volume and forms a heavy ribbon. To test for a ribbon, hold the whisk stationary above the batter. The batter should fall slowly and fold back and forth on itself as a thick silk ribbon would. (If you are working over the stove, remove the ready batter immediately, and continue to beat it until it is cooled.) Beat in the lemon rind if using and the vanilla.

Sift a third of the sifted flour into the batter, and fold it in (use a large rubber spatula for the best results). Repeat with the second and then the third addition of flour. Work quickly, so as not to deflate the mixture, but be sure all the flour is well incorporated. Hold the bowl close to the bottom of the prepared pan, and carefully pour the batter into it so as not to deflate it. Tap the pan gently on the counter once, to break any large air bubbles that would leave holes in the cake. Bake for 35 to 40 minutes for a round cake or about 20 to 25 minutes for a sheet cake, until the sides of the cake shrink slightly from the pan and the cake tests done when poked with a metal cake tester or toothpick; insert the tester in the center of the cake, and leave for 5 seconds or so; it should come out clean and feel slightly warm when touched to the palm of your hand. Invert the cake onto the sugar-dusted towel on the cooling rack as soon as it is baked.

VARIATION: The cake can also be baked in a 10½-by-15½-inch or 17½-by-11½-inch sheet pan. It depends on how you intend to use it. The larger the pan, the thinner the cake. To bake the sponge cake in sheet cake form, butter the bottom and sides of the pan and line the bottom with parchment or wax paper (the paper helps keep the baked cake from breaking when it is turned out of the pan). Butter the paper, sprinkle it with flour, and then tap out the excess. Bake the cake at 325° F for about 20 to 25 minutes or until it begins to shrink from the sides and tests done as above. Turn it out onto a large cooling rack covered with a sugared towel to cool. Peel the paper off the sheet cake.

Tiramisù

SERVES 8 TO 10

Created more than 30 years ago by the owner of the Venetian restaurant El Toulà, this creamy *delizia* quickly became one of Italy's most popular desserts. Reproduced, redesigned, and re-created by chefs and homemakers all over the world, *tiramisù* translates to "pick-me-up"—and why wouldn't it, with such a delicious combination of ingredients. I have created my own version, which avoids the use of raw eggs, a standard ingredient in the original recipe.

You can build the *tiramisù* in a 5-by-10-inch loaf pan or layer the cake free-form on a serving platter.

MAKING AHEAD

1 sponge cake baked in a 10½-by-15½-inch sheet pan (preceding recipe)

THE FILLING

1 pound mascarpone cheese, at room temperature

1 cup confectioners' sugar

1 teaspoon pure vanilla extract

⅓ cup dry Marsala

1½ cups heavy cream

THE SOAKING SYRUP

⅔ cup espresso or strong coffee

⅓ cup sugar

2 tablespoons dark rum, or more to taste

FOR THE FINISH

2 tablespoons unsweetened cocoa mixed with 2 tablespoons confectioners' sugar, or 4 tablespoons sweetened cocoa

When the cake has cooled, cut it crosswise into three even pieces, each about 5 inches wide and 10 inches long. If you plan to build the cake in a loaf pan, then use the pan to determine the width; the pieces should be wide enough to fit snugly into the pan. If the sides of the loaf pan are slanted out, use the bottom of the pan to measure the bottom slice, and the top of the pan to measure the top piece. Line the loaf pan with a sheet of plastic wrap long enough so the ends hang well over the sides.

Scoop the mascarpone into a mixing bowl, and stir it with a wooden spoon until it is homogeneous. Sift the confectioners' sugar on top of the cheese, and stir it in. Then stir in the vanilla and the Marsala. In a separate bowl, using a whisk or electric beaters, beat the heavy cream until it has soft peaks. Continue to beat on low speed as you add the mascarpone mixture to the whipped cream, about ½ cup at a time. When it has all been added, use a large rubber spatula to reach to the bottom of the bowl and make sure all the mascarpone is mixed into the cream.

To make the soaking syrup, heat the coffee, if it is cold, and stir in the sugar so that it melts. Remove from the heat, and pour in the rum.

Lay one slice of the cake in the loaf pan or in the center of a serving platter. Using a pastry brush or a spoon, cover the top of the cake with one-third of the soaking syrup. Spread half the cream filling over the cake, and cover with a second piece of cake. Soak that with another third of the syrup, and cover with the rest of the filling. Use the remaining syrup to soak one side of the last piece of cake and place the soaked side down on top of the filling. Refrigerate for at least 2 hours or overnight.

If you have formed the *tiramisù* in a loaf pan, tip it upside down on a serving platter and use the plastic wrap to help ease the dessert out of the pan. A free-form cake can remain as is. Sift the cocoa over the top of the cake. Serve in slices.

SUBSTITUTION: Use 4 tablespoons sweetened cocoa powder to finish.

VARIATION: If you want a stronger chocolate flavor, fold about 4 ounces of finely chopped bittersweet chocolate into the filling.

VARIATION: To make a round dessert, bake the cake in a 9-to-10-inch round pan, cut it horizontally into three slices, and then build the dessert in a springform pan that is the same size as the baking pan. Refrigerate as above, and remove the outer ring to cut and serve. Or bake the sponge cake in a square pan, and build the *tiramisù* in the same pan; cut it into squares to serve.

VARIATION: Substitute packaged, soft ladyfingers for the sponge cake. You will need about twenty-four of them. Split the ladyfingers in half, and line them up in the pan or on the platter with flat sides facing up, leaving a tiny bit of space between them. Saturate with the soaking syrup, and build the dessert as above. Place the top layer on with the rounded sides up.

VARIATION: Sicilian Cassata. The Sicilian *cassata* has experienced as many interpretations as *tiramisù,* many of them quite elaborate. To make a simple version, bake and cut the cake as above. For the filling, push 2 pounds of ricotta cheese through a strainer into a mixing bowl. Sift in 1 cup of confectioners' sugar, and mix it into the cheese. Fold in ½ cup each finely chopped bittersweet chocolate, candied citron or other candied fruit or peel, and chopped almonds or hazelnuts. For the soaking syrup, use ⅓ cup water, ⅓ cup sugar, and ½ cup rum or orange liqueur. Form the cake as above, and dust with the cocoa powder mixed with powdered sugar, or sweetened cocoa powder.

VARIATION: Brandy is often substituted for the rum, and it is quite good.

Soaking Syrups

Italians love their desserts flavored with sweet syrups laced with spirits. Rum, brandy, Maraschino, Marsala, as well as sweet liqueurs, sooner or later find their way into *dolci.* If you wish to omit the alcohol in the recipes for *delizie,* you can use a simple sugar syrup to soak the cake. Each of those composed cake desserts needs more or less 1 cup of soaking liquid. To make a simple sugar syrup, pour 1 cup of sugar and ⅔ cup of water into a perfectly clean small saucepan. Add 2 or 3 drops of lemon juice; the acid will discourage the sugar from crystalizing. Bring to a simmer, and cook until the sugar has completely dissolved. Let cool before using. The syrup will keep at least 2 weeks in the refrigerator, so if you plan to make the cake desserts often you should double or triple the recipe. You can substitute lemon, orange, or lime juice for the water for a flavored syrup, provided it complements the cake filling.

Berry Mascarpone Delight

DELIZIA DI BACCHE E MASCARPONE

If berry shortcake is your family's idea of the perfect dessert, try this Italian version. The tanginess of the mascarpone enhances the sweetness of the pastry cream and the fruit. The directions below show you how to build the *delizia* in a loaf pan for unmolding, but you can also make it free-form or in a round or a square pan, like the *tiramisù*.

The filling is based on a moderately thick pastry cream, *crema pasticcera*, flavored with lemon. For a quicker whipped-cream version, see the variation below.

MAKING AHEAD

1 sponge cake baked in a 10½-by-15½-inch sheet pan (page 438)

GETTING READY

1 large lemon

1⅓ cups whole milk

4 cups mixed berries (blueberries, raspberries, black raspberries, strawberries, etc.)

¼ cup sugar

1 tablespoon lemon juice

THE FILLING

½ pound mascarpone cheese, at room temperature

The lemon milk from above

4 large egg yolks

⅓ cup sugar

3 tablespoons flour

Pinch salt

1 teaspoon pure vanilla extract

THE SOAKING SYRUP

⅓ cup water

⅓ cup sugar

⅓ cup Maraschino, kirsch, or orange liqueur

FOR ASSEMBLING THE CAKE

The sponge-cake slices from above

The fruit from above

FOR THE FINISH

Confectioners' sugar

The milk will be used in the pastry cream for the filling, but it must be infused with the lemon peel 45 minutes to an hour before it is used. It can sit longer, so do it first and let it steep while you prepare the cake. Wash the lemon, and remove the rind with a vegetable peeler, being careful not to take any white pith with it. Put the milk and the lemon peel in a small saucepan, and bring to a simmer. Turn off the heat, cover the pan, and let steep for at least 45 minutes. Remove the lemon peel, and reserve the milk in the saucepan.

If you are using strawberries, slice them in half or thirds. Mix all the berries together in a bowl. Measure about 1 cup of the mixed berries, and puree them in a blender or a food processor with the sugar and lemon juice. Strain the puree to remove the seeds, and fold the pureed juice into the reserved whole berries.

When the cake has cooled, cut it crosswise into three even pieces each about 5 inches wide and 10 inches long. Line a 10-by-5-inch loaf pan with a long sheet of plastic wrap; it should be long enough that pieces hang well over the sides and can eventually wrap back over the top of the pan when it holds the dessert.

Put the mascarpone in a mixing bowl, and stir it with a wooden spoon to smooth it out. Reheat the lemon milk until small bubbles appear around the edges. While the milk is heating, whisk the yolks, sugar, flour, and salt together in a heavy-bottomed saucepan. Whisking constantly, dribble small amounts of milk into the yolks until all the milk has been added. Put the saucepan over medium heat, and bring to a boil, continuing to whisk so the cream will thicken evenly. Once it has thickened, continue to cook and whisk for about 1½ minutes, until it is quite thick. Remove the pan from the heat, and stir in the vanilla. Push the *crema* through a sieve into the bowl with the mascarpone, and stir the two together well, making sure that all the cheese melts into the *crema*.

Make the soaking syrup by heating the water and sugar together until the sugar has melted and the liquid is clear. Remove from the heat, and pour in the Maraschino.

Tuck one slice of cake into the bottom of the loaf pan. Brush or spoon one-third of the soaking syrup evenly over the cake. Spread half of the cream on top, and spoon half the fruit over the cream. Place a second piece of cake on top of the berries, and press it down gently. Soak with one-third more syrup, cover with the rest of the cream and fruit. Before placing the third cake slice on top, brush one side with the remaining syrup, and place it, soaked side down, on top. Pull the overhanging plastic wrap over the top, and refrigerate for at least 2 hours or overnight.

When you are ready to serve the cake, pull back the plastic from the top, and turn the pan upside down on a serving platter. Use the long ends of the plastic wrap to coax the cake out. Sift confectioners' sugar over the top and serve in slices.

VARIATION: You can use any combination of berries or just one type. If peaches are in season and nicely ripe, add thin slices of one or two peeled peaches to the berries.

VARIATION: You can use a mascarpone-and-whipped-cream filling in place of the pastry cream. Scoop ½ pound mascarpone into a mixing bowl, and stir it with a wooden spoon until it is homogeneous. Sift in 1 cup of confectioners' sugar, and stir it into the cheese, then stir in the 1 teaspoon of vanilla extract and ¼ cup Maraschino, kirsch, or orange liqueur. In a separate bowl, beat the heavy cream until it has soft peaks, and then beat in the mascarpone mixture, adding about ½ cup at a time. Use a large rubber spatula to reach to the bottom of the bowl and make sure all the mascarpone is mixed into the cream. Layer the mascarpone cream with the berries, cake, and soaking syrup as above.

VARIATION: Substitute ladyfingers for the cake. You will need twenty-four of them, split in half.

"English Soup" or Italian Trifle

ZUPPA INGLESE

SERVES 6 TO 8

Once upon a time, *zuppa inglese* was all the rage in Italian restaurants both abroad and in the United States. Perhaps it was the mysterious name that made this homey dessert so intriguing and popular. "English soup" may be a reference to the fact that the dessert resembles the popular English trifle, or it may be a playful interpretation of an Italian *zuppa* in which the cake replaces the bread and the custard the broth. There are numerous theories as to the origin of the name, but what concerns me is why its popularity should ever have waned! It is a delicious dessert, and one that lends itself to untold variations. The cherry-almond variation that follows the classic recipe below is a family favorite.

Alchermes is an Italian spicy, crimson-colored liqueur that is a treasured ingredient in *zuppa inglese,* not only for its flavor but also for the red hue it imparts. The brand I use is Luxardo. Ask for it in specialty-liquor stores (and see Gasbarro's in Shopping Online, page 29). Morello cherries are called *amarene* in Italian, and you may find the preserves so labeled. Unlike eating cherries (*ciliegie*), morellos are tart, dark-red fruit used for baking and in making jams and liqueurs, such as Maraschino.

I like to build this *delizia* in a glass bowl so the vibrant red is visible. I use a stemmed glass bowl that holds just over 6 cups and the dessert mounds just above the top. But you can build it in any bowl or free form on a platter. It cannot be unmolded like the *tiramisù,* however, since the *crema* is too soft.

MAKING AHEAD

9- or 10-inch round or square sponge
   cake (page 438)
1 recipe vanilla-flavored *crema* made
   with 2 tablespoons flour (page 450)

FOR ASSEMBLING THE CAKE

1 cup heavy cream
2 tablespoons confectioners' sugar
The *crema* from above
The cake slices from above

Cut through the cake from top to bottom so you have slices about ½ inch thick. Then cut the slices into pieces 4 to 4½ inches long by 3 inches wide. Make the *crema* according to the directions.

Beat the heavy cream with the sugar until it forms soft peaks. Fold half of it into the *crema* and set the rest aside for the finish. Arrange several slices of cake in the bottom of a serving bowl so they fit snugly and cover all the surface. Drizzle a few tablespoons of the liqueur over the cake, and then spread on about a third of the *crema*. Turn more slices of cake quickly in the Alchermes or Maraschino, and put them on top of the cream. Cover with more cream, and continue to layer all the ingredients, ending with a layer of cream.

Spread the remaining whipped cream over the top, cover, and refrigerate 2 hours or overnight. I always decorate this *delizia* with a few spoonfuls of morello-cherry preserves scattered on top.

VARIATION: The chef's version of *zuppa inglese* calls for a baked-meringue topping. Build the cake layers on an ovenproof platter or baking sheet, and omit the heavy cream from the finish. When you are making the *crema,* set the whites aside and then beat them with 2 tablespoons of sugar until they form stiff peaks. Spread the meringue over the entire cake, sift some confectioners' sugar on top of it, pop the whole platter into a 400° F oven, and bake for 5 to 7 minutes, or until the meringue is lightly colored.

VARIATION: **Cherry-Almond Zuppa.** For our favorite cherry-almond *zuppa,* you will need one sponge cake cut as above, 1 recipe for almond-flavored *crema* (page 451) and 1 cup morello-cherry preserves. For the soaking syrup, use 1 cup of Maraschino, or make a syrup of ¼ cup water, ¼ cup sugar, and ½ cup Maraschino, kirsch, or orange liqueur. Layer the cake as above, dabbing the cherries on top of the cream on each layer. Cover with the whipped cream as above.

VARIATION: In either the classic recipe or the cherry-almond variation, substitute the Dried Tart-Cherry Sauce on page 454 for the morello preserves, or use one of the berry sauces on pages 452 and 453.

Some Simple Italian Meal Endings

There are some lovely, simple things you can fix for dessert that involve no cooking.

CHEESE AND HONEY: Put a thin slice of sweet Gorgonzola cheese on each dessert plate, and drizzle a few tablespoons of acacia honey over the top.

PEACHES AND WINE: For each person, slice a perfectly ripe peach into six or eight wedges, and put into a bowl. Sprinkle 1 tablespoon of sugar per peach on top, toss together, and then pour on 3 tablespoons of chilled dry or sweet white wine per peach. Keep chilled until ready to serve.

STRAWBERRIES AND BALSAMIC VINEGAR: Measure ⅔ to 1 cup of strawberries for each diner. Cut the strawberries in half, and toss each serving of berries with a scant tablespoon of sugar and 1 teaspoon of best-quality balsamic vinegar. Let sit for 10 to 15 minutes before serving, and offer the pepper mill with the berries. Freshly ground black pepper adds a lovely zip to them.

ICE CREAM WITH CHOCOLATE AND ESPRESSO: Place a scoop of store-bought or homemade coffee or vanilla ice cream in a small bowl for each person. Sprinkle 2 tablespoons of shaved bittersweet chocolate (preferably Italian) on top of each serving. Pour 1 tablespoon of very hot and strong espresso on top, and serve immediately.

FRUIT, CHEESE, AND SWEET WINE

You can put a bowl of whole fruit and a plate with a wedge of cheese on the table and sit most contentedly nibbling and chatting, or get out your prettiest dessert plates, make an artful arrangement of fruit and cheese on each, and offer a splendid, chilled sweet wine. Either way makes a fine Italian ending to a meal. Be sure that the fruit is ripe and the cheese is at room temperature. Some suggestions for slightly fancy but simple presentations follow.

Comice Pears and Gorgonzola: Pears and Gorgonzola love each other. Comice are particularly "peary," but you can also use Anjou or Bartlett. Put slices of perfectly ripe pears and a dollop of room-temperature cheese on each plate. If you want, you can make them a bit fancy: peel the pears, if you like, and cut each in half lengthwise. Rub the cut side with lemon juice to prevent discoloring and use a melon baller or spoon to remove the core and make a shallow trench. Place a generous spoonful of Gorgonzola cheese—sweet or mountain variety—in the trench and run the pears under the broiler a minute or less until the cheese is warm and slightly melted. Serve the pears with a chilled Malvasia di Lipari or Passito di Pantelleria.

Pears with Mascarpone or Ricotta: Serve a whole or half pear per person. Cut each pear in half and use a melon baller or spoon to remove the core. Cut the pears into long, thin slices and fan out on dessert plates. If you wish to peel the pears, do so as close to serving time as possible and rub the flesh with lemon juice to prevent browning. Measure about ¼ cup of room-temperature mascarpone or ricotta cheese per serving and stir 2 teaspoons of orange liqueur or maraschino and 1 tablespoon powdered sugar into it. Put the cheese next to the pear and decorate with fresh mint leaves if your garden grows them. Serve with either of the wines suggested for Comice Pears and Gorgonzola.

Taleggio and Berries: Arrange a small rectangle of room temperature Taleggio and a mixture of perfectly ripe strawberries, blackberries, and raspberries on each plate. Add a sprig of mint leaves and a lemon biscotti. Serve a chilled, sparkling red Brachetto d'Acqui.

Oranges and Fontina: Cut the peel and pith off seedless (navel) oranges; go right down to the flesh. Then cut the oranges into slices about ¼ inch thick and overlap them slightly on a plate (lemon leaves underneath would be nice). Place a wedge of room-temperature Fontina on the side. Serve with a chilled, sweet Vin Santo or Muscato d'Asti.

Parmigiano Reggiano with Honey and Jam: According to my friend Lombard Gasbarro, this is all the rage in Verona. Break egg-size pieces of Parmesan from a large piece; do not cut them off since you want the ragged edges. Put them on plates and circle them with a generous teaspoon each of honey, raspberry jam, and strawberry jam. Serve with a chilled, sweet Recioto della Valpolicella, Classico.

I think it is a very good idea to have a handy repertoire of quick dessert sauces and toppings that you can call upon. That way you can turn fresh berries or poached fruit or even store-bought ice cream or pound cake into an Italian *dolce*. These are some of my standards.

Custard Sauce

CREMA

MAKES ABOUT 2 CUPS

Italians flavor and thicken a custard sauce depending on how they intend to use it. A thin, pourable *crema* is delicious over fresh berries or poached fruit, and it's a lovely accompaniment to the firm-textured Italian baked puddings. Slightly thicker versions are equivalent to the creams that fill pastries or are layered with sponge cakes and ladyfingers for composed desserts. They can be flavored in a number of ways and enriched with whipped cream. Very thick *cremas* are eaten as puddings. Learn how to make this versatile sauce by rote and you will always be ready to turn a simple dessert into an occasion.

Just a note on the starch used to thicken the sauces: The presence of a starch—all-purpose flour, potato starch, or cornstarch—is what allows the custard sauce to boil and thicken without causing the eggs to scramble. A thin custard sauce, *crema,* called "stirred custard," or *crème anglaise* in French, is usually made without any starch, in which case the custard is cooked to a point below boiling. Most Italian home cooks add a small amount of starch to a *crema* sauce and allow it to boil. Potato starch or cornstarch will yield the silkiest thin *crema,* but all-purpose flour will also do the trick. For thicker pastry-cream custards, I use all-purpose flour, as do most Italians.

1½ cups whole milk

4 egg yolks

⅓ cup sugar

1 tablespoon potato starch or all-
purpose flour

Dash salt

1 teaspoon pure vanilla extract

Put the milk in a small saucepan, and set it over medium heat until small bubbles appear at the edges—i.e., scald the milk. Turn off the heat. While the milk is heating, whisk the egg yolks in a medium-sized, heavy saucepan until they are broken and liquid, and then whisk in the sugar and salt. To assure that unwanted clumps of flour do not spoil your *crema,* pour the flour through a fine sifter into the saucepan. Whisk the ingredients just until they are homogeneous. Add the hot milk gradually so it does not curdle the eggs, and set the pan over medium-high heat. Whisk continuously, and cook until the cream comes to a slow boil and thickens. Continue to cook, whisking constantly, for a minute, to remove any taste of uncooked flour. Remove from the heat, and strain into a clean bowl. Stir in the vanilla. Use warm, or refrigerate up to 3 or 4 days.

VARIATION: Add 2 to 3 tablespoons of spirits such as rum or brandy or flavored liqueurs to the above recipe. Do not eliminate the vanilla, since it not only adds flavor but also balances the egg-yolk flavor.

VARIATION: **Orange- or Lemon-Flavored Crema.** To make an orange- or lemon-flavored *crema,* remove the peel from 1 large orange or lemon, being careful not to take any of the white pith. Heat 1⅓ cups milk with the peel until the milk bubbles, then remove from the heat, cover the pan, and let steep for 45 minutes to an hour. Strain, reheat the milk, and proceed as above.

VARIATION: **Almond Crema.** For an almond *crema,* add 1½ teaspoons of pure almond extract to the above recipe.

VARIATION: **Pastry Cream.** For a pastry cream that is thick enough to spread, use 2 tablespoons of starch in the above recipe. For a very thick *crema* that will hold its shape, use 4 tablespoons.

Quick Berry Sauce

CONDIMENTO DI BACCHE

I regularly make this quick berry sauce in summer, when berries are at their best. It is delicious served over ice cream, poached fruit, or pound cake, or with *panna cotta* or thick *crema pasticcera*. Actually, the berries themselves are quite good with lightly sweetened mascarpone cheese or whipped cream.

4 cups berries, one kind or a combination
¼ cup sugar

1 tablespoon lemon juice
3 tablespoons Maraschino, kirsch, or orange liqueur (optional)

If you are using strawberries, cut them in half. Mix the berries together, and then put 1 cup of the mixed berries into a blender or food processor with the sugar and lemon juice and optional liqueur. Puree the berries until they are smooth, and then pour them through a strainer to remove the seeds. Pour over the remaining berries. Fold together carefully, and refrigerate until needed.

VARIATION: Fresh ripe peaches and nectarines can be added to and pureed with the berries.

VARIATION: Once the puree has been poured over the berries, they are best eaten that day or the next. The puree, however, will keep for a few weeks in the refrigerator or about three months in the freezer. Make a large batch of it when berries are at their best, and dress fresh berries or peaches when you want to serve them. The puree itself is delicious on pancakes and waffles.

Cooked Berry Sauce

CONDIMENTO COTTO DI BACCHE

MAKES ABOUT 2½ CUPS

This cooked berry sauce can be used just as you would the uncooked berry sauce (preceding recipe). When the blueberries are cooked, they release a bit of pectin into the syrup, so the resulting sauce is more gelatinous than the uncooked sauce.

About 1 pint blueberries
½ cup water
½ cup sugar

2 tablespoons Maraschino, kirsch, or
  orange liqueur (optional)
6 to 8 ounces raspberries (about
  1¼ cups)

Wash the blueberries, and pick off any stems; discard any unripe ones. Put the water and sugar in a medium-size frying pan, and bring the water to a boil, swirling the pan gently so the sugar will melt. Add the blueberries to the simmering liquid, and cook just until they begin to pop, about 2 minutes. Then pour them into a strainer set over a bowl. Shake the strainer gently to release all the liquid, and return the strained juices to the frying pan. Turn the heat to medium high, and boil and reduce the juices until about ¼ cup remains; the bubbles should be large and the juices thick and syrupy. Pour in the liqueur—carefully, lest it flame—and reduce again to a thick syrup. Pour the syrup over the remaining blueberries, and gently fold in the raspberries. Serve cold or at room temperature. The sauce will keep in the refrigerator for up to 4 days.

VARIATION: Substitute other berries—blackberries, black raspberries, strawberries—for the raspberries. Cut large strawberries in half.

Dried Tart-Cherry Sauce

CONDIMENTO DI CILIEGIE SECCHE

MAKES ABOUT 1 CUP

This method will work for any dried fruit. The fruit should be cooked in the syrup long enough for it to soften. This slightly tart sauce is delicious served over the Ricotta and Semolina Puddings. Or make the Neapolitan Bread Pudding on page 429 without the raisins and pine nuts, and serve it with this sauce. When I serve this sauce on any one of these puddings, I usually pour an equal amount of almond *crema* on top. The combination is delicious.

1 cup water

⅓ cup sugar

¾ cup dried tart cherries

2 tablespoons Maraschino, kirsch, or orange liqueur

Pour the water and the sugar into a medium-size frying pan, and bring the water to a boil, swirling the pan gently so the sugar will melt. Add the cherries to the liquid, and simmer for 7 minutes, then pour them into a strainer set over a bowl. Shake the strainer gently to release all the liquid, and return the strained juices to the frying pan. Turn the heat to medium high, and boil and reduce the juices until about ⅓ cup remains; the bubbles should be large and the juices thick and syrupy. Pour in the liqueur—carefully, lest it flame—and reduce again to a thick syrup. Pour the syrup over the cherries.

VARIATION: **Dried Cranberry Sauce.** Substitute dried cranberries for the cherries.

VARIATION: Substitute 1 cup of red wine for the water in the poaching liquid. Omit the Maraschino. Or, in place of the wine, use grappa, Marsala, or orange juice.

Chocolate-Espresso Sauce

CONDIMENTO CIOCCOLATO

MAKES ABOUT 1 CUP

There are many complex methods for making chocolate sauces, but this almost instant one is my standard. If you do not regularly brew espresso, then buy a high-quality Italian brand of instant espresso powder and stir it into boiling water. Serve this sauce over ice cream or *panna cotta*. For a double chocolate hit, serve it over the Chocolate Bread Pudding. The sauce will keep a week in the refrigerator but will be too cold to pour, so reheat it on top of the stove. It can also be frozen for a few months and reheated slowly.

½ cup heavy cream

¼ cup sugar

5 ounces bittersweet chocolate

3 tablespoons strong brewed espresso

Put all the ingredients in a small saucepan, and cook over low heat, stirring occasionally, until the chocolate and sugar have melted. Beat well with a whisk to make a smooth sauce. The sauce will keep a week in the refrigerator.

BISCOTTI

In Italy, *biscotti* is a general term for cookies and sweet biscuits. Here, we think of biscotti as lean, crunchy cookies that are baked first in a loaf, then cut and baked again. The word actually means "twice-baked"—*bis*, "twice"; and *cottare*, "to cook"—so we are quite justified in our thinking. This double baking creates a hard, crisp cookie that is perfect for dipping into sweet wine, coffee, latte, or cappuccino.

There are a number of very good reasons to bake your own biscotti: they are quite simple to make, you can flavor them in a multitude of ways, they keep for a long time, and they make a delicious gift.

Anise Biscotti

MAKES ABOUT 60 BISCOTTI 3 INCHES BY 1 INCH

A freestanding, heavy-duty mixer is the best tool for mixing the stiff dough. If you do not have one, use a bowl and a sturdy wooden spoon or your hands. This recipe can be doubled, and if you don't want to bake all of the dough at the same time, wrap the logs in plastic, slip them into a freezer bag, and store for 3 weeks.

THE DRY INGREDIENTS

2 cups all-purpose flour

1 cup sugar

¼ teaspoon salt

2 teaspoons baking powder

THE LIQUID INGREDIENTS

3 large eggs, at room temperature

1 teaspoon pure vanilla extract

1½ teaspoons anise extract

Position an oven rack in the center of the oven, and preheat the oven to 350° F. Line a baking sheet or cookie pan with either parchment paper or aluminum foil, shiny side down. I use a baking sheet that is 12½ by 17½ inches. A smaller one is fine, but you will have to form three shorter logs.

Put the dry ingredients into the bowl of a heavy-duty mixer fitted with a paddle attachment. Run the machine on low for several spins, to blend the ingredients together. In a small separate bowl, with a fork or whisk, beat the liquid ingredients together until the eggs are quite runny. With the mixer running on medium speed, pour the eggs into the bowl and let the machine run until the eggs have mixed completely with the flour and form a mass of soft dough. The dough should be moist enough to hold together but not so wet as to cling to the bowl or your hands. If it is too wet to hold together, sprinkle small amounts of flour over it and run the machine until the dough pulls itself together. On the other hand, if the dough is too dry to form a mass, either add a small amount of water or beat another egg and add small amounts until the dough is the right consistency. If only a small amount of dry ingredients have not been incorporated, you can knead them in once the dough is out of the bowl.

Turn the dough out onto a lightly floured counter, and knead it a few times to make it smooth and to chase away any air pockets. Divide the dough in half, and use your hands to roll each half into a rope about 15 inches long and 1½ inches round. Place them on the prepared cookie sheet, leaving at least 3 inches between them, and keeping them a couple of inches from the sides of the pan. Pat the top of the dough to flatten slightly, and straighten the sides of the logs if necessary to make them uniform.

Put the pan in the oven and bake the logs for 25 to 30 minutes, or until they are firm when pressed and have begun to turn lightly brown on top. Remove the pan to a wire rack. Reduce the oven temperature to 300° F.

After about 10 minutes, or as soon as the logs are comfortable to handle, transfer them from the pan to a cutting board, and discard the paper from the baking sheet. Use a serrated knife to cut angled pieces ½ inch wide. Put the cookies back on the baking sheet, cut side down. They can be close to each other. Bake the second time, for 15 to 20 minutes, until the biscotti are beginning to color lightly and feel hard. They will continue to harden as they sit. Cool the biscotti in the pan on a wire rack until they are no longer even slightly warm. Store in an airtight container for up to a month or so.

VARIATION: If you would like to make larger biscotti, form the two pieces of dough into 12-inch-long, 2½-inch-round logs, and bake the first time for about 40 minutes. Cut the logs into 1-inch-thick slices, and rebake for about 20 minutes, or until lightly colored.

VARIATION: For a stronger anise flavor, add 1 tablespoon of crushed aniseed to the above recipe.

VARIATION: To make softer biscotti, beat 4 tablespoons of butter or of vegetable oil into the dry ingredients with the eggs.

Some Very Good Biscotti Combinations

Lemon-Nut Biscotti: In the basic recipe, substitute 1½ teaspoons of lemon extract for the anise extract, and add the grated rind of one large lemon and 1½ cups of toasted, chopped walnuts or pistachios to the dry ingredients.

Orange-Walnut Biscotti: In the basic recipe, use 1½ teaspoons of orange extract instead of the anise extract, and add the grated rind of one large orange and 1½ cups of toasted and coarsely chopped walnuts to the dry ingredients.

Chocolate-Nut Biscotti: Omit the anise from the basic recipe. Add ½ cup unsweetened cocoa powder, ¼ cup chocolate chips, and 1½ cups toasted, peeled, and coarsely chopped hazelnuts (see box) or toasted almonds to the dry ingredients. To punch up the almonds, use 1½ teaspoons almond extract.

Cinnamon-Raisin Biscotti: In place of the anise extract in the basic recipe, use 2 teaspoons of ground cinnamon. Mix ½ cup of dark raisins into the dry ingrediens.

Adding Nuts to Biscotti

Almonds are probably the most common addition to biscotti, but any variety of nuts can be used. A combination is lovely. I keep nuts well wrapped in the freezer, and when I have several bags of different varieties, I mix two or three types together.

For the proportions in the recipe on page 456, use about 1¼ cups of nuts. In order to release the nuts' natural flavor, toast them before adding them to the dough. To toast nuts, spread them out in one layer on a baking sheet, and toast in a 350° F oven for about 10 minutes, or until the nuts are lightly browned and emit a nutty fragrance. Let them cool completely before chopping them; leave the pieces quite large. Blend the nuts with the dry ingredients before pouring in the eggs.

ALMONDS: You can use whole unpeeled almonds or peeled slivered ones. I prefer the whole ones with their skins attached. Toast them as above, and cut each roughly into three pieces. Leave slivered almonds whole.

HAZELNUTS (FILBERTS): When you buy hazelnuts, they will most likely have their skin attached, and it is not at all palatable. To remove it, toast as above until the skins begin to crack. Enclose the hot nuts in a kitchen towel, and let them sit for 5 minutes to steam, then rub them vigorously in the towel. Not all of the skin will come off, and you can squeeze some of it away with your fingers, but don't worry about small stubborn pieces.

WALNUTS AND PECANS: Use black or green walnuts, or pecan halves, and toast as above.

PISTACHIOS: Use unsalted pistachios.

A Note on Measuring

In most of cooking, a little more of this or less of that is not going to matter. Baking, on the other hand, needs more precision.

Because I have so often seen students reach for the wrong tool to measure ingredients, I think a remark is warranted. There are "wet" measures and "dry" measures. Wet measures are usually made of glass and have spouts for pouring. They should be used to measure all liquid ingredients accurately. Dry measures are straight-sided and made of either metal or plastic.

When you are measuring liquids, place the measure flat on the counter and pour in the liquid until it reaches the proper measured line indicated on the side. Do not pick the measure up to eye level or the liquid can slosh and give you an imprecise reading.

When a recipe calls for a dry ingredient—1 cup of flour, for example—press the 1-cup "dry" measure into the bag or bin of flour until it is full. Use the flat side of a knife to scrape off whatever comes above the rim, and do not tap the cup down before or after doing so; what you have scooped and leveled is the right measurement. If the recipe calls for "1 cup flour, sifted," measure it as above and then sift it. On the other hand, when a recipe asks for "1 cup sifted flour," sift the flour into the measuring cup and level it off. Use the same scoop-and-level technique for tablespoons and teaspoons.

BIBLIOGRAPHY

Anderson, Jean, and Elaine Hanna. *The New Doubleday Cookbook*. New York: Doubleday, 1985.

Artusi, Pellegrino. *The Art of Eating Well*. Trans. Kyle M. Phillips III. New York: Random House, 1996.

Barrett, Judith. *From an Italian Garden*. New York: Macmillan, 1992.

Bittman, Mark. *How to Cook Everything*. New York: Macmillan, 1998.

Bugialli, Giuliano. *Classic Techniques of Italian Cooking*. New York: Simon & Schuster, 1982.

———. *The Fine Art of Italian Cooking*. New York: Times Books, 1989.

Carnacina, Luigi, and Luigi Veronelli. *La Cucina Rustica Regionale,* vols. 1, 2, 3, 4. Milano: Rizzoli, 1978.

Child, Julia. *Cooking with Master Chefs*. New York: Knopf, 1993.

———. *In Julia's Kitchen with Master Chefs*. New York: Knopf, 1995.

David, Elizabeth. *Italian Food*. New York: Penguin Books, 1989.

Del Conte, Anna. *Gastronomy of Italy*. London: Bantam, 1987.

———. *The Italian Pantry*. New York: HarperCollins, 1990.

Della Salda, Anna Gosetti. *Le Ricette Regionali Italiane,* settima edizione. Milano: Solares, 1967.

Fant, Maureen B., and Howard M. Isaacs. *Dictionary of Italian Cuisine*. New Jersey: The Ecco Press, 1998.

Francesconi, Jeanne Caròla. *La Cucina Napoletana*. Naples, Italy: Delfino, 1977.

Hazan, Marcella. *Essentials of Classic Italian Cooking*. New York: Knopf, 1992.

Jenkins, Steven. *Cheese Primer*. New York: Workman Publishing, 1996.

Malgieri, Nick. *Great Italian Desserts*. New York: Little, Brown, 1990.

Mariani, John. *The Dictionary of Italian Food and Drink*. New York: Broadway, 1998.

Plotkin, Fred. *The Authentic Pasta Book*. New York: Simon & Schuster, 1985.

Rombauer, Irma S., Marion Rombauer Becker, and Ethan Becker. *All-New All-Purpose Joy of Cooking*. New York: Scribner, 1997.

Roden, Claudia. *The Good Food of Italy*. New York: Knopf, 1990.

Schwartz, Arthur. *Naples at Table*. New York: HarperCollins, 1998.

Scott, Jack Denton. *The Complete Book of Pasta*. New York: Bantam, 1983.

Willinger, Faith. *Red, White & Green*. New York: HarperCollins, 1996.

Wells, Patricia. *Patricia Wells' Trattoria*. New York: William Morrow, 1993.

INDEX

Note: Primary Recipes are indicated by (PR) following the recipe title; variations are indicated by (var.) following the recipe title.

A NOTE ON THE TYPE

This book was set in Garamond, a type named for the famous Parisian type cutter Claude Garamond (ca. 1480–1561). Garamond, a pupil of Geoffroy Tory, based his letter on the types of the Aldine Press in Venice, but he introduced a number of important differences, and it is to him that we owe the letter now known as "old style."

The version of Garamond used for this book was first introduced by the Monotype Corporation of London in 1922. It is not a true copy of any of the designs of Claude Garamond, but can be attributed to Jean Jannon, a Protestant printer working in Sedan in the early seventeenth century, who had worked with Garamond's romans earlier but who was denied their use because of Catholic censorship. Jannon's matrices came into the possession of the Imprimerie nationale, where they were thought to be by Garamond himself, and were so described when the Imprimerie revived the type in 1900. The italic is based on the types of Robert Granjon, a type cutter and printer active in Antwerp, Lyons, Paris, and Rome from 1523 to 1590.

Composed by North Market Street Graphics
Lancaster, Pennsylvania
Printed by Tien Wah Press Ltd.
Singapore
Designed by Johanna S. Roebas